The Railway King of Canada

During the first two decades of this century, Sir William Mackenzie was one of Canada's best-known entrepreneurs. He spearheaded some of the largest and most technologically advanced projects undertaken in Canada during his lifetime – building enterprises that became the foundations for such major institutions as Canadian National Railways, Brascan, and the Toronto Transit Commission. He built a business empire that stretched from Montreal to British Columbia and to Rio Janeiro and São Paulo in Brazil. It included gas, electric, telephone, and transit utilities, railroads, hotels, and steamships as well as substantial coalmining, whaling, and timber interests. For a time Mackenzie also owned Canada's largest newspaper, *La Presse*. He accumulated an enormous personal fortune, but when he died in 1923 his estate was virtually bankrupt as a result of the dramatic collapse of his Canadian Northern Railway during the First World War.

In an era when the entrepreneur has come to be seen as a media hero and when struggles about the role of state enterprise in the transportation and energy sectors consume public policy debate, it is ironic that Mackenzie is largely forgotten by all but a few historians and railway aficionados. He left no papers to guide biographers. After a decade of gathering and piecing together fragments from an immense array of sources, Rae Fleming has written the first biography of the man that the German press extolled as 'the Railway King of Canada.'

R.B. FLEMING is a professional historian who was raised in Eldon Township, Ontario, Mackenzie's native area. He has taught at several Canadian universities and is currently honorary visiting fellow in Canadian Studies at the University of Edinburgh.

R.B. FLEMING

The Railway King
of Canada
Sir William Mackenzie, 1849–1923

UBC Press
Vancouver

ISBN 0-7748-0486-6

Canadian Cataloguing in Publication Data

Fleming, Rae Bruce, 1944-
The railway king of Canada, Sir William Mackenzie, 1849-1923

Includes bibliographical references.
ISBN 0-7748-0486-6

1. Mackenzie, William, Sir, 1849-1923.
2. Railroads–Canada–History. 3. Industrialists
–Canada–Biography.   I. Title.

FC556.M32F63 1991   971.05'6'092   C91-091162-2
F1033.M32F63 1991

This book has been published with the help of a grant
from the Social Science Federation of Canada, using funds
provided by the Social Sciences and Humanities Research
Council of Canada.

UBC Press
University of British Columbia
2029 West Mall
Vancouver, BC V6T 1Z2
(604) 822-5959
Fax: (604) 822-6083
Email : info@ubcpress.ubc.ca
www.ubcpress.ubc.ca

For Grandfather Mitchell, a storyteller;
for my parents, Myrtle and Victor, in memory;
and for Joanna and John, who also enjoy stories

Contents

Illustrations

MAPS

Abbreviations

AGOL	Art Gallery of Ontario Library, Toronto
BA	Brascan Archives, Toronto
BLCU	Butler Library, Columbia University, New York
CAR	*Canadian Annual Review*
CACPR	Corporate Archives of Canadian Pacific Railway
CBT	City of Birmingham Tramway Company
CHR	*Canadian Historical Review*
CNoR	Canadian Northern Railway
CNoOR	Canadian Northern Ontario Railway
CNoPR	Canadian Northern Pacific Railway
CNoQR	Canadian Northern Quebec Railway
CPR	Canadian Pacific Railway
CRMW	*Canadian Railway and Marine World*
CTA	City of Toronto Archives
CWA	City of Winnipeg Archives
EDCO	Electrical Development Company of Ontario
GAA	Glenbow-Alberta Archives
GDC	German Development Company
GTR	Grand Trunk Railway
GTPR	Grand Trunk Pacific Railway
HBCA	Hudson's Bay Company Archives, Winnipeg
JJHRL	James Jerome Hill Reference Library, St. Paul, Minnesota
LMRCC	Lake Manitoba Railway & Canal Company
MEGLC	Manitoba Electric and Gas Light Company
MHECA	Manitoba Hydro Electric Commission Archives, Winnipeg
MTL	Metro Toronto Library, Toronto
NA	National Archives of Canada (formerly PAC), Ottawa
NWMP	North West Mounted Police
OHA	Ontario Hydro Archives, Toronto

OPC	Ontario Power Company
ORMB	Ontario Railway and Municipal Board
PAA	Provincial Archives of Alberta, Edmonton
PABC	Provincial Archives of British Columbia, Victoria
PAM	Provincial Archives of Manitoba, Winnipeg
PAO	Provincial Archives of Ontario, Toronto
QLLSR	Qu'Appelle, Long Lake & Saskatchewan Railway
QUA	Queen's University Archives, Kingston
RCSL	Royal Commonwealth Society Library, London, England
RMW	*Railway and Marine World*
RSW	*Railway and Shipping World*
SAB	Saskatchewan Archives Board
SRO	Scottish Records Office, Edinburgh
TCA	Toronto City Archives, Toronto
TELC	Toronto Electric Light Company
TF	Thomas Fisher Rare Book Room, University of Toronto
TLC	Trades and Labor Council
T&N	Toronto and Nipissing Railway
TPC	Toronto Power Company
TRC	Toronto Railway Company
TTC	Toronto Transit Commission
TTCA	Toronto Transit Commission Archives, Toronto
UBL	University of Birmingham Library, Birmingham, England
UAA	University of Alberta Archives
UHR	Urban History Review
UNBA	University of New Brunswick Archives, Fredericton
UTA	University of Toronto Archives, Toronto
UTL	University of Toronto Library
VVE	Vancouver, Victoria & Eastern Railway
WER	Winnipeg Electric Railway Company
WESR	Winnipeg Electric Street Railway
WGN	Winnipeg Great Northern Railway

Acknowledgments

I owe many debts, not least of which is to several institutions which provided funds for travel and research. The J.S. Ewart Memorial Fund, University of Manitoba, provided travel and accommodation funds for research at the National Archives, Ottawa. The Ontario Arts Council, Toronto, gave two grants to complete the manuscript. The James Jerome Hill Foundation in St. Paul, Minnesota, donated travel and research funds. The Faculty of Graduate Studies, University of Saskatchewan, provided scholarship and research funds, and the History Department came up with research money. Archives and libraries in Canada, the United States, and Britain deserve thanks, especially the National Archives and the National Library, Ottawa; the Royal Commonwealth Society, London; and the James Jerome Hill Reference Library, St. Paul.

The following read drafts: Michael White, Margaret Mackay, Kathleen Bowley, Anthony Griffin, Elwood Jones, Munroe Scott, Marjorie Kennedy, Robert Elliott, Hugh Grant, Robert Sims, Ron Rees, Diana Rees, Mary Rubio, Gilberta Nicholls, Jennifer Brown, Jay Cassel, John Eagle, and Marjorie Porter. T.D. Regehr, History Department, University of Saskatchewan, supervised the PH.D. thesis from which this book emerged. I must also thank the three anonymous SSFC readers whose comments sharpened the argument and filled gaps. In addition, teaching social history at the University of Guelph in the autumn of 1990 helped me clarify some of the social issues in this biography.

Hugh Macmillan, formerly liaison officer with the Archives of Ontario, deserves praise for his enthusiasm and for introducing me to interested scholars and obscure sources; Robert Stacey generously shared his voluminous knowledge of Canadian art and history, and gave me the pen-and-ink illustration of William Mackenzie,

drawn by Stacey's grandfather, C.W. Jefferys in 1908; Mike Filey
sorted out details of street railway history and technology; W.B.
Arnup and Jay Cassel threw light on Mackenzie's mysterious medical problems; Ron Poulton gave up his idea of a biography of Mackenzie and gave me his research notes; Irene Spry made available
her collection of books concerning hydroelectricity; Kathleen
Bowley worked tirelessly on her Mackenzie genealogy and turned
over her discoveries to me; Douglas McCalla, Hugh Grant, George
Murphy, and Michael Bliss made suggestions on accounting and
economics; and Evelyn Tolmie, Margaret Mackay, Diana Rees, Ron
Rees, and Colin Read gave encouragement, as did Duncan Mc-
Dowall, Ken Munro, and Michael Bliss. Scores of people in Canada,
Britain, and the United States offered friendly conversations, good
food, and comfortable beds during the research. Mackenzie descendants in Canada, New York, the UK, and Africa were unfailingly
helpful and hospitable, especially Gilbert Griffin, whose kindness
and joie de vivre I will never forget. Ged Martin's kindness and
generosity brought me to the University of Edinburgh in early 1991
as Visiting Fellow at the Centre of Canadian Studies where I
finished work on this book.

Three people deserve special praise. Elwood Jones gave encouragement and introduced me, when I was in a slough of despond, to
Marjorie Kennedy, retired copy-editor, biography aficionado, and
bonne vivante. Biographer Munroe Scott was writer-in-residence at
Lindsay Public Library during the months leading up to my PH.D.
thesis defence, and like Marjorie Kennedy he devoted countless
hours to the manuscript and offered much appreciated moral support. My thanks to all three.

Jean Wilson, executive editor at the University of British Columbia Press, deserves top marks for guiding the manuscript through
the various stages leading to publication. I could not have had a better editor. And Frank Chow, copy-editor for UBC Press, made valuable suggestions which greatly improved the final version. It was
also a pleasure to work with Peter Milroy, director of the Press, Berit
Kraus, assistant marketing and promotion manager, and Holly
Keller-Brohman, associate editor. The fine maps were done by
Geoffrey Matthews and Chris Grounds, Department of Geography,
University of Toronto. My thanks to the Social Science Federation of
Canada for helping to fund this publication.

From my parents I inherited three prerequisites for writing a
book: intelligence, perseverance, and money. They would have been
quietly proud.

Introduction

A few days after Sir William Mackenzie's death in December 1923, his lobbyist and friend, Billy Moore, predicted that 'when the history of the time is written, the relation of Sir William Mackenzie's achievements will reveal the side of his character which he studiously shielded from the public, and revealed only to his intimate associates.' Moore did not elaborate and few of Mackenzie's family or colleagues left clues to the veiled side of his character. Except for a few undated letters and many fantastic stories promoting himself and his business endeavours, Mackenzie himself left posterity almost nothing. Thus, while researching and writing this biography, I often felt like a voyeur peering through the windows of a dimly lit mansion, observing the man, his family, and his partners in animated mime. Occasionally, years later, I was able to interview one or two of the participants in the drama, but Mackenzie himself remained elusive. Some of his papers were lost; other records were never created. When Agnes Deans Cameron, the Arctic traveller, met Mackenzie in Edmonton in 1908, she noted that he wrote few letters and travelled without his secretary. He was too rushed to worry about posterity, and would have dismissed any attempts to recreate his life. His contemporary, Augustus Bridle, once said that if a Boswell had ever tried to record Mackenzie's life, Sir William would have done one of two things: thrown him out the window of his office on King Street in Toronto, or given him a job 'so useful that he would have no time for biography.'[1]

Why, then, have I spent ten years reconstructing the life of an unwilling subject? First of all, I am fascinated by lives, and especially by people like Mackenzie who can be interpreted so diversely. Most historians who deal with the Laurier period usually claim that Mackenzie, like one of the thieves, should be damned. In his home

township in Ontario, his memory is not treated so unsympatheti-
cally. Mackenzie gave the local people work and his wealthy and
flamboyant family gave them stories, repeated and embroidered for
years after Sir William's death in 1923. My grandfather, born in the
same township in 1864, was one of the storytellers. His cousin was
estate manager for the Mackenzies in nearby Kirkfield, Mackenzie's
birthplace in 1849. Grandfather used to visit his cousin and return to
his large and curious family with stories of fast cars, fancy clothing,
mansions, and grand furniture. He also talked about other local
characters such as the formidable tavern keeper, Biddy Young, who
had known the Mackenzies in pioneer days before there was
money. One of the fascinated young listeners was my mother, who
years later repeated the stories. By the 1950s, when I began to listen,
no one could tell me how Sir William Mackenzie had acquired a title
and money. To satisfy my curiosity, I wrote this biography.

In his day, Mackenzie was a household word, admired for his financial wizardry and resented for his wealth and failures. With his
railway partner, Sir Donald Mann, he built a transcontinental railway from Quebec City to Vancouver; he was president of several
street railway companies in Canada and abroad; he sponsored the
world's first feature-length documentary film; and he was the
trusted adviser to three Canadian prime ministers and many provincial premiers. At one time, he and Sir Donald Mann owned *La
Presse*, then Canada's largest newspaper and the most important
voice of French Canada. He was toasted by the House of Lords,
made a Knight of the Realm by George v in 1911, and called the Railway King of Canada by the press in Berlin. One of his daughters
married into one of France's most prominent families. In 1917 Mackenzie helped Prime Minister Borden form the Union Government,
which saved Borden from electoral defeat and which may have
saved the country from more violent civil disturbances over the
question of conscription. Until his death in 1923, he remained a
close friend of both Sir Robert Borden and Arthur Meighen.

Mackenzie's meteoric rise dazzled millions of Canadians, Americans, Brazilians, British, and Europeans. His business empire was
compared to the British Empire, and it was said that the sun set on
neither. At his death, however, his empire had all but vanished. Today, he lies in the Kirkfield cemetery in a grave that shows the effects of time and neglect.

My version of Mackenzie challenges traditional historical interpretations. T.D. Regehr's *Canadian Northern Railway*, the only sympathetic study of Mackenzie and his transcontinental railway,
paints a cheery picture, influenced by stories invented by Macken-

zie in order to sell himself and his businesses. By contrast, many historians and journalists believe that Mackenzie and Mann were melodramatic crooks who took politicians and the people of the Laurier and Borden era for a long railway ride, then dumped them off at some dark crossing, leaving them to pick up unpaid bills – a Canadian version of Mark Twain's King and Duke in *Huckleberry Finn*. Mackenzie, I admit, was wily, crafty, and manipulative. He was forthright, quick to anger, and apparently very intimidating. According to one of his accountants, many people, including his closest partner Donald Mann, were often frightened of him. But I doubt if he was a criminal deserving posthumous damnation. If Canada ended up with too many kilometres of railway lines, it was the fault of politicians and voters, as well as promoters. Thus my Sir William Mackenzie is neither a saint nor a scallywag. In this biography, he is a human being with his share of the flaws and strengths common to us all.

By focusing on personalities and interpersonal relationships, biography enriches history, and often takes issue with interpretations that deal with issues and events rather than with the human participants. While appreciating and admiring the groundbreaking work of historians Christopher Armstrong and H.V. Nelles, I challenge some of their interpretations of the Toronto Street Railway, strikes, crowds, and bicycles, as well as the process that led to the creation of Ontario Hydro. The Toronto Railway Company, the predecessor of the Toronto Transit Company, was a good, soundly managed company that, in spite of many differences with councils and journalists, provided Torontonians with speedy, inexpensive service that was the envy of visitors from the United States and Britain. The work of historians such as Donald Davis and John Weaver on street cars, reform, jitneys, and the expansion question in Toronto modifies the work of Nelles and Armstrong. I hope that this life will add texture to the debate.

Inevitably, steam railways play an important role in this story. While construction was almost always lucrative, operation of railways rarely made a company wealthy. I have attempted to show how that construction money was made. This biography, I believe, puts the Canadian Northern Railway in perspective: while it is true that it was a mammoth undertaking, it was only one of about a half-dozen important enterprises that engaged Mackenzie. T.D. Regehr's study of the railway implies that it was the only important business, which leads to the conclusion that with its failure, Mackenzie failed. The truth is that most of his other businesses, notably street railways in Winnipeg, Toronto, and Brazil, were admirable successes whose profitable stocks Mackenzie sold in a futile attempt to keep the Canadian Northern afloat.

One of the myths of Canadian historiography is that of the hatred that met the Canadian Pacific Railway in western Canada, and of the adoration that greeted its competitors, the Canadian Northern and the Grand Trunk Pacific. While agreeing with John Eagle's recent study of the CPR and western Canadian development, which indicates that there was competition, I suggest that a good deal of that competition was promoters' rhetoric designed to impress politicians and voters in order to obtain government subsidies and bond guarantees for railway construction. It was always good politics to be anti-CPR. While there is no doubt that the CPR often competed with the Grand Trunk Pacific and several northern American railways, there is biographical and interpersonal evidence to suggest that the CPR and the Canadian Northern often co-operated with each other.

Although Mackenzie has been dead for almost seventy years, many issues and debates of his time remain with us, especially the role of the state in transportation, energy, communications, and the arts. Some of Mackenzie's most virulent battles were fought with agents of the state such as Sir Adam Beck, who in the name of the people created public corporations and made privately controlled corporations public. Thus Canadians have inherited government-owned corporations such as Ontario Hydro, Hydro Quebec, the Toronto Transit Commission, VIA Rail, the Potash Corporation of Saskatchewan, the Canadian National Railway, and Air Canada. Now after five or six decades of government control, the wheel has turned. Governments are privatizing many state-controlled corporations, and the state is again playing the role of observer and regulator. Although the Canada Council and other government granting bodies are necessary and appreciated, in Mackenzie's day the arts were supported almost solely by business; and the pages of the *Canadian Annual Review* dispel doubts that Canadian culture flourished before the founding of the Canada Council. As the twentieth century draws to a close and governments seek ways to trim budgets, we may have to encourage more active business support for the arts.

Historians who demand definitive explanations of character will be disappointed. With so few Mackenzie papers, his biographer can only suggest motivation: why, for instance, he felt compelled to build a transcontinental railway, or what he so 'studiously shielded from the public.' I imply that a good deal of the infrastructure of Canada – railway lines and hydro generating stations, to name two examples – was born of the hostilities and friendships that characterized the relationships of men such as Sir William Mackenzie, Sir William Van Horne, Sir Clifford Sifton, and Sir Adam Beck. Government policy and public rhetoric played important roles, but so did fantasy, folly, ruse, bluff, jealousy, role playing, and other facets of personality.

Inevitably, the biographer shows a world as perceived by the subject of the biography. Because this is the life of a capitalist, historians of fields such as labour may feel that the role of workers and unions is treated in a cursory fashion, especially since labour played a critical role, as protagonist and antagonist, in the life of Sir William Mackenzie. Within the limits of biography, I hope that I have been as fair as possible to workers and navvies, as well as to politicians, journalists, women, newcomers, and artists, all of whom participated in this man's life. But biography insists that the one life itself remain the focal point.

Because I believe it impossible to say that a thing happened exactly this way or that, or that a person is exactly this or that, I have introduced chapters with epigraphs from a variety of sources – novels, autobiography, poetry, and essays – which suggest that the line separating history from fiction, or truth from invention, is very fine, and perhaps non-existent. What these epigraphs also suggest is that this biographer does not have a monopoly on truth, and that he realizes that no biography is immortal.

Finally, let me say that I hope that these various debates have remained subservient to the narrative line. Mackenzie's life is a good story, and I trust that the reader will take pleasure in reading this version.

THE RAILWAY KING OF CANADA

CHAPTER ONE

Shanties, Schoolhouses, and Townhalls, 1849–82

The trawling net fills, then the biographer hauls it in, sorts, throws back, stores, fillets and sells. Yet consider what he doesn't catch: there is always far more of that.

(Julian Barnes, *Flaubert's Parrot* [1985] 38)

William Mackenzie began his life on one of two dates: he always claimed 30 October 1849 as his birthdate; however, according to the parish records of the Reverend McMurchy, the Presbyterian minister who baptized William, the boy was born on 17 October. It's a small thing, this difference of several days, but it suggests the difficulties of recreating the life of a man born into a culture that relied on storytellers rather than accountants and lawyers to preserve community memory. In such a culture, the story of the birth was more important than the actual date of that birth. And in such a culture, the child often grows up with a love of storytelling.

The folk of William's birthplace, Eldon Township, Victoria County, Ontario, loved to tell stories – a trait that they brought with them from their native Scottish Highlands in the 1820s, '30s, and '40s. Their stories were of ghosts that arose from graves at night, of suicide victims buried in unmarked graves on which no grass grew, and of corpses that revived during a wake, frightening slightly inebriated mourners. They believed in the curse of the evil eye, and they were highly superstitious – it was bad luck to sweep the kitchen floor after lighting the kerosene lamp, or to seat thirteen at a supper table. They developed maxims, often humorous and self-deprecating, such as 'If we were the makings of ourselves, we'd be a pretty perfect lot,' or 'Better the day, better the deed,' an apology for Sabbath labour. At the marriage of an older couple or a couple whose ages differed considerably, neighbours would gather at midnight with wash tubs and wooden spoons to 'shivaree' the couple. Like all pioneering townships, Eldon had its clearing and threshing bees, barn raisings, excursions, and church suppers, which provided the setting to retell old stories, and the grist for new ones.

The fact that William Mackenzie grew up among storytellers helps to explain his lifelong ability to enthral listeners with stories of his rise from the backwoods of Canada, his business successes, and his optimistic predictions for the future. His storytelling ability helps to explain what one historian has called his 'entrepreneurial dexterity,'[1] his ability to turn his vision of a company into the reality of hydroelectric plants generating power for cities, or of street cars moving people through the streets of those cities. To do so, he had to convince a variety of people, from stockbrokers to investors, engineers, managers, and politicians, that the vision could be realized. As a storyteller, he understood his audience instinctively, telling them what they wanted to hear. He knew how to flatter them with stories shaped to suit the moment of telling. He knew too that it was not the exact memory of things that counted, but what the storyteller made of that memory. Growing up among the Highlanders of Eldon Township taught him that the heart enjoys fantasy, and that distinguishing illusion from reality is unnecessary, and often impossible.

William's father, John Mackenzie, was a man of little means and no education who seldom wrote his name, and when he did, it came out as 'Mckenzy' or 'Mckenzey.' Born about 1810 in Ross-shire, a few kilometres northwest of Inverness, Scotland, John grew up in a community of poor tenants who eked out a subsistence living on a soggy piece of land aptly named 'Faebait,' Gaelic for 'drowned bog.' The once-powerful Mackenzie clan was in decline, the Highlands were being turned over to Cheviot sheep, and the future for Highlanders looked bleak.

About 1832, with his wife Mary, relatives, and connections, John Mackenzie left Scotland for the Canadas. They settled first in Montreal, then moved to Toronto in 1834, where according to family legend they lived near the corner of Lot (Queen) and Bay, inhabited at that time by other people of little means, probably fellow migrants. In late 1836, after two years of working in the little city to support a family and to acquire capital, John Mackenzie and his brother-in-law applied for land, and were assigned two lots in Eldon Township, about 120 kilometres northeast of Toronto.

Mackenzie Sr. must have had an affinity for poor farmland. From a drowned bog in Scotland he came to a narrow bit of sandy land running steeply uphill in North Eldon Township. He built the required 16 x 20' shanty and added to his family, which already included Duncan and Catherine, born in Montreal, and Alex, born in Toronto in 1836. Rod followed in 1839, John in 1841, twins Janet and Mary Anne in 1845, and Maggie in 1846. William, born in 1849, was the ninth child, and Ewan would follow two years later. The large family remained on their narrow, sandy farm, even though there was fertile farmland ready for clearing in townships a few kilometres south.

There were good reasons to remain in Eldon. The township, along with Thorah Township immediately to the west, was beginning to attract fellow Highland settlers, who carried on familiar customs and 'had the Gaelic,' the language of the Highlands. Furthermore, the area held promise of good times. The Colonial Office in London, fearful of American invasion, commissioned a report on the possibility of a canal from Georgian Bay to Lake Ontario to take ships and troops across the heartland of Upper Canada, a few hundred miles north of the international border. In 1835 engineer N.H. Baird reported that such a canal could be built following the valley of the Trent. John Mackenzie's farm was located close to the proposed canal.[2]

Part of the canal would run parallel to an old portage that Hurons, French traders, and missionaries had used in the seventeenth and eighteenth centuries in order to circumvent an impassable stream running between Lakes Simcoe and Balsam. The portage, which the Hurons called 'Ouskebawkning,' or 'the green leaf place where we leave the river,' had been an artery of Montreal's fur trade network. In 1615 Samuel de Champlain had walked the trail, accompanied by Hurons en route to raid Iroquois camps in what is now New York State.

Although the Hurons were dispersed by the Iroquois in 1649, the Trent system, including the portage trail, remained a link between the Northwest fur lands and Montreal, Paris, and London.[3] In the 1790s French names were anglicized by Lieutenant Governor Simcoe. 'Lac Aux Claies' became 'Simcoe' in honour of Simcoe *Pere*; and the impassable stream that ran into Lake Simcoe was changed to 'Talbot,' after Simcoe's private secretary. The portage trail, however, retained its French name. When the first European settlers reached North Eldon in the late 1820s, the portage was almost completely hidden by new growth. At first the township's surveyor ignored the trail and incorporated it into 200-acre lots. Settlers protested, and surveyor Ewing made the narrow portage the focal point of long, narrow lots on each side, in the style of lots along the St.

Lawrence and Red rivers. Consequently John Mackenzie's farm, fronting on what settlers called 'the Portage Road' or simply 'the Portage,' was narrow and long. And it was on that farm, in a shanty overlooking the Portage, that William Mackenzie was born in 1849.

The Highlanders incorporated stories from the area into their own tales. Champlain became a character of Eldon township,[4] along with drunken surveyors, unscrupulous settlement officials, lascivious clergymen, and rebellious politicians. The first surveyor of Eldon Township left many abrupt double curves in the quarter roads, which settlers attributed to his fondness for whiskey. 'As crooked as a dog's hind leg' was how they described these roads running east to west. Donald Cameron, the superintendent of settlement for Eldon and Thorah townships, had ended up in the York jail in 1830, accused of mishandling settlement. For two decades he fought, un-successfully, to clear his name. In the 1830s Eldon township was rocked by a ministerial scandal, always good material for stories. The Reverend Campbell had been convicted in Scotland of 'fornica-tion, fraud and wilful imposition.'[5] In early 1837, shortly after John Mackenzie's arrival in Eldon, it was discovered that the young woman with whom the clergyman was living was not his wife. Hor-rified newlyweds scurried off to the nearest legitimate minister to make holy their conjugal beds. A few weeks later, a heavy fall of snow caused the roof of the fornicator's log church to cave in, a fit-ting conclusion to the story.

The Rebellion of 1837 touched the area. A few Highland farmers of Eldon and Thorah, not including John Mackenzie, sympathized with William Lyon Mackenzie, who was no known relation. During the elections of 1841, some Eldoners marched over sixty kilometres to vote against George Boulton, a member of the Family Compact.[6] In 1844, the Canadian version of the Scottish Presbyterian Disruption divided the Church into two factions, those who supported the con-nection with the traditional, established Presbyterian Church of Scotland, and others who opted to form the Presbyterian Church of Canada, known as the Free Church. John Mackenzie opted to re-main with the more conservative Established Church.[7] When Wil-liam Mackenzie was growing up, the two Presbyterian groups kept a wary watch on each other, rarely attending each other's services. Membership determined party support: Established Kirk members voted Conservative, and Free Churchers, Liberal. In his early years, like his father, William Mackenzie was an Established Kirk Presby-terian and thus a Tory.

The location of his birth, a few metres from the narrow trail which led to distant forts and metropolitan capitals, was important in giving the child a mental map that transcended backwoods limitations. He was born in 1849, an auspicious year for railways, both urban and interurban. Toronto's first organized transit system was inaugurated. Thomas Keefer's *Philosophy of Railways*, which promised that railways would solve economic woes, was published. The Guarantee Act of 1849, by which government would guarantee private railway bonds, and the 'Baldwin Act' of the same year helped to divert money to railway construction, thereby supporting the railway boom of the 1850s.[8] In 1849 Sandford Fleming went to Montreal to obtain his government licence as a land surveyor, later returning to Toronto to form the Canadian Institute, whose topics of discussion were surveying, engineering, and the Northwest. In the Northwest, Guillaume Sayer's cry, 'Le commerce est libre,' challenged the Hudson's Bay Company's right to preserve the vast prairies for the fur trade. At the same time, old Ontario, then known as Canada West, began to fear that the last of its fertile territory was being rapidly settled. George Brown of the *Globe* began to see agricultural possibilities in the land beyond Lake Superior, and realized that railways would be needed to link the manufacturing centres of the east with this fertile land of the west. William Mackenzie's attention was to be drawn towards these various methods of transportation and communication, which were also conceived and born in the 1840s.

When William was three, his mother died suddenly, perhaps worn down by rigorous pioneer conditions and too many children. She is one of the mute millions whose biographies can never be written, for she left no records and died too long ago to be recorded in photograph albums or even in family stories. The effect of the sudden and mysterious departure of his mother on the three-year-old must have been traumatic, and may account for Mackenzie's constant search for stability, security, and control.

When Mary Mackenzie died, seventeen-year-old Kate took charge of the older children. William was taken to the nearby farm of Donald McDonald, then to his mother's sister, Catherine, who with her husband, Donald Munro, lived a few kilometres away. In a way, the death of his mother was a stroke of luck, for by living with the Munros, he was close enough to walk to the first state supported or public school in North Eldon. Had his mother lived, he would have remained on the family farm and probably not attended the school in Bolsover, several kilometres from Kirkfield. And when he was ready to attend school, the educational system of Eldon was beginning to improve.[9] Teachers were better qualified and more schools were being built. Egerton Ryerson's search for order was beginning to shape educational patterns in remote Eldon township.

In January 1866, when William was seventeen, a new school opened in his native Kirkfield, where he completed his local education. The curriculum included morning Bible reading, spelling, reading, arithmetic, grammar, history, bookkeeping, algebra, and mathematics. The school had a library of about 200 books.[10] On wall maps, William could run his fingers over the Red River Colony, the vast Northwest, the colonies of Vancouver Island and British Columbia, and cities such as Toronto and Montreal. During the mid-1860s, railway capitalists and the Fathers of Confederation were formulating plans to strengthen the east-west axis created by geography and reinforced by the fur trade.

One of the students in the Kirkfield Common School was little Patrick O'Byrne, six years William's junior. In 1864, when Pat was nine, the family settled on the harsh limestone plains on the southern edge of the Canadian Shield, a kilometre north of the Portage. In later life, long after he started to call himself 'Burns,' perhaps because in the nineteenth century a Scottish name was associated with success, Pat liked to tell the story of the potato contract. Mackenzie agreed to dig a field of potatoes, then hired Pat as the subcontractor who did most of the work while Mackenzie collected most of the money.[11] The potato episode was the beginning of a long personal and business relationship.

After finishing common school in December 1866, William moved thirty kilometres southeast to attend grammar school[12] in Lindsay, an attractive town with a few thousand souls and well-stocked stores. Since its chief industry was lumbering and milling, the pleasant fragrance of cedar permeated the place.[13] One of William's fellow students was John McDonald, son of Donald McDonald, who with his wife had helped to look after the younger Mackenzies after Mary's death in 1852.

The two boys enrolled in the 'Classical Course,' which meant that each could read 'intelligently,' spell accurately, write legibly, and solve certain mathematical questions as well as parse 'an easy sentence.'[14] They studied Caesar and Cicero, English history, English literature, arithmetic, geography, writing, drawing, algebra, and even some elementary Greek. The quality of education and student discipline improved greatly in 1867, thanks to the strict new headmaster, Henry Reazin. By the second term, beginning 1 August 1867, the 'unqualified' students were gone, and those remaining, including Mackenzie and McDonald, were 'such as ought to be in Grammar School,' according to the school inspector.[15]

Beginning in January 1868, William taught for one year in his old school at Bolsover, where he apparently gained the respect of the students for being 'very thorough.'[16] That he left the profession after only one year suggests that he was searching for new challenges. He was back in Kirkfield in October 1870, when at twenty-one he launched a new career. With his brother Alex, classmate John McDonald, and John's brother, Angus, he opened the 'Shoofly Store,'[17] a name derived from William's habit of shooing away houseflies, for which he bore an intense dislike.

Since the days of survey and first settlement, the area had remained relatively isolated – what historians of development like to call the backwoods. But now, stimulated by transportation links with the outside world, the young village of Kirkfield was beginning to develop. A few kilometres to the east, the Victoria Road had been constructed during the years 1856 to 1866, one of several colonization roads built between 1855 and Confederation in an expensive, ultimately unsuccessful attempt to turn millions of acres of Canadian Shield country in North Victoria and Muskoka into productive farms.[18] Mackenzies, Munros, and McDonalds supplied timber for bridges and corduroy roads through swampy land. Wages for manual labour were one dollar a day,[19] respectable for the 1860s, and the Victoria Road did attract settlers who bought supplies from general stores such as the Shoofly Store.

Of greater importance to Kirkfield was the construction of the Toronto & Nipissing Railway, linking Kirkfield and Toronto, whose retail merchants (Eaton), grain merchants and distillers (Gooderham and Worts), and wholesalers (Merchant Prince McDonald) were anxious to develop trade with a growing hinterland. The 'Nip and Tuck,' the line's popular name (suggesting precarious financing and uncertain completion), was incorporated in 1868. Kirkfield's lumber baron, A.P. Cockburn, was a director. So too were Bolsover's lumber merchant and MPP, Duncan 'the Member' McRae, and George Laidlaw, colleague of Gooderham and Worts. The T&N was financed by private capital and by government guarantees and subsidies. So anxious was Eldon Township to host the line that it donated the enormous sum of $44,000, almost 30 per cent of Toronto's bonus of $150,000.[20] Thus the line ran the length of the township, from Woodville to Argyle to Kirkfield, then east to Coboconk, its northern terminus hundreds of kilometres short of Nipissing. (By the 1870s, railway promoters had learned how to impress voters and politicians with grandiose titles suggesting geographic places reached only in the imagination.) Nevertheless, the line encouraged the young timber industry of the Kirkfield area, as well as spin-off industries such as saw and lath milling, and shingle and turpentine manufacturing.[21] Like many other railway communities during the immediate post-Confederation period, the 100 inhabitants of Kirkfield, no longer backwoods people, exuded what one historian has called 'an observable gain in confidence that led people out a little beyond the timidities of the colonial state.'[22] By 1873 the North West, British Columbia, and Prince Edward Island had joined the four original provinces. The years immediately following Confederation seemed full of optimism.

In 1872, Mackenzie married Margaret Merry. Although there is no known photograph of her at the time of her marriage, a family photograph taken about 1889 shows a woman whose beauty had not faded even after giving birth to her ninth child. The photographer captured her quiet dignity, the perfect foil for her energetic husband. It is easy to see, in a photograph of Mackenzie taken in his twenties or early thirties, why Margaret found him attractive. His compact body and compelling face exudes an animal magnetism; his deep-set, dark eyes peer enigmatically at the camera, his right eye slightly darker and more penetrating than the left, which is disconcertingly gleeful. The eyes are shrewd. Under the bushy moustache and the long, black beard, the bottom lip is pursed. The left hand resting on the left thigh is clenched. The right hand holds a newspaper, as if even then he was learning that control of information is a key to business success. The fingers are long and elegant, more like the hands of an artist than those of a contractor or storekeeper. They were theatrical hands, or perhaps the hands of a magician who seems to be mesmerizing the camera lens as it records him for posterity.

The marriage raised a few eyebrows in Kirkfield. Perhaps because she was Roman Catholic and he Presbyterian, no family member attended the wedding in Lindsay. The only witnesses were two strangers. The ceremony was performed without a mass, since William remained Presbyterian. He was not likely pleased by the presence of a priest, but would have consented to the Catholic marriage in order to please his beautiful bride.

The question of religion may not have been the sole reason for raised eyebrows. Apparently the bride was pregnant. The couple claimed 8 June 1872 as the date of their marriage, but that date was invented. According to Ontario marriage records, they were married on 8 July 1872, exactly one month later.[23] Mackenzie never let a fact or two stand in the way of a good story. Who would ever know that little R.J. Mackenzie was conceived, as is the wont of many a first born, a trifle too soon? You couldn't fool the local folk, though.

The wedding and birth provided them with a witty way of illustrating the character of William Mackenzie. 'Just like the Mackenzies,' they would remark. 'Always in a hurry.'

During the mid- and late 1870s, William Mackenzie began to make his mark in contracting. Shortly after Confederation, some of his brothers had set themselves up as 'Mackenzie Brothers,' a contracting company that built the new structures required as the community moved from isolation to integration into the Ontario and Canadian economy. In Kirkfield the company ran a sawmill, a sash and door factory, and a small furniture factory, and sold stumping machines to remove stumps remaining from clearing days in order to prepare sites for new construction. Mackenzie Brothers was the 'right combination'[24] that William Mackenzie later created in his railway and utilities companies: the integration under one company of all parts of the industry from raw materials to finished product, with an exclusive monopoly that kept away competitors. The monopoly was usually part of the franchise in the case of urban utilities. In Kirkfield, however, monopoly was created partly by an exclusive licence to cut timber in areas off limits to others, and partly by the goodwill that Mackenzie Brothers had built up in the area, which made it difficult for competitors to enter the market.[25] In addition, the company ran a grist mill in Kirkfield, which suggests that it even supplied the ingredients for the daily bread consumed by families occupying Mackenzie Brothers' houses. Except for brief mentions in the Kirkfield columns of local newspapers, no records survive of this company; because of the verbal nature of contracts in rural Canada at that time, few written records existed.

Sometime in the 1870s, perhaps shortly after his marriage, William joined Mackenzie Brothers. Besides houses in Kirkfield, the company built brick schoolhouses and hotels throughout the area, an Agricultural Society building at Glenarm, and grain warehouses in Kirkfield and Lorneville. During the 1870s, William Mackenzie began to invest in local real estate; in 1880 and 1881, he constructed a hotel in Kirkfield and a fine brick residence and store, where he planned to sell furniture and hardware.

For the 300 or so residents of Kirkfield, and especially for Mackenzie Brothers, the first decade of railway service proved prosperous. Mackenzie was proud of the booming little town, which besides the grist mill and Shoofly Store had a harness shop, a confectionery and bake shop, a flour and feed store, a brickyard, and a tinsmith shop. The town acquired a new brick schoolhouse. Margaret Mackenzie could now have her hats and clothing made at a new millinery and dressmaking shop. When the couple took their young family out for a stroll on the new wooden sidewalks, some of which had been built by William Mackenzie, they must have marvelled at the town's growth: over sixty new houses under construction; at the west end of town, a new Methodist church; and across the road, a new Presbyterian manse. Mackenzie no longer had to go to Lindsay or Beaverton to buy a carriage. The little town was in touch with the world through its new telegraph office. Before it was purchased in 1881 by the Midland Railway, the Toronto & Nipissing had erected a fine, new station on the northern edge of town. Residents no longer expressed surprise that it was possible to travel to Toronto in the morning, shop at Eaton's in the afternoon, and return to Kirkfield that same evening. Hides were being turned into leather in new tanneries. A shoemaker had set up shop to turn that leather into shoes and boots. With the new-found prosperity, Kirkfield residents began to worry about property values and household security. An insurance agent, who doubled as a real estate agent, set up shop on Nelson Street, the town's proud main street. There was even a small professional class. If any of Mackenzie's young children needed a doctor, there was now one in Kirkfield.[26]

This success story, repeated many times in post-Confederation Ontario, removed any doubt that railways were, as Keefer had predicted in 1849, a great economic panacea. And this local growth was occurring during a period of sluggish national growth. The Kirkfield pattern of railway-inspired growth was typical of Canada in the 1870s and 1880s. It would be repeated hundreds of times during the next three decades, when Mackenzie himself would create dozens of booming railway towns throughout the prairies.

In 1871 Ontario began to provide subsidies of $2,000 to $4,000 per mile in order to encourage the construction of colonization railways, which, it was hoped, would help to settle vast tracts of barren Shield country in Muskoka and elsewhere.[27] Railway builders took advantage of the subsidies and devised grand plans. George Laidlaw obtained a charter to build the Victoria Railway from Lindsay to the Ottawa River. In reality, it went as far as Haliburton, about 100 kilometres north of Lindsay. If his friend, Sir John A. Macdonald, returned to office and succeeded in building a transcontinental railway from Montreal through Northern Ontario to Vancouver, then Laidlaw would be ready with a Toronto link.[28]

From 1874 to 1876, William and Alex Mackenzie built bridges for the Victoria Railway, as well as the station and engine house in Kinmount, north of Lindsay. It was William Mackenzie's introduction to railway construction and to two men instrumental in his rise in the railway world – James Ross, chief engineer for Victoria Railway, and Herbert Holt, a young land surveyor and office boy.

When Laidlaw moved on to build the Credit Valley Railway, to connect Toronto to points in Western Ontario and possibly to be a link in a transcontinental from Montreal to BC via Chicago and Winnipeg, Mackenzie followed. Laidlaw was very pleased that Mackenzie was undercutting rates charged by Toronto contractors. He built cedar cribwork for the Credit Valley Railway's wharf at the Toronto harbour and, with his brothers, several stations.[29] His ability to work to schedule within cost estimates was appreciated, and he became one of Laidlaw's 'principal contractors.'[30]

There were already signs of the self-confidence and daring that would later drive him to create his international business empire. According to the station agent at Brampton, west of Toronto, Mackenzie and his brothers had built the platform too high. Passengers were inconvenienced by having to take a large step down in order to enter a passenger car. On 16 March 1880 chief engineer Bailey ordered that the platform be lowered. Mackenzie was furious. He had not been consulted and renovations would be at his expense. In less than an hour he was in Bailey's office.

Bailey was his superior, but it was Bailey who backed down. Within three hours, Bailey ordered the platform to be left as it was. The step problem was solved by James Ross, manager of construction, who suggested that some minor renovations would make the platform safer.[31]

His work completed on the Credit Valley Railway, Mackenzie returned to Kirkfield to play a role in municipal politics – not a surprising turn since business and politics have always been bedmates. Throughout the 1870s, the Mackenzies had been active in politics, supporting Conservative candidates. The support took different forms, from debates to bribes. For instance, during the Ontario election of 1875, Mackenzie campaigned for Duncan McRae. McRae won, but the election was rendered void because some of the candidate's workers, including John Merry, Mackenzie's father-in-law, had offered voters free liquor and food on election day. The ensuing by-election confirmed McRae in office.

Politics was a serious affair. The few Kirkfield area Grits who dared to vote against Macdonald in 1878 were burned in effigy.[32] (The secret ballot never did prevent country folk, whether in Mackenzie's Eldon or Leacock's Mariposa, from knowing how neighbours voted.) Since he was so active throughout the 1870s, Mackenzie may very well have helped to put together a straw-filled effigy and helped to string the Grit facsimile over the branch of a Kirkfield tree, where it was set on fire.

From January 1876 to December 1877, Mackenzie was a councillor for North Eldon, and thus dealt with local questions such as schools, tavern licences, assessment appeals, indigents, and roads. He did so with ability and tact.[33] At the same time, he learned a lesson in railway financing. The township held a $6,000 Toronto & Nipissing bond. The Midland Railway, which was about to take control of the T&N, refused to honour the old railway's promise to exchange the bond for a new and more valuable bond. The Township of Eldon took the railway to court, but lost and was forced to sell the old bond at a 50 per cent discount. In January 1878 Mackenzie ran for reeve, but was defeated, possibly because voters were displeased with the $3,000 loss on the bond, a considerable sum in 1877.

While he was out of office, the $44,000 bonus given to the Toronto & Nipissing in 1869 began to raise concern. The township had sold twenty-year bonds to raise the money, and the principal would be due in 1889. The council had voted to create a sinking fund that by 1889 would be sufficient to pay off the bondholders. Unfortunately, the sinking fund was not growing quickly enough, and ratepayers became anxious.

In January 1880 Mackenzie made a second bid for the reeveship. The nomination meeting, held in Woodville on Monday, 29 December 1879, was lively. Reeve Carmichael called the Woodville *Advocate* a 'miserable little sheet,' because it had called him stupid, incapable, and ignorant.

It was Mackenzie's turn to address the packed town hall. 'I am running for reeve because a large number of friends have asked me to be nominated as a candidate,' he began in his quiet tenor voice, whose gentle, musical lilt owed something to the rhythms of Gaelic, which in the 1870s was still the working language of Highland migrants and some of their children. He already had a good deal of support, he reported. 'I am not prepared to make any charges against the retiring Council,' he continued, 'but I do think that the affairs of this Township have been badly managed.' If the electors were dissatisfied, then they should vote for new representatives. 'But make sure you choose the best men,' he added. If he were elected, he would 'strive to do his duty to the Township.'

'But would you fire the Clerk and Treasurer?' shouted someone in the audience. Yes if they were found wanting, but no if they had performed well. And what about the discount on the $6,000 bond?

After all, was it not Mackenzie who had helped carry out the negotiations? His elusive answers satisfied the audience.

He addressed the two issues that had been exercising the *Advocate*: he would be in favour of fall, as opposed to spring, assessment, in order to facilitate the process of drawing up assessment rolls and voters' lists; and he would allow no work on roads after the first of September, in order to avoid irritating quagmires such as the one that year at Morrison's Hill in Woodville.

A week later he won the election by a landslide. Only one person in his ward voted against this 'young man of ability, intelligence and energy,' as the Kirkfield correspondent to the *Canadian Post* called him. At age thirty he was reeve of Eldon.

Reeve Mackenzie met monthly with council in one of the dozen village hotels of Eldon. Once a year, usually in late spring or summer, the council presided over a Court of Revision that heard assessment and enumeration appeals. Along with fellow reeves, Mackenzie was a member of Victoria County Council, whose debates on county roads, bridges, finances, assessment, and education often lasted two or three days at county headquarters in Lindsay.

The electors of Eldon were so happy with Mackenzie's first term in office that they acclaimed him reeve for another year. When he retired from politics in December 1881, he left the township in remarkably sound financial shape.[34] He had learned a great deal: how to deal with the passions of electors, how to please taxpayers, and how to deal with railway financing. He had gained the respect of the county of Victoria and had thereby built a solid and loyal foundation from which to launch his national career. Although he could easily have won a third term, he chose not to run. At age thirty-two, he was still searching. His role as reeve was his fourth vocation, following teaching, storekeeping, and several kinds of contracting. In later life, he claimed that he had thought of becoming a clergyman, an unlikely idea probably told to enhance a story or to deflect attention from his wealth.

His growing family also kept him busy. After R.J. in 1873 came Mabel in 1874, Gertrude in 1875, then Alex in 1877, Bertha in 1879, and Ethel in 1881. Six children in less than ten years. Three more would be born in the 1880s. The town of Kirkfield also provided ample entertainment. There were baseball games, hunting expeditions, the Queen's birthday, Dominion Day, and the Glorious Twelfth. From time to time, someone would host a fancy-dress ball. Occasionally the town would celebrate a political victory or the birth of a child with a torchlight procession through the dark streets. The rituals of birthdays and weddings were a good excuse for an oyster supper, after which the men would retire to a separate room to sip whiskey punch. The Maple Leaf temperance club was formed in Kirkfield in the 1870s, a partially successful attempt to discourage drinking. Soirées and concerts were popular. Travelling lecturers would introduce topics such as phrenology. The Mackenzies could take the train to Niagara Falls, to the Toronto Industrial Exhibition, or to the Philadelphia World's Fair of 1876. In 1878 the family sent father John, sixty-eight years old, widowed for the second time, and father of two young children, on a trip to the 'Old Country,' Scotland.

If Mackenzie wanted to get away from Kirkfield for an hour or two, he could hitch up the horse and carriage and head down the Portage to Biddy Young's Hotel, built in 1866, near Bolsover. The proprietress, Julia Young, was known as 'Biddy,' Irish for an unusual woman. Short, stout, and formidable, she ran her hotel and tavern, acted as her own bouncer, and kept a whiskey still hidden among the gnarled roots of an ancient elm. Once a judge told Biddy that she had enough brass in her head to make a huge kettle. 'Yes,' replied Biddy, 'and you've got enough sap in yours to fill it.'

She was not intimidated by judges; she was not impressed by the Mackenzies and their new wealth. She liked to remind Margaret Mackenzie that she had once worked as an upstairs maid at Biddy's hotel. Biddy also liked to mount a soapbox in Kirkfield to preach against people who had acquired too much too soon. Like the ancient Brahan Seer who foresaw the demise of the Highland Mackenzie clan, Biddy predicted the downfall of the Kirkfield Mackenzies. She entertained the community and no doubt embarrassed some of the Mackenzies. She became a legend in her day and for generations afterwards.

William Mackenzie was probably more amused than insulted by Biddy's sharp tongue. In any case, she did not limit his political and business activities. In 1882, as his second term as reeve was coming to an end, he headed out to Winnipeg, where he planned to establish a branch of 'Mackenzie Brothers' in the booming Manitoba capital. In spite of a lingering recession which had begun with the crash of 1873, Canada appeared healthy and confident. In 1876, Alexander Graham Bell, a Canadian of Scottish birth, was given credit for inventing the telephone; Manitoba was beginning to export wheat; and urban centres were growing rapidly. The arrival in November 1878 of the new governor general, the Marquis of Lorne and his wife, the Princess Louise, daughter of the Queen, confirmed to Canadians their important status within the Empire. In 1879, Canadian Ned Hanlon became the world's champion sculler. In 1880 Sir John A. Macdonald and George Stephen signed a contract to build a transcontinental railway to the Pacific. The times were right for a man of ambition and ability such as William Mackenzie.

CHAPTER TWO

Seeking Newer Worlds, 1882–91

It isn't so different, the way we wander through the past. Lost, disordered, fearful, we follow what signs there remain; we read the street names, but cannot be confident where we are.

(Julian Barnes, *Flaubert's Parrot* [1985] 60)

In April 1882, Mackenzie took the train to Winnipeg to set up a branch of Mackenzie Brothers.[1] Perhaps because he foresaw the end of the boom, he abandoned expansion plans and in June was back in Kirkfield, where he soon became re-engaged in politics. In the Dominion elections of 1882, Hector Cameron was running for the Conservatives. Mackenzie campaigned for him and was promised extensive timber concessions in north Victoria County should Cameron and Sir John A. Macdonald be victorious. They were, but Cameron's opponent claimed voting irregularities. At a subsequent trial, at which Mackenzie testified, Cameron was charged with 'boodling,' a term covering anything from political corruption to vote buying. Mackenzie was found blameless,[2] and ended up with a licence to cut valuable timber northeast of Kirkfield,[3] apparently the result of his association with Cameron.

In 1884 Mackenzie and his partner, his former schoolmate John McDonald, acquired an even richer contract, thanks to Mackenzie's friendship with James Ross, now manager of the western division of CPR construction. With a gang of men, a portable saw mill, and a supply of horses, Mackenzie and McDonald headed for the Rockies to build bridges for the CPR. The workers from Eldon Township soon became recognized for their loyalty to Mackenzie and McDonald, and were dubbed the 'Eldon Reserve' by other gangs, who sometimes did not view their own bosses with the same respect. Mackenzie and McDonald's office and sleeping quarters were located in a large tent. Between worksites in the Rockies and the Columbia Valley, the two men moved their equipment along a temporary tote road, a narrow and precipitous pathway carved into the side of the majestic mountains.[4] Of the dozen or so bridges constructed in western BC that year, Mackenzie and McDonald built two–one at the third crossing of the Kicking Horse River, and a large two - deck bridge, 150 feet long, at a town called Donald.[5] They also built telegraph offices, eating houses, water tanks, a gunpowder factory at Moberly, and coal sheds; and they dug a well.

In 1884 Mackenzie met his future partner, Donald Mann, who had been working with the CPR since 1879. Their meeting was nothing unusual; during the construction of the CPR, almost every contractor in Canada must have met almost every other contractor at least once. Because these two men later became one of the most famous teams in Canadian history, however, their first meeting became legend. Each contractor had ordered seven mules to transport goods. In one story, only seven mules arrived. In another version, there were enough mules, but they were all in the same pen. The two contractors agreed to divide the mules by selecting one or two at a time, so that each would end up with seven mules of similar quality. Although Mann outwitted Mackenzie and got the pick of the mules, Mackenzie ended up admiring his brash opponent. The truth of the stories lies not so much in the details but in Mackenzie's ability to spot a good man, even if an antagonist. The fact that there are at least three different versions of their first meeting suggests the difficulty of discovering the truth in any event, especially in the life of a promoter and self-inventor such as Mackenzie.

Railway construction days in the 1880s were zesty. By June 1884 three thousand men, including some of the 'hard lot' who had worked on the Northern Pacific Railway, had arrived in the mountains.[6] Theft and an occasional murder resulted, and whiskey flowed in from Idaho and points east. Prostitutes set up shop in saloons adjacent to construction sites, but were dispersed to the edge of a zone sixteen kilometres wide on either side of construction, where whiskey and prostitution were prohibited. In September 1884 no man's land was extended to thirty-two kilometres when sixteen kilometres proved inadequate to prevent lusty construction workers from visiting tents and saloons of ill repute and returning to worksites early the next morning.

And yet construction sites retained a remarkable air of civility, thanks partly to the North West Mounted Police and the intrepid Sergeant Sam Steele from Orillia, a few kilometres west of Kirkfield.[7] Priests came by to say mass, Governor-General Lord Lansdowne toured construction sites in the summer of 1885, and journalists from as far away as Fleet Street noted living conditions, breathtaking scenery, and the railway that would give the Empire a land route to the Pacific. Mackenzie received mail from his wife by packhorse; and itinerant photographers captured workers, Indians, and Mounties, all posing sternly amid magnificent mountains, lacy railway trestles, muddy main streets, and police barracks built of logs. One photograph shows Mackenzie dressed in trousers, vest, and jacket, posing with engineers. He is wearing what appears to be a pith helmet, protective headgear for supervising bridge work.

Hardy contractors and their men overcame a rainy spring and summer and early fall snows to complete the line to Donald by January 1885.[8] In Donald, Mackenzie, McDonald, and Mann built attractive log houses on higher ground overlooking the public buildings, two churches, several hotels, saloons, and gambling houses near the station. According to D.B. Hanna, railway mythmaker par excellence, Donald Mann's house was furnished with a piano which sometimes accompanied William Mackenzie's clear tenor voice in Sunday evening singalongs of gospel hymns such as 'What a Friend We Have in Jesus.' They may have even performed popular Scottish songs such as 'Loch Lomond.'

In January 1885 Mackenzie and McDonald were back in Kirkfield to recruit more men.[9] They returned to BC with Ab Boynton, Kirkfield's livery man, who in a railway car set up a general store in the Selkirks. As tracks were laid, his store moved westward, selling to contractors an array of goods from sides of beef to longjohns.[10] Later that spring, Margaret Mackenzie and Sophia McDonald, wife of Mackenzie's partner, took their families to live in Donald, where Sophia gave birth to baby Jack shortly after her arrival. The two women apparently never ran into Henry Norman of London's *Pall Mall Gazette*, who told his English readers exactly what they wanted to hear, that Donald was 'the toughest place in the Dominion' and that there was 'not a respectable woman in the place.'[11] Margaret Mackenzie no doubt disparaged the invitations to excess in downtown Donald, but she also recognized a good investment. She bought and managed one of the town's log saloons,[12] though it was not, one hopes, a place where temptations proved so 'particularly trying' for several Mounties who deserted after getting themselves into 'trouble,' according to the circumspect language of the NWMP annual report.

Mackenzie's project for 1885 was the construction of the massive

Mountain Creek Bridge, one of the largest wooden structures ever built. The gorge through which Mountain Creek tumbled was almost half a kilometre wide. The bridge was built with over 300,000 metres of Douglas fir, taken from surrounding forests and planed in one of Mackenzie's mills, which operated night and day in order to avoid construction delays.[13] Observed from each end, the completed bridge, sixty metres high, resembled an elongated A with a flattened top on which tracks were laid.

This bridge and other structures proved more costly than expected, and in early 1885 the CPR ran out of money. Contractors went unpaid and so, therefore, did their workers, who grew restive. Mackenzie may have been at the mill in Donald at the end of March when news reached him that several hundred men, engaged in clearing and grading west of Mountain Creek, were on the march. They soon arrived at Mountain Creek Bridge. From on high, Mackenzie's men stared down in silence. Loyal to their boss, they refused to strike. One strike leader ran to the block and tackle, whose ropes and pulleys hauled timber up to worksites above, and cut the rope. Lumber came crashing to the ground. The Eldon Reserve continued to resist silently. Balfour, manager of bridge construction, called the men down, but they still refused to join the strike.

The frustrated strikers continued on to Beaver, where James Ross promised free room and board until the railway could find more funds. Most workers dispersed, but about 300 remained in Beaver, harassing track layers, teamsters, and bridge workers. On 1 April, James Ross mounted an engine and rode full tilt through defiant strikers, who scattered as the engine approached. A volley of bullets hit the engine, which stopped just past the narrow canyon of Beaver Creek, at the end of track. Ross's purpose was to prevent the strikers from reaching other workers further down the track. The 300 angry strikers tried to break through the gap, but were stopped by Mounties. The strikers turned back to Beaver and headed for the Mountie barracks. Sam Steele rose from his sickbed and posted himself at one end of a bridge separating the police barracks from the centre of Beaver. The Riot Act was read, and Steele threatened to shoot the first man to put a foot on the bridge. A couple of Mounties dragged the strike leader across the bridge to jail. The strike ended. A pay car arrived. The Riel Rebellion, which began a few days later, ensured that the CPR would not be short of money.[14] The Mountain Creek Bridge was completed, and on schedule.

Mackenzie's men built other bridges in the Selkirks, and at Cascade Mountain a snowshed that was also a marvel of engineering, its massive walls and roof strong enough to withstand tons of snow hurtling down the mountains. Each snowshed, up to a third of a kilometre long, was built of enormous logs and cedar timbers. Inner walls were fixed securely to mountain sides, and outer walls, left open to let in light, looked like delicate latticework.

On 9 November 1885, Mackenzie and John McDonald were at Craigellachie to watch Donald A. Smith drive the last spike.[15] The following January, they were in Van Horne's office in Montreal to collect their profits, about $200,000 for each contractor for two years' work.[16] Railway contracting was a lucrative game. Small wonder that the railway company itself lived on the edge of bankruptcy.

Mackenzie could now play the role of part-time gentleman farmer. In February 1886 he purchased a large farm on the edge of Kirkfield from his connections, the Armstrongs, and a trotting mare from Matthew Perry. Social and political affairs kept him busy. On Monday, 22 February 1886, Margaret and he celebrated the double wedding of her brother and sister, John and Annie Merry, to Brigit and William Mitchell, feasting and dancing long past midnight. In early March Mackenzie journeyed to Ottawa with a delegation from Victoria County to persuade the Dominion government to complete the Trent Canal.

Later that month, with McDonald and about sixty men, Mackenzie headed for BC to build snowsheds on the east side of the Selkirks. His contract stipulated that the sheds were to be completed in eight months. He completed the job a month ahead of schedule, though other contractors had predicted that even eight months was not enough time – at least so he claimed in later life. Years later, no doubt, Mackenzie exaggerated dangers and obstacles. Nevertheless, his qualities of leadership and organization stand out, and during the construction of the CPR, he emerges as a confident, competent contractor, and as a good field person who maintained the respect of his workers.

In 1886, though contractors were yet to complete the snowsheds, trains began to run to the Pacific. In mid-July the Mackenzie-McDonald men caught a view of Sir John A. and Lady Macdonald, she on the cowcatcher, as their westbound train struggled up the east slope of the Selkirks. If C.W. Jefferys' illustration, composed years later, is based on an actual scene, the occasion was festive, with workers waving from the top of stationary railway cars, from the crevices of rocks, and from limbs of overhanging trees.[17]

Sir John A. was not the only visitor. Canadian artists such as William Brymner and Lucius O'Brien were commissioned by William Van Horne to paint CPR scenery in order to decorate hotels such as the Banff Springs and to advertise the railway and Canadian scenery in Britain. William Mackenzie's father, John, still active at seventy-six, travelled across the North West Territories to visit his son in the Selkirks,[18] then returned to Kirkfield with Margaret Mackenzie at the end of August. The following October, Katharine, William and Margaret's eighth child, was born in Kirkfield.[19] That same month, Mackenzie and McDonald travelled to Montreal to collect payment for the snowshed contracts, each having made the admirable sum of about $150,000.[20]

As contracting money returned to Kirkfield, the little town revelled in prosperity and respectability. Each time that Mackenzie returned from the mountains, he could stroll the main street, catch up on the latest gossip, and admire the changes that had occurred in his absence. In 1886 Messrs. Ritchie and A.C. ('Big Archie') McKenzie of Brechin bought the general store once owned by Rod Campbell, a member of the Eldon Reserve killed in October 1885 while unloading timber in the Rockies. The income of harnessmaker Wright increased in 1886, thanks to a $200 order shipped to Mackenzie in July. (D.B. Hanna's story that Mackenzie used old harness in mountain construction is probably another example of railway mythology.) The town acquired the trappings of a leisured society – a music teacher, watchmaker, and jeweller, all in one man named Richardson. In the Buckner block, Margaret Mackenzie and her daughters could have their billowing Victorian dresses made in a new dressmaking shop. That fall, the town established a debating society. 'Which is the more useful member of society, the farmer or the mechanic?' one of its early debates asked. In November Edward Mosgrove was hired as the new Kirkfield teacher for 1887, at a salary of $450 per annum.[21] His contract came into effect in January, the first month of the school year. Also in January 1887 Mackenzie made an attempt to enter Dominion politics, but failed to wrest the nomination away from his former benefactor, Hector Cameron. In February he and John McDonald, with their wives and children, were off to Montreal to attend Carnaval.

In early March, Mackenzie was in Maine, where he and Donald Mann united their contracting companies for the first time to build an eighty-five-kilometre section of the Maine 'short line,' designed to give the CPR a route from Montreal to Saint John. James Ross was manager of construction, P. Turner Bone was assistant engineer,

Pat Burns supplied the meat, and Hugh Lumsden was chief engineer. The Eldon Reserve, as well as six carloads of horses to pull scrapers and haul ties and rails, followed Mackenzie to Maine.[22]

Contractors were not always guaranteed hundreds of thousands of dollars in profit, as Mackenzie discovered in Maine. The surveying had been improperly done and instead of loose soil, Mackenzie and Mann found nothing but rock and hardpan. It was soon obvious that their cost estimates were too low. Mackenzie appealed to Tom Shaughnessy of the CPR, who raised their mileage payments, allowing them to break even.[23]

In December 1888, when Mackenzie and his men finished two seasons in Maine, they brought back little money, but they were rich with the tall tales of giants such as Paul Bunyan, told in the lumbering country through which the railway had been constructed. In Kirkfield Paul Bunyan became 'Big Jim,' who with his blue ox Babe was credited with creating lakes such as Balsam and Simcoe, which were Jim and Babe's footprints. Versions of the Bunyan fable reached Minnesota and Manitoba, perhaps carried by Pat Burns and other Kirkfield men who migrated to Manitoba in the 1880s and '90s.[24]

When Mackenzie returned to Kirkfield from Maine, he joined Margaret and the children in a splendid three-storey mansion on Nelson Street. It had cost $18,000 to build, four or five times the average cost of brick houses of 1888. Downstairs were large rooms serving as parlour, reception, and dining rooms. The entrance hallway was almost five metres wide. At the top of the finely crafted oak staircase were fifteen large rooms, including one huge bathroom. The house was heated and ventilated by a large forced-air furnace.

There were other improvements: Mackenzie Brothers were building an addition to their grist mill and planned to put in rollers to produce rolled oats. They continued to operate their saw mill and a sash, door, and planing factory, and in 1887 they erected fifty-six buildings in the area. McKay's woollen mill opened in the spring of 1888, and that same year, a veterinarian set up shop. Two general stores competed, as did two hardware stores. A.C. McKenzie risked bankruptcy by slashing profits in an unsuccessful attempt to destroy his competitors, Shields and Perry.

There were new enterprises each time Mackenzie returned: a bakery, a boot and shoe shop, tin shop, blacksmith and wagon shop, furniture store, stove and pump store, two harness shops, two hotels, seven carpenters, one tailor, three dressmakers, an insurance agent, a medical doctor, two teachers, two butcher shops, a superintendent of municipal works, two Protestant churches, and a livery stable with stylish rigs. The Burns brothers, Dominic of Vancouver and Pat of Winnipeg, returned to Kirkfield periodically to visit their parents, the O'Byrnes. In March 1889, Pat bought a carload of horses from Kirkfield and shipped them to Winnipeg to sell to homesteaders, livery owners, and perhaps to the street railway.

The town was more than pleased with Bill Mackenzie, who continued to 'employ his home friends,' thus building up 'his own village and county.' In Kirkfield, the Mackenzies were playing the role of the town gentry. Besides the mansion, Margaret Mackenzie built a community hall, developed a park and a Catholic burial ground next to the Protestant cemetery, and began to line the streets with hard maples. Her new steamer took friends and family for excursions on nearby Balsam Lake. In 1888 the Mackenzies enrolled their eldest son, R.J., in Toronto's prestigious Upper Canada College. In May 1889, Mabel, the eldest daughter, gave 'quite a select picnic' for a few friends from Lindsay. On 15 December 1888, Margaret Mackenzie gave birth to their last child, Grace.[25]

The death of George Laidlaw on 6 August 1889 provided a fitting conclusion to this period of Mackenzie's rapid climb through the ranks of Canadian business and society. During the 1880s, Laidlaw had spent a good deal of time on his 5,000-acre ranch, 'The Fort,' east of Kirkfield, breeding cattle, playing gentleman rancher, and corresponding with Sir John A. Macdonald. Laidlaw had introduced Mackenzie to the world of railways. He had recognized Mackenzie's strengths – his penchant for meeting deadlines, for doing the job economically, and for dealing with gangs of men and new engineering concepts. For Laidlaw, Mackenzie had constructed bridges, wharves, and stations. At Laidlaw's death, his former protégé had already surpassed him in wealth and was at least his equal in accomplishments.

When his old mentor died, Mackenzie was at work on the Qu'Appelle, Long Lake & Saskatchewan Railway (QLLSR), which was to link Regina to Prince Albert. It would be 'one of the most important roads in the Northwest,' Sir John A. Macdonald told the House of Commons in 1889. Poet Charles Mair, a resident of Prince Albert in 1889, was in favour of the line, since it would increase the value of his real estate. His friend and connection Colonel George Denison was also pleased, since a wealthier Mair could then return to a 'Christian community,' Denison's Toronto. Territorial politicians, Mounties, and sober residents of the tiny Temperance Colony of Saskatoon wondered, 'Will we have the Railway next summer?' When construction began in August 1889, after seven years of false starts, Mackenzie was in charge of timber supplies for ties, bridges, and stations; Mann took charge of grading; and Herbert Holt, of track laying. James Ross was general manager.[26]

Throughout his life, Mackenzie was always in too much of a hurry to worry about small details. His object was to get the job done, to make his profit, and to begin the next contract. In the fall of 1888, the Crown Timber Agent discovered Mackenzie's men taking out green timber instead of dry timber. The next year he and Holt left brush and debris lying on the ground after timber operations, claiming that 'it would cost more than the ties were worth.' And although he made a profit of about $25,000 on timber and ties in 1889 and 1890, Mackenzie owed $741.81 to the Crown Lands Department, apparently because it had slipped his mind. James Ross covered the amount.[27]

In his biography of Sir Joseph Flavelle, Michael Bliss borrows the title of a 1970 television series to describe the close business relations enjoyed by a small group of Montreal and Toronto businessmen and bankers who, during the Laurier and Borden years, directed millions of dollars of business in Canada and elsewhere. In business terms, they were 'All in the Family.' The QLLSR was constructed or supervised by William Mackenzie's 'family': Pat Burns was beef contractor; Ewan Mackenzie had a grading contract south of Prince Albert; John, another Mackenzie brother, was in charge of a saw mill in Donald, BC, where he was killed in November 1889; Malcolm McTaggart, son of William's eldest sister, Kate, was awarded a contract, as was Hugh John Montgomery, a relative by marriage. John McTaggart, Kate's second husband, was Crown Timber Agent for the Prince Albert district, responsible for supervising the cleanup of 'The Pines,' where Mackenzie and Holt had left the debris in 1889. Hugh Lumsden, Mackenzie's friend from Woodville, Ontario, was Chief Inspecting Engineer for the Dominion government. Thus, even the inspectors were 'family.'

John McTaggart had moved from Kirkfield to Prince Albert in 1884 to act as Dominion Lands Agent. In 1885, after the battle of Batoche, his wife, Kate, their family, and Mary McRae, Kate's only child from her unhappy first marriage in Kirkfield, followed McTaggart to Prince Albert. Mary married Hugh John Montgomery, a widower from Prince Edward Island, who in the 1890s sent for his fifteen-year-old daughter, Lucy Maud. The budding young writer, passionate and headstrong, enjoyed the company of Mabel and Trudie Mackenzie, William's eldest daughters, and Mary Jane Mackenzie, William's half sister, who were Maud's age. She never liked her stepmother, however, and may have used her as a model for the stern Marilla of *Anne of Green Gables*.

On 2 September 1890, Maud and her Mackenzie connections welcomed the first through train from Regina. Though absent from the celebrations, William Mackenzie played a role in Maud's diary entry. She guessed correctly that he was a millionaire. The $100,000 made on QLLSR construction pushed his accumulated tax-free income over the million mark, a remarkable sum even today.

By the time the last spike was driven on 22 October 1890, Mackenzie and his three partners had begun work on their next project, a railway from Calgary to Edmonton. They were too busy to attend sod-turning ceremonies in Calgary on 21 July 1890, and thus avoided the tainted roasted ox that played havoc with the digestive systems of VIPs such as Edgar Dewdney, Minister of the Interior, and Senator James Lougheed. The railway was to reach Edmonton or a point nearby by 1 July 1891, and the CPR agreed to operate and manage it for the first six years. A land grant of 6,400 acres per mile of construction and an annual payment of $80,000 for carrying Mounties and mail would finance construction and subsidize operations, Prime Minister Macdonald announced in the House on 5 May 1890.

The four contractors were moving up in the world of railways – as well as being contractors, they were four of the seven directors of the Calgary & Edmonton. Mackenzie mills in BC supplied timber for culverts, stations, water tanks, and bridges over the Bow and the Red Deer rivers. By early December 1890, track-laying had reached Red Deer. In five months, the efficient contractors had laid 370 kilometres of track.

Mackenzie returned to Ontario for the rest of the winter. In Kirkfield he hired over thirty men to work in the Northwest and made contact with the Liberal regime of Sir Oliver Mowat. Before returning to Calgary, he entertained the Provincial Treasurer and his wife in Kirkfield. Although he had always supported Conservatives, and no doubt had voted for Sir John A. Macdonald's party the previous March, Mackenzie always kept in touch with those in power, no matter what the party or the ideology. Politicians were also members of the 'family.'

Both Alex and Ewan Mackenzie had contracts on the Calgary & Edmonton in 1891, Alex as superintendent of station construction, and Ewan as a grading contractor. Several of Mackenzie's nephews from Kirkfield worked on the railway and his cousin from Bolsover, Dan Munro, built the Strathcona Hotel on Whyte Avenue and finished the interiors of several stations. That year, both man and beast were subject to disease. In 1891, typhoid killed many subcontractors' horses; fifteen NWMP constables contracted malaria and six others caught gonorrhea, though happily all were cured and eventually resumed duties.

On Saturday afternoon, 15 July 1891, an Edmonton pioneer named Ross drove the last spike. Eight days later the CPR began to operate the line. In late September, with James Ross and Augustus Nanton, Mackenzie took an overnight train from Calgary. At St. Albert, near Edmonton, the three men enjoyed a day of prairie chicken hunting. Edmonton journalist Frank Oliver was disgusted, not at the killing of prairie chickens – in 1891, they were plentiful – but at the fact that the hunters brought a team and wagon from Calgary instead of renting them in Edmonton.[28]

Oliver's nose had been out of joint for several months, ever since he discovered that the 400 or so Edmonton residents were to play second fiddle to Strathcona, then a separate municipality across the North Saskatchewan River. Although the railway company used the word 'Edmonton' in its title, the cost of building a bridge over the river was prohibitive. The agreement stipulated that the railway be built to a point at or near Edmonton, and since Strathcona was a Calgary & Edmonton townsite, the railway company had every intention of causing a boom there rather than north of the river.[29] Calgary papers were amused. Oliver charged the Calgary & Edmonton and the CPR with acquiring excessive land grants, with selling $2 million worth of bonds in excess of construction costs, and with low quality construction and high freight rates – charges mostly the product of Oliver's overheated imagination, which cooled considerably when Edmonton gained its first railway, several years later, courtesy the same Mackenzie and Mann.

The line reached Strathcona, and once again Mackenzie had come in contact with the northern prairies. Contracting was a lucrative business, and he had risen to the rank of director of a railway company. He had noted the propensity of Canadian governments to reduce financial risks in railway construction by means of subsidies and government-guaranteed bonds. But in 1891, no matter how much he wanted to construct more railways through the prairies, a weak domestic and international economy discouraged agricultural settlement and railway construction. During the early 1890s, Mackenzie turned his attention to urban transportation.

He had already learned that it was necessary to advertise his wealth in order to assure the business and investment world that he was a successful contractor and a good investment risk.[30] In 1889 he acquired a second house, a two-and-a-half storey brick house at 623 Sherbourne Street, Toronto, south of Bloor, and thus became a neighbour of John Ross Robertson, Joseph Flavelle, A.L. Gooderham, Henry Pellat, and architect E.J. Lennox. Not far away, on Jarvis Street, lived the Masseys, the Mulocks, and George Gooderham.[31] With the move to Toronto came a change in spelling of the family name, from 'Mckenzy' (old John Mackenzie's misspelling of the name) and from variations of 'Mckenzie' and 'McKenzie,' to the more genteel, more Scottish and Protestant 'Mackenzie.' In Toronto, country matters and manners were camouflaged and refined: the marriage date was altered; and Margaret Mackenzie took lessons in deportment and accent. To take tea with Toronto's 'FF's, its First Families, it was de rigueur to avoid faux pas that might reveal log-shanty origins in the hinterland.

In 1891 Mackenzie reached his forty-second birthday. With his fortune, he could have retired to Kirkfield to become a gentleman farmer and sitting member at Queen's Park or on Parliament Hill. His name arose several times during the 1890s as a potential Conservative candidate. He chose to call himself a businessman, however, which meant, of course, that he was still engaged in politics. In 1889 he became president of the C.J. Smith Coal Company, whose headquarters were on King Street East, the financial centre of Toronto and, to a growing extent, of the Dominion. Toronto was helping to settle and insure the vast prairies: also on King Street were the headquarters of the Saskatoon Temperance Colonization Society, and nearby, at Richmond and Victoria, was the new and magnificent Confederation Life Building.

Coal generated electrical power which provided light and heat for Toronto, and ran some of its factories. Two years after investing in coal, Mackenzie and three others purchased the horse-drawn Toronto Street Railway. These two acquisitions suggest that he was beginning to see that electrical power and transportation companies could be united under one management. His urban utilities empire was taking shape.

CHAPTER THREE

The Electric 1890s

Hypothesis is spun directly from the temperament of the biographer.
(Julian Barnes, *Flaubert's Parrot* [1985] 40)

The excitement had been building all morning. Rumour had it that an electric trolley might travel up Toronto's Church Street that day. Sure enough, on that warm Wednesday, 10 August 1892, a horseless trolley sailed effortlessly out of the Toronto Railway Company's car barns at Front and Frederick streets. Its dark chocolate exterior and spring-cushioned seats, its handcrafted maple interior, mirrors, plate-glass windows, and five electric lamps shimmered in the sunlight. It moved west along Front Street past city hall at Jarvis, headed towards the new Gooderham Flatiron office tower at Church and Front, then curved to the right and headed north on Church Street. It was loaded to the brim. William Mackenzie, president of the Toronto Railway Company, was enjoying his new toy. Beside him sat his wife, and nearby, several young Mackenzies. City engineer E.H. Keating, other officials of the city and the railway company, journalists and former MPP, John Leys, who had been a passenger on Toronto's first horse-drawn tram car in 1861, were all proud and pleased.

As the trolley approached the Metropolitan Methodist Church at Church and Queen streets, an inquisitive drunk climbed aboard, offered his fare, and squeezed in beside an amused William Mackenzie. 'Congrashulate you,' he confided to Mackenzie. 'It's a fine 'speriment. Been street car man m'self.' The tension was broken; the guests laughed. Keating leaned over and shook hands with Mackenzie. People strolling along Front or Church streets stopped in their tracks to marvel. A young lad watching at Church and Wilton streets raised a cheer for the trolley.

Young Alex Mackenzie, middle son of William, was hanging on for dear life at the rear end of the trolley, which was so overloaded that the front end was higher than the back. Alex's cousin, little Viola Mackenzie, never forgot the magic of that horseless ride[1] past red-brick cottages on tree-lined Church Street, east onto posh Bloor Street, past the large house where Alex's best friend, Arthur Hills, lived. While the Hills family stood waving from their verandah, Arthur's grandmother exclaimed, 'Isn't it just wicked!'[2] The trolley whisked its laughing passengers towards Sherbourne Street and north into lower Rosedale, the end of the line.[3]

It was a typical Mackenzie show, the grand gesture combined with a whiff of disorganization. No one had been quite sure whether the trolley would actually run the whole distance that afternoon. As a precaution, two horses pulled a tram a hundred metres in front of the trolley. Mackenzie had even forgotten to invite the mayor.

Word of the electric trolley spread quickly. During the return trip, crowds lined the sidewalks. One youngster attempted to keep up, but to no avail. Some daredevils tempted fate by running across the track in front of the oncoming trolley. Others placed piles of dirt on the track, having been told that the trolley would lose power if the wheels broke contact with the tracks. It headed down Church Street, and the motorman began to run it a bit faster, probably at the urging of Mackenzie. 'We're now going fifteen miles per hour!' he exclaimed to the excited passengers. (If so, the car was travelling at almost twice the speed recommended by city council. Mackenzie was never averse to stretching rules.) At Church and King streets, where the spire of St. James Cathedral kept watch, passengers noticed Mayor R.J. Fleming. 'Come on! Get on!' they shouted and waved. The big, outspoken, bearded mayor rode with them to the barns on Front Street.

The casual observer might have supposed that harmony had always informed the relationship of the Toronto Railway Company and the city of Toronto. The harmony, however, was an illusion. By 1890 Toronto had become a beautiful city of tree-lined streets, green and leafy parks, fine brick residences, and majestic church spires keeping watch on the city. In 1891, when Maud Montgomery, en route from Prince Albert to Prince Edward Island, visited her Mackenzie connections, she thought Toronto a 'beautiful city,' much more attractive than Ottawa. A Scottish visitor found it 'in every respect a very beautiful place.'

Lovely yes, but also complacent, Godly, and goodly. It wanted to emerge from the recession of the early 1890s that threatened violence whenever knots of unemployed men huddled around the city hall; it yearned to play the leading role in the economic and cultural life of Canada; and yet Toronto seemed to enjoy the leisurely pace represented by horse-drawn trams and gas lamplighters. It desired and yet feared change. Its political system reflected that ambivalence – untrained, unpaid aldermen were expected to make big-city decisions requiring the knowledge of a mechanical engineer and the morality of a preacher.[4]

What William Mackenzie brought about in Toronto was nothing short of revolutionary. He helped to speed up the pace of life there; he helped to shift economic power from Montreal to Toronto; and by doing so, he helped to give birth to a new era of prosperity in the Queen City. He dared to fulfil the inchoate longings of Torontonians. He was their agent of change. They admired him, yet they also mistrusted him and the new power he wielded. City officials often reflected this ambivalence in their dealings with Mackenzie over the following three decades.

Mackenzie had not planned to invest in Toronto transportation. In 1891 his chief interest was the completion of railway work in the District of Alberta. Opportunities often lay across his path, and his imagination and foresight led him to see possibilities and profit in developing what he had stumbled upon. In May 1891 he was in Toronto en route to Ottawa, on Calgary & Edmonton Railway business. His lawyer, Nicol Kingsmill, a director of the Calgary & Edmonton, mentioned that a couple of Americans were at the Queen's Hotel on Front Street. One of them, Henry Everett, a Cleveland entrepreneur of electric street railways, was acquainted with electric trolleys and with engineers who understood the new technology. Everett had come to Toronto in January 1891 at the request of Toronto city council, in order to determine a selling price for the old horse-drawn tramway franchise, due to expire in May. Senator Frank Smith was asking $5 million for his company. Everett evaluated it at $1,453,788, which the city paid to Smith in May 1891.

The city's fractious relationship with Smith's company made some members of council wary of private ownership of the transit system. But the majority of aldermen had no intention of operating a street railway; and Toronto ratepayers had turned down this option, perhaps because they knew that public ownership of utilities did not guarantee satisfactory service – witness the city-owned water system, which from time to time spat forth polluted harbour water. Furthermore, the city did not have the financial means to convert the street railway system to electricity at an estimated $30,000 to $35,000 per mile. New trolleys, heavier rails, and overhead copper wiring were expensive, as was a power generating plant, its long pipes extending into Lake Ontario to bring in the water that the huge coal-powered boilers would convert to steam in order to generate electricity. Private companies had access to the necessary capital. In return, they insisted on monopoly franchises over a given period, usually thirty years. These monopolies were carefully regulated by city by-laws that controlled fares, rents paid to the city, and hours of operation.

A month before Mackenzie met Everett at the Queen's Hotel, Toronto council had considered several offers of purchase, all unsatisfactory. Near the end of April, when council made a second call for tenders, Everett decided to act. He persuaded George Kiely, a member of the old tramway syndicate, to join him. Everett and Kiely sought a second man from Toronto. They spoke to Nicol Kingsmill, who recommended William Mackenzie. A few days after their meeting at the Queen's Hotel, Everett, Kiely, Mackenzie, and Chancey Woodworth, Everett's friend from Rochester, submitted an offer to purchase the old Toronto Railway Company.[5]

Of the three groups tendering in this second round, Everett and Mackenzie made the most attractive offer. They combined financial and technical expertise and should have won in May, when the second-round tenders were opened. They were willing to raise their own capital, whereas the other competing syndicates, though composed of wealthy men such as George Cox and S.H. Janes, wanted the city to borrow the millions of dollars required for electrification. Instead of awarding the franchise to the Mackenzie group, however, council called for a third round to allow Cox and Janes time to find their own sources of capital.

The two rival syndicates were now aware of the details of Mackenzie and Everett's offer. Council insisted that they emulate one of the attractive features of Mackenzie's offer: as income rose, so would the percentage of that income paid to the city. The deadline for the amended tenders was 30 June. The second Mackenzie offer was even more attractive than the first: the minimum percentage paid on earnings was raised from 7.1 per cent to 8 per cent, and the maximum from 10.1 per cent to 20 per cent, in addition to $800 per mile for single track paid to the city as a form of street rental. The three city officials examining the tenders decided that Mackenzie's was the 'best straight offer,' for it provided the city with about a million dollars more over the lifetime of the franchise than did Mackenzie and Everett's first offer.[6]

Throughout this June bidding period, the Everett-Kiely-Mackenzie syndicate managed to maintain good press relations.[7] Had they then disappeared for a month, had Mackenzie spent July in Kirkfield, the syndicate might have avoided the gossip that plagued them in August. On Saturday, 4 July, with Everett and Noel Marshall, his partner at the C.J. Smith Coal Company, Mackenzie visited several aldermen to preach the merits of private ownership. They were asked many questions. Which school system, the public or the separate, would their taxes support? (In 1891 the company had the right to choose.) Why, the public, not the Roman Catholic system, Mackenzie assured the concerned Protestant alderman. Many of the questions were of a similar subjective nature.[8] One alderman refused to talk to them; another was 'not at home'; Alderman Graham, whom they visited at his store, continued to favour municipal ownership. They may have influenced Aldermen Bell and Jolliffe, who later voted for Everett and Mackenzie.

When council met on Tuesday afternoon, 21 July, Mackenzie was present with Everett, Kiely, lawyers Laidlaw and Kingsmill, and Mahler, Everett's lobbyist from Cleveland. After a heated debate, council decided by a vote of twenty-four to fourteen to accept the Mackenzie tender. Mayor Clarke was one of the nays. Amid the confusion and jubilation, Alderman Boustead muttered, 'Gentlemen, you have just thrown away a million and half,' his estimate of the profit that might have accrued to the city during thirty years of municipal ownership.[9]

Mackenzie returned to Kirkfield. Rumours began to circulate that the Mackenzie syndicate had spent up to $50,000 to win the franchise. No doubt money was spent by all tendering syndicates, 'tens of thousands,' according to Mackenzie's friend, Sam Hughes.[10] The money bought advertising space in newspapers, legal counsel, engineering advice, and other transaction costs.[11] Hughes was probably thinking also of questionable expenditures. Fred Coleman, an associate of Mackenzie and Marshall, made a bet with Alderman Gowanlock that the Mackenzie tender would not win. In September, after the awarding of the franchise, Everett or Kiely 'lent' an alderman $10,000 and purchased real estate from another.

Into the midst of the fray strolled the flamboyant E.A. Macdonald, sporting his floppy black sombrero. He had been defeated by Mayor Clarke the previous December and was seeking to embarrass city hall. A real estate speculator and a 'child of fate and turmoil,' as *Saturday Night* dubbed him, he was constantly in need of cash and attention. During a decline in property values, his suburban land – some on Bellamy Road in Scarborough, and hence his nickname, 'Baron of Bellamy' – had brought him to the edge of bankruptcy. On 21 July, the day of the council decision, he sought an injunction to prevent the Mackenzie syndicate from winning the franchise, then dropped the legal action.

The delighted press had a marketable issue, and in a city where six newspapers competed for the attention of a population[12] no larger than 200,000, the Baron was always good press. On Saturday evening, 25 July, Macdonald went to Noel Marshall for money. Marshall lent him $4,000, provided that he drop his injunction. Macdonald gladly took the cheque, photographed it, cashed it, showed the photo to a few friends, then asked Marshall for more money – $15,500 in all.

Fred Coleman leaked the story of Macdonald's extortion attempt. The press published a photograph of the cheque. On Monday, 3 August, Mackenzie returned to Toronto. He chastised Marshall.[13] At the corner of King and Yonge, on his way to his office, he ran into Alderman Hewitt, who had made it clear that if bribery of any sort were proven in the awarding of the franchise, he would not hesitate to call for another round of tenders.[14] The conversation between the two men went unrecorded. Mackenzie reimbursed Marshall for the loan to Macdonald, but only because Marshall had believed that he was acting in Mackenzie's best interests. The fact that the money was offered to Macdonald by cheque, not in anonymous cash, suggests that Marshall was indeed making a loan rather than a bribe, although the two are as close as dang is to swearing, as the folks in Eldon Township liked to say.

The second week in August, Mackenzie left for Calgary, where the Calgary & Edmonton Railway was about to begin operations. During his absence, a brief investigation took place. Macdonald continued to insist that aldermen had been bribed, but refused to give names. Council was satisfied with the testimony of Marshall and William Laidlaw, one of Mackenzie's lawyers. The courts refused the *World*'s owner-editor, Billy Maclean, an injunction to postpone council's decision. On 26 August, by a convincing vote of twenty-two to eight, council awarded the franchise to the Mackenzie syndicate.[15] Selling price was $1,453,788. The syndicate made a down payment of $475,000 in cash, assumed responsibility for $600,000 worth of debentures inherited from the Smith company, and agreed to pay the remaining $378,000 within a year at 5 per cent interest. At the end of the thirty-year franchise, the city had the right to buy the railway at a price set by arbitration. The city guaranteed principal and interest of $2,000,000 Toronto Railway Company bonds to finance the electrification of the railway's 110 kilometres (sixty-nine miles) of lines. Mackenzie was in Toronto on 1 September to participate in signing ceremonies at the city hall at Front and Jarvis streets (now the St. Lawrence Market). He spent a few days in Kirkfield, then headed back to Calgary.

On 2 September the street railway began to operate under its new owners. Passengers were pleased – ticket prices were reduced and they could now transfer free of charge. In September the company opened a new Belt Line on Sherbourne, Bloor, Spadina, and King. Lower fares, free transfers, speedier trams, and the Industrial Exhibition resulted in increased gross and net earnings. Council was pleased, for the city was now being paid $8,000 in mileage rental payments, and, more importantly, 8 per cent of rising gross earnings.[16]

The new transfer system, however, caused some problems, based as it was, until paper transfers were developed, on the word of the passenger and the credulity of the conductor. One day in September, Baron Macdonald and his sombrero attempted to board a southbound Yonge tram at King, claiming that he was transferring from a King Street tram. A sceptical conductor threw him off. Macdonald laid assault charges. In late 1893 a new paper transfer system solved most of these problems.

The franchise did not permit Sunday transit unless a majority of ratepayers voted for Sunday cars, and before the vote could be held, the company had to obtain 5,000 signatures. It did so with the help of newspaperman Billy Maclean, once the harshest of critics but now so pleased with the new Toronto Railway Company that he opted for Sunday cars. From the company's point of view, it made little sense to have cars sitting idle one day a week. Potential revenue was lost, and horses had to be fed and cared for, even when idle in their stalls at Front and Frederick streets. Mackenzie's bid for Sunday cars was not novel, for street railways in cities such as Hamilton already ran on Sundays. But when the vote was taken in January 1992, during the annual municipal elections, a large majority voted down Sunday cars and Toronto stayed good.

In the heat of the December campaign, Mackenzie made a questionable deal. Alderman Hewitt, who had supported Mackenzie during the summer of 1891, needed $13,000 to retire a mortgage. Mackenzie was approached. He hesitated. When asked a second time, he consented. While there was never any proof that Mackenzie used this loan to maintain Hewitt's support, the loan is another example of Mackenzie's walking the fine line between profit and propriety. It must be pointed out, however, that during the tough times of the early 1890s, banks were not willing to lend such large sums, especially when the collateral was only real estate. One of the few sources of capital was businessmen. No doubt Mackenzie and other businessmen were approached frequently for loans, and no doubt when they made those loans they expected unspecified political favours.

In April 1892 the Toronto Railway Company was incorporated by the Ontario Legislature and capitalized at $1 million or 10,000 shares with a par or paper value of $100 each.[17] Mackenzie replaced Kiely as president, which suggests that Mackenzie's interest had shifted from steam railways to street railways. No records remain from the early days of the TRC, but later records show that he controlled several thousand shares and that Joseph Flavelle, Sir William Van Horne, James Ross, L.J. Forget, and Senator George Cox were also major shareholders, having paid $25 for each share, or $25,000 for every 1,000 shares. At their first meeting, the directors raised the equity capital from 10,000 to 60,000 shares, to a total of $6 million.[18] If the TRC was floated in the same manner as other Mackenzie companies later in the 1890s, these extra 50,000 shares were worthless and were used as 'sweeteners.' They were given to the syndicate of Mackenzie colleagues in Toronto and Montreal, and to directors of large Canadian insurance companies that bought most of the bonds. It was these bonds, not the common stock, which provided the greater part of the capital required to pay for electrification. The practice of overcapitalization, or 'watering' capital, was used by industrial capitalism to generate the large pools of capital which fuelled the industrial boom prior to the First World War. As the Toronto Railway Company prospered and the common stock increased in value, syndicate members and members of the boards of insurance companies, often the same men, carefully sold small quantities of the stock to small investors in Canada and Britain. Profit from sales of the now valuable stock encouraged members to handle bonds for the next big utilities project requiring millions of dollars of capital.[19]

In May 1892 council voted to allow the TRC to install the trolley, or Edison, system, as it was sometimes called in honour of one of its inventors. The term 'trolley' originally referred to the arm that reached up from the car to the wires overhead to conduct electrical power to each car. There were two other choices of traction – a battery system, in which a rechargeable battery was installed under each car, and the conduit system, in which power was transmitted to cars via a buried third rail. Unfortunately the huge batteries added much weight to each car and often lost power while in service, and the buried third rail of the conduit system often became filled with the snow and dirt of city streets. The trolley system was chosen in Toronto because it was the best workable system. Once the decision was made, the TRC went ahead with electrification, installing poles and lines, purchasing new trolleys, electrifying some of the old horse-drawn cars for temporary use, and constructing lines to the Polson Iron Works, its first source of electrical power. The first electrified routes, after Church Street, were King Street West to the Exhibition grounds and the Belt Line.[20]

For several months, Mackenzie and city engineer Keating had been having discussions, often heated, on the subject of poles. The day before the inaugural run of the first electrified trolley up Church Street, they had words at city hall. Keating wanted iron poles, and so did Mackenzie. But in order to get the electric system working, Mackenzie was installing wooden poles. Keating laid down the law. If Mackenzie did not remove the wooden poles, he would chop them down.

The problem was not unique to Toronto. In Quebec, a pole dispute had resulted in a clearing bee. Keating did have right of final approval before any line could be operated, but the company argued that this right did not extend to the poles. City solicitor Z.A. Lash obtained a stop-work injunction, only to have it cancelled on 19 August. Lash persevered, and in late October obtained a court ruling giving the city the right of final approval of all street railway construction, including poles.

In early November Mackenzie left for Winnipeg on business. The street car company continued to erect wooden poles east on Queen Street at the Don River. Keating dispatched his street commissioner and half a dozen men to Queen Street East. On their shoulders they carried axes. East to the Don they marched and began to chop poles, twenty-three in all. Keating warned the company that he would soon do the same thing on King West. Mayor Fleming initiated a suit. The city obtained an injunction preventing the erection of further poles without Keating's approval.[21]

Mackenzie hurried back to Toronto. He inspected the damage and consulted Keating. They came to an agreement. The company would continue to erect wooden poles provided that Mackenzie immediately order iron poles from England. He did. The pole dispute was the first of scores of differences between the company and the city over the thirty years of the franchise. If lawyers for either side had had the foresight to predict clashpoints, they would have been pleased to incorporate into the charter methods of solving these disagreements. Disputes aired in public tarnished the image of both city council and the company. Had they developed mechanisms to deal with these various problems, they might have solved them in camera, away from the front pages of the daily newspapers. But no proper forum had evolved; no suitable negotiators had been appointed to examine complicated legal questions affecting the relationship between a city and privately-owned utilities. It would take a managerial revolution to develop the necessary negotiating structures in the form of commissioners and a Board of Control for the city, and a hierarchy of managers for the TRC.

The brilliant lawyer Z.A. Lash is often given the credit or the blame for making Mackenzie's contracts so seamless that municipalities could seldom win in court. Ironically, during the early 1890s Lash worked for the city itself. What is remarkable about the pole dispute is that each of the three principals for the city would eventually work for Mackenzie: Z.A. Lash as his chief solicitor, E.H. Keating as an engineer, and the ebullient R.J. Fleming as manager of the Toronto Railway Company. Even S.H. Blake, who helped to draw up the franchise agreement on behalf of the city, would become one of Mackenzie's lawyers in the next century. One of Mackenzie's strong points was a keen ability to spot good men, even if they had once worked for an antagonist. He took great delight in battling with his peers, then hiring their representatives for the next battle.

There was one other dispute in 1892, concerning 'permanent' pavements. In May 1892 council agreed to install permanent pavements on newly electrified streets. That the city owned the pavements, no one doubted; and mileage payments were a form of rent. The city, however, was also in charge of replacing the old pavements, mainly cobblestones set in sand, with new, permanent ones which had to be much more substantially built because of the weight of the trolley cars.[22]

In the 1990s we take for granted transfers and asphalt pavements. A century ago, however, these transit questions found no easy solution. Did cobblestones laid on a bed of sand constitute a permanent pavement, as Keating contended? Or did 'permanent' mean, as the company contended, a solid concrete foundation supporting cobblestones and asphalt?[23] After all, acting engineer Rust had told Mackenzie that the city would lay down asphalt pavements on King and Yonge streets. Mackenzie assumed that the city would do likewise for all electrified lines.[24] The pole dispute, which simmered from August to November, made it more difficult to reach agreement on the pavement question. The approach of winter postponed the discussion until 1893.

Mackenzie must have assumed that the paving problem would be solved. In January 1893 he gave Keating a list of streets to be converted to electricity that year, and ordered rails from England and motors from Canadian General Electric in Peterborough, Ontario. In

early February, Margaret and he, with Mabel and Trudie, set off
from New York on the ss *Bismarck* for a three-month tour of the Med-
iterranean and Europe: Alexandria, Constantinople, Athens, Ge-
noa, Naples, Paris, and the British Isles. They left no record of their
tour. Like the young Lytton Strachey, who was visiting Egypt at the
same time, they no doubt enjoyed the carnival atmosphere of Cairo,
the grand pyramids, and the mysterious Sphinx.[25]

On his return to Toronto in early May,[26] Mackenzie discovered that
the pavement dispute had intensified and that a minor dispute with
the Grand Trunk Railway had developed during his absence. In
early April the railway company had refused the TRC permission to
cross its tracks at Queen Street and the Don River. Neither company
would agree to provide safety gates, which, according to the Railway Act, were the TRC's responsibility. As a result of the dispute,
residents east of the Don River had no street car service. Council
was unable to find a solution. In late April one alderman stated that
the only person who could solve the problem was William Mackenzie, and that he would do it 'speedily.' As soon as he returned, Mackenzie met GTR officials and agreed that the TRC should build the
gates. Queen Street trolleys began to cross GTR tracks.[27]

But the pavement issue eluded easy solution. Because of the economic recession, the city could not raise the necessary money,
through either taxes or bonds, to build kilometres of concrete bases.
In March, Keating decided that all streets to be converted to electricity in 1893 were already permanently paved. It would therefore fall to
the company to replace the cobblestones after removing the old
tracks. A stretch of Spadina Avenue between Queen and King was
the first test of Keating's policy. In mid-April the courts agreed with
the TRC that 'permanent' meant 'concrete and asphalt.' Now the TRC
insisted that the city lay concrete under all new rails, including a
proposed extension of the King line to High Park. Keating refused,
and the company halted construction.

Soon after his return from Europe, Mackenzie made a proposal.
Why not allow the company to lay the concrete under new tracks and
to place cobblestones adjacent to the tracks? In return, the city might
forego mileage payments.[28] Some of the press thought this a ploy to
gain possession of the streets. Could the TRC be trusted to do the job
properly wondered the *Globe*? The Board of Works, however,
thought that under supervision, Mackenzie's idea might work. In
early June, Mackenzie assured the *Globe* that he had no ulterior mo-
tive in proposing that the company do its own paving; he simply
wanted to finish the job of converting to electricity. The paper was

sceptical and so was Keating. The dispute simmered throughout the summer until 14 August, when council decided to accept a Board of Works report recommending what was essentially the street railway company's definition of permanent. The city agreed to lay a concrete base under all tracks laid in 1893.

During this impasse, the Sunday car question reappeared. In June Professor Goldwin Smith predicted that Sunday cars would be running before the first fleck of snow fell on Toronto. On the morning of Monday, 19 June, Mackenzie and Billy Maclean presented council with a petition of 5,389 signatures, including those of George Gooderham and the Anglican archbishop of Toronto, requesting a referendum. Mackenzie suggested an early vote instead of waiting until the January municipal election. The 26th of August was selected. But who would pay? Mackenzie volunteered TRC money, only to be accused of attempting to buy victory. Soon the Sabbath Observation Association regrouped. A second group, composed of people such as E.E. Sheppard of *Saturday Night*, was formed to fight for Sunday cars.

Throughout July and August 1893, the debate raged, touching on issues such as the quality of urban life and the human need to slow down one day a week, whether in a church or a park or at home. Both sides argued for morality, equality, and the plight of the working-man (and sometimes the workingwoman). Proponents argued, for instance, that cars would allow all Torontonians, not just those with private rigs, to spend Sundays in a park, at friends' homes, or in the church of their choice. E.E. Sheppard was certain that the good taste of Torontonians would ensure decent Sundays.

The sides were evenly drawn. Fundamentalist Protestants tended to support the anti-car side. Methodists Timothy Eaton and Hart Massey favoured closed Sundays, perhaps for religious reasons or perhaps because they feared that workers would show up Monday morning not sufficiently rested; but retailer Robert Simpson favoured Sunday cars. So, too, did the Roman Catholic and Anglican bishops of Toronto. Women expressed themselves at public meetings and at social teas. Some shop clerks and many domestic servants favoured Sunday cars. After all, one clerk asked, what had fundamentalist clergymen done to help them?[29] The Working Women's Protective Association supported Sunday cars. Mrs. Chester Massey's 'progressive conversation party,' held in her Jarvis Street home the last week in July, discussed various topics – the weather, the Chicago World's Fair, fashion, and, inevitably, Sunday cars. Each topic lasted ten minutes, then it was on to the next subject.[30] Opinions were not reported, but one can imagine that few guests would dare to favour Sunday cars, lest they offend Mrs. Massey's Methodist sensitivities.

Academic and editorial opinions were also divided. Sir Daniel Wilson was opposed; Professor Goldwin Smith and the Reverend Doctor Clark of Trinity College were in favour. Cartoonist J.W. Bengough thought that the workingman should be using his own back yard on Sundays instead of travelling by trolley to High Park. Newspapers generally supported the Sabbatarian Observance Society. The *Globe* wooed the *World*'s labour readership by taking up the cause of TRC conductors. Billy Maclean fought back with a few lines of doggerel:

> O, give us the Sunday street car
> Hear the workingman's voice
> As he swelters hot 'mid city's jar,
> For he has no other choice.

Labour groups were, by and large, in favour of Sunday cars. But what about the 600 employees of the TRC? Would they be forced to work extra hours, beyond the ten-hour day and sixty-hour week guaranteed by the 1891 agreement between the city and the company? Was it possible for the company to add an extra day without breaking the old agreement on maximum hours of work? The Trades and Labor Council (TLC) of Toronto, which united representatives of various trades and occupations in the city, grew concerned. In early July, Mackenzie assured the TLC that no worker would be forced to work on Sundays. Not all members of the TLC were satisfied, since Mackenzie's promise was not in writing. In mid-July, however, the TLC voted thirty to sixteen to support Sunday cars.

The first week in August, Mackenzie got some high-profile assistance – Ellen Terry and Henry Irving were passing through Toronto with London's Lyceum Theatre Company. Irving contended that Sunday should be a day of joy and pleasure, as it had been before the Puritans spoiled everything.[31] The actor did not still the battle. Until mid-August, Mackenzie had taken relatively little part in the debate, since he had been spending a good deal of time in Montreal on business. A couple of times he had replied to criticism by writing letters to the *World*. The question of Catholic investors arose. In Orange Toronto, Mackenzie was vulnerable. Why, not a dollar's worth of stock was held by a Roman Catholic, he announced.[32] Catholic shareholders such as George Kiely and Margaret Mackenzie kept their mouths shut.

On Friday, 18 August, Mackenzie made an appearance at a public meeting at the Pavilion, Toronto's 'Crystal Palace,' in Allan Gardens. Each speaker was to address a resolution that Sunday cars not be adopted until a written agreement was made with the city and with the railway employees, in order to ensure that employees would not be forced to work more than sixty hours per week. It was a raucous meeting. Mayor Fleming presided. He was cheered and booed. William McCabe, who had publicly accused Mackenzie of being unreasonable and uncompromising, was there on behalf of Toronto ratepayers. Goldwin Smith, Billy Maclean, Nicol Kingsmill, and George Bertram intended to address the crowd in support of Sunday cars.

Mackenzie arrived at the steamy, smoky hall with William Laidlaw. He had not intended to speak. He was not an effective public speaker, and he disliked crowds, especially one so exercised. But when the mayor asked for speakers, Laidlaw and he made their way through the crowd. Sunday car advocates let go a thunderous cheer that threatened to break the glass walls. The two men sat down on the platform and listened to the other speakers. Robert Jaffray of the *Globe*, a paper unsympathetic to Mackenzie, agreed that Sunday street car men needed written protection. He noted, half in jest, that both Mackenzie and he were 'Scotchmen,' who often kept the Sabbath and anything else they could lay their hands on. Jaffray wondered if the company was not too anxious to gain extra revenue. Amidst cheers, Jaffray resumed his seat.

William Laidlaw addressed the throng. There was no need for further agreements, he said. Sunday cars were covered by the 1891 agreement, which did not stipulate that a further agreement be drawn up to cover Sunday operations. One of his opponents grew so incensed that he rushed the stage. 'Get back into your seat,' Mayor Fleming shouted. The meeting was reaching fever pitch. Goldwin Smith tried to soothe the crowd. He had not decided how he would vote. He thought the street car service good, the employees obliging, and the management adept at running such a large system. Nevertheless, he thought that a separate agreement regulating Sunday cars was needed.

Several speakers followed. Billy Maclean strode to the podium. He was greeted by cheers, groans, and hisses. He contended that no city in the Empire had grown as large as Toronto without Sunday cars. 'Belfast,' a voice cried out. 'Edinburgh,' intoned another. Maclean told the crowd that Belfast did have Sunday cars and that Edinburgh was about to get them.

Several more speakers kept the crowd stirred up. Then came

Mackenzie's turn. It was the first time that he had stood before a crowd since the night in December 1879 when he had accepted the nomination for reeve of Eldon Township. That evening the crowd had been unruly, but Mackenzie had been the popular opponent of an unpopular incumbent. This time, the circumstances were not as propitious.

As he approached the podium, the crowd settled down a bit. 'Mr. Mayor, ladies and gentlemen,' he began hesitantly, 'I am the poor, miserable creature that has been painted so black for the last few weeks.'

His opening tactic was clever. He was always a good actor, who could dip into his reservoir of memories and come up with a suitable role. Now he was the little guy, perhaps even the motherless child alone in a pine and tamarack forest. The quiet tenor voice and his soft Scots-Ontario accent may have resembled Canadian accents described by Rupert Brooke as rather soft and lovely.[33] Not for Mackenzie the stylish mid-Atlantic accent favoured by his wife and daughters. Although he was an actor of many masks, he was a man of few pretensions.

'I always thought I was a kind of respectable sort of fellow, but probably others know better than I do,' he continued. He wondered if he might ask Torontonians to judge him a little more fairly.

The crowd grew more sympathetic. He drew them back to the summer of 1891. The preconditions of the franchise were so strict that he and his syndicate had hesitated before submitting a tender. But they had won because theirs was the most attractive offer. 'We have tried,' he went on, 'to the best of our ability to carry out that agreement in every particular, and I defy and challenge any man in this room or in this city to show in any one particular where we ever violated that agreement.' He was beginning to cast his spell. They were listening to him. A few started to clap, then the whole audience burst forth in applause. He grew more confident.

Then someone in the crowd heckled him. He stopped momentarily. 'Gentlemen, I don't know as I ever before stood up before an audience to speak.'

A voice shouted encouragement: 'You're doin' fine. Go on.'

He begged their indulgence. He collected himself, then challenged the idea that Sunday cars were not covered by the agreement of 1891. 'If I can,' he promised, 'I will apply every condition of that agreement to the Sunday car service.' He was a man of his word who did not enjoy being 'reviled and blackguarded' from every platform. 'I am willing to put my record beside any man's record in this room,' he told them. The crowd broke into applause again. He caught his breath. He seemed to have won them over.

A voice cried out, 'Give us Sunday cars.'

He looked in the direction of the voice, a hint of a smile washing over his face. 'I have nothing to say about Sunday cars,' he continued. 'The citizens of Toronto will decide that.' But he did want to defend his company from the 'base insinuations' made during the past few weeks. He knew that the citizens of Toronto would not pay these insinuations the slightest attention. That was all he had to say, except that he would carry out the agreement with the city to the best of his ability. He was finished. He returned to his seat, and the crowd burst into sustained applause. He had won them over. Or so it seemed. Shortly thereafter, amidst other speeches, he quietly left the Pavilion.

At the end of the meeting, the mayor asked for a standing vote on the resolution that a written agreement be drawn up with the city and the employees before Sunday cars could be operated. The audience was almost unanimous in its support of the resolution.[34] They may have favoured Sunday cars, but only with a written agreement to protect conductors and motormen.

Just before leaving for Montreal the next morning, Mackenzie dispatched a letter to Mayor Fleming, with copies to both the *Globe* and the *World*, stating emphatically that the 1891 agreement did indeed cover Sunday operations, and that the company would never surrender any of its legal rights guaranteed by that agreement. The letter inspired the *Globe*'s Jaffray to chide Mackenzie for exaggerating the vindictiveness of his opponents. Torontonians were really not ill-disposed towards him. Quite the opposite – they greatly appreciated the new transit company and its president.

While Mackenzie was in Montreal, another mass meeting was held at the Pavilion. His name was slandered to such an extent that Lindsay's John A. Barron, for years a political opponent of Mackenzie, Hector Cameron, and Sam Hughes, was prompted to express his distaste for the nastiness of the debate. He certainly owed Mackenzie 'less good than harm,' he claimed in a letter to the *World*, then proceeded to defend Mackenzie, whose reputation was 'high and honorable,' and who was incapable of 'a mean or unworthy act.'

But the question remained – how would Mackenzie and the company arrange the new seven-day work week, which would add ten to twelve hours of operation to the system, without breaking the 1891 agreement setting maximum working hours? For several weeks he resisted requests to put an agreement in writing. His attitude towards labour may have informed his decision. The conductors on the cars and craftsmen at the shops had few collective rights except those assigned to them by city council in 1891. The Trades and Labor Council played no more than a watchdog role. Like most capitalists in the 1890s, Mackenzie saw no reason why any organization or union should act as liaison between him and his men, any more than an institution should question the right of the male head of a household to deal directly with his wife and children. As an entrepreneur, Mackenzie and his syndicate were taking large financial risks. He was responsible for keeping the system in good working order, and that system, including all its component parts – trolleys and conductors – should work in harmony under his direction to provide sound transportation for passengers and a good rate of return to investors. Only a few brave members of that patriarchal society a century ago questioned Mackenzie's capitalist attitude.

While he rejected unions, he was prepared to negotiate with his workers, either individually or in small groups. On Sunday, 13 August, he had been warmly received when he met about 400 of them to explain the company's position. He emphasized the voluntary aspect of Sunday work and offered to allow the York County judge to adjudicate any differences. He asked that a committee of six workers be delegated to negotiate with the company.[35] (The next day, council decided to settle the paving dispute on Mackenzie's terms. He was very much in charge of events that weekend.)

After Mackenzie left the meeting, a committee nominated by the workers began to negotiate with company officials, and together they arrived at an agreement. The company agreed to drop the provision that each worker be required to work one Sunday in seven; in return, the committee of railway employees agreed that during the Industrial Exhibition or snowstorms, the company might ask men to work extra hours. The company agreed to reduce speed and keep all trolley bells silent near churches on Sundays. The agreement was signed by the six committee members and by Mackenzie and James Grace.

The Trades and Labor Council, however, was not impressed. D.J. O'Donoghue, the seasoned labour leader who had fought a losing battle during the violent street railway strike of 1886, would have nothing to do with an agreement hammered out by non-union workers and capitalists. A TLC meeting passed a resolution that the railway employees should have the right to form or join any labour organization of their own choosing.[36] The city was vexed too. When Mackenzie returned from Montreal on Thursday, 24 August, he discovered that before city solicitor Biggar would allow the referendum, he wanted Mackenzie to sign an agreement guaranteeing Sunday workers' rights. The city's proposal was almost identical to the agreement arrived at by Mackenzie and the employees' committee. To reach a final agreement, both parties agreed to submit to arbitration. Solicitor Christopher Robinson was chosen arbitrator, and on Friday evening Mackenzie, William Laidlaw, and Biggar took the train to Orillia, where Robinson was vacationing.

This flurry of last-minute negotiations brought about an agreement stipulating that employees could not be forced, or even 'permitted,' to work more than sixty hours or six days in any seven consecutive days. The company was denied the right to require employees to work extra hours at Exhibition time or during emergencies. The agreement of 1891 was altered to make it clear that it applied to Sunday operation also, and that the city could rescind Sunday service if the company did not live up to this agreement.[37]

The referendum went ahead. The voters turned down Sunday cars, but only by a majority of under 1,000, down from the 4,000 margin of the last vote. The tide was turning, noted Professor Smith, and the *World* could hardly wait for the next vote. The *Globe*, however, thought that the margin of victory would have been even greater had not the company handed out so many free tickets. Street cars did run on Sunday, 3 September, when two lads broke into two of them and drove them down fashionable Bathurst Street to King, east to Government House and Upper Canada College, then south on Simcoe, where they were abandoned. No trolley would run again on a Sunday for several more years.

CHAPTER FOUR

Toronto, Montreal, Winnipeg, and Birmingham Trolleys

How do we seize the past? Can we ever do so? When I was a medical student, some pranksters at an end-of-term dance released into the hall a piglet which had been smeared with grease. It squirmed between legs, evaded capture, squealed a lot. People fell over trying to grasp it, and were made to look ridiculous in the process. The past often seems to behave like that piglet.

(Julian Barnes, *Flaubert's Parrot* [1985] 14)

The results of the Sunday vote ended any hope of operating seven days a week, for the moment at least. There was one residual problem. Before the vote, while Mackenzie was in Montreal, his roadmaster, Nix, had dismissed Megginson, a motorman, for reasons which can only be guessed today. Megginson was an organizer and leader, and may have been perceived by Nix as insubordinate in some way.

Some employees threatened to strike. Mackenzie rushed back from Montreal. Two days before the Sunday car vote, he discussed the matter with Megginson, then reinstated him. He wrote to Nix that he could not allow an employee to suffer 'any injustice.' The letter was made public (Mackenzie's real intent was to win over public opinion) in the same edition of the *World* as Barron's laudatory letter, the day before the vote on Sunday cars. Mackenzie's timing was almost perfect.[1] It appeared that he had dealt with the matter as efficaciously as he had dealt with problems in the Selkirks during the construction of the CPR. There his Eldon Reserve had never considered striking. The situation was different in Toronto, for instead of a score of acquaintances who had known the Mackenzies in Kirkfield for half a century, Mackenzie was dealing with hundreds of men, most of them strangers, whose loyalty to him and to his company was subordinate to questions of working conditions, cost of living, and wages.

More so than Mackenzie, Megginson realized that loyalties were shifting. He formed a union of conductors, motormen, and trans-fermen. For more than twenty years unions had been legal, ever since the government of Sir John A. Macdonald had passed the Trade Unions Act of 1872. The problem for union organizers, how-ever, was the absence of any act to force employers to recognize their union as a legal bargaining tool.

The first week in September, men representing the new union went to Mackenzie's office to present a memorandum of agreement between the Toronto Railway Company and the 'Employees' Union & Benefit Society.' Among other things, the union wanted all re-ports critical of employees to be in writing and made available to the union, so that the accused might appeal dismissal. It asked that no employee be suspended without an investigation, and that employ-ees not be charged for broken trolley poles, lights, or couplings un-less the damage was proven to be the fault of the employee.[2] The union's requests were moderate.

Mackenzie listened as George Streeter, secretary of the union lo-cal, read the memorandum. He agreed that it was unfair to charge conductors for all broken poles, or to force a man to wait around for fifteen hours whenever his trolley was temporarily out of service in order to put in ten hours of work. He promised to look into such matters, but he would not sign the proposals. Doing so would have meant recognizing the union as a bargaining tool.

In mid-September, about 600 employees, in other words, most conductors, motormen, and transfermen, held a rally at the Pavil-ion. Mayor Fleming presided. Several clergymen, most of whom had fought against Sunday cars, encouraged the men and compli-mented them on their orderliness, proving that paternalism was not unique to entrepreneurs. After one clergyman announced that he never knew a corporation with a soul, the men lifted their voices to God, brought in a few sheaves, and gathered at the river. The secre-tary of the union announced that the company had already rectified a couple of grievances. *Saturday Night*'s E.E. Sheppard, once a staunch supporter of unions, wondered if the churches were not simply trying to strike a blow at the Toronto Railway Company be-cause of its attempt to run on Sundays. Men do not invest millions in public enterprises, he added, only to have their affairs managed by public meetings.[3]

Later in September, after a brief holiday in New York City with his wife and family, Mackenzie again met the union executive, now more militant because the Toronto Railway Company had dismissed three employees. (Reports do not name the charges, but since the dismissed were two conductors and one transferman, there may have been irregularities in the collection of money and tickets and the issuing of transfers.) The executive agreed that the charge against one employee was serious and, if proved, was just cause for dismissal. Mackenzie refused to discuss the other two, and the union made strike plans.

Mackenzie played for time. Suspecting that a great deal of Megginson's support was soft, he quietly worked out a deal. In November the company established a corporate union called the Street Railway Employees' Benevolent Society, which would pay the medical expenses of workers and their families and guarantee a regular salary for sick employees. The offer was generous and shrewd, for there was one proviso – all employees had to join the new company union before the plan could be instituted. By early December about a hundred men had joined the company union. A few days later that number had doubled. Soon even the strongest supporters of the old union decided to postpone any further attempts to implement their definition of a union. The word 'strike' was no longer heard. Without a strike, the old union lacked a focal point and disbanded.[4]

Mackenzie had something else to be pleased about. At first, many Torontonians had not taken kindly to electric trolleys. Accustomed to the clip-clop of horseshoes on cobblestones and to the smell of horse manure on tramway routes, some passengers discovered that the odourless, almost soundless trolley confused their senses and worried their central nervous systems. Disoriented, they sometimes ran in front of a moving trolley, having misjudged its speed. Others jumped from a moving trolley, as they had safely done from trams, only to be injured by heavy wheels or by another trolley. Occasionally a pedestrian would stand transfixed in front of an oncoming trolley, frozen in some kind of 'future shock.' During the first months of operation, a sinister nursery rhyme was heard in Toronto: 'Oh, look papa, strawberry jam!/Oh, no my dear; it is your aunt, run over by a tram.'[5]

However, after initial anxiety and hostility, the Toronto press and passengers became more sympathetic to the TRC. Even the *Globe*, once one of Mackenzie's harshest critics, decided in January 1894 that Toronto had a street railway system 'unequalled on the continent;' the Belt Line and the paper transfer system, recently introduced, were working admirably; the cars were well-lighted and heated, and were very speedy. Torontonians rode further for less money than any other North Americans, and the city treasury benefited to a greater extent than that of any North American or European city. If the company continued to improve its service, the paper concluded, the citizens of Toronto and its press would have to find something else to complain about.[6]

In July 1894, Allan McDougall, a longtime critic and former chairman of the city's Railway Committee, who in 1891 had pushed for a public commission to run the street railway, now had nothing but praise for the TRC. Its equipment was state-of-the-art; its fares were among the cheapest in North America. According to his calculations, riders and the city were making about $610,000 from the company in reduced fares, free transfers, and percentage and mileage payments. The city, McDougall contended, had made a very good deal.[7]

By August 1894 the horse trams on McCaul Street were removed, and by December the Toronto system was completely electrified. In 1894 the TRC also acquired the Mimico Electric Railway & Light Company, the first of several such acquisitions in towns adjacent to Toronto. The same year, F.M. Bell-Smith's oil painting, *Lights of a City Street*, was unveiled. It depicted trolley passengers during rush hour at King and Yonge streets, the city's busiest intersection, now completely at ease with, perhaps even slightly bored by, the speedy, punctual, and efficient electric trolleys. During the early and mid-1890s, ridership increased dramatically, even though the last of the long recession retarded the growth of Canadian urban populations.[8]

There was only one important difference with the city during the last half of 1894. The city was making plans for a grand boulevard linking Union Station on Front Street with the new Parliament Buildings in the Queen's Park. (During the 1890s, the definite article was still used.) Old College Avenue, which ran from the park south to Queen Street, would be pushed through to Front Street. In 1894 College Avenue was a chestnut-lined residential street of small, handsome two-storey brick homes inhabited by skilled working families such as the Smiths, whose daughter Gladys, born about 1890, would later change her name to Mary Pickford and subtract three or four years from her age.[9] The street name, too, would soon be changed to the grander 'University Avenue.' Mackenzie thought it a splendid idea for a trolley to sweep visitors and legislators from Union Station up the boulevard to the park.[10] It was. He proposed that the line carry on through the ravine on the west side of the Queen's Park, then up Avenue Road north of Bloor. The idea was voted down by city council, however.

In September 1894, the city asked for tenders for lighting Toronto. Three companies responded, including Henry Pellatt's Toronto Electric Light Company, which had sold electricity to Toronto for several years. Consumers' Gas submitted a bid, as did the Toronto Railway Company, whose large new power plant, in its former horse barns at Front and Frederick streets, could produce more power than the street railway company consumed.

When the tenders were opened on 17 September, the Electric Light Company was found to have submitted the lowest bid – $74.825 per city lamp per annum, slightly below the ceiling of $81.78 set by engineer Keating and well below the same company's old rate of $108.59. Soon, however, rumours of corruption and influence peddling involving Alderman Stewart began to circulate. Council asked Judge McDougall to conduct an inquiry, which opened on 5 November at the Adelaide Street Court House, a few blocks east of Yonge Street. A week later, Judge McDougall found Alderman Stewart guilty of soliciting bribes.

Before the inquiry was adjourned, word of another bribery incident emerged. In 1891 Alderman Hewitt, a Mackenzie supporter, had claimed to be acting as agent for the Toronto Railway Company. If John Inglis & Sons Company would pay him $1,000, he could make sure that the TRC would buy only Inglis engines and boilers for their new power house. Apparently he had not discussed the matter with Mackenzie beforehand, and Mackenzie would have nothing to do with the deal. He bought equipment from Canadian General Electric, but the alderman kept the money anyway.

Council gave Judge McDougall the widest possible powers to probe what council called 'aldermanic corruption' over the previous three years. The investigation lasted until Christmas. It examined all aspects of Mackenzie's dealings with councils and mayors from 1891 to 1894 – the awarding of the franchise to Mackenzie, Everett, and Kiely in 1891; the TRC's 1892 contract with Edison Electric for motors; a paving contract in 1893; and the electric lighting contract of 1894. Mackenzie testified several times, acquitting himself well. At no time, he claimed, did he resort to bribery. He reiterated that he had found out about the Marshall-Macdonald case only after his return from Kirkfield, and reimbursed Marshall only because he had acted in good faith, though completely without Mackenzie's permission. He knew nothing of Kiely's supposed loan of $10,000 to an alderman in 1891. He was in Calgary at the time. Nor, until after the fact, did he know about Coleman's 'bet' with Alderman Gowanlock. He had canvassed various aldermen in the summer of 1891, he told the judge, in order to promote his syndicate's bid for the street railway franchise. But he certainly did not pay them to vote for him. And what about the $13,000 lent to Alderman Hewitt in 1891? He denied that the money was used to influence the alderman's vote.

The villain of the piece seems to have been Coleman, owner of a paving company and Mackenzie's colleague in the C.J. Smith Coal Company. He had used his influence and Mackenzie's money to obtain paving contracts. On one of his frequent trips to Montreal in 1893, Mackenzie had received a telegram from Coleman asking him to honour a bank draft for $7,000; Coleman told him only that he was in financial trouble. Mackenzie wired the bank in Toronto to honour Coleman's draft. Coleman used the money to bribe aldermen, and planned to buy a mortgage owed by Mayor Fleming to the Traders' Bank, in order to influence the mayor. When Mackenzie found out, he told Coleman that his intentions were 'contemptible and mean,' and ordered him to stop.

Judge McDougall questioned Mackenzie about paving contracts in 1893. Did Mackenzie not aid Coleman by preventing a Detroit contractor from laying pavement, even though the city had awarded the American a contract? Mackenzie explained that he had refused all companies, including Coleman's, the right to lay pavement until the dispute with the city was resolved.

Mackenzie was quite willing to have all records, his own personal records and the TRC's, scrutinized. He explained various bank withdrawals and denied that any of his money lined aldermanic pockets. Compared to the reaction of other men involved in the investigation, Mackenzie's attitude seems exemplary. Alderman Gowanlock resigned, Alderman Hewitt fled to California, and Alderman Bailey disappeared. Everett took refuge in his native Detroit, and Coleman soon disappeared, leaving his insolvent wife and family in Toronto. These reactions do not prove either innocence or guilt, but Mackenzie's willingness to co-operate suggests that he saw the investigation as a push for much-needed urban reform.

When singled out by historians a century later, the inquiry appears to have dominated Mackenzie's life for several weeks. It was, however, only one of several events in his business and personal life. On 13 October he attended the unveiling by Prime Minister Thompson of a statue of Sir John A. Macdonald at the Queen's Park, and rubbed shoulders with S.H. Janes, Robert Simpson, Alexander Muir, Lucius O'Brien, Sam Hughes, and Lieutenant Colonel Otter.

With his wife, he attended a social tea in early November at the home of Ontario Chief Justice Meredith, and in the same month participated in the fortieth anniversary ball of the Royal Canadian Yacht Club. At their home on Sherbourne Street, Margaret gave a tea and, a week or so later, an evening of Italian music. They attended the New York Horse Show and, on 30 November, the St. Andrew's Ball at the Pavilion, hosted by the governor general and Lady Aberdeen. In mid-November, Mackenzie purchased the Kiely Building at the northwest corner of King and Church streets, to be used as TRC offices.

Of course Mackenzie might have been using these events to divert attention from the scandals and investigation, and from his own role in the affairs. His biographer believes that even an expert at the game of smoke and mirrors like Mackenzie would have had difficulty weaving such an elaborate social and business tapestry. So apparently did Wallace Nesbitt, Judge McDougall's 'able counsel,'[11] who soon became a friend.[12]

The city's journalists also found other games in town. On 13 November American evangelist Dwight Moody pounded a pulpit in the new Massey Music Hall, damning all 'backsliders,' a vague term that might have included bribe-takers. Two weeks later in the same venue, Professor Goldwin Smith introduced Scottish novelist, Dr. Arthur Conan Doyle, who read from his Sherlock Holmes stories. Even the clever Baker Street detective would have been perplexed by the sensational murder that grabbed as much newspaper space as the McDougall inquiry – a young woman, Clara Ford, was tried for the murder of a man called Westwood, a close friend of rising Toronto architect, E.J. Lennox. On 12 December, a month after Mackenzie saw him at the Queen's Park, Prime Minister Thompson died suddenly at Windsor Castle. News of the deaths of Count Ferdinand de Lesseps, builder of the Suez Canal, and novelist Robert Louis Stevenson also competed for attention.

In December Professor Goldwin Smith chaired a large meeting at the Pavilion to deal with the question of civic reform. Prominent among those on the stage were businessmen, most of them friends and associates of Mackenzie, including W.R. Brock, George Bertram, Timothy Eaton, and George Cox. No doubt they too had encountered avarice in their dealings with city hall. No doubt some of them had responded to it. To clean up city hall, Professor Smith suggested a commission-style government similar to Washington's in order to reduce the likelihood of bribery.

Judge McDougall's report, released on 3 January 1895, would never have won a Leacock award for humour. It makes clear, however, that corruption of the early 1890s was due to more than aggressive, self-righteous plutocrats. 'Improper relations,' noted the judge, existed between council members and contractors. Contracts and franchises had been obtained by illegal and corrupt means. The judge singled out eight individuals for blame, most of them aldermen. Judge McDougall decided that Everett had lent money fully aware that its purpose was to influence aldermen. Coleman, too, was found guilty of bribery.

And Mackenzie? Although the judge had reason to be suspicious about Mackenzie's loan of $13,000 to his friend Alderman Hewitt in December 1891, he could find no evidence of bribery. He commended Mackenzie for his willingness to open the company's books as well as his own personal accounts. He also commended him for chastising Coleman after he had attempted to use Mayor Fleming's bank debt as leverage in 1893. Although two of his business associates and six aldermen, including Hewitt, were severely reprimanded, Mackenzie himself emerged from the investigation free of blame. To claim that the investigation's conclusions 'blackened' Mackenzie's name and 'seriously damaged' the reputation of the Toronto Railway Company is to misread or ignore the evidence.[13]

Toronto was only one of four cities in which Mackenzie was actively interested during the 1890s. In 1893, during the debate on Sunday cars in Toronto, he spent a good deal of time in Montreal. In February and March 1892, he had been quietly working with James Ross to acquire control of the Montreal Street Railway. By 1 April their efforts were successful. Ross became president and Mackenzie managing director. Everett and L.J. Forget of Montreal were important shareholders. Forget had been president of the old horse-drawn system that Mackenzie and Ross proposed to electrify. To become contractors, Mackenzie and Ross had to resign their positions on the board of directors. As the only tenderers, they won the contract handily, and soon began to convert 160 kilometres of lines to electricity,[14] a three-year project that, when completed, was the end of Mackenzie's active association with the Montreal transit system.

He was also interested in Winnipeg power and transportation. As early as 1890, with Ross, Holt, and Mann, he investigated the hydro power potential of the Assiniboine River,[15] though nothing came of it. In September 1891, a few days after Mackenzie and Everett took control of the Toronto Railway Company, Mackenzie and Ross made an offer to Winnipeg council to construct and operate an electric street railway system.

Winnipeg already had an electric system of sorts, an experimental mile of trolley operating since January 1891 on River Avenue. In 1882 its proprietor, A.W. Austin of Toronto, had been granted a twenty-year franchise to operate horse trams in Winnipeg. Austin promised to electrify his system if council would provide him with an exclusive thirty-year extension of his present contract, which ended in 1902.[16] In late August 1891 Austin issued an ultimatum, giving council one week to accept his offer.[17] Council called on lawyer J.S. Ewart, who decided that Austin's franchise did not guarantee him a monopoly.

Three days later, on 6 September, Mackenzie and Ross arrived, not by chance, in Winnipeg. With them were the New York architect who had built Montreal's Windsor Station and a representative of a Toronto loan company. During their five hours in Winnipeg, they inspected the main thoroughfares, then headed out to Alberta for some prairie chicken shooting near Edmonton. The following evening, their Winnipeg agent, G.H. Campbell, made an offer to council on behalf of 'anonymous' clients who wanted to build and operate eight miles of 'first-class' electric street railway.

In October, council asked for tenders for an electric system, and J.S. Ewart drew up a by-law that set forth construction deadlines, routes, pole regulations, fares, and trolley schedules. Austin was understandably reluctant to tender, since he continued to believe that his company had a monopoly on transportation. G.H. Campbell, an experienced railway lobbyist, was unmatchable: he attended council meetings; he leaked news that Mackenzie's friend, William Van Horne, was part of the syndicate, which suggests that, at least in 1891, the CPR was not as much disliked in the West as historians like to think; he kept in touch with Ross and Mackenzie in Toronto and Calgary; and he made the Mackenzie-Ross offer more attractive by offering free transportation to uniformed policemen, firemen, and postal workers, by reducing ticket prices, and by promising night cars when the city reached a population of 100,000. Austin refused to match these new concessions, and on 1 February council awarded the franchise to Mackenzie and Ross.

On Sunday, 10 April, William Mackenzie stepped off a CPR train at the station on Winnipeg's Main Street, having visited his relatives in Prince Albert, where he had just presented a handsome pulpit and clerical chair to the new Presbyterian church. He checked into the Manitoba Hotel, Winnipeg's new, luxurious seven-storey hotel at Main and Water streets. Recognized by a couple of reporters, he had little to say except that he had great faith in the future of Winnipeg and the whole country, provided that capital was available for resource development.[18]

He had come to Winnipeg to oversee the final passage of the bill chartering his new company. The following Thursday he strolled over to the legislature on Kennedy Avenue to watch Thomas L. Morton, member from Gladstone and chairman of the Private Bills Committee, speak on behalf of the bill incorporating the Winnipeg Electric Street Railway (WESR).[19] The same day in Toronto, his Toronto Railway Company also received its charter from the province of Ontario. He was now president of street railways in the country's second and third largest cities. The following July, a couple of weeks before the inauguration of Toronto's first electric line on Church Street, Campbell officially opened the Winnipeg Electric Street Railway by running its first electric car up Main Street to Selkirk Avenue and into the Exhibition Grounds. A few weeks later, he opened a line on Main between Portage and Broadway; and in November he held a gala opening of Winnipeg's 'Loop Line,' down Notre Dame to Nena (Sherbrook), Logan, and Main.

Two days after the opening of the Loop, Mackenzie was back in Winnipeg to attend sessions of the Manitoba Court of Appeal. Still claiming that he had a monopoly, Austin had filed suit to prevent Mackenzie's WESR from operating on streets already served by horse trams and from building tracks across his company's tracks. The Court of Appeal rejected Austin's argument, as did every other court including the Privy Council in London, which left Austin little recourse but to sell to Mackenzie. This he did for $175,000. Bitter and frustrated, Austin contended that Mackenzie's success was due to powerful connections, conveniently forgetting that he had once bragged that he controlled city hall. Mackenzie did indeed have good connections, including Premier Greenway[20] and the province's attorney general, Clifford Sifton, who on 8 September 1892 urged Greenway to allow Winnipeg Electric Street Railway to build tracks across Austin's tracks,[21] at the time an illegal act of trespassing.

On 11 May 1894, Winnipeg's last horse car was removed from the streets. This drove a local poet to write a 'Lament for the Horse Car,' in which she warned that when women got the vote, the horse cars would return. Most passengers, however, appreciated the quiet, clean, and speedy service of the electric cars, what the *Free Press* called their 'general excellence' and 'inestimable convenience.'[22] In November 1895 the company opened a new thermal (coal-generated) power house with three times the generating capacity of the old. In 1897, with Ross and Van Horne, Mackenzie gained control of Manitoba Electric & Gas Light Company, which provided a power distribution system in the city. In 1898 he united gas, electrical power and distribution, and passenger transportation under one management, and a few months later bought out a 'troublesome competitor,' the Nor-West Electric Company. Thus WESR lighted, heated, and transported Winnipeggers, and provided them with fuel to cook their meals. The 'right combination' – the creation of a large company under one management with an exclusive franchise lasting a fixed period of time, uniting power generation, transmission, and distribution with the city's transportation, heating, and lighting – soon gave consumers a welcome reduction of 25 per cent in gas prices.

During expansion and consolidation, labour-management relations were good. Admittedly, the company employed fewer men than did the Toronto Railway, about 50 serving fewer than 32,000 Winnipeggers, compared to Toronto's 600 employees[23] serving almost 200,000 people. Manager Campbell worked hard to retain worker loyalty. For instance, he helped to organize the inaugural ball of car conductors in November 1893. Winnipeg Street Railway workers of the 1890s did not attempt to organize union locals. Campbell's relations with the council were usually amicable. Thus, whenever Mackenzie met Winnipeg council, outstanding issues such as timetables, extension of the Portage Avenue line to Armstrong's Point, the condition of the road beds, and the laying of a second track on Broadway were discussed in a constructive manner.[24]

In late June 1895, Mackenzie sailed to England with his oldest daughters, Mabel and Gertrude, who were embarking on a study tour of Britain and Germany. The McDougall Investigation and other business had placed considerable strain on their father, and his colleagues were concerned that he was 'not himself.' They encouraged him to take a holiday. Once in Britain, he received reassuring words from his associates in Toronto: 'There is nothing to bring you back,' they told him, and encouraged him to forget his worries, to enjoy himself, and to get the most out of his trip. Senator George Cox planned to meet him in London in July to keep him up-to-date with Canadian business news. In these communiqués from Toronto, there is a note of pleading, which suggests that his colleagues wanted him to stay away for a few weeks for their own benefit as well as his. Day-to-day management of street railways could be carried out more efficiently with Mackenzie in London.

He toured England and Scotland with Mabel and Trudie, who then went off to study in Dresden. Soon their father's restive and inventive mind saw possibilities for street railway development. His partners in Toronto held their breath while he looked over the systems of two of England's largest cities. On 8 July he toured the London transportation system, operated by a combination of horse trams, steam engines operating in subways and cuts, and one short, inefficient electrical underground line, the City & South London, which since its opening in 1891 had suffered from badly designed underground 'tubes' and low voltage at points furthest from the generating plant.

Compared with North America and Germany, electrical technology in Britain was fragmented and uneconomical. As late as 1913, when its foreign competitors had long enjoyed the benefits of economy of scale and rationalization of electric generation and transmission, Greater London had 'sixty-five electrical utilities, seventy generating stations' and 'forty-nine different types of supply systems, ten different frequencies, thirty-two voltage levels for transmission and twenty-four for distribution, and about seventy different methods of charging and pricing.'[25] Entrepreneurs were content with sizeable profits from surface trams, which carried the majority of London's commuters. In 1895 Mackenzie seriously considered buying part of the underground system, probably the City & South London company. His idea was not quite as preposterous as it sounds, given his experience in modernizing trolley systems in Canada, his acquaintance with North American electrical engineers, and his ability to raise capital. In 1896 rumour had Mackenzie putting together a financial consortium that included the Rothschilds, to buy and operate the London system. That the transportation system of the Empire's capital came close to colonial control is rich with irony.

In early July Mackenzie also examined Birmingham tramways. He may have been told about the city's transportation problems while examining the London system. In 1895 Birmingham was served by seven transportation companies operating what some Birmingham residents called 'abominable steam trams with their filth and stench.'[26] Mackenzie was interested in gaining control of these companies, amalgamating them, and converting the lines to electricity. He asked Charles Porteous, his business manager, to sell 3,000 to 4,000 shares in the Toronto Railway Company so that he might buy Birmingham stock. Since TRC shares at the time sold for between $80 and $85 per share, Mackenzie would have realized about $30,000 from the sale. He asked his colleagues in Montreal and Toronto to join him in investing in Birmingham.[27] 'Now don't jump to the conclusion that I am going to rush right in without due precaution ...,' he promised Porteous.[28] But having seen in Toronto, Montreal, and Winnipeg how electricity meant lower operating costs, rising revenues, and therefore rising stock values, Mackenzie was ready to throw precaution to the wind.

When he returned to Canada in early September 1895, his friends remarked that his three months in England had not cured his distress. Nevertheless he continued to deal with Canadian business affairs until the end of February 1896, when Margaret and he sailed from New York to Liverpool aboard the *Campania*, with their four youngest daughters, Ethel, Bertha, Katharine, and Grace, and their niece, Josephine Wheeler. Alex and Joe remained at Ridley College, a private school in St. Catharines, Ontario. R.J. also stayed in Canada, as his father's chief field man. In July 1895 he had explored for minerals on the southwestern shore of Hudson Bay, and later in the Prince Albert area.

In London the Mackenzies made the Queen's Hotel, near Regent's Park, their place of residence. In April, with Mabel and Gertrude, they travelled to Rome, where they toured the Colosseum, the newly unearthed Forum, the Capitol, and other tourist sites. Back in London later that month, Mackenzie cycled in Regent's Park with his daughters and niece, and accompanied them to plays such as *For the Crown*, starring Forbes Robertson. Had his business interests in Britain grown as quickly as his Canadian affairs, he would have made London his home, and 'Mackenzie and Ross' might have become better known than 'Mackenzie and Mann.'

His colleagues in Toronto and Montreal, especially Porteous, remained concerned about his health. 'Trusting you are well and having a pleasant time,' Porteous wrote in April 1896, 'and that you feel benefitted by your trip.' Take care of your health and don't get involved in anything as difficult as Birmingham, Porteous advised in May. R.J., Porteous assured Mackenzie, was attending to any necessary business in Canada.

Mackenzie's mysterious illness, which grabbed hold of him when business pressures grew heavy, was never named in surviving documents. No doctor's report has survived. His symptoms – fever and headache, greyish-green complexion, and knotted veins at the temple – could have been those of malaria, or the ague (its popular name in the nineteenth century, when swamps and sloughs bred malaria-bearing mosquitoes). Malaria's symptoms, including fever and bad colour, often manifested themselves under duress, which was the case with Mackenzie. He could have contracted the disease in Eldon Township or at one of several construction sites in the 1870s and '80s.[29] One other possibility is that Mackenzie suffered from hypertension, which periodically incapacitated him and reduced his resistance to disease and infection. In order to protect his reputation as a successful businessman, his wife and family removed him from the public eye for a few days during times of stress. Investors and politicians would lose confidence in a company if they knew that it was directed by a man subject to periodic breakdowns.

Often his stress was self-generated. Mackenzie's strength as a businessman was also his fatal flaw. He was a creative, visionary individual who took risks. He combined imagination and foresight, two important characteristics of the successful entrepreneur. He had an instinct for markets and profits. He could often predict, with remarkable accuracy, the future of a business. The problem with vision is that it is often dependent for its success on luck or coincidence. Mackenzie knew the value of secrecy, which provides the successful entrepreneur with unshared knowledge and, therefore, power over his competition. As an entrepreneur, he also knew that he had to share his business secrets with carefully selected colleagues. The problem was that he sometimes failed to discuss his investment ideas and knowledge with even his closest business friends, on whom he depended for capital and direction. His colleagues knew that Mackenzie was brimful of energy, spontaneity, and ambition; they also knew that at times he could be very impractical. Small wonder that they were always fearful that he might commit them and their money to highly speculative investments without telling them beforehand.

Until 1891 Mackenzie's contracts had spelled out the specifics of his work. He had been a good field worker, willing to accept orders from entrepreneurs such as George Laidlaw. And he had been a good administrator and manager of small groups of men during CPR construction in the 1880s. During the 1890s, however, he himself began to play the role of entrepreneur. With that came the pressure of choices and judgment. His business affairs began to grow too large to manage by himself, but he found it painful to delegate authority, even to competent managers. In the early 1890s James Ross recognized Mackenzie's weaknesses and made sure that men such as G.H. Campbell in Winnipeg and Charles Porteous in Toronto took hold of his companies. Mackenzie had no choice but to accept the management revolution that big business had thrust upon him. The learning process was painful; hence, his periodic breakdowns. He was capable, however, of the most remarkable recoveries, which caused his colleagues in Toronto and Montreal to hold their collective breaths, for it was often during these periods of recovery that his creative, entrepreneurial urges were at their strongest.[30]

In April 1896 Mackenzie returned to Birmingham in the company of James Ross, whose practical good sense instilled confidence. If

Ross approved of investing in Birmingham, Canadian colleagues would concur. Ross saw good prospects in Birmingham. Negotiations went ahead, but very slowly. This did not surprise Porteous, who remarked that the English always moved slowly. On 1 July 1896, at Donald Smith's Dominion Day reception at the Imperial Institute in London, Ross and Mackenzie met the colonial secretary, Joseph Chamberlain, who, as former Lord Mayor of Birmingham, remained interested in the progress of his home city, especially because his family had large investments there. The electrification of the Birmingham street railways by Canadians nicely combined urban modernization with what Chamberlain called 'imperial intercourse.'[31]

Whether by coincidence or design, negotiations were renewed. On 7 July the council of the Corporation of Birmingham voted to accept Mackenzie and Ross's offer. The Canadian company, called the City of Birmingham Tramway Company (CBT), would convert the tramways of Birmingham to electricity, using overhead wires on all streets except for those in the city centre, where the conduit, or buried third rail, system was to be used on thirteen kilometres of streets. (Birmingham's winters, milder than Toronto's or Winnipeg's, made the conduit system more feasible.) During the following months, Mackenzie and Ross discovered that council was a fractious lot. Although a majority supported Mackenzie and Ross, a vocal minority wanted municipal ownership and a complete conduit system. Some councilmen were bothered by the idea of colonial ownership of Birmingham's transportation.

On 20 July 1896 shareholders of the various steam-powered companies voted to accept the sale of their shares to Mackenzie and Ross's company. Mackenzie must have been confident of the vote, for he was already on his way to New York, having left Liverpool three days earlier.[32] He called on Fred Pearson in Boston and asked this leading electrical engineer to draw up plans to convert Birmingham's transportation system to electricity. Back in Canada, Mackenzie found the Canadian press somewhat sceptical. 'You get some queer things in the papers' was his reply in the lobby of the Manitoba Hotel in August 1896 when reporters asked him about the attempts by some Birmingham councillors to have the British parliament rule against the sale of Birmingham's tram companies. There was not a grain of truth in that statement, he contended, as he edged towards the hotel elevator, which whisked him up and out of sight.

He returned to England in November, full of optimism. He had found his sea legs on the passage to Liverpool, he boasted to Porteous, even though the rough Atlantic had caused seasickness in other passengers. He was happy to discover that revenues in Birmingham were increasing by the remarkable sum of 300 pounds weekly.[33] As in Toronto in 1891, the introduction of free transfers and speedier service had increased ridership, even though the Birmingham system was still steam-powered. At company headquarters, 119 Colmore Row, Mackenzie and his Birmingham Manager, Edward Langham, formerly with the TRC, drew up proposals which would allow the company to convert to electricity as soon as possible.

Some city officials continued to hesitate. If the company was willing to construct and operate thirteen kilometres of conduit, why not the remaining forty-six kilometres too? Mackenzie and Ross argued that if forced to build and operate fifty-nine kilometres of conduit, more than the total of conduit systems worldwide at the time, they would have to ask for a franchise of up to forty-two years. Council grew more intransigent and deleted a clause giving CBT the right to sell surplus power to industry and to electrical lighting companies. All these problems were hard on Mackenzie. On Monday, 4 January 1897, his niece recorded in her diary, 'Uncle is ill, sent for the doctor.'[34] A few days later, a worried telegram arrived from Porteous in Toronto, advising Mackenzie to take care of himself.

Three days later, his powers of recovery at work again, he hosted a dinner for several people, including the Duke of Marlborough's solicitor. He continued to spend the middle three or four days of each week in Birmingham, returning to his family in London for Thursday dinner. One evening in February, Sir Joseph Pope, former private secretary to Sir John A. Macdonald, dropped by. Mackenzie continued to enjoy London theatre. On Friday 12 February, he took Bertha, Ethel, and Jo Wheeler to see *Daughters of Babylon*.

In March, however, back in Canada, he was once again 'worried and run down,' trying to do far too much, according to Porteous. He remained in Canada for three months, from mid-March to mid-June, long enough to tend to his Canadian affairs. He journeyed to British Columbia, down to Chicago, and out to Winnipeg. In mid-June he sailed back to England, in time to witness the Queen's Jubilee parade through London on 22 June 1897. Porteous hoped that the Imperial spirit of the Jubilee would make Birmingham officials more hospitable.

There was no mellowing. In June, Ross leaked news of the negotiations to the Birmingham *Daily Post*. Some council members took umbrage. Negotiations raged on throughout June 1897. In the press, engineer Fred Pearson and the city engineer debated the relative merits and costs of conduit and trolley systems. Pearson offered to build an experimental trolley line along the Bristol Road from Colmore Row to the city boundary. An exhausted Mackenzie returned to Canada in the second week of July. Porteous met his ship at Quebec and escorted him to the Porteous Norman-style summer home at Ste. Petronille, on the west end of l'Ile d'Orléans. There, surrounded by gentle farmland and bountiful orchards sweeping dramatically to the majestic St. Lawrence, Mackenzie recuperated before proceeding to Toronto.

Late in 1897, he returned briefly to Birmingham, where Ross and he decided to build a power house and an experimental trolley line to demonstrate the cleanliness and convenience of the trolley system. The power house was erected and a beginning made on overhead lines and tracks. Mackenzie returned to Canada, then sailed back to England in May 1898, this time in the company of Sir William Van Horne. When they arrived in London, he met with Ross to plan their next offensive.

On 5 June the *Daily Post* published a letter from Ross to the Lord Mayor of Birmingham. Ross claimed that the trolley system was superior, and that Manchester, Glasgow, and Leeds, among others, had opted for it. He also claimed that in November 1896 one of the members of the public works committee had given the company verbal permission to erect an experimental line on Small Heath and Sparkbrook streets, a total distance of just over eight kilometres. Council was meeting that evening. Councillors opposed to Mackenzie and Ross were outraged. An air of 'mutual indignation' reigned over the meeting.[35] One alderman decided that there was only one thing worse than a Canadian, and that was a Scots-Canadian. In Canada, another claimed, Mackenzie and Ross's conduct might be acceptable, but certainly not in England.[36] Britannia ruled the waves in the 1890s, but here were two colonials attempting to rule the streets of Birmingham. Between the raucous lines of council debates, it is possible to catch glimpses of the insecurities and fears that haunt an imperial power. In June 1898 council voted by a narrow margin to terminate negotiations, thus leaving residents of Birmingham with noisy, dirty steam tramways for years to come.

Mackenzie was back in England in late October 1898, accompanied by Mabel, Ethel, and Bertha, who were en route to Florence to rent a room with a view during the winter. Before their departure, Mackenzie accompanied them to the theatre, concerts, and art galleries. They shopped for prints in the Strand. At an antique shop on Soho's Wardour Street, then the home of antique and antiquarian shops operated by Continental émigrés, he bought a pair of antique brass candlesticks for the family home in Toronto.[37] When he arrived in Birmingham in early November, the company was no closer to electrification than at the time of purchase in 1896. In fact, Mackenzie and Ross never would succeed in converting the city's transportation to electricity, and, during the first decade of the next century, as leases terminated they sold component parts of their company to the city, which by 1911 owned and operated the system.

During his rise in business, Mackenzie and his family also climbed into Toronto Society, the 'Four Hundred,' as they were dubbed by E.E. Sheppard's alter ego, 'Don,' of *Saturday Night*. It was a zesty and powerful little group composed of old names (Strachan, Jarvis, and Robinson), the not-so-old (Gooderham and Nordheimer), and the nouveaux (Eaton and Massey). It was mainly a Toronto group, with business and family connections across the country. One of the strongest ties existed between Winnipeg and Toronto – the Mowats of Toronto were related to the Ewarts of Winnipeg, the Vankoughnet name united the piano Nordheimers with Winnipeg politician, Hugh John Macdonald, son of the prime minister. Banks and businesses in Victoria, Calgary, Winnipeg, and Montreal were often managed by sons of the Four Hundred. Politicians in Ottawa and in provincial capitals were connected with these families. The world of letters and ideas was also connected; by association, sponsorship, and blood. Goldwin Smith was a member; so, too, was Ernest Thompson (later he would add Seton to his name). The Four Hundred sponsored poetry readings (Pauline Johnson and Louis Fréchette), and art exhibitions (F.M. Bell-Smith, Lucius O'Brien, I Iomer Watson, and Paul Peel). Toronto was their stage. They paraded in horse-drawn victorias through the Queen's Park and showed off their latest fashions at the Queen's Plate at Woodbine Race Course. They enjoyed lectures, theatre, and concerts. Madame Albani, the Canadian opera singer, thought them the best-dressed audience in North America.

It was by no means a static, inbred group. There were Roman Catholics, German Jews, and Protestants of almost every shade. There were English, Irish (Green and Orange alike), Welsh, and Scots (Highland and Lowland), Germans, and Poles. It seemed a tolerant group, accepting uncommon names such as Gzowski. Politics counted for little. Conservatives mingled with Grits. Continentalist Goldwin Smith rubbed shoulders with Canadian Imperialist George Denison. Descendants of Susannah Moodie and Bishop Strachan conversed and danced with William Lyon Mackenzie's grandson, Willie King.

The Mackenzies of Kirkfield quickly moved into the Four Hundred. Soon after moving into their house on Sherbourne Street, they began to appear at teas or literary conversaziones. They were seen among guests when Governor General Lord Stanley or Prime Minister Macdonald were in town. They began to appear at society weddings. In 1893 Margaret Mackenzie joined Professor Smith, Mrs. Joseph Cawthra, the Reverend Doctor Scadding, and A.A. Macdonald at the annual distribution of prizes at Upper Canada College. The Mackenzies joined the Royal Canadian Yacht Club. By the end of 1893, Don confided that Mrs. Mackenzie was 'one of the most hospitable hostesses on the east side.'

The week of the Queen's Plate, founded by Sir Casimir Gzowski in the 1860s, was a high point in the calendar of the Four Hundred. *La crème de la crème* – Gzowskis, Simpsons, Denisons, Cassels, Ridouts, Coxes, Janes, Otters, Gooderhams, and so on – played their roles during the five days of festivities. Occasionally, European nobility attended. In May 1893, Prince Roland Bonaparte of Monte Carlo was a guest.

In 1893, for the first time, thousands of race fans could travel to Woodbine Race Track on the fast and splendid trolleys that ran along Queen Street.[38] One grand day William Mackenzie brought out the luxurious, chocolate-coloured private car. On board were the James Grace family, the J. Enoch Thompsons, William, Margaret (in a tan costume with a bonnet, noted Don), Mabel, and Gertrude. The fifth race that day was the Street Railway Steeplechase, a two-and-a-half mile race with two water obstacles. Mackenzie threw in an extra $100 in prize money. It was wise to keep the Four Hundred happily entertained, as well as the thousands of others in attendance, including the mayor. After all, in May 1893, the pavement dispute with the city was just beginning to heat up.

In December 1893 the *Globe* published Archibald Lampman's 'The Railway Station.' Its theme is the increasing speed that was beginning to characterize the lifestyle of Canadians during the 1890s. The narrator is saddened by the flight of crowds hurrying to catch a train and the increasing isolation created by the age of speed.[39] F.M. Bell-Smith's *Lights of a City Street*, unveiled shortly after the publication of Lampman's poem, also suggests the faster pace of urban life in the 1890s. As light drains from the sky, crowds hurry to catch two waiting trolleys. Newsboys scurry to sell the latest bulletins. A few brave cyclists wait at the intersection. Few people have time to chat. Poem and painting have more in common with this century than with the nineteenth, for the quickening pace of the twentieth century began during the 1890s, as cities became wired, as electric trolleys began to regiment the lives of city dwellers, and as electric lights began to replace natural light in cities.

The Chicago World's Fair of 1893 featured a miniature house in which electricity performed many wonders, from heating to washing, cooling, cooking, disposing of garbage, and playing phonographs. Electricity was compared to the 'divine, unsearchable power of Christ.' It was recreating the world. In 1893 a new electric clock was installed at King and Yonge streets. Visible in Bell-Smith's painting, the clock stated time more precisely than older mechanical clocks, such as the one in St. James Cathedral tower, visible in the distance. The trolley and the electric clock imposed punctuality and speed on a public accustomed to neither. At the heart of *Lights of a City Street* lies a tension between the natural light of God and the artificial light of Prometheus, between fading twilight and the glowing eye of a trolley headlight.

Mackenzie owned that trolley. He made up his mind with the speed of light. He was an aggressive, ambitious man whose mind worked like a steel trap. Back on the Portage Road in pioneer days, when the majority of Canadians governed their lives according to the rhythms of nature, there seemed to dwell in Mackenzie a clock that governed his life in minutes and seconds. No matter what the project, whether procreation or recreation, Mackenzie was always in a hurry. Coinciding with his own personal development during the three decades after 1870, electrical energy and the horseless trolley were invented and developed. At the same time, capital accumulation in the 1880s and 1890s provided the means to finance large enterprises. Character and circumstance intersected and interacted. In the 1890s Mackenzie married capital to invention, thereby transforming the lives of urban Canadians.

CHAPTER FIVE

Dauphin Iron and
Yukon Gold, 1895–8

> It's impossible to say a thing exactly the way it was, because what you
> say can never be exact, you always have to leave something out, there
> are too many parts, sides, crosscurrents, nuances; too many gestures,
> which could mean this or that, too many shapes which can never be
> fully described, too many flavours, in the air or on the tongue, half-
> colours, too many.
>
> (Margaret Atwood, *The Handmaid's Tale* [1985] 144)

Dreams of transporting Manitoba grain to Europe through Hudson
Bay began soon after the first surplus crop was harvested in the
1880s. Like too many Canadian dreams of the North, it was impractical and expensive but politically attractive during elections from
the 1880s to the 1930s, when a railway finally reached Fort Churchill.
The railway and its northern port never fulfilled the promises of its
advocates, however, and today little grain is shipped through Churchill.

During the 1880s and '90s William Mackenzie played an important role promoting such a railway. As contractors, he and Donald
Mann had been associated with two failed attempts, in 1886 and
1891, to build a branch railway from Winnipeg to Hudson Bay. In
1895, as another election approached, the weak Conservative government of Prime Minister Mackenzie Bowell decided to revive the
Bay railway, apparently agreeing with the old departed chieftain, Sir
John A., that the promise of Dominion monies for a railway would
gain votes in the most intractable ridings. And the visceral question
of language was making Manitobans decidedly intractable. The
charter to build to the Bay was held by promoter Hugh Sutherland,
who first hired contractors Mackenzie, Mann, Ross, and Holt, then,
for various reasons, fired them. Denied the potentially lucrative

contract, Mackenzie and Mann decided to seek their own contract, and quickly gained powerful support: Sam Hughes and Winnipeg MP, 'Fighting' Joe Martin; the Honourable John Haggart, Minister of Railways and Canals; Senator Sir James Lougheed; and, in Winnipeg, Clifford Sifton, T.A. Burrows, and T.L. Morton.

On 22 July 1895, as Parliament was about to prorogue for the summer, several bills incorporating railways were hurried through the House and Senate, with what P.B. Waite has called 'malodorous haste,'[1] and given vice-regal assent. One bill created a charter for the Lake Manitoba Railway & Canal Company (LMRCC), allowing it to build 160 kilometres from Gladstone or Arden north into the Dauphin plains. Since it was headed in the direction of the Bay, it was eligible for a Dominion land grant of 6,400 acres per mile and a transportation subsidy of $80,000 per annum. The man who controlled the new charter was Donald Mann. There were now two active charters to build north to Hudson Bay, the second controlled by Mann's rival, Hugh Sutherland.

Like the Qu'Appelle, Long Lake & Saskatchewan and the Calgary & Edmonton Railways, the Lake Manitoba Railway & Canal Company was conceived as a branch of the Canadian Pacific Railway's main line to Vancouver. In October 1895, when Mackenzie returned from Birmingham, he was accompanied to Winnipeg by Sir William Van Horne and other officials of the CPR, as well as by the general manager of the Bank of Montreal, the CPR's bank. In 1896 Van Horne's son, Benny, joined one of the survey parties north of Gladstone, and the CPR opened its Winnipeg repair shops to Mackenzie and Mann during construction of the Dauphin line.[2] There was little doubt which charter and which promoters the CPR favoured.

But which of the two charters would get the nod to build a railway to the Saskatchewan River and on to the Bay? Mackenzie solved that problem when he met Sutherland in Ottawa on Wednesday, 29 January 1896. Several months earlier, they had parted on bad terms. Sutherland owed Mackenzie money, but when the meeting was over, Sutherland had agreed to put his own charter on hold and to join Mackenzie and Mann.[3] No doubt Mackenzie made Sutherland an attractive offer, perhaps even forgiving the debt.

The same day, Mackenzie attended a meeting of the provisional directors of the Lake Manitoba Railway & Canal Company. As treasurer, he announced that the new company would be capitalized at $800,000, or 8,000 shares at par value of $100. The meeting was adjourned. A couple of hours later, at a shareholders' meeting, Mackenzie announced that 25 per cent of the capital stock had already been subscribed and that 10 per cent, or $20,000, as Dominion government regulations required, had been deposited with the Canadian Bank of Commerce in Ottawa. Mackenzie and Mann became the majority shareholders. Five colleagues, Charles Porteous, James Gunn, A.J. Sinclair, J.M. Smith, and Fred Nicholls, held twenty shares each and were appointed directors. Fred Nicholls became the first president. As contractors, Mackenzie and Mann were prevented by Dominion regulations from becoming directors. But by controlling the majority of subscribed shares, they controlled the company.[4]

Mackenzie's name was already noted by those who counted in Ottawa society. He had made it into what Sandra Gwyn has called the 'outer circle' of perhaps a thousand invited guests at Rideau Hall. On Saturday, 25 January, a few days before establishing the new railway company, Margaret and he attended the governor general's annual skating party, where inevitably the fine line dividing social gossip from political influence vanished in the chill Ottawa air. A few months later, he sent a photograph of Clifford Sifton accompanied by a laudatory article to the Buffalo *Illustrated Express*. When it was published, Mackenzie sent a copy of the newspaper to Sifton in Winnipeg, telling him that 'we are all anxious to see you down here as soon as possible.' (The letter is, typically, undated, apparently written after the Laurier victory of June 1896. Mackenzie was suggesting that Sifton consider joining the Dominion Liberals, which he did, in 1896.)[5]

As attorney general of Manitoba, Sifton was already a colleague of Mackenzie. Back in February 1896 Mackenzie had been in New York. While his family shopped and sat for photographs, he was busy at the Hotel Brunswick sending telegraph messages across the continent, one of which urged Sifton not to add 'restrictive clauses' to the Lake Manitoba Railway Bill that the legislature was debating that day in Winnipeg.

Sifton succeeded in steering the bill through the legislature with few restrictions. In addition to exempting the railway from taxes for thirty years, the province promised to guarantee $1 million in construction bonds for 200 kilometres of railway to Lake Winnipegosis. In return, the government asked that the railway company submit their freight rates for approval.[6] Some members found the bond guarantees excessive, but Gladstone's T.L. Morton, whose Westbourne riding stood to benefit from the new line, thought the agreement 'fair and reasonable.' T.A. Burrows, Sifton's brother-in-law and MPP for Dauphin, where he held large timber rights, was tickled pink.

Not surprisingly, the LMRCC chose as its contractors its two major shareholders and gave them 6,000 unsubscribed shares as a bonus. To pay for construction, Mackenzie and Mann received the transportation subsidy, as well as construction bonds of up to $1 million guaranteed by the land grant of 6,400 acres per mile of construction. In June 1896 Mackenzie scouted the London bond market to sell a third issue of bonds, $1 million second-mortgage bonds whose interest would be paid by the transportation subsidy.[7] The potential bonded indebtedness of the Lake Manitoba line thus rose to a maximum of $3 million. Governments anxious to construct railways and maintain power were more than willing to guarantee large amounts of construction bonds. It seemed like a good way to build railways, for initially it cost governments nothing, gained them votes, and provided low-risk money for railway contractors.

Mackenzie himself was rarely seen on construction sites, for his chief role was that of company representative in investment houses and Parliament. Donald Mann supervised construction more frequently, although he too was an effective political lobbyist in Winnipeg and Ottawa. They made a formidable team, the stocky Scots-Canadian from Kirkfield and the big, brawny Scots-Canadian lumberjack from Acton, Ontario, near Guelph. Supervisory jobs in Manitoba were left to Mackenzie's oldest son, R.J. With chief superintendent D.B. Hanna, R.J. made sure that the work was done on time. A 'regular taskmaster,' he often carried a repeating rifle. One day in Dauphin country, Ukrainian workers decided to celebrate a religious holiday not part of the Presbyterian calendar of observances. 'Get back to work or you don't get fed,' he ordered, brandishing his rifle. The workers quickly decided that their stomachs took precedence over their souls.[8]

In August Mackenzie inspected the first dozen miles of track north from Gladstone. The next month, accompanied by Margaret, R.J. and Donald Mann, he rode in the *Sea Falls*, Mackenzie and Mann's first private railway car, to the end of the line somewhere south of the present town of Dauphin, which had not then been surveyed as a townsite. Mackenzie must have been pleased with Dauphin country. Its fertile plains, dotted with woods and fed by freshwater streams and creeks, looked somewhat like the fertile and gently rolling land of his native Victoria County, Ontario. Over to the west, the deep blue Riding Mountain brooded over the plains, a smaller version of the Scottish Highlands he had visited the year before. It was a historic area, which like his own Portage Road had connections with France, Old and New. Fort Dauphin, named by fur trader and explorer La Vérendrye in honour of the eldest son of Louis XVI, dated from 1741.[9]

In early November 1896, the first shipment of cattle was made
from Dauphin. In late December, passenger service was inaugurated,[10] and by mid-September 1897 the rest of the line, to Lake Win-
nipegosis, was completed. From the beginning the Lake Manitoba
Railway & Canal Company made small operating profits: $1,202 in
January 1897, its first full month of operation,[11] and about $6,000 in
1897.[12] By 1897, however, there was no doubt that the real profits
were in construction. Mackenzie, Mann & Company's profit for
constructing the Dauphin line was about $200,000, in line with ear-
lier construction profits in BC and the Northwest.[13]

Any evidence suggests that the quality of construction was good.
Mackenzie knew that shares in sound railways often rose in value.
Toronto Railway Company shares had reached a high of $89 in 1895,
a few months after going public, providing shareholders, those who
had bought shares at $25 and those who had received shares as bo-
nuses in 1892, with an attractive profit.[14] Mackenzie and Mann had
paid an average of $2.50 for each of their 8,000 shares in the Dauphin
Railway. It might take a few years, but some day the population of
Dauphin country would justify the building of this railway. Some
day these shares would rise, perhaps to $30 or $40 each, and the two
contractors would profit a great deal.

In early January 1898, William Mackenzie hosted a gala tour of the
Dauphin line. In the *Sea Falls* rode Donald Mann, Premier Greenway, D.B. Hanna, Lieutenant Governor Macmillan, opposition
leader Rodmond Roblin, and General Superintendent Whyte of the
CPR. When the train stopped at the new town of Dauphin, which
had been assembled 'pre-fab' style by moving buildings from two
nearby towns established a few years earlier, Mackenzie announced
that he was ready to build to Swan River country and on to the Bay.
The assembled men cheered.

In the late 1890s, Mackenzie and Mann acquired other railway
charters, which promised to provide more contracting. The charter
of the Ontario & Rainy River Railway allowed it to build in north-
western Ontario towards the Lakehead; and that of the Manitoba &
South Eastern Railway provided for a line from Winnipeg to the
southeastern part of Manitoba. With a couple of small gaps, these
two lines could join Winnipeg and Port Arthur. Fred Nicholls was
appointed president of the new companies and the board of directors was roughly the same as for the Dauphin Railway, with the addition of Mackenzie's twenty-one-year-old son, Alex, who had just
completed two years at the University of Toronto. In order to pay for
construction, the directors turned over 'all the stock, bonds, subsidies and bonuses from whatever source' to Mackenzie and Mann.

During Mackenzie's mid-summer visit to England in 1897, he floated construction bonds for the Rainy River line.[15]

In July 1898 Prime Minister Laurier told Mackenzie that he would ask Parliament for a subsidy of $1,312,000 to finance construction of the Rainy River line. 'Though this letter is private and confidential,' Laurier added, Mackenzie was free to inform his banker, the Canadian Bank of Commerce.[16] The railway was also subsidized by the government of Ontario's Premier Hardy at $4,000 per mile,[17] increasing the total subsidy to $10,400 per mile of construction, or $2,132,000 for the 205 miles.

A few days after Laurier's welcome communication, Mackenzie, his wife and family, joined Laurier at Stanley Junction, the eastern terminus of the Rainy River Railway, thirty-two kilometres southwest of Port Arthur. Laurier turned the first sod.[18] The 'rascally french [sic] crowd,' as the alarmed Porteous had labelled the victorious Liberals in June 1896, were proving loyal supporters of Mackenzie and Mann. In opposition, Laurier had been suspicious of their intentions. In power, however, leaders often find it politically expedient to support people and ideas once rejected. Sifton, Laurier's Minister of the Interior, helped to make Laurier sympathetic to western railways.

In August 1898 Mackenzie, Mann & Company purchased the bankrupt Port Arthur, Duluth & Western Railway, which ran from Port Arthur to Stanley Junction, continuing southwest to the Minnesota border.[19] It appeared that at last Mackenzie had a vision of a coordinated railway company, which on paper linked Winnipeg to the Saskatchewan River system in the west, to Hudson Bay in the north and by water to Europe, and to the Great Lakes at Port Arthur and thence by water to Toronto and Montreal. And yet, according to Porteous, when Mackenzie acquired the Port Arthur, Duluth & Western, he was 'somewhat aimlessly wandering about.' If Mackenzie had a clear strategy, he did not divulge it. He seemed to be a man directed more by chance than by design. The historian Macaulay once argued that the British Empire was acquired in a fit of absence of mind. In *The Sleepwalkers*, Arthur Koestler suggests that important ideas are often stumbled upon, as if in a sleeping state. Mackenzie's empire appears to have been created in similar fashion. Perhaps most empires are.

On 17 October Mackenzie sent a telegram to Sifton. Had an order-in-council extending the time limit for earning the land grant of the Winnipeg Great Northern Railway Company been passed?[20] Hugh Sutherland controlled the charter for the WGN, but the deadline for completing construction to the Saskatchewan River was 31 December 1898. If Sifton could extend the deadline, then Mackenzie would unite the WGN and the LMRCC. In December 1898 the two companies were amalgamated and the Canadian Northern Railway (CNoR) was born. The new company inherited all the rights and privileges – bond guarantees, land grants, and mileage subsidies – of the two antecedent companies. The Canadian Northern Railway now had two charters to build to the Saskatchewan River, with two land grants at 6,400 acres per mile and two transportation subsides. It also acquired an old land grant of 256,000 acres connected with one of the failed attempts to build to the Bay a decade earlier.[21] The railway's capital stock rose to $16 million.

Mackenzie and Mann's ambitions were not limited to Manitoba and Northwestern Ontario. The same day that Mann obtained the LMRCC charter in 1895, he and Mackenzie, with Senator Cox, Fred Nicholls, and Hugh Lumsden, obtained a charter for the James Bay Railway Company, to link Toronto to James Bay via Sudbury and Parry Sound. The company was allowed to issue up to $1 million in common stock, and also to sell or lease the railway to other companies, including the CPR.[22] After constructing the railway line, Mackenzie may have had two plans in mind. One was to lease the line to the CPR, thereby reducing travelling distance between Toronto and Winnipeg by hundreds of kilometres, since the CPR would no longer have to depend on the Grand Trunk's line from Toronto to North Bay in order to connect with its own main line from Montreal to the west. Mackenzie may also have had long-range plans—perhaps a railway of his own. Parry Sound's harbour on Georgian Bay was excellent. Did he envisage a railway from Toronto to Parry Sound, with a connecting water link to Port Arthur? After all, the James Bay charter permitted construction of grain elevators and operation of steamboats in Georgian Bay. Although Mackenzie and Mann did not immediately build the James Bay line, it would later play an important role in their transcontinental railway plans.

In the summer of 1896, gold was discovered in the Klondike. Canadians, particularly retailers in Vancouver, Victoria, and Toronto, wanted an all-Canadian route, by water and land, to the gold fields. In October 1897 Clifford Sifton inspected various routes. The Chilkoot and White passes might have provided railway corridors, but the nearest port towns, Dyea and Skagway, were in territory claimed by both Canada and the United States. Sifton decided on a more southerly route through the American town of Wrangell, where steamers could enter the Stikine River without having to land on American territory (see map, opposite page). After passing

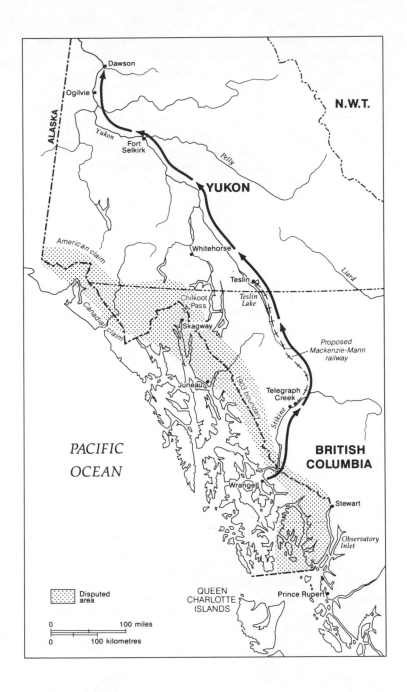

Proposed water-rail route, Wrangell to Dawson, 1897-8

through the narrow Alaska Panhandle, miners and their goods would disembark at Telegraph Creek, BC, then board a train for Teslin, on the east side of Lake Teslin. Another steamer would take them up the lake and down the Teslin and Yukon Rivers to Dawson. Technically, the route was all-Canadian, since free navigation of the Stikine River through the Panhandle was guaranteed by the Treaty of Washington.[23] Although the international boundary would not be settled for another six years, the plan would work, even if the boundary were fixed as far inland as Americans demanded.

On New Year's Day 1898, Mackenzie and Mann announced that they were about to apply for a charter to build the 'Stikine and Teslin Lake Railway Company' from Telegraph Creek to Teslin.[24] On 25 January 1898, they were in Ottawa to sign the contract. It provided no cash subsidy, but to cover their estimated $5 million costs for the 150 miles (240 kilometres) of railway and sleigh road, they would receive 25,000 acres of land per mile of railway, or 3,750,000 acres. The Dominion government would keep alternate blocks of land in order to share any veins with the contractors, who would pay 1 per cent royalty on gold, rather than the usual 10 per cent paid by miners. As a guarantee that the railway would be completed by 1 September 1898, the contractors deposited $250,000 with the government.[25]

'We have three outfits en route already, and a line has been located,' an ebullient Mackenzie announced in February. Seventeen hundred tons of steel track had been ordered. Rock blasting was to begin in April. Four thousand men would be employed, and the line would be completed in September, 'without a doubt, or we should not have undertaken the job.'[26] As was his wont, Mackenzie had the railway built before the final contract was signed.

Mackenzie overlooked one important condition of the agreement – both Houses of Parliament had to ratify it. Stacked with Conservatives from years of Macdonald rule, the Senate was ready to turn it down. In February debate began in the Commons. The Laurier Liberals were generally in favour. At first, opposition leader Tupper approved, but he could not carry a divided Conservative party with him. Some newspapers suggested that Tupper had investments in Mackenzie, Mann & Company.

The *Globe*, on the other hand, thought that William Mackenzie was the only Canadian with the courage to play such high stakes at such short notice, for he did not suffer from that Canadian disease, St. Vitus' dance, a metaphor for indecision and confusion. Of course, the paper argued, Mackenzie and Mann would make a great deal of money, but at the same time, Pacific Canada would be revitalized. Not surprisingly, Clifford Sifton's *Free Press* thought that the Yukon railway venture would eclipse the building of the CPR, and that Mackenzie was a man 'possessed of unsurpassed nerve and unparalleled business enterprise.' Other papers developed the theme of the invincible magician-businessman: Mackenzie was the swiftest and most clear-headed man in Canada, and he was about to overshadow Lord Mount Stephen and Lord Strathcona, and even Sir William Van Horne.

Mackenzie travelled to Ottawa several times to watch the debate in the House of Commons. He heard his friends George Bertram and Sam Hughes speak in favour of the bill. If the Americans would not abide by the Treaty of Washington, Hughes thundered one day, then Canada should build an all-Canadian railway from Port Simpson in British Columbia, north into the Klondike.

The Americans were indeed willing to abide by the letter of the Treaty of Washington. Unfortunately for the Canadians, in order to steam up the Stikine River, an ocean vessel had to unload goods onto a river vessel, and the treaty made no mention of transshipping. In early March, Congress announced that it would allow trans-shipping of Canadian goods through Wrangell only if Canada allowed each American gold miner to import half a ton of American equipment duty free, scarcely an acceptable arrangement for Canadian manufacturers and retailers.

The Yukon Bill became the talk of Ottawa. On the evening of Wednesday, 9 March, *le tout* Ottawa crowded into the Visitors' Gallery for the debate and vote on the bill's third reading. Lady Laurier was there. Donald Mann strolled over from the Rideau Club. George Taylor Denison reported in his diary that Sir Wilfrid, whose hospitality he was enjoying for a few days, did not return home to Theodore Street (now Laurier Avenue) until six in the morning. The bill passed the House, and was sent to the Senate.

In the States these debates were watched with alarm. The bill's five-year monopoly clause would bar American railways through Skagway or Dyea. When the bill went before the Senate, Ottawa was deluged with American lobbyists representing transportation and retailing interests in San Francisco and Seattle, who distributed copies of a slick 125-page booklet called *An Appeal of the Yukon Miners to the Dominion of Canada*. The lobbyists claimed that Yukon miners, 40 per cent of whom were American, would be more than upset if Ottawa interfered with their rights as American citizens – in territory that was indubitably Canadian! Small wonder that Canadians donned their seldom-worn cloak of nationalism. In Ottawa there was cause for concern, for by 1898 Americans were experts at infiltrating foreign territories then calling on Washington to annex them.

Mackenzie and Mann grew concerned at the intensity of the American lobby. Just after the House passed the bill, they travelled to Montreal to meet two men representing a proposed railway from Skagway through the White Pass to Whitehorse. The Canadians proposed amalgamating the schemes and sharing land grants. They suggested a meeting with Sifton in Ottawa, but the Americans turned them down.[27]

American lobbyists might have stayed home, for the Senate was unco-operative. Only one Conservative, Sir Frank Smith, owner of the old pre-1891 Toronto Railway Company, supported it. Mackenzie, Mann, and Sifton were hectored: Sifton had given away $8,000 per mile to Mackenzie and Mann for constructing the Dauphin Railway; the Yukon land grant was monumental; and the contractors got the best choice of the gold lands. And what about the Toronto Street Railway? – acquired by bribery and operated with indifference. Senator Mills rose in the afternoon of 30 March to declare that he had never witnessed such a partisan and nasty debate in the Senate. Senator George Cox defended Mackenzie, Mann, Sifton, and the Toronto Railway. But to no avail – as the crowded and hushed gallery leaned forward in seats above, the Senate voted down the bill by fifty-two to fourteen.

Mackenzie was exhausted. 'Your heart would have softened to the unfortunate man,' Porteous wrote to James Ross in Birmingham. Mackenzie was losing control of himself. 'His face was ghastly, a grey greenish colour, pulled out of shape, with the veins standing out like knotted string.' He complained of cold and headache.[28]

Defeated he was, but failure, as much as success, indicates a man's intentions. At Wrangell the railway was to link with the CPR ferries that plied the west coast between Vancouver, Victoria, and Wrangell. The Yukon railway was another branch line to tie into the CPR.[29] Was Mackenzie planning to operate the railway line after constructing it? Or had he planned to make his money on construction and gold? The evidence is ambiguous. Although House debates assumed that the two contractors were responsible for operation of the line, Laurier's solicitor general warned the prime minister that the contract, drawn up by Z.A. Lash, made no provision for operating the road for any definite period.

Despite the defeat in the Senate, the Yukon railway was not dead. Sifton was determined to push another version through Parliament. Sam Hughes suggested to Sifton that an altered bill, which included provision for building the railway completely through BC, would pass the Senate. Principal Grant of Queen's University and 'Klondike' Joe Boyle spoke in favour of an all-Canadian route. Many Canadians were furious at the loss of business to Americans. Recovered, Mackenzie was back in Ottawa the first week in April.

Prior to sailing to England with Van Horne in May 1898, Mackenzie told Porteous that a railway, 720 kilometres long, from Observatory Inlet, just south of the present-day BC-Alaska boundary, was being planned. Since Laurier's and Sifton's hands were tied by the Senate, the new proposal was being promoted by Premier Turner of BC. The northern section from the Stikine River to Teslin Lake was to be completed by 31 August 1899; the southern section to a BC port by the end of 1901.[30] It was a grandiose scheme, fortunately never attempted. When Mackenzie landed in England in late May, he learned that because Parliament had refused a subsidy, the railway scheme was finished. The BC government, however, still wanted a wagon-sleigh road built into the Yukon. Mackenzie and Mann's construction crews had already built part of the Teslin Trail when Turner in Victoria was forced to resign in mid-1898. There were signs that the gold rush had peaked, and in August the new government of Premier Semlin ordered the work halted. Ironically Mackenzie and Mann's idle rails were incorporated into the American-built White Pass railway through Alaska to the Yukon gold fields.[31]

In August 1898 Premier Semlin also put a temporary stop to Mackenzie and Mann's plans to construct the Vancouver, Victoria & Eastern Railway (VVE), from Vancouver to Midway, in the Kootenay district of southeastern BC. The line was designed to give west coast businesses access to the mining areas of the Kootenays, where since 1893 Mackenzie, Mann, and other Toronto and Montreal businessmen had controlled silver, lead, and iron-ore mines. In 1897 the two contractors had bought a controlling interest in the charter of the VVE, which at Midway would make connections with the proposed Crow's Nest Pass Railway from Nelson to Lethbridge. The VVE, leased to the CPR, would have provided that company with a route through southern BC to Vancouver, thus allowing it to compete with J.J. Hill's Great Northern along the international border. But since the provincial subsidy was conditional on a subsidy from Ottawa, which did not materialize, Semlin was forced to postpone the scheme. And Laurier refused Mackenzie and Mann's proposal to build and operate the Crow's Nest Pass Railway, for without their own line to Winnipeg and the Lakehead, they would not have been able to offer reductions in freight rates – the 'Crow Rates' – to the Lakehead. Thus the Crow line was built by the CPR. In 1901, when it became clear that neither Ottawa nor Victoria would aid the construction of the VVE, Mackenzie and Mann sold their interest to J.J. Hill, whose Great Northern proceeded to build the line from Penticton to Vancouver, to the great displeasure of the CPR.[32]

The Toronto Railway Company remained one of Mackenzie's most profitable companies. Torontonians used the system in increasing numbers, from about 16 million in 1891, to 22,610,000 in 1894, and 28,710,000 in 1898.[33] Operating expenses as a percentage of gross earnings declined from a high of 72 per cent in 1892 to about 50 per cent by 1895; and net earnings doubled between 1892 and 1898.[34] Share values reached par of $100 in early 1898.[35] In March 1895, the TRC gained control of the small Scarborough Railway Company, the second acquisition of a neighbouring tramway company. Shareholders of the Scarborough line, such as Henry Pellatt, were paid with TRC shares.[36]

When the TRC went public in January 1895, listing itself on the Toronto Stock Exchange (located then on the second floor of a building on King Street East near Yonge), its stockholders increased to about 300,[37] including Le Séminaire de St. Sulpice, which had begun life in Canada as proprietor of the island of Montreal. In the eighteenth century, the seminary had operated a mission in Toronto. The Sulpicians' investment in the TRC turned out to be as solid as the Rock of St. Peter.

Behind the scenes, a struggle for management control of the company was beginning to create factions. On the one hand, there was Mackenzie, who thought that he could run the growing company by making ad hoc decisions and by examining the books in a casual way at month's end. He was spending up to half of each year in London and Birmingham, and the company's performance worried Porteous and Ross, especially in 1896, when net revenues fell slightly. On a day-to-day and route-by-route basis, the company needed to know exactly why this was happening. James Gunn, superintendent in 1896, oversaw the company too casually, Porteous complained to Ross. In January 1897, without consulting Mackenzie,Ross and Porteous created a new position of manager, and appointed W.L. Wanklyn, who had both CPR and Grand Trunk connections and represented the new generation of managers with 'thorough mechanical experience,' James Ross told shareholders in January 1897. The *Globe* published the name of the new manager before Mackenzie, in Birmingham, had been informed. Furious, he began to distance himself from Ross and Porteous. Mackenzie's speculative business style would soon be unrestrained by the careful investment style of James Ross, who was never part of the Canadian Northern Railway Company, the most speculative of all Mackenzie's investments.

During the first two or three years after electrification, from 1892 to 1895, the TRC basked in public praise and good relations with council, but after 1895 relations with aldermen were often fractious. The mileage question became a bone of contention. In 1896 the city demanded back payment of $800 per mile, or $20,000 on curves and intersections, which the company, understandably, had never counted as mileage. Professor James Mavor, who was acquainted with both Toronto council and Mackenzie, blamed both sides. 'The City Council,' he noted, 'was perhaps unduly harassing in its demands, and the direction of the Company was perhaps tactless in its relations with the Council.'[38]

A few passengers and journalists complained that cars were unheated on chilly fall days, or that some conductors lacked courtesy. There were complaints about overcrowding during late afternoon rush hour. Inexpensive rush hour tickets for labourers, one aspect of the agreement of 1891, exacerbated the problem, since cheaper tickets encouraged rush hour travel. Most passengers, however, enjoyed the efficiency of the system and the low cost of the tickets. For a system that carried about thirty million passengers per annum by the end of the 1890s, there were remarkably few complaints.

And many compliments. In March 1895 the *Monetary Times*, often the TRC's harshest critic, praised Toronto's 'rapid street car service.'[39] In early July the *Globe* called street railway service 'magnificent,' and said that the trolleys were unsurpassed for comfort and accommodation. The *Street Railway Review* of New York liked the TRC. In September 1896 J.C. Lane of Birmingham expressed his appreciation of the ease and speed of the 'first class' cars. A year later the *Globe* called street car service along King to the Exhibition grounds 'admirable.' The same month a professor from Liverpool noted that what impressed him most about Toronto, next to its loyalty to the Mother Country, was the 'perfection' of its street railway system. Glasgow railway officials also admired Toronto trolleys. Many people continued to agree with the sentiments expressed in *Toronto Illustrated*, published a few years earlier, that Mackenzie had brought 'health, comfort and convenience' to Torontonians, and that he was a public benefactor, deserving of all financial benefits derived from the TRC.[40]

The Sunday street car issue had been shelved, but only temporarily. A third vote took place in May 1897. This time Mackenzie made no impassioned speeches to unruly crowds, and Torontonians were less exercised than in 1893. The head of the anti-Sunday car forces remained friendly with the TRC.[41] The sky did not fall when John Massey joined the pro-Sunday side. Upper Canada College's principal, Dr. Parkin, explained that he was in favour of Sunday cars, which meant, he said, that he was in favour of an orderly British Sunday, and not a raucous American Sunday.[42]

The vote was held on Sunday, 16 May. The pro-Sunday car side won, even if by only a few hundred votes. The 'Saints' could no longer scare the voters with stories of sacrilegious Sundays and overworked motormen. Sunday could be a day of rest, or a day for visiting friends, or for strolling in one of the city's lovely parks. Ever aware of the value of good public relations, Mackenzie donated the receipts from the first Sunday to charity, and let the press know of his generosity.[43]

The following Tuesday, Mackenzie was in Montreal. Didn't the TRC use underhanded tactics to obtain its majority? he was asked by reporters as he stepped from the train in Windsor Station. 'Oh,' he replied, 'you can't believe everything you hear,' and blamed the clergy for some of those allegations. The TRC, however, was not entirely innocent of coercion, though of a much more sophisticated kind than pulpit oratory. Porteous had 'donated' $3,700 to the Toronto Star to ensure its support during the campaign.[44] He arranged 'literary matters' with Saturday Night, and would have 'donated' 200 TRC shares to each of three newspapers had Ross not scotched the idea.

Sunday operations proved an immediate success and helped to increase profits. The popularity of the equal-wheeled bicycle had little or no effect on profits, for there was really little danger that a few hundred, even a few thousand, cyclists dashing through Toronto streets on pleasant days would endanger the robust health of a company that carried an average of 74,000 passengers daily in 1897. The contention advanced by Professors Nelles and Armstrong a few years ago that the bicycle was a form of Methodist 'revenge' on the Toronto Railway Company for operating on Sunday should be treated with levity. Many of Mackenzie's Methodist colleagues and friends, such as John Massey, supported Sunday cars; George Cox and Joe Flavelle, also staunch Methodists, invested in both bicycles and the Toronto Railway Company. Cox was president of the Canadian Bank of Commerce, Mackenzie's chief source of loan money, a stockholder in the City of Birmingham Tramway Company,[45] and a partner with Mackenzie in BC railways and mines. In 1897 the TRC was making plans to install trolley bicycle racks for the convenience of cyclists,[46] which suggests that it perceived no threat from the two-wheeled conveyances. Mackenzie himself was a cyclist.[47]

If there was any 'revenge,' it was on the part of the 'Saints,' who wanted to keep Sunday a day of rest. They succeeded beyond their wildest expectations, for as late as the 1960s, Sunday street cars had not enlivened Toronto's indecently boring Sundays.

Benvenuto: Italian for 'welcome.' The name had been chosen by the S.H. Janes family, who in 1891 had moved into their Norman castle at the top of Avenue Road hill, south of St. Clair. The bleached, rough-surfaced limestone mansion, with its four baronial towers, was designed by two architects affiliated with McKim, Mead and White, New York architects of Broadway and Newport mansions. From near the top of a sweeping rise of land that had once been the shoreline of long-vanished Lake Iroquois, Benvenuto surveyed the city below. Casa Loma would later join it on the same bluff, a couple of kilometres to the west. Archibald Lampman bristled poetically at such conspicuous extravagance,[48] but Mercer Adam thought Benvenuto a 'splendid piece of masonry,'[49] and years later, historian Arthur Lower thought it 'the last word in magnificence.'[50] The Mackenzies purchased it and its contents in June 1897 for about $100,000, in part, apparently, with TRC shares.[51] (Ironically, Janes had been a member of one of the syndicates bidding against Mackenzie in 1891 for the TRC.) Benvenuto's size and location bespoke solidity and self-confidence, assuring investors, brokers, and politicians that Mackenzie's risk of default was low.[52]

In June 1897, when the mansion was purchased, William Mackenzie was en route to England. It was Margaret Mackenzie who made the deal. As one of her husband's managers, in charge of his social and personal life, Margaret played a role similar to that of Porteous, Campbell, and Keating. Her small tavern business in Donald in the 1880s suggests that she too had entrepreneurial instincts, which she expressed as best she could within the confines of a patriarchal society. For years she had been noted for her teas, dinners, and trolley parties, popular in the 1890s when clubs or individuals often hired five or six open trolley cars, set up a band on one of them, then paraded around the Belt Line. Her guest lists were drawn up with consummate skill. She made certain that colleagues from the political, legal, business, and scholarly world remained on good terms with her husband.

Powerful men and their spouses from Canada, the United States, and Europe, along with friends and relatives from Winnipeg, Prince

Albert, Victoria, Dauphin, Paris, London, and Kirkfield were welcomed into the mansion's entrance hall, the largest room of the
house. The hall's fireplace warmed guests; its panelled walls and
ceilings impressed them. Its dining room featured rare seventeenth-century French tapestries, part of the Janes collection that
had come with the house. A drawing and music room was decorated
in Louis xvi style, its walls 'hung with damask, its white woodwork
picked out with gold,' unusual at a time when drawing rooms were
often dark and ponderous.[53] Other rooms featured Florentine, *ancien
régime*, and Victorian objets d'art and an enviable art collection. The
mansion became a focal point for Toronto society.

On Tuesday, 13 December 1898, Mrs. Mackenzie hosted a tea
party at Benvenuto. Between four and six o'clock, Toronto Society,
bundled up in furs and muffs against the subfreezing weather, arrived in Victorias and sleighs. The lights of the snow-covered city
below were beginning to sparkle in the cold, blue air. Over to the
west, the sky glowed with streaks of gold and crimson. Inside,
Toronto's d'Alsandro Orchestra entertained George Taylor Denison
III, Lady Thompson, widow of the late prime minister, Mrs. Hardy,
Judge Falconbridge; and Cawthras, Kingsmills, Gzowskis, among
others. They chatted in the library, in the conservatory, in the three
drawing rooms, in the entrance hall, and in the dining room; they
nibbled on salted almonds and candied fruit, and sipped steaming
tea.[54]

Margaret Mackenzie also oversaw the conversion of the once rug-
ged and ribald Kirkfield into a lovely little garden town. In 1895 the
large Kirkfield home had its lawns and gardens improved by a Scottish floriculturist, and her gardeners planted over 600 maples and
elms along Kirkfield streets that not so long before had stubbornly
refused to give up the last of their ancient pine and maple stumps,
reminders of clearing days sixty years earlier. In 1896 she bought
land on Balsam Lake, east of Kirkfield, where she supervised the
construction of a rambling stone and frame mansion, over ninety
metres long, which would not have looked out of place at Saratoga or
Newport. It contained over forty rooms, including fourteen bathrooms, had five fireplaces, and employed a staff of fifteen servants.
Some rooms featured tongue-and-groove Douglas fir panelling,
transported over prairie and Shield from Mackenzie's mills in BC.
Other rooms were decorated with French silk wall coverings.

Margaret Mackenzie's social graces were married to an iron will
that did not please all who met her. One day after her husband had
been knighted, she demanded to use the party telephone line in the
countryside near Kirkfield. 'I'm Lady Mackenzie and I want the

line,' she announced. But the druggist in Beaverton, who was talking to a local farmer, told her that even if she were Lady Halifax, she wasn't getting the line.[55]

The acquisition of mansions and a yacht, together with the beautification of Kirkfield, suggests that Margaret Mackenzie realized, perhaps before her husband did, that to be acknowledged successful, one must first create the illusion of success. The old Kirkfield, with its log shanties, huge stumps, and alcoholic excesses, had to be eradicated, since it evoked the days of poverty, insecurity, and limited prospects when little Maggie Merry, her feet wrapped in potato sacks, walked behind her father as he gathered the meagre harvest of turnips and potatoes.

Electric street railways in Birmingham, Toronto, and Winnipeg, and steam railway construction connecting cities to hinterlands in Manitoba, Ontario, British Columbia, and the Yukon were William Mackenzie's chief business interests from 1895 to 1898. He also invested in over thirty other businesses: street railways in Montreal, Halifax, Hamilton, London (Ontario), Saint John, Minneapolis, and Havana; power projects in St. Catharines, Halifax, Chicago, Kingston (Jamaica), and Keewatin; mines in BC, Ontario and Minnesota; land and real estate in the Yukon, Minneapolis, Lindsay, and Toronto; timber and pulp and paper in BC and Quebec; gas in Vancouver; asphalt in Chicago; Sam Hughes' Pullman ventilating system; and coal retailing and cold storage in Toronto. With the help of Porteous and estate manager Billy Mitchell, Margaret Mackenzie's brother-in-law, he imported sheep and cattle – Gloucesters, Shropshire Downs, and Guernseys – from England to Kirkfield.

He rarely relaxed. During these four years, he crossed the ocean six times and his country at least a dozen times. He visited the Roman Forum and the Scottish Highlands. He was at home in the Manitoba Hotel and on the golf course at St. Andrews, Scotland. He enjoyed window shopping on the Strand as much as inspecting mines in frontier towns such as Rossland, BC. At home with colonial secretaries and prime ministers, he enjoyed solving the world's problems over the oak counter of Shields' General Store in Kirkfield.

At the same time, he remained an enigmatic, often disorganized dreamer, a man in the midst of building the foundations of a large business empire, and yet one who was known to send orders for running that empire in telegraph codes that made no sense, since he used, on one occasion, at least, no recognized code book.[56] He remained a man who could put together multi-million dollar deals in a few hours, then absent-mindedly take the documents with him to

Winnipeg or Vancouver. He would often forget to sign cheques and stock certificates, leaving his managers with the task of finding him and the documents. During the 1890s Mackenzie learned, often with difficulty, to appreciate managers and codes. The hard lessons of Birmingham, BC, and the Yukon were teaching him how to play the entrepreneurial game of turning fantasy and vision into the reality of a successful business.

CHAPTER SIX

Masked Ball, 1899–1903

To create success one has first to create the spirit of enthusiasm; that is, the spirit of success. This works miracles.
    (William Dieterle, director of the film *The Hunchback of Notre Dame*)[1]

The Mackenzies loved a party, and on 31 December 1903, they gave a masked ball at Benvenuto. This New Year's Eve was special, for the following year was leap year. At midnight, the invitations announced, 'the customs of Leap Year may prevail.'[2] Guests disguised themselves as figures from the world of opera, theatre, and romance. Mrs. Cawthra arrived as Carmen in a crinolined red dress with a black veil and fan. Her husband, in pantaloons, turban, and sword, was Omar of Afghanistan. Colonel Lessard was the Sultan of Turkey. Two bachelors were dressed as babies. One of William Mackenzie's daughters was Lady Teazle from *School For Scandal*. Gilbert and Sullivan's Three Little Maids From School scuttled across the ballroom on Japanese wooden getas. At midnight masks were removed and the New Year was welcomed with cheers and good wishes.

The customs of leap year! Standards and formalities were turned on their heads. The unexpected and the unusual became the norm. All evening, behind masks, the revellers worked out their schemes, made their deals, plotted, cajoled, dared to act out fantasies. The Three Little Maids were typical of many guests, 'up to all sorts of pranks, and plainly inciting each other to further mischief,' according to *Saturday Night*. At midnight fantasies were realized, pretence became reality, rules were ignored, and all that was once solid and fixed melted into air (Marx's phrase). Those blessed with quick wits and a spirit of mischief were the most successful, for they were well prepared to invent new standards and to benefit by them. At midnight women gained the right to ask waiting men to dance.

The Mackenzies' masked ball was a microcosm of a national

masked ball whose setting was the Laurier era. There was Laurier, the grand conjurer with a magic wand,[3] presiding over the masked guests – politicians, businessmen, and voters who carefully camouflaged their identities, their motives, and their aspirations. Provincial capitals held their own masked balls. In Toronto, Professor James Mavor likened the debate on hydroelectric power to a piece of theatre in which the actors attempted to create reality from illusion.[4]

Mackenzie, Laurier, Adam Beck, and Premiers Whitney of Ontario and Scott of Saskatchewan were intelligent, visionary people. But vision remains illusion and fantasy until translated into practice. To convince others to believe in his dreams, the politician or businessman becomes an actor. He learns to use facial gestures, body language, and costumes to convince an audience that his assumed character is his real character. The mask camouflages the intentions of the actor and is, at the same time, an extension of the actor. The mask, as Yeats tells us in his poem of the same name, engages the minds of the audience and sets its hearts to beat. The audience is then prepared to suspend disbelief and to become enchanted by the actor's character and vision, whether that vision be a transcontinental railway, government-owned hydroelectricity, state medicare, a bilingual country from sea to sea, or a sovereign *pays* on the banks of the St. Lawrence, to name some of the visions that have engaged the minds and stirred the hearts of Canadians during the past century.

During the 1890s William Mackenzie was learning the importance of theatre in dealing with politicians, other businessmen, and the Canadian public. At the same time, he also gained control of himself. His breakdowns appeared to grow infrequent, because he learned how to handle executive stress. During the period from 1899 to 1903, he finally became a master of illusions and a creator of realities.

D.B. Hanna, superintendent of the Canadian Northern Railway, was a clever storyteller. He, too, understood the importance of dreams in creating reality. In his memoirs, *Trains of Recollection*, published in 1924, he compared the creation of Mackenzie's Canadian Northern Railway to a motion picture whose leading character was a juggler. At the film's première, enchanted Canadians watched as the juggler tossed a few 'projections of steel' into the air, then caught them as they fell. The magic of film made each piece of steel hang in suspense for a few seconds. Then in dreamlike slow motion the pieces began to fall into place, into what Hanna called an 'ordered announcement.'[5] (Hanna's imagination was formidable – his 'film' reminds one of Norman McLaren's animated films, produced decades later, in which objects and people seem to hang in space. His imagination also prefigured television, which has mastered the fine art of selling a product by means of magic and illusion.)

Mackenzie was the juggler who tossed up sticks and then connected them to create the Canadian Northern Railway. During the first months of 1899, he was busy lobbying politicians and promoting the CNoR in Toronto, Ottawa, New York, Winnipeg, and Dauphin. In February 1899 he attended the first directors' meeting of the new company, which reconfirmed Fred Nicholls as president. Mackenzie himself was still not interested in assuming the presidency. At that time he and Mann were contractors and promoters, not operators of railways, and in 1899 the Canadian Northern's chief purpose was to provide construction contracts for Mackenzie, Mann & Company. The creation and growth of the CNoR was more haphazard than Hanna liked to believe when he wrote his memoirs a quarter-century later.

In 1899 Mackenzie continued to claim that the railway's intention was a line to Hudson Bay. 'I have great faith in the feasibility of that route,' he told the Dauphin *Weekly News* in April, adding that he was convinced that most prairie grain, flour, and cattle would be shipped to Europe through the Bay.[6] Well into the present century, he continued to claim that the Canadian Northern would be constructed to Hudson Bay, probably in order to satisfy the Manitoba government that its generous bond guarantees would be of benefit to the province. He also had to satisfy politicians in Ottawa, since hundreds of thousands of acres of Dominion land had been granted for the purpose of constructing such a railway.

In 1899 Mackenzie was gaining control of more unconnected pieces of railways – the Edmonton, Yukon & Pacific Railway,[7] the Inverness Railway on Cape Breton Island, and the Halifax & South Western Railway from Halifax to Yarmouth and from New Germany to Caledonia Corners.[8] That same year Mackenzie and Mann acquired the charter of a short Minnesota line to link Ontario and Manitoba lines by way of the American state. In September Mackenzie travelled from Toronto to Winnipeg with a steamship promoter, apparently to acquire a Great Lakes shipping link from Port Arthur to Parry Sound. In 1900, the CNoR purchased from Mackenzie, Mann & Company the Manitoba & South Eastern Railway, recently completed from Winnipeg to Lake of the Woods, and the Ontario & Rainy River Railway. Authorized capital stock of the CNoR rose to $24 million. In September the Gilbert Plains branch line of the Dauphin railway, running from Dauphin west to Gilbert Plains, Manitoba, was opened. Further north, a line through the Swan River country was being pushed in the direction of Prince Albert. Mackenzie, Mann & Company was busy.

While most of the Dominion land grants had become the property of the CNoR, the construction company reserved about 100,000 acres for itself, to sell to homesteaders and to create townsites. Two small pieces were turned into ranches, one at Minitonas in Swan River country and a second at Dauphin, where in 1899 Mackenzie and Mann began to develop a 1,000-acre farm to raise cattle and racing horses and to take care of work horses and construction equipment. The Dauphin 'Company Farm' was managed by men from Kirkfield – Jack 'Reddy' Campbell and Matthew Perry, who, during his tenure from 1901 to 1910, made the farm the social and literary centre of Dauphin.[9] One of his daughters, Eugenie, extolled the virtues and vices of the town, its river, and its residents in iambic pentameter.

Railway construction could go ahead only if bond markets continued to absorb millions of dollars worth of construction bonds to build railways in Canada and throughout the hemisphere. The muskeg and granite of northwestern Ontario, through which the Rainy River railway was being constructed, pushed costs to $28,000 per mile,[10] the equivalent of over $300,000 per mile today. During the spring of 1900 Mackenzie went to London to float more construction bonds—about $6 million for the line to Port Arthur.

But the Boer War and the Boxer Rebellion were making markets nervous. The fact that the bonds were guaranteed not by government but by the CNoR itself further frightened investors. Even at 4.5 per cent interest, a half point higher than usual, neither New York nor London markets were interested.[11] Mackenzie had borrowed a great deal of money from the Bank of Commerce, expecting to pay it back through the sale of these bonds. If they did not sell, Rainy River construction would grind to a halt, and Mackenzie, Mann & Company would have to turn elsewhere for construction contracts.

On returning to Canada from London in August 1900, Mackenzie was again exhausted. And yet during these uncertain months, he decided to acquire another symbol of success. In Chicago, Mackenzie and Mann purchased an official railway car which they christened the *Atikokan*, after a townsite about 200 kilometres west of Port Arthur. The purchase of this second private car when the future of the railway and the construction companies was in doubt seems an act of folly. Mackenzie, however, knew that real success was often engendered by apparent success. When times are tough, illusions are all the more necessary. The private railway car would create the illusion of self confidence.

For a while the illusion seemed to fail, even though Mackenzie did his best to make it work. He travelled thousands of kilometres, down to the Maritimes, out to Winnipeg, trying to convince politicians. He even considered purchasing the Kingston Locomotive Works. But prospects remained gloomy. He began to exhibit 'bad colour'; once again his supportive daughters came to the rescue. Three of them, probably Mabel, Gertrude, and Ethel, whisked him off in the *Atikokan* to spend September on the west coast.[12]

Then the illusion turned into success. The province of Manitoba came to the rescue. It had little alternative. If the railway did not reach the Lakehead, the province would be left with a local railway and millions of dollars in debts. In 1901 Premier Roblin provided government guarantees for the unsold $5,800,000 of Rainy River bonds and for new bonds at $8,000 per mile for the short section through Minnesota. The province also acquired 562 kilometres from the insolvent North Pacific & Manitoba Railway, whose Manitoba lines ran from Winnipeg to the American border, from Winnipeg to Portage la Prairie, and from Morris west to Hartney in the southern part of the province. Roblin then leased these lines to the CNoR for 999 years. In return the CNoR agreed to submit to provincial regulation of freight rates on the Winnipeg to Port Arthur line.[13] The company also agreed that rates on grain between Winnipeg and the Lakehead would fall to an unprecedented ten cents per hundredweight, four cents lower even than the new Crow rate charged by the CPR for shipping grain to the Lakehead. The Canadian Northern Railway promised reductions of between 15 and 25 per cent on some goods shipped from the Lakehead to Winnipeg.[14] Thomas Shaughnessy and J.J. Hill found the new lower rates reckless. Mackenzie and Mann probably agreed, but the Canadian Northern had little choice. If it turned down the Manitoba offer, it would remain a feeder network for the CPR, and Mackenzie, Mann & Company would be left holding CNoR stock of little value, as well as large debts on incomplete lines. Furthermore, the rate would not come into effect until 1 July 1903, and the Manitoba government promised that if the new rate structure created operating losses, the province would reimburse the Canadian Northern.

Small wonder that Mackenzie and Mann signed the deal with such enthusiasm, and that Donald Mann, assisted by Clifford Sifton and J.J. Hill, spent $5,000 to encourage the Senate to pass it.[15] (Hill, apparently, no longer found the rates so reckless!) The Canadian Northern even threw in for good measure the usual rhetoric about being the 'long-awaited competitor for the CPR.'[16] (Or so Mann claimed years later, when he and Mackenzie had perfected the art of railway mythologizing. Thomas Shaughnessy was probably closer to the truth when he said privately in February 1901, a month after the Manitoba deal was signed, that a CNoR line to the Lakehead would benefit the CPR.)[17] Thus it was a good deal for the CNoR and particularly for the construction company, for it could continue building and making profits, which on the Rainy River line turned out to be at least $400,000.[18] And by 1903 freight rates had declined on their own, so the agreement of 1901 imposed no penalty on Mackenzie and Mann.

By the end of 1901, Mackenzie, Mann & Company had completed construction of the Rainy River line. The last spike was driven at noon on Monday, 30 December, a mild winter's day, about zero degrees celsius. The private car *Dauphin* (probably the *Sea Falls* renamed) brought journalists, politicians, CNoR and banking officials such as Hanna, John Aird, and Hugh Sutherland from Winnipeg. From Toronto came the *Atikokan* with Mackenzie, Mann, Moore, Lash, Edmund Walker, Mackenzie's son Alex; as well as E.J. Davis, Ontario commissioner of Crown Lands, and George Graham, president of the Rainy River Navigation Company. The two private cars met centre stage at Atikokan. Mackenzie led a tour of the roundhouse, then handed Davis a silver spike. The minister pretended to drive it home, then stooped, retrieved it, and returned it to Mackenzie, who thanked both the Bank of Commerce and governments in Winnipeg, Toronto, and Ottawa for backing the railway. The ceremony ended with three cheers for King Edward, the new road, Mackenzie and Mann, governments, and the Bank of Commerce. Mackenzie and Mann tipped the stagehands and carpenters – $2 to each workman, $5 to each gang foreman, and $25 to each district supervisor of construction. After a rousing rendition of 'God Save the King,' the men headed for Port Arthur. Along the way little knots of pioneers and lumberjacks gave Mackenzie and his troupe a standing ovation.

That evening, Port Arthur's Northern Hotel was festooned with Chinese lanterns and evergreens, potted plants, flags, and bunting. At one end of the banquet hall hung a huge painting of a Canadian Northern passenger train. At the other end huge portraits of Mackenzie and Mann were flanked by banners bearing the words 'Energy, Enterprise, Ability,' 'Port Arthur, the Silver Gateway to the Golden West,' and 'Port Arthur by water to Liverpool, 4,000 miles; by rail to the Pacific, 2,000 miles.' Mackenzie managed to get through a short speech, promising rapid completion of the new Port

Arthur grain elevator, with a capacity of 1,250,000 bushels. Mann
promised that next year the CNoR would ship all its grain through
Port Arthur rather than through Duluth, and expected that the last
spike of the transcontinental CNoR would be driven within seven
years.[19]

A year later Mackenzie and Mann's optimistic predictions were
being realized. By 1 January 1902 the CNoR had grown to 1,309 miles
(2,095 kilometres) of operating railway – 354 miles (566 kilometres)
in Ontario, 50 miles (80 kilometres) in Minnesota, 883 miles (1,413
kilometres) in Manitoba, and 22 miles (35 kilometres) in Saskatch
ewan.

Every eight to ten miles, a new village was created and named
with an eclectic mix of the local and international: Erwood, west of
the Manitoba border in the district of Saskatchewan, for E.R. Wood
of National Trust; Cowan, Manitoba, for W.J. Cowan, subcontractor
and Mackenzie connection from Victoria Road, near Kirkfield; Vassar, in southwestern Manitoba, for William Mackenzie's sister-in-
law, Rose (Vassar) Mackenzie; Ethelbert, between Cowan and Dauphin, for Mackenzie's daughter Ethel and his half-brother Bert; Baden, Powell, and Mafeking for the South African hero and siege, all
prominent in the news of 1901; Laurier and Sifton for friends and
patrons in Ottawa; and Roosevelt, Minnesota, for the man who had
taken over as American president from the recently assassinated
McKinley. Dauphin acquired a Mackenzie Street; the main intersection of Ochre River became Mackenzie and Mann, one of the rare examples of William Mackenzie's name on Canadian maps. Winnipeg, which by 1901 was home to Mackenzie relatives and connections who had moved from Kirkfield and Prince Albert, gained a
Kirkfield Park and streets named for Mackenzie's daughters. In 1897
Canadian poet F.G. Scott wrote 'The Unnamed Lake,' in which a no-
mad comes across a northern lake, enjoys its beauty, then moves on
without naming it. Mackenzie and Mann, however, were empire
builders who named and renamed as they imposed their transportation and communications order on the older 'measureless West'[20]
of the Indian, Métis, and fur trader.

From its base in Manitoba, the CNoR was now poised to penetrate deeper into what Rudyard Kipling called the 'far-flung fence-
less prairie, where the quick cloud shadows trail.' With charters in
the Edmonton district, in BC, Ontario, and Nova Scotia, and with
the completion of its huge grain elevators in Port Arthur, the CNoR
had national aspirations. Only for a fleeting moment was the Canadian Northern limited to the role of pioneer railway of the northern
prairies.[21] In March 1902 the company moved its headquarters from

Winnipeg to Toronto, and Mackenzie became president. The railway company had become too large to be considered a mere appendage to the construction company.

Also in March 1902 Mackenzie and Mann incorporated their construction company as a joint stock company under the name Mackenzie, Mann & Co. Ltd. Since they were no longer 'contractors personally' – construction thenceforth was carried on by subcontractors – they could legally become officers of both the construction and the railway companies.[22] Mackenzie thus became president of both the CNoR and Mackenzie, Mann & Co. Ltd., and Donald Mann became vice president of each company. After March 1902 Mackenzie Mann & Co. Ltd. hired subcontractors, especially the second Mackenzie and Mann construction company called the Northern Construction Company Ltd., owned and operated by Sandy Mann, bother of Donald, and 'Big Archie' McKenzie, husband of William Mackenzie's niece, Minnie. Mackenzie, Mann & Co. Ltd. now made profits by buying real estate, grain elevators, coal docks, and rolling stock, which it later sold to the Canadian Northern Railway or other interested companies such as Canadian Northern Land & Townsites Company.

June 1902 was a busy month for Mackenzie. He was dealing with the directors of the Canada Atlantic Railway, which he and Mann were attempting to buy.[23] He was also trying to head off a threatened strike against the Toronto Street Railway. In Winnipeg a labour dispute had been simmering for several weeks. Machinists and freight handlers had been complaining about wages and working conditions.

Mackenzie arrived in Winnipeg on Monday evening, 16 June. As he emerged from the *Atikokan*, a reporter spotted him. The interview was carried out on the run.

'What about a possible [Toronto Railway Company] strike?,' the reporter shouted.

'No, I don't care to talk at long range,' Mackenzie told him, and referred him to a recent interview in Toronto.

Reporter: 'Then you will not deal with the men as a corporation [union] but only as employees of the company?'

Mackenzie: 'You saw my interview.'

Reporter: 'But what are your views regarding the labor question?'

Mackenzie: 'Oh you can't make me say anything further than that.'

Reporter: 'In regard to the men striking here.'

Mackenzie: 'No, nothing about that.'[24]

Mackenzie had always been willing to deal with his men, but only as individuals or in small groups, never as members of official unions. He did exactly that in Winnipeg and began to negotiate for a new wage scale that would meet CPR standards. His paternalism was typical of owner-management attitudes at the time. As the *Monetary Times*, voice of the employer, once opined, 'no business can be conducted which is subject to the dictation of a union.'[25] Like fellow capitalist Hart Massey, Mackenzie found trade unions 'incomprehensible.'[26]

In Winnipeg, A.G. Broach, local chairman of the railway union, met Mackenzie and Hanna. The meeting was tense. Broach later claimed that Mackenzie had told him that if he did not like the company's offer, he could go to hell. Although Hanna denied that such strong language was used, Mackenzie was quite capable of telling Broach where to go, and probably did.

Mackenzie remained in Winnipeg for about five days, then headed back to Toronto and out to Nova Scotia with his daughter Mabel, her husband, and Donald and Mrs. Mann, for the official opening of the Halifax-Yarmouth railway. He was confident that Hanna could handle any problems in Winnipeg. Hanna couldn't. The strike began in earnest, although Hanna did manage to confine it mainly to Winnipeg. The newly opened Canadian Northern Telegraph lines proved an effective weapon to control strike information. The company brought in strike-breakers from Montreal. Strikers tampered with switches, derailed a car, set fire to the CNoR bridge over the Assiniboine, and hounded landladies who boarded strike-breakers. The company erected a huge tent near its freight sheds between Main Street and the Red River. On Hudson's Bay Company property where Broadway met the Red River, the strikers erected a tent within shouting distance of the CNoR tent.

In July, Hanna claimed that the strike was over, while Broach claimed that hundreds were still out. A few days later, strikers, reinforced by some CPR men, attacked the CNoR roundhouse at Water Street and the Red River. The strike threatened to become a general strike when over 800 workers from various Winnipeg trade unions gathered at Broadway and the Red to sympathize with Broach and his strikers.[27] The company raised wages but refused to recognize the union. In August the strike lost steam and the CNoR got up enough steam of its own to inaugurate its passenger service between Winnipeg and Port Arthur.

The Canadian Northern's vigorous expansion vexed the Grand Trunk's general manager, Charles Melville Hays, who hoped that the Grand Trunk would be able to absorb this upstart. In London, Charles Rivers-Wilson, president of the Grand Trunk, was kept informed of Canadian Northern intentions. In March 1902 Mackenzie called on Rivers-Wilson in his London office. The meeting was friendly. The president of the GTR assumed that he had Mackenzie 'in his pocket.'[28] Mackenzie probably led him to believe just that. Rivers-Wilson no doubt agreed with Hays that Mackenzie was still only a contractor, and may even have been unaware that just before leaving for London, Mackenzie had become president of the CNoR. (During the CNoR's fifteen-minute meetings, a good deal was accomplished, often unreported by the press.) A few weeks after the meeting in London, the CNoR submitted to Parliament plans to build from Port Arthur to Quebec, with lines to Montreal, Ottawa, and Toronto.

In early September, at the urging of Hays, Senator George Cox sounded Mackenzie and Mann out, and concluded that the only way for the Grand Trunk to acquire the CNoR was by obtaining a charter to build a line to the Pacific, parallel to the CNoR. Once Mackenzie and Mann realized the hopelessness of their situation, Cox told Hays, they would sell.[29] Mackenzie may have given Cox the impression that he might sell if boxed in. He no doubt knew that Cox would report the conversation to Hays. Cox's strategy was apparently the genesis of the Grand Trunk Pacific.

A few days later, on a mellow autumn day, Mackenzie was riding over a pasture in Earlscourt, west of Toronto (near the intersection of Dufferin Street and St. Clair Avenue today), with his lobbyist, Billy Moore. 'Cox has made an offer for the Canadian Northern,' he told Moore as their horses slowed to a walk. 'But there is not enough money in the world to buy my share – until the railway is completed.'[30]

There are few clues to explain why Mackenzie embarked upon one of the greatest acts of daring and grandeur in Canadian history – the building of a transcontinental railway whose shares were controlled by himself and Donald Mann. Billy Moore, who knew Mackenzie intimately, claimed that it was his quest for success that drove Mackenzie to seek new worlds, and that money had nothing to do with it. Edmund Walker of the Bank of Commerce thought that Mackenzie hated the very idea of losing control.[31] Up to the turn of the century, his life had many moments of disorder and chaos, interspersed with successes in Winnipeg and Toronto. Now at last he seemed to be lord of all he surveyed. Memories of Yukon and BC failures, the intransigence of Birmingham council, and even the bouts of nervous exhaustion, were safely locked away. Now the world would take notice. Now he really could eclipse Donald Smith and William Van Horne.

Underestimating the resolve of the taciturn Mackenzie, Hays began to construct an elaborate ruse to force him to sell. Laurier was drawn in, as was A.G. Blair, Minister of Railways, and officials of the Bank of Commerce. While Cox was encouraging Hays, Edmund Walker of the same bank was assuring investors that the Commerce stood firmly behind Mackenzie and Mann.[32] Israel Tarte, Laurier's recently deposed Minister of Works, reported to Governor General Lord Minto that J.J. Hill, Senator Cox, Mackenzie, and Mann had bought off Laurier and Sifton, and thus controlled the Northwest, Manitoba, and the Yukon.[33]

There was no stopping Mackenzie. On Monday evening, 17 November 1902, he tried to put through a long-distance telephone call to Sifton in Ottawa[34] to discuss government subsidies of $13,000 per mile for a railway line from Edmonton to Vancouver. That same evening he planned to drive down Avenue Road to Holwood, Joseph Flavelle's mansion overlooking Queen's Park, to discuss a loan from National Trust, which along with the Commerce was Mackenzie's main source of loan money. A few months later, in February 1903, when Mackenzie was in London, he met the Reverend Doctor Barr, who was making plans to settle 10,000 English immigrants in the Northwest. Mackenzie offered land on his proposed line between Battleford and Edmonton, an offer that resulted in the settlement of Barr colonists near the present city of Lloydminster. On his way home Mackenzie met J.J. Hill in New York City. Hill promised that his Northern Pacific Railway would not compete with the Canadian Northern in Manitoba.[35] In Quebec Mackenzie and Mann were attempting to gain control of the Great Northern Railway, to link lines in Ontario and the Maritimes. They were assembling land for stations in Edmonton and Winnipeg, and in early 1903 surveyors were at work east of Port Arthur. The company was expanding in southern Manitoba, and in Ontario, the James Bay Railway was reincorporated. On a trans-Canada basis, Mackenzie was assembling a gigantic 'right combination.'

Rivers-Wilson began to realize that Mackenzie and Mann were not about to withdraw from battle. In February 1903, when Mackenzie was in London, Rivers-Wilson wrote to Hays. Why not offer Mackenzie the presidency of the merged CNoR and Grand Trunk Pacific?[36] But the stubborn Hays was not going to ask the 'impossible' Mackenzie to head any new company and continued to favour Cox as president of any amalgamated company, hoping that Mackenzie and Mann would soon sell the CNoR.

In London Mackenzie was apparently playing a cat-and-mouse game with Rivers-Wilson. He twice postponed meeting the president of the Grand Trunk, and when he tried to contact him in February, Rivers-Wilson had left for Rome. Mackenzie thus missed being informed of Rivers-Wilson's proposal to let him have the presidency of a merged CNoR-GTPR company. Had it taken place, the meeting might have changed the course of Canadian railway history. In March 1903, as the railway situation grew more complex, the Laurier government established a Board of Railway Commissioners, whose role was to supervise and regulate freight rates and to help sort out railway rivalries.

On Monday evening, 23 March 1903, Laurier invited Hays to meet Mackenzie and Mann at the prime minister's residence. The three railway men met again the next day in Montreal in Hays' office. Lash apparently favoured railway union but Mackenzie and Mann demanded par value of $25 million for their stock, which Hays thought overvalued. Mackenzie and Mann were calling Hays' bluff, and may have thought that he would drop his idea of a parallel line through the prairies. Unfortunately no one backed down and the Laurier government found a typically Canadian solution: it refused to take sides and funded both projects, guaranteeing millions of dollars of construction bonds for both the CNoR and the GTPR, and promising to build the National Transcontinental Railway from Moncton to Winnipeg, an eastern link for the GTPR. The country was to be blessed and cursed with two parallel railway lines to Edmonton and the Rockies.

This solution touched off more rumours and intrigue in the national capital. Laurier was thought to be meeting with Hays without consulting Blair, who was reported to be in the rather large pocket of Mackenzie and Mann. In mid-July Blair suddenly resigned. Hays and Rivers-Wilson heard dreadful rumours that Sifton was to replace Blair as Minister of Railways. Laurier promised Mackenzie that he would sign nothing with Hays without consulting Mackenzie, but quickly forgot that promise.[37] Lord Strathcona and Mackenzie were seen travelling together between Ottawa and Montreal, touching off speculation of a CNoR sale to the CPR. Mackenzie and Shaughnessy were rumoured to be discussing an agreement of some sort. Shaughnessy told opposition leader Robert Borden that the CPR might share its line north of Superior with the CNoR and the GTPR.[38] Hugh Sutherland and Clifford Sifton were reported to be attempting to cancel Laurier's agreement with the GTPR.[39] In early December, Mackenzie was said to have told the prime minister about rumours that Grand Trunk Railway shareholders in Britain were unhappy that Moncton rather than Portland, Maine, the Grand Trunk's eastern port, was to be the National Transcontinental's Atlantic port.[40] If these shareholders refused to ratify the agreement between the GTP and the Dominion government, Mackenzie and Mann alone would build to the Pacific. Mackenzie and Mann were determined, they told the prime minister, to build through Ontario and Quebec, and reminded him of his promised subsidy for the James Bay Railway to be built from Toronto to Sudbury.[41] In November 1903 the Laurier government offered further subsidies to Mackenzie and Mann's Halifax & South Western Railway Company, and considered subsidizing a line from southern Manitoba to Regina.

In 1902, Mackenzie and his staff moved into the Toronto Railway Chambers at 1 Toronto Street, east of King and Yonge. This honeycomb of offices, located on one of the city's most beautiful streets, became the setting for momentous decisions made by a handful of Montreal and Toronto businessmen – Sir Henry Pellatt, Senator George Cox, Joseph Flavelle, Sir William Van Horne, James Ross, R.B. Angus, Donald Mann, Alex Mackenzie, and his father, William. Here Mackenzie and Mann, with R.J. Mackenzie and D.B. Hanna, the four executives of the Canadian Northern Railway, discussed lines in Alberta and Nova Scotia. Here boards discussed trolley riders in Winnipeg and Toronto, electric lights in Winnipeg and Havana, and, a few years later, power generation at Niagara Falls and Pinawa, Manitoba. During the two decades leading up to the Great War, Toronto was capital of a transportation and communications empire that transcended national, linguistic, and political boundaries. The Toronto Railway Chambers was a Colonial Office, and Mackenzie a Colonial Secretary. Out in the colonies, skilled managers and engineers worked tirelessly to manage daily affairs. Like the British Empire, Mackenzie's empire enjoyed constant sun, or so the press of the day liked to imagine. Before the Great War, both empires seemed immortal.[42]

All empires have their detractors. In Toronto issues such as overcrowding and expansion dogged Mackenzie. On 13 February 1899 he explained to city council that the agreement of 1891 had spoken of 'comfortable accommodation' for each passenger. The company simply could not give every passenger a seat, especially during rush hours. He suggested that council pass a by-law prohibiting passengers from entering already overcrowded cars.[43] 'We can't prevent the people getting on the cars,' he told a reporter one day as he hurried off to meet board members. The problem of overcrowding was not unique to Toronto at the turn of the century, when a more vibrant

North American and international economy was causing cities to grow at a rapid rate. Commuters eventually learned to accept uncomfortable overcrowding during rush hours as one of the norms of urban life. Councils and legislatures, whose members often rode in private conveyances, took longer to learn.

There were other differences with council, such as mileage payments on curves at intersections[44] and heating in street cars in early fall. There was also the question of which body, company or city, had final authority to determine the number of stops made by each street car. Some of the press called Mackenzie and R.J. Fleming obstreperous. Mayor Coatsworth, however, thought the press 'absolutely idiotic in dealing with street railway matters,' because it printed rumours and innuendo.[45] In November 1905 the Privy Council in London ruled that the city engineer had sole power over the number of stops. The eliminated stops were rescheduled.[46]

Then there was the delicate question of expansion. Between 1883 and 1889 Toronto had more than doubled its land area by annexing areas such as Riverdale, Parkdale, the Annex, and Yorkville. The agreement with the Toronto Railway Company in 1891 had specified service within the boundaries as defined at that time. In 1905 and 1906 the city annexed three more adjacent neighbourhoods: Rosedale and two areas adjacent to Avenue Road north and south of St. Clair Avenue, where some of the city's merchant princes and utilities barons lived, including Mackenzie himself. He refused to expand the TRC beyond the 1891 boundaries or to amalgamate it with the Scarborough or Mimico systems in order to make greater Toronto a one-fare zone, because he realized that only densely populated urban areas could be served profitably.

The issue went to the Privy Council, which in 1905 decided that council had no power to alter the 1891 agreement. The only passengers inconvenienced by the decision were the few who travelled from Scarborough or Mimico to Toronto and were forced to pay an extra fare. Mackenzie's emphasis on profitability and good service within a compact area has contributed to the viability of modern Toronto with its compact, liveable neighbourhoods and its 'high riding habit that made mass transit uniquely viable.'[47] And although the company refused to expand beyond the 1891 boundaries, it did develop the system within those boundaries.

In spite of differences, the company and the city were more often than not in agreement. Bad news makes great copy whereas good news often goes unreported. Or, if reported at the time, it is sometimes ignored by historians. In 1901 'Don' of *Saturday Night* urged passengers to withhold fares as a protest against worn-out cars and unannounced schedule changes, but in April 1902 he wrote warmly about the new street cars of Toronto, admiring the perfume of flowers carried by passengers, as well as the lively gossip exchanged on board.[48]

Both company and city council were keen on radial railways in order to consolidate the metropolitan dominance of Toronto over the surrounding countryside and towns, and to increase company revenues. In early 1900 Mackenzie and the chairman of the City Works Department agreed in principle to build radials to Oshawa, Rice Lake, and Beaverton.[49] In August 1904 Mackenzie formed the Toronto & York Radial Railway Company by amalgamating the Mimico, Scarborough, and Metropolitan Railway systems. In 1906 the line to Newmarket was extended to Jackson's Point on Lake Simcoe.[50]

Relations between the company and its men were usually good, with one important exception – the strike of 1902. Once the economy grew robust, cost of living rose and workers asked for a raise. Local 113 of the Amalgamated Association of Railway Employees had been organized during the labour-management differences of 1893. A decade later, about 90 per cent of the 950 men working for the TRC were members. In June they began to agitate for union recognition and for an increase in wages. Management offered a wage increase of between 20 and 25 per cent per hour, and offered improvements in working conditions. The company also offered to provide the men with the right to appeal a dismissal, albeit to the general manager of the TRC and not to an independent arbiter.[51] But the men were militant, partly because one employee had been dismissed for taking money from fare boxes. They demanded an across-the-board increase of twenty-five cents per hour, and refused an offer of arbitration from the Board of Trade, probably because they feared a business bias.

Mackenzie was in Winnipeg attempting to head off the CNoR strike when the Toronto strike began on Saturday, 21 June. He arrived in Toronto Sunday morning. As he emerged from Union Station on that overcast, cloudy spring day, it must have seemed that the old closed Sundays had returned to Toronto. For the first time since June 1897, no Sabbath trolleys ran. This was the first transit strike since 1886, when the city had been much smaller and less dependent on the old horse-drawn trams. Anxious and apprehensive Torontonians held their breath. Safe inside his home on Walker Avenue, north of Yonge and Bloor, Toronto lawyer Larratt Smith awaited news. Rumours began to circulate about 'rioting in town,' Smith recorded in his diary.[52] Large crowds gathered at each of the three trolley barns – on Yorkville Avenue, on Roncesvalles in the west, and at King near the Don, where Billy Moore drew a volley of stones when he attempted to put a trolley in operation. The drama was captured by the ubiquitous C.W. Jefferys, whose illustrations appeared in the Toronto *Star*.

It was never clear what motivated the throngs to attack company property. They may have been demonstrating solidarity with strikers. They may have been out for a good time. Toronto police lost control, and the police commissioner read the Riot Act and called in the militia from Niagara. The arrival of 1,400 soldiers on Monday morning brought peace and order without loss of life.

Mackenzie made no public statement. By Friday, manager Keating for the TRC, motorman Pickles for the Men's Committee, and the Board of Trade, represented by A.E. Ames, Joseph Flavelle, J.D. Allan, and Paul Jarvis, achieved a negotiated settlement. The company would not recognize the union, but agreed to discuss future grievances with suspended men. Wages rose to eighteen cents per hour for the first year and twenty cents thereafter; and the company, not the motormen, would be responsible for cleaning trolleys each night.[53]

In his *Arcadian Adventures of the Idle Rich*, Canada's gentleman-socialist, Stephen Leacock, who through his wife was related to Sir Henry Pellatt, poked fun at the nouveaux riches whose wealth had been created during the booms of the late nineteenth and early twentieth centuries. At their summer home, Castel Casteggio, Leacock's Newberrys consume conspicuously, congratulate themselves endlessly, and admire their perfectly manicured gravel walkways. They also manage to blow up Italian labourers while hacking out a road to their summer home. The only Italian story at the Mackenzies' summer home on Balsam Lake concerned a chef who served a dish that displeased Ethel and Mabel. They knew Italian cuisine from firsthand experience in Florence and Rome. With bravado and gesticulations, the chef told them that if they did not appreciate his cooking, he would quit. Within an hour the two women had him seated on the Toronto-bound train.[54]

Mackenzie enjoyed his family at the lake. Sometimes the grandchildren and young friends 'got up' a piece of theatre. An audience of adults assembled in boats in a semi-circle near the shoreline, where the nervous youngsters would recite their memorized lines. On one occasion, a young actor forgot his lines. He was prompted. He mumbled something and stopped. From one of the boats came

an impatient question, 'What's he trying to say?' William Mackenzie's stage whisper carried across the water. The poor lad never did
get his line straight, and the play concluded self-consciously without him.[55] Often Mackenzie used the summer home as an office and
would carry on negotiations with fellow businessmen on the large
verandah facing the lake. Even on sweltering summer days, he insisted on dressing in a dark three-piece suit, making only one concession to the heat – he often bargained in his bare feet.[56]

As the country folk observed, the Mackenzies were always in a
hurry. Mackenzie's children were no exception. Hatted and veiled,
Mackenzie women were often chauffeured down dusty concession
roads, laughing at the startled reaction of people. Farmers shook
their fists at them for dusting their crops. Wide-eyed children ran to
get a closer look. Once a Mackenzie car frightened a horse so badly
that its driver was killed. Another time Grace was ripping through
the countryside in her red roadster and killed some hens pecking
away contentedly on the road, blissfully unaware of the new age of
fast motor cars. She stopped and peeled off a dollar bill for each dead
hen. The shocked farmer said afterward that he wished that more
hens had been on the road that day. 'Don't play near the road,' little
Francis Lindsay's mother warned him, 'Joe Mackenzie might come
speeding by today.'

In 1905, when his railway had reached Gamebridge, Mackenzie
would have his chauffeur, Pogson, drive him to catch the train to
Toronto. Mackenzie always tried to beat his previous best time to
Gamebridge, about twenty kilometres west of Kirkfield, and urged
Pogson to drive faster and faster over the dirt and gravel Portage
Road, whose curves, often abrupt, were better suited to portaging
canoes than to racing English motor cars. On one occasion, Arthur
Hills was in the back seat with an elderly gentleman. As the car
bounced and the dust billowed, the old man flew up and cut his
head on the metal ribbing of the canvas roof. 'Stop!' shouted Hills,
as blood started to drip from the cut. Mackenzie looked around,
puzzled. 'Well, what on earth was he doing up there anyway?' he
asked, then ordered Pogson on to even greater speeds.

One day in 1906, R.J. Fleming and Mackenzie were being driven
up Church Street in Toronto by Arthur Grantham, Gertrude Mackenzie's first husband. At Queen, they hit a horse-drawn rig. No one
was hurt. During the ensuing court case, the driver of the rig testified that Mackenzie and friends had been speeding. A motorman
driving one of Mackenzie's street cars testified that the rig driver
had been gazing at the street car instead of watching the traffic.

Mackenzie and Fleming both testified that Grantham could not have been driving more than two or three miles per hour. Grantham was exonerated.

Mackenzie even played golf, his favourite sport, with a sense of urgency. Cyril Andrewes, Gertrude's second husband, remembered seeing him in his spiked golfing shoes, jumping up and down on the hardwood floor of the Kirkfield home in anticipation of a game. In 1902 he hired George Cumming, a professional golfer from the Toronto Golf Club, to lay out a nine-hole course in Kirkfield. The ninth hole was located a few metres from the new Presbyterian church in which ministers, intoning interminable prayers and didactic sermons, had to listen to shouts and laughter whenever Mackenzie and a friend reached the ninth hole.

Wyndham Lewis once claimed that speed, as in quick movement, was the drug of the twentieth century. Mackenzie had helped to introduce speed, punctuality, efficiency, consumerism, and transience to the late nineteenth and early twentieth centuries. In his business dealings, he used speed to mesmerize and to confuse his opponents. Masks, magic, and fantasy had became the stock in trade of this man whom the press called a financial wizard. Like the revellers at the Benvenuto masked ball on New Year's Eve 1903, Mackenzie knew that a spirit of mischief and quick brains to direct it were useful in achieving success in Canada and around the world.

By 1904 he was president of five companies. He had finally learned how to delegate authority and to accept deference, two difficult concepts for a man born in a log shanty. He seemed to understand the advantages of allowing effective managers to run his companies. Good managers, such as E.H. Keating and R.J. Fleming, Toronto's former mayor who became manager of the TRC in 1904, helped Mackenzie to act the role of president. They helped him to find his misplaced keys, to organize meetings, and to find lost stock certificates; and they left to him the role of turning prophecy into reality.

CHAPTER SEVEN

La Presse and Other Affairs, 1904–6

Man is never so truly himself as when he is acting a part.
(William Hazlitt)

It's all theatre; once I understood that, I was all set.
(Prime Minister Brian Mulroney)

I am far from sure when I am acting and when I am not, or, should I more frankly put it, when I am lying and when I am not. For what is acting but lying, and what is good acting but convincing lying?
(Sir Laurence Olivier)

Throughout the period from 1904 to 1906, quick-witted politicians and businessmen jostled and lobbied. Mackenzie and Mann wanted to acquire the Canada Atlantic Railway in order to link the Great Lakes with the Ottawa Valley. The Grand Trunk also coveted the Canada Atlantic in order to scuttle Canadian Northern expansion plans. Rumours abounded in May and June 1904. Mackenzie and Mann were thought to be dealing with Canadian Atlantic directors. No, they were not, the Canada Atlantic's general manager informed the press. In June, however, J.R. Booth, president of the Canadian Atlantic, told C.M. Hays that Mackenzie and Mann were willing to pay $14 million for the Canadian Atlantic, and that the Liberals in Ottawa would guarantee a bond issue to cover that amount. Hays could not very well stop the sale, he wrote to Rivers-Wilson, since Mackenzie and Mann had contributed more money than the Grand Trunk to the Liberal party.[1]

With Laurier's assistance, the Canadian Northern continued to expand. In June 1904 H.R. Emmerson, the new Minister of Railways and Canals, signed an agreement with Mackenzie for a charter from Edmonton to the Yellowhead Pass.[2] Later that year the Laurier government agreed to subsidize the James Bay Railway from Toronto to Sudbury at a maximum of $6,400 per mile, a supplement to the provincial bond guarantee of up to $20,000 per mile.[3] In July, Mann was making arrangements with his brother, Sandy, and with Big Archie McKenzie, whose Northern Construction Company was awarded the subcontract to build the James Bay Railway. 'I want the beef contract,' that old Kirkfield boy, Pat Burns, wrote from Calgary to Sandy Mann in November 1904.[4]

So successful were William Mackenzie and Donald Mann in 1904 that Hays grew quite frustrated and confused. Sifton was a bit more friendly, he told Rivers-Wilson. Did that mean that Mackenzie and Mann were ready to make a deal? Later, he had the idea that he could gain Mackenzie's favour by offering Sir Henry Pellatt a place on the board of the Grand Trunk. To make matters more confusing for Hays, in October 1904, Blair resigned as chairman of the Board of Railway Commissioners and seemed about to join with several Saint John and Montreal Conservatives in a grand conspiracy to defeat Laurier.

On 11 October 1904 these Conservatives purchased control of *La Presse* of Montreal, which enjoyed the largest circulation of any Canadian newspaper and was one of the most influential voices of French Canada. The newspaper's owner and president, the nervous and fretful Trefflé Berthiaume, emboldened by an ever-increasing readership,[5] had overexpanded. In 1901 he had asked Sir Wilfrid Laurier for $300,000. Laurier had turned to wealthy Ontario Liberals, and had passed up a trip to Niagara Falls with the Duke and Duchess of Kent and Cornwall in October that year in order to consult with Senator George Cox. Cox and the Bank of Commerce, however, considered Berthiaume a poor risk.

Berthiaume's financial problems were worrisome to Laurier. *La Presse* was a recent convert to Laurier Liberalism. In 1898 it had been critical of Mackenzie and Sifton's Yukon railway. Only in February 1899, when Laurier's friend Arthur Dansereau became the paper's 'directeur politique,' did *La Presse* begin to provide editorial opposition to the Conservative Montreal *Star*, and to *La Patrie*, published by Israel Tarte, whom Laurier had removed from cabinet in October 1902.[6]

'L'affaire *La Presse*' was a tangled event, with a cast of characters from the highest ranks of journalism and politics. Hugh Graham, proprietor of the Montreal *Star*, had failed to defeat Laurier in the election of 1900, and was all the more determined in 1903 and 1904. His new ally was A.G. Blair and two of Blair's Saint John colleagues, David Russell and William Pugsley. J.N. Greenshields, Mackenzie and Mann's Montreal lawyer, was part of the group. Senator Rodolphe Forget was rumoured to be a member. Opposition leader Robert

CPR engineers' camp at Summit, BC, 1885, showing William Mackenzie, standing far right, with P. Turner Bone, 2nd from left, and C.A. Stoess, 2nd from right

Earliest known photograph of William Mackenzie, ca. 1875, during early contracting days in Ontario

William and Margaret
Mackenzie, ca. 1889, and
their nine children: Grace
the baby, R.J. and Gertrude
standing at back, Mabel far
left, Joe on stool in front of
Mabel, Ethel standing
between her parents,
Katharine on William's
knee, Bertha far right and
Alex in front

Kirkfield house of William
Mackenzie, opened in 1888,
a sign of a man on the rise
after making a fortune
contracting for the CPR in BC

Winnipeg's Portage and Main, ca. 1900, showing street cars of the Winnipeg Electric Railway Company

Toronto Railway Company street cars at the intersection of Yonge, Carlton, and College streets, mingle with cyclists, buggies, automobiles, and pedestrians, Toronto, ca. 1900

Benvenuto–'the last word in magnificence' according to historian Arthur Lower–was purchased by the Mackenzies in 1897. It overlooked the city from near the top of Avenue Road hill in Toronto until torn down in the 1930s

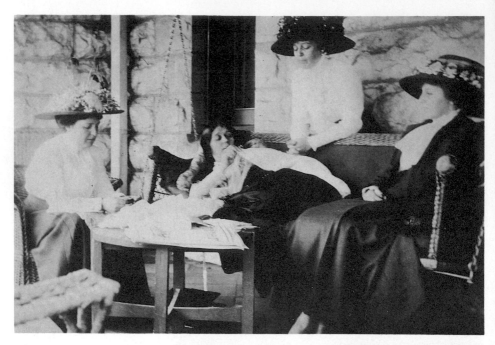

Four Mackenzie sisters in
Edwardian finery on one of
Benvenuto's verandas, ca.
1905

Summer mansion on
Balsam Lake, Ontario, near
Kirkfield, ca. 1905

Wawinet, Mackenzie's
yacht, purchased in 1903
from Polson Iron Works,
Toronto. In 1910, it helped
to entice a French count to
marry into the Mackenzie
family

Portrait of William
Mackenzie, ca. 1905, by
H. Harris Brown, who
thought that he had never
seen such penetrating eyes

Canadian Northern workers
with foreman, Jim Laidlaw
Sr., on front of CNoR freight
car 36102, ca. 1905

Some of the Eldon Reserve
working for Canadian
Northern Railway in the
prairies, ca. 1906,
including, back row, left to
right: Jack Moran, Lachie
McKerral, Alex Spence, and
Bill MacMillan; front row:
Dan Nicholson

Generating station of the Electrical Development Company of Ontario, which produced Toronto's first hydroelectricity in November 1906

Mr WILLIAM MACKENZIE ADDRESSING THE COMMITTEE

MR R.J. FLEMING MINUS HIS BEARD

C.W. Jefferys

MR S.H. BLAKE K.C.

"Dont interfere with the efforts of Canadians to get capital in England."

The Triumphant Triumvirate Street Railway Advocates before The Private Bills Committee, Friday

Dont Rub this drawing make good cut. 11 a.m. sure

Illustration by C.W. Jefferys, *Mr. William Mackenzie Addressing the Committee*, pen and ink [1908], Mackenzie speaking to the Private Bills Committee of the Ontario Legislature, 3 April 1908, with R.J. Fleming and S.H. Blake; originally published in the Toronto *Star*, 4 April 1908

Sir William Mackenzie,
January 1911, in suit of
knighthood

Lady Mackenzie at time of
her husband's knighthood

Borden played an indirect role in the conspiracy.[7] Since $200,000 worth of their bonds was part of the purchase deal when Hugh Graham and fellow Conservatives bought the paper, Mackenzie and Mann appeared to have been members of the anti-Laurier cabal. Historians, beginning with Liberal apologist O.D. Skelton, have assumed that the two railway builders were caught in the act and chastised by Laurier.

Quite the contrary seems to be true. Mackenzie and Mann had no reason to defeat Laurier, for his railway policy had been of great benefit to them. Although the Canada Atlantic Railway did fall to the Grand Trunk in September, that sale was made between Booth and Hays. The prime minister later asserted that if the Grand Trunk had not purchased the Canada Atlantic, his government would have acquired it for the CNoR.[8] Furthermore, even if they had wanted Laurier out, Mackenzie and Mann were astute enough to realize that buying a paper in the hopes of defeating a government just two weeks before the election was an act of monumental folly. By 1904, French-speaking Québecois had decided that Laurier and the Liberal party guaranteed their *survivance*, and even Tarte decided that it made good business sense to return *La Patrie* to the Laurier fold in 1905.[9]

One key to unmasking Mackenzie and Mann's role is their Montreal lawyer, Greenshields, an influential confidant of Laurier's. In 1897 he had supplied money to Tarte to buy *La Patrie* in order to keep it Liberal. In September 1903 it was Greenshields, along with Lomer Gouin, Minister of Public Works, who broke the news to Laurier that Hugh Graham and Rodolphe Forget were attempting to buy *La Presse*. It was also Greenshields who suggested to Laurier that Liberals should purchase the paper in order to keep it Liberal.[10]

Greenshields, however, appeared to be a member of the Russell-Graham gang that bought the newspaper in October 1904. He was apparently playing the role of spy for Laurier and for Mackenzie and Mann. Did he pledge Mackenzie and Mann bonds in order to convince Graham and Russell that the Canadian Northern was on their side? Did he play host to a party on the night of 11 October, when Berthiaume signed the deal, in order to keep an eye on Russell? 'If there was any plot or scheme,' the *Canadian Annual Review* noted, 'it certainly appears to have been given away by someone.'[11] Greenshields? Quite possibly. He remained Mackenzie and Mann's Montreal lawyer and a Laurier confidant.

Arthur Dansereau's role may be the other key to the mystery. According to Berthiaume, Dansereau accepted money to deliver *La Presse* to Graham.[12] Dansereau was to remain chief editor and was to be allowed to write pro-Laurier editorials.[13] Was Dansereau, like Greenshields, a Laurier mole? Did Dansereau force Berthiaume to sell in order to save the paper for Laurier? In a leap year, when traditional roles are reversed, were the apparent victors, Graham and Russell, really the grand dupes? To make matters worse for the Montreal–Saint John cabal, Laurier won convincingly on 3 November.

If Greenshields and Dansereau were reporting to Laurier and to Mackenzie and Mann from September 1903 to January 1905, as surviving documents suggest, small wonder that the conspirators appeared so 'amateur and leaky' (O.D. Skelton's phrase), or that Laurier's intervention appeared so 'decisive and timely' (J.W. Dafoe).[14] Not long after the purchase, the business affairs of Graham and Russell were, to say the least, 'pas brillantes,' as Thomas Côté, cartoonist of La Presse, told Laurier on 19 November 1904. On the same day Liberal Senator Raoul Dandurand penned a witty note corroborating Côté's assessment: 'Je suis convaincu,' he informed Laurier, 'que le courtier qui offrirait son argent à Russell n'aurait pas de difficulté à le lui faire prendre. La seule question pour moi est de trouver l'argent.'

Laurier knew where to find money. He would consult 'une ressource pour La Presse,' a wealthy Torontonian. Coincidentally, Mackenzie postponed a trip to Europe.[15] So confident was Laurier that the situation was well in hand that he left for his vacation retreat in Monterey, California. The Torontonian, whom Laurier referred to as 'D.M.,'[16] was probably Donald Mann. Mackenzie and Mann gained a controlling interest in the newspaper. The details were worked out at the St. James Club in Montreal on 18 January 1905, after which the two Torontonians sent a telegram to Laurier promising that La Presse would give him 'a generous support.' The fickle Berthiaume was dumped as president,[17] and Graham gained a lasting reputation as a Judas. Conservatives never forgot that he had once betrayed the party by selling out to Mackenzie, Mann, and Laurier in 1904.[18]

The irony of the situation was delicious. The newspaper's francophone owner and founder had been willing to sell to anglo-imperialists, and it was two Toronto Protestants who had saved the paper for a francophone prime minister. It is not known if readers of La Presse knew whose money controlled the paper after 1904. No more, perhaps, than Orange riders of Toronto street cars were aware, at the same moment, that Montreal, and to a great extent francophone and Catholic money, owned the majority of shares in the TRC. Behind our northern masks lie many layers of untold irony.

Mackenzie and Mann stabilized the financial affairs of the newspaper and tolerated the complaints of the aggrieved former owner. Berthiaume warned Laurier to make sure that the paper was back in French-Canadian hands as soon as possible, for once Laurier was gone, there would never be another French-Canadian prime minister.[19] (Berthiaume's prescience was as sound as his business sense.) In return for their favour, Mackenzie and Mann received Laurier's continued support, including tens of millions of dollars in bond guarantees, which helped to build almost 2,000 kilometres of lines in Ontario and Quebec. By the end of 1906, with Laurier's help, the Canadian Northern acquired the Qu'Appelle, Long Lake & Saskatchewan Railway from David Russell, a member of the unsuccessful anti-Laurier cabal in 1904. 'L'affaire *La Presse*' was a grand triumph for Mackenzie and Mann.

In provincial capitals too Mackenzie and Mann's reputation rose to record heights. When the new provinces of Alberta and Saskatchewan were officially inaugurated in 1905, Mackenzie was an invited guest. Near the end of August he took the *Atikokan* to the end of steel at Vegreville. From there, with Edmund Walker, novelist Sir Gilbert Parker, and English journalist H.A. Kennedy, Mackenzie drove a motor car over prairie trails and graded roadbed comprising the remaining hundred or so kilometres into Edmonton, through countryside where 'the prairie merged into an undulating territory' and 'hill and wood rolled away from the banks of the Saskatchewan,' to use Sir Gilbert's description in a short story published four years later.[20]

After hours of being jostled by the roadbed, the four must have been relieved to reach the bustling little capital, set so beautifully on the north bank of the North Saskatchewan River. Mackenzie declared that he was 'delighted and surprised' by Edmonton's progress. The four men were 'highly pleased' with the entertainment 'got up' for the inauguration of Alberta – a concert that featured the 'Soldiers' Chorus' from Gounod's *Faust*, followed by a reception for a thousand people, including Lord Grey, Sir Wilfrid and Lady Laurier, Premiers Rutherford and Scott, Lieutenant Governors Bulyea and Forget, Senator Lougheed, and Calgarian R.B. Bennett, who thought Edmonton a poor choice for capital. The several days of celebrations, which culminated in the official inaugural day on Friday, 1 September, also featured a Mountie Musical Ride, baseball games, and a grand ball.

On Saturday morning, 2 September, Mackenzie and his guests boarded the *Atikokan* and on the CPR line, the old Calgary & Edmonton, headed down to Calgary, then east to Regina to celebrate the new province of Saskatchewan on Monday, 4 September.[21] Mackenzie and the new premier, Walter Scott, enjoyed a close personal and working relationship that dated back to 1902, when Scott had been the Dominion MP for the District of Assiniboia West (now part of southern Saskatchewan). The two men had worked out mutually beneficial railway and land deals, perhaps too successfully, for when Mackenzie met Scott in Regina that September, the cultured and urbane premier was about to face an embarrassing trial involving newspapers, railway charters, and bribery.[22]

Less than three months after these inaugural celebrations, Donald Mann was in Edmonton to celebrate the coming of the CNoR. Alberta's Lieutenant Governor Bulyea drove a silver spike, fashioned from a Mackenzie and Mann mine at Fort Steele in southeastern British Columbia. That evening, at a banquet held at the Queen's Hotel, R.J. and Alex Mackenzie accepted on behalf of their absent father a silver tray from Edmonton's mayor. By the time the CNoR reached Edmonton, Frank Oliver, Sifton's successor as Minister of the Interior, had forgiven Mackenzie and Mann their sins of twenty-five years earlier, when they had made Strathcona the northern terminus of the Calgary & Edmonton.[23]

By 1905 Boers, Boxers, and the 1903 recession had receded in memory and Canadian railways found favour with British investors. In June 1906 Mackenzie took Ethel, Bertha, and Grace to England on the ss *Kaiser Wilhelm*.[24] In London he had great success in floating about $5 million worth of construction bonds for the Canadian Northern Ontario Railway (CNoOR), the new name for the James Bay Railway.[25] Even at the relatively low rate of 3.5 per cent, British investors were attracted to these bonds, guaranteed by Ontario. By the end of July about 25 per cent had been subscribed.[26]

Mackenzie was back in Canada in late July. In August he travelled to the west coast. Premier Scott, with electoral promises to keep, wanted the Hartney extension from Brandon to Regina rerouted through Moosomin, whose mayor and Liberal voters were anxious to be on a CNoR route. From Vancouver, Mackenzie sent a telegram to Scott: he would arrive in Regina the following Tuesday morning. He travelled back through Calgary, then up to Edmonton to call on Premier Rutherford. Telegrams flew back and forth between Scott and Mackenzie. But Mackenzie was moving around so quickly that he kept missing Scott's telegrams. Finally the two met in Winnipeg on Wednesday evening, 22 August. The Moosomin delegation, however, never did catch up with the fleet-footed Mackenzie, and the Saskatchewan town had to content itself with one railway line – it was already served by the CPR.

In October 1906 there was more good news. A new bond issue of a million pounds sterling ($4,680,000) was snapped up in Britain. The investing public could not get enough Canadian railway bonds. The Canadian Northern's popularity was due to its enviable increase in gross earnings for September, up 64 per cent from the year before – a greater increase than either the GTR or CPR.[27] Even Hays became friendly, and in November he met Mackenzie, Mann, and Lash in Montreal. The CNoR agreed to share Edmonton and Winnipeg terminals with the GTPR; and Hays offered to share harbour facilities on Georgian Bay.[28] In November 1906 the first passenger train left Toronto for Parry Sound for the official opening of the first half of the Canadian Northern Ontario Railway. By the end of 1906 Mackenzie and Mann had received bond guarantees for the astounding sum of $24 million.

One late December evening in 1900, George Beardmore, Master of Fox Hounds at the Toronto Hunt Club, gave a dinner party at Chudleigh, his large home at Dundas and Beverley. Guests included Donald Mann, Wallace Nesbitt, William Mackenzie, and Scott Griffin, opposition leader Whitney's private secretary. One of the topics of conversation was the transmission of Niagara Falls hydro power to Toronto. Would it ever be possible to transmit electrical power over so many miles? Toronto was lagging behind other cities, since it was the last of the large eastern Canadian cities to convert from coal-generated to water-generated power. For several years Buffalo and San Francisco had been receiving long distance power, and the latter was further away from its source of power than Toronto was from Niagara. The debate ended inconclusively, although Wallace Nesbitt, newspaper editor and former chief counsel for the McDougall inquiry, was certain that Toronto was too far from Niagara for effective transmission.[29]

The discussion at Chudleigh was friendly. The public discussions soon became intense, however. In fact, Ontario Hydro, which today powers the province's industries and lights and heats its houses and businesses, emerged from some of the most bitter debates ever witnessed by the province. Mackenzie was in the thick of them. Had the players been different, had their dislike for each other not prevented them from reaching compromise, Ontario might have ended up with a different hydro system, perhaps a mix of public and private companies whose competition could have prevented the development of the behemoth that Ontario Hydro is today.

Mackenzie's contribution to the debate at Chudleigh was unrecorded. He no doubt offered some comment, for he was already familiar with power generation, transmission, and distribution. The

Toronto Railway Company did all three. During the first five years of this century, the coal-burning generators at Front and Frederick streets were reaching maximum capacity. Although the trolley system added little extra mileage after 1900, it operated many extra street cars which required more power. The TRC's power station also supplied power to Mackenzie's suburban street railways. Hydro power promised to be cheaper and more reliable. Thus it was essential that Mackenzie and his partners find a method of bringing Niagara power to Toronto.

During the early 1890s the TRC had introduced Mackenzie to Henry Pellatt and Fred Nicholls. Beginning in 1892 Nicholls' Canadian General Electric, of which Mackenzie was one of ten major shareholders, supplied generators for the TRC's power house. Pellatt's brokerage firm bought and sold TRC bonds and stock. It was the bidding war in 1894 between Pellatt's Toronto Electric Light Company and Mackenzie's TRC to supply lighting to Toronto that had precipitated the McDougall investigation. The lighting and transit companies consumed most of the power generated in Toronto. Pellatt was a director of the TRC. Until 1902 Nicholls was president of the Canadian Northern Railway. All three were well acquainted with the best educated electrical engineers in North America, understood the workings of capital markets, and had the necessary personal connections with those markets in Toronto, Montreal, New York, and London. It was not, therefore, surprising that they should team up to bring power from Niagara to Toronto.

At first they tried to buy electricity from the Ontario Power Company (OPC), one of the two American companies already operating on the Canadian side of the Falls. In early 1902 the Dominion Parliament incorporated the Toronto & Niagara Power Company to transmit power from Niagara to Toronto. When negotiations with OPC reached an impasse, the three Canadians obtained a franchise from the Queen Victoria Niagara Falls Park Commission, authorizing them to generate up to 125,000 horsepower of electricity at Niagara at an annual rental of $80,000. The commission agreed not to engage in electrical generation, which the three men assumed to mean that the Ontario government itself would forever refrain from generating electricity at Niagara.

With this franchise, Pellatt, Nicholls, and Mackenzie formed the Electrical Development Company of Ontario (EDCO), chartered by Queen's Park in February 1903. EDCO became the third generating company, and the first Canadian company, at Niagara. It was capitalized at $6 million in common shares, and issued $5 million in bonds.[30] In 1903 the three men also created the Toronto Power Company (TPC) to distribute power to the Toronto Electric Light Company (TELC) and to the TRC. The new distribution company was capitalized at $6 million common shares.[31] The stock of TPC and EDCO was purchased, probably at ten to twenty-five cents per share, by the family of capitalists who ran the Toronto Railway Company and other such companies. Some stock may have been retained for bonuses to those who bought and sold large blocks of bonds, which, as usual, provided the real source of capital for the company.

From its magical generation, to its split-second transmission, to its wondrous and mysterious illumination of cities and powering of trolleys, hydro power was the stuff of legend and theatre. Although it was the product of science and technology, electricity was more akin to the fantastic stories told by the country folk of Mackenzie's Eldon Township; and by Mackenzie himself. Fred Nicholls called electricity a 'genie out of the bottle.'[32]

Meantime, in 1901 fretful representatives of several municipalities joined with urban reform representatives to create the Union of Canadian Municipalities. Like J.P. Whitney, Toronto's Mayor Howland, the union's first president, preferred government regulation to government ownership. Westmount mayor and versifier, W.D. Lighthall, was appointed honourary secretary. On 9 June 1902 a motley collection of southern Ontario manufacturers and wholesalers gathered at Berlin (now Kitchener). F.S. Spence, for years a proponent of publicly owned power and an enemy of all things Mackenzie, was the guest speaker. Adam Beck, who was Conservative MPP, mayor of London, and a cigar box manufacturer, was also in attendance. The convention set up a committee, headed by D.B. Detweiler and E.W.B. Snider, a friend of Premier Ross, to investigate the power question. The committee recommended that the Ross government construct and operate a transmission line and buy power from private generating companies, then sell it to interested municipalities.

Premier Ross modified Snider's recommendation by placing the onus on municipalities. His Power Act of June 1903 gave them the right to form municipal co-operatives to buy power directly from any one of the three private generating companies at Niagara and to transmit and distribute that power to the municipalities comprising the co-operative. The province, however, refused to finance or subsidize any such works. In August representatives of seven municipalities and several manufacturers met in Toronto to set up the Ontario Power Commission in accordance with the June act. The commission's role was purely advisory. Snider was selected chairman, to be assisted by three men, one of whom was Adam Beck.

The Ontario election campaign of January 1905 brought the issue of hydro power to the fore. Premier Ross relied on competition, market forces, and minimal government intervention to regulate Niagara power, while Whitney advocated a slightly greater government role. For the private operators, there was nothing to fear, for Whitney was 'not enamoured of the public ownership principle,' according to his private secretary, W.R. Plewman.[33] For years Mackenzie had known Whitney, who had supported him in the legislature as far back as 1895, when Everett and Mackenzie had attempted to amalgamate the London Street Railway with the Port Stanley railway.[34]

In 1905 when the Conservatives under Whitney defeated the minority, scandal-plagued Liberals, few Ontario voters were surprised or alarmed. True, the new government refused to ratify a franchise granted during the last days of the Ross government, which would have allowed EDCO to develop an additional 125,000 horse power, providing that half the additional power be reserved for municipalities at prices regulated by Queen's Park. True, the new Whitney government did institute a tax on electric railways and prevented the Toronto & York Railway from entering Toronto. True, Adam Beck was appointed to the cabinet, but without portfolio; he was also appointed chairman of a second commission on hydro power, but with limited powers. On 19 April 1905, Whitney did say in the legislature that Niagara power should be as free as the air, but since voters seemed satisfied with private ownership of transportation and communications, Whitney was no more expected to act on political rhetoric than was Laurier expected to expropriate the twentieth century, even if he did claim it for Canada.

Scott Griffin was an important liaison between William Mackenzie and Ontario's new premier. As Whitney's private secretary, Griffin had reported the December 1900 Beardmore dinner to his boss, then the opposition leader. Griffin was a bright and witty lawyer with impeccable Loyalist connections – he was related to Egerton Ryerson and to the Harris family of Eldon House in London. He had been a law partner of Sir William Meredith. He was also a lawn tennis fan and player, who wrote articles about the increasingly popular game.[35] Throughout the 1890s he hobnobbed with the Toronto Four Hundred, among whom he met Mabel Mackenzie, eldest daughter of William and Margaret Mackenzie. In October 1901 they were married. Wedding guests arrived from Winnipeg, Toronto, Kirkfield, and London (Ontario and England). The Horne-Paynes sailed across the Atlantic to attend. During the festivities guests at

Benvenuto could watch the electric light show provided by gigantic spotlights on the clock tower of the new city hall at Queen and Bay in honour of Prince George and Princess Mary, who were visiting Toronto.

In July 1902 Griffin was posted to Winnipeg, where he worked for his father-in-law as superintendent of the Canadian Northern Telegraph and Express Company. He kept in touch with Whitney, and thus kept Whitney in touch with Mackenzie, who was, all things considered, as Griffin once jested, a loyal Tory.[36] In August 1905 he wryly chided Whitney for cutting into his 'respected Father-in-law's bank account on the [electric railway] tax question.' Griffin invited the Ontario premier to attend CNoR 'orgies' in Edmonton to celebrate last spike ceremonies in November.

Whitney enjoyed Griffin's correspondence and understood the problems of private capital. His problem was the growing municipal power movement, orchestrated and conducted by Adam Beck, whom Whitney privately called his 'obstacle.'[37] Beck had a mission, the zeal of the missionary, and the haunting memory of family bankruptcy in 1879, when his father's water-powered foundry at Baden, Ontario, could no longer pay its bills. His father had fled to Detroit, a city that Adam visited frequently for his pleasure.

Whitney was no Laurier. The prime minister had also faced internal dissent, but he had dismissed Tarte in 1902 on the question of protectionism, and he had cornered Blair on the railway question. Beck was Tarte and Blair combined. Whitney had not yet learned to play the strong leader, however, and thus during the first years of his mandate, it was Beck who controlled the situation. Unlike Blair, Beck was certainly not about to resign in protest, though he would temporarily retire to London in a huff if he thought the premier was not listening to his every whim. Mackenzie and his colleagues were left with little leverage, not even a newspaper to purchase for the premier.

Another problem for Whitney was that Mackenzie and the Toronto Railway Company suffered from a mixed reputation among Toronto councillors and journalists. 'I may say in passing that I think one cause of the prejudice which today undoubtedly exists in Toronto against Mackenzie,' Whitney told Griffin on 16 February 1906, 'has been the fact that in the past – not at present – the Street Railway Co. steadily and unceasingly fought against anything in the nature of carrying out the details of their agreement, or perhaps I should rather say, would do nothing until compelled.'[38]

A few days later Whitney had yet another example of the seeming omnipotence of Toronto capitalists. Mackenzie was a director and major shareholder of Manufacturers' Life Assurance Company, of which the former premier, the Honourable George Ross, was president. Mann, Pellatt, and Hanna were also shareholders. In 1902 Manufacturers' Life had lent money to Mackenzie and Mann for the purchase of CNoR bonds. The McTavish Royal Commission, which began its deliberations a few days after Whitney's February letter to Griffin, also revealed that Senator Cox's Canada Life Assurance Company had invested in the web of Cox, Pellatt, and Mackenzie companies, including the Electrical Development Company of Ontario and Manitoba-guaranteed CNoR bonds. In most cases, with the notable exception of Canada Cycle and Motor Company (CCM), the unsuccessful bicycle and automobile company founded by Flavelle and Cox, the insurance money was well invested. Even though Sir Clifford Sifton had condoned the transactions,[39] they were illegal, for the Insurance Act of 1899 had forbidden directors of insurance companies to invest in other companies having the same directors.

The problem for the young utilities companies was a tight capital market, as Mackenzie had discovered in London in 1900. During the first few years of the new century, British money was invested in its own expanding domestic market.[40] And yet Canadian cities were growing rapidly. Street railway systems needed to expand and upgrade quickly. City councils demanded improvements. Where to find the investment money? Insurance companies had built up considerable capital, which they were quite happy to invest in safe securities. Since the same men sat on both insurance and railway boards, the transactions were carried out in the most casual way – a suggestion, a handshake. Done. The old oral, interpersonal culture of the general store would soon be at loggerheads with the new print culture of government regulations, which forbade such intimate transactions.

Just as the insurance question was becoming a public issue, Beck chose to exercise his position as chairman of the Hydro Power Commission. His timing was inspired. He demanded to see the account books of the Electrical Development Company. He announced that the government was thinking of establishing its own generating plant at Niagara for distribution to municipalities, and also that at the next session the government was about to debate the legal rights of existing power companies. Whitney had already assured Pellatt that the government had no such intention.[41] Beck accused private companies of expecting to make huge profits from Niagara by selling power to the Toronto Electric Light Company and to the Toronto

Railway Company for thirty-five dollars per horsepower per annum, the same rate as thermal power. What he did not explain was that the $35.00 rate was merely a tentative figure, to help Mackenzie to sell company bonds.[42] EDCO was in the midst of building transmission lines and had not yet laid the cornerstone of its generating plant; therefore, no firm price could be established.[43] Henry Pellatt and others protested to Whitney, but Beck continued his public scolding.

As might be expected, Beck's public utterances were frightening investors.[44] Whitney was caught between his personal predilections and his unruly 'Minister of Power.' He tried to explain the Hydro-Electric Power Commission to Griffin. It was set up to save private power from its own excesses and to preserve its image in the face of adverse public opinion.[45] The commission was designed not to replace private power but to regulate it in order to ensure fair consumer rates for electricity. In that way the sting would be removed from Beck's movement.

In March 1906 Beck released the reports of the two commissions. From these emerged the genesis of a Hydro Act that created a Hydro Commission with power to set rates charged by private companies and to expropriate these companies. The Conmee Act, which had placed limits on municipal expropriation, was annulled for municipalities obtaining power from the Hydro Commission. The onus for transmission was shifted from the municipalities to the province, which would guarantee all loans for construction. Importantly, however, the commission was responsible to the legislature. Whitney assured the press that private power would survive under these new regulations. It appeared that he might yet contain Beck. Satisfied, Mackenzie left for London in June to reassure British investors that Electrical Development Company bonds remained a good investment, even though the new Hydro Act had caused a drop in the company's share and bond values.

In a *Star* cartoon, C.W. Jefferys' trenchant pen bade Mackenzie au revoir. Big Daddy Mackenzie, about to board a train, encourages little Bobbie (R.J. Fleming) to take care of little Emmie (Mayor Coatsworth).[46] The cartoon implied that Mackenzie and his managers took care of government officials, which may have been true. To his credit, Mackenzie never seemed to take umbrage at cartoonists' innuendoes – he sponsored Jefferys on a sketching tour of the prairies the next year.

In the January 1907 municipal elections six months later, ratepayers were asked to approve or reject a by-law based on the Hydro Act

of 1906. The by-law proposed giving municipal councils the power
to negotiate a contract with the Hydro-Electric Power Commission.
No minimum quantity of power was stipulated. Estimated cost
would be about half the thirty-five dollars per horsepower per annum paid by TELC and TRC for thermal power. Both sides campaigned vigorously. It was obvious that Beck would win the referendum of January 1907. It did not matter that his cost estimates were
challenged by some of the very people who had worked with him on
the commission. Few ratepayers would vote against 'Cheap Light,
Cheap Heat, Cheap Power.' Even the *Monetary Times*, a voice of
business, conceded victory to Beck.

Ultimately, however, Beck would fail. Whitney had chosen his
two fellow commissioners carefully. Both Mayor Hendrie of Hamilton and engineer Cecil Smith were sympathetic to private capital.
Furthermore, only twelve municipalities expressed support for the
Hydro-Electric Power Commission in 1906. Several important cities
disapproved, including Niagara Falls, Brantford, Hamilton, Peterborough, and Berlin. Engineers scoffed at Beck's cost estimates. A
fellow cabinet minister snubbed Beck by leasing several water
power sites to private companies.[47] C.W. Jefferys summed up the
opposition to Beck in a *Star* cartoon – Beck in dressage costume riding the Niagara Power horse, harassed by eastern Ontario, the corporations, the city of Niagara Falls, and a strong current of 'anti-
socialist' sentiment.[48]

The important thing for Mackenzie, Pellatt, and Nicholls was
Whitney's loyalty. Although he had declined to attend the
cornerstone-laying ceremonies for the Electrical Development Company's generating station at the Falls on 8 May 1906, the day after the
Hydro-Electric Power Commission Bill was given first reading at
Queen's Park, he did make it clear that he agreed with sentiments
expressed by the lieutenant governor, who in laying the stone expressed sympathy for private utilities.[49] Soon thereafter Whitney
was rubbing shoulders with Mackenzie, Pellatt, and Nicholls at the
King's Plate and at a vice-regal dinner at the end of May. Throughout 1906 he continued to participate with them in social events. During the rather nasty by-law campaign, he met Mackenzie at least
twice. On Thursday afternoon, 29 November, he and Mrs. Whitney,
Sir Henry and Lady Pellatt, William and Margaret Mackenzie, Colonel Denison, Colonel Otter, Edmund Walker, and others attended a
vice-regal tea to welcome the Countess Grey and her daughters to
Toronto.[50] Less than a week later, the premier and Mrs. Whitney
dined with William and Margaret Mackenzie and Colonel Denison

at Government House at King and Simcoe.[51] Whitney publicly praised Mackenzie at a banquet in early December. As Whitney learned how to play the masked ball game of political leadership, he would surely learn how to outmanoeuvre Beck.

Like its Toronto counterpart, the Winnipeg Electric Street Railway expanded within boundaries established by the agreement of 1892, creating a new Loop Route (Main, River, Osborne, and Broadway) in 1899, and expanded east of the Red River in 1902. In 1904 the Winnipeg, Selkirk and Lake Winnipeg Railway Company, controlled by the WESR, inaugurated a steam railway service from Winnipeg to Selkirk, thirty-five kilometres north. Street cars were purchased from the TRC's plant in Toronto or constructed in the company's Fort Rouge plant in Winnipeg. In July 1904, the Winnipeg Electric Railway Company (WERC) was formed, an amalgamation of the trolley company WESR and the Winnipeg General Power Company. The amalgamation of 1904 created the right combination with monopoly powers not only in Winnipeg but also throughout Manitoba.

Hydroelectric power from the new Pinawa Power House, ninety-six kilometres northeast of the city, on the Winnipeg River, sizzled into the Mill Street power station in June 1906,[52] five months before the first Niagara power reached Toronto. In all respects, the Winnipeg Electric Railway was successful. Even the Sunday issue was solved peacefully when Sunday service was voted in after a short, polite debate in 1906. One notable supporter was the Reverend Charles Gordon, better known as Ralph Connor. Like fellow novelist-moralist Charles Dickens, he realized that Sunday cars benefited workers, for whom Sunday was often the only day of leisure. Voters also opted for municipal generation of power, and in 1906 Premier Roblin's government allowed the city of Winnipeg to generate and transmit power from Pointe du Bois, northeast of the city.[53] But Manitoba had no Beckish empire builder and Winnipeg no provincial rival; consequently public and private sectors continued to co-operate.[54]

The system grew from fifty-one kilometres in 1906 to fifty-four in 1907 and eighty-five in 1908. There were a few debates, such as the question of hours and frequency of trolley operation. In Winnipeg, however, company and council reached agreements without years of expensive litigation. WERC suffered from the same problems as other systems during the recession of 1907–8, and new trolleys were difficult to build or buy because of the shortage of materials. The company did, however, manage to expand, and in 1908 it built a line to suburban Charleswood. Its dividend in 1907 was 8 per cent, rising to 10 per cent in 1908. Mackenzie's dividend income was about $250,000 for the two years.[55]

The only exception to these successes was a brief strike. In March 1906 the Winnipeg Electric Railway dismissed ten men on charges unknown today. The ten men were officials of the International Union of Street Railway Workers, which had been asking for thirteen changes in relations with the company, including union recognition, an increase in wages, and a discussion of who should pay for damages to streetcars – conductors or the company. The men obviously did not agree with manager Phillips' claim that wages were the best east of the Rockies, and they voted to strike. To operate the cars, the company began to bring in strike breakers from Montreal and from cities west of Winnipeg.

The same pattern of violence occurred in Winnipeg as in Toronto four years earlier. Crowds, composed of youths – a fourteen year old, in one instance – the very well dressed, and some 'toughs' congregated in the streets to enjoy the early spring sunshine and to observe and participate in the street theatre. When the company attempted to keep the cars running, mobs damaged several of them, and set them on fire. The system closed down. According to press reports, few if any of the 250 conductors and motormen participated in the violence. The company hired detectives from Chicago as secret agents. When the city's small police force lost control of the crowds, the Riot Act was read. The Fort Osborne Militia rode out from the barracks, located on the site of today's legislature, and restored order. Partial service resumed. Charles Gordon deplored the violence on both sides and offered to negotiate a settlement.[56]

Mackenzie remained in Toronto, which was probably a wise decision. In the hurly-burly of a strike, he was given to speaking his mind too forthrightly. By 1906 he had learned to delegate authority and to make his appearances significant by their infrequency. In early April the Free Press printed an interview with him in Toronto. No, he would not go to Winnipeg unless the situation grew more serious. His board of directors in Winnipeg was competent to handle the dispute. 'We gave them an increase last February,' Mackenzie told the reporter. 'They were apparently satisfied and went back to work without the settlement of the point regarding recognition of their union. From what I am informed now, they demand another increase, also recognition of their organization. Labor organizations are gaining great influence in the West at present.'[57] He was expressing the alarm felt by Canadian capitalists in the first decade of the century when Canadian locals were growing stronger because of affiliation with large international organizations such as the American Federation of Labor.

The strike lasted a few more days. More cars were damaged when the company attempted to resume night service. The public now demanded a settlement. Royalty was coming in from Edmonton on the first Canadian Northern passenger train between the two cities, and it would be unseemly to greet Prince Arthur and his host, Scott Griffin, with burning trolleys at Portage and Main. On Saturday 7 April, ten days after it had begun, the strike was settled. The men gained an increase of one cent an hour, in addition to several changes in their contracts. But the union remained unrecognized. The strike had been costly for both sides.

Why all these violent strikes and threats of strikes during the first decade of this century? Beneath the surface of wage debates and union recognition lay the altered relationship between labour and capital. When Mackenzie supervised his Eldon Reserve in the 1880s, he was in daily touch with men from his home town and county. But during the 1890s, industrial monopoly capitalism relied increasingly on scientific management; aloof superintendents and managers began to focus on cost accounting and labour efficiency.[58] As migrants swelled the labour pool, the workplace became a buyer's market, especially during the recessions of 1903 and 1907, and workers tended to view the new work world 'with suspicion and hostility.'[59] When times were good and cost of living rose, workers demanded improvements in working conditions and wages, and often withdrew or threatened to withdraw their participation in the work process by means of strikes.

Not all threats resulted in strikes. When motormen threatened to strike in Winnipeg in 1908, company and employees came to an agreement in April, thereby frustrating American union organizer Emma Goldman, who had arrived in the city to lend a hand to the motormen. The new Industrial Disputes Investigation Act, passed the year before under the aegis of Deputy Minister of Labour William Lyon Mackenzie King, may have helped to avoid a strike. The act postponed strikes while representatives of employers, employees, and the public discussed a possible settlement. The union could choose to strike later, but in Winnipeg in 1908, the International Union of Street Railway Employees accepted the negotiated settlement.

When the Canadian Northern Ontario Railway reached Parry Sound, the Toronto Board of Trade decided to celebrate the achievements of Mackenzie and Mann. On 14 December 1906 it held a grand banquet in the large and majestic banquet hall of the three-year-old King Edward Hotel on King Street East. The main entrance of the hotel looked north towards the handsome neoclassical Toronto Railway Chambers on Toronto Street.

The guests that evening paid tribute to the 'pluck, perseverance and ability' of William Mackenzie and Donald Mann. It was a celebration of several years of success. For Mackenzie and Mann, the banquet celebrated the first decade of continuous partnership. Exactly ten years earlier, the first train of the Lake Manitoba Railway had made its way from Gladstone to Dauphin. From that humble beginning of about 160 kilometres, the system had grown at an average rate of just over a mile a day to 6,400 kilometres (4,000 miles). It stretched from the Rockies to the Lakehead, by water to Parry Sound and by rail to Toronto, with lines scattered throughout Quebec and Nova Scotia. Soon the Canadian Northern would connect its eastern lines and poke through the Rockies to the Pacific. Toronto was assuming what it knew was its rightful role as the headquarters of a transcontinental railway.

The King Edward's banquet hall was decorated with a huge floral Canadian Northern locomotive emblazoned with 'Transcontinental' and 'Mackenzie and Mann.' At seven-thirty the two guests of honour stood near the large entrance doors of the hall to welcome the guests, who included representatives from Parliament Hill and Queen's Park, city hall and King Street. Toronto's Mayor Howland was there. So, too, were Lieutenant Governor Sir Mortimer Clarke and, notably, Premier Whitney. Opposition leader Ross attended, as did Timothy Eaton, Joseph Flavelle, and George Gooderham, Sir Henry Pellatt, and Chester Massey. The mayor of Edmonton wired his greetings.

When the guests had assembled at tables, Howland introduced Mackenzie and Mann, and proposed a toast to the Canadian Northern. Rising to reply, Mackenzie was greeted by prolonged and hearty cheering. He stood in silence. At age fifty-seven, he was beginning to show his years. The spade beard and the bushy moustache were now completely grey. The hairline had receded considerably. He was always nattily dressed in carefully tailored three-piece suits. Brisk walks, riding, and frequent games of golf had kept his compact body fit. He often used his long, artistic hands effectively, sometimes placing the right hand in his trouser pocket and gesticulating with the left, singling out a face in the crowd or pointing to a businessman or politician. But it was the eyes that people noted. Hector Charlesworth, editor of *Saturday Night*, remembered them as the visionary eyes of a dreamer and the cool, alert eyes of an eagle.

These amazing dark blue eyes combined a look of youthful curiosity and reckless courage. A British portrait artist once remarked that he had never encountered such a pair of penetrating and profound eyes.[60]

Always uncomfortable in front of a crowd, he seemed more like a shy schoolboy delivering a five-minute speech in English class. Yet his very inability to dazzle a crowd with rhetoric became a positive feature. He begged the listeners to meet him halfway, to indulge him as he collected his thoughts and checked his 'manuscript,' as he called his typed speech. Haltingly, he started to read the speech. After a few minutes, he paused. 'This is ten times harder than building a railway,' he told his audience, then set aside his text and made a few remarks. He was a proud Canadian, he told them in his quiet, Scots-Ontario lilt, but not to the point of 'provincialism,' for the country continued to require imports of both men and money. He reminded them that in London, the world's financial centre, Canadian securities were highly respected, so far; that the Canadian Northern's subsidies were less than those of the other two transcontinentals; and that the company earned enough to pay the interest on government-guaranteed bonds. He thanked the Bank of Commerce for its assistance.

Then with a smile of 'ineffable relief,' according to one observer, he sat down to another round of sustained applause.[61] Donald Mann spoke of the benefits to Toronto of a transcontinental line. Z.A. Lash said it was about time that Mackenzie and Mann's undeserved reputation for milking the public trough was put to rest, that their control of the shares of the railway had very positive results, for they were able to make rapid decisions while other railway companies had to go to a board, thereby losing momentum and secrecy.

Premier Whitney praised the 'splendid' work of these two great railway men in developing Ontario and Canada. Mackenzie's eyes must have shone as he listened to the premier. Niagara power had arrived in Toronto, more by arrangement than by good luck, on 19 November, the very day that the first train ran between Toronto and Parry Sound. Surely Whitney was praising the splendid work not only of Mackenzie and Mann, but also of Mackenzie, Pellatt, and Nicholls.

At midnight the Qu'Appelle, Long Lake & Saskatchewan Railway, which Mackenzie had helped to build fifteen years earlier, became part of the Canadian Northern system. The *Monetary Times* reported that the whole deal had been arranged in a few hours. Mackenzie had likely arranged that the final papers would be signed at Benvenuto immediately after the banquet, so that the press would carry both stories the next morning. By what seemed like a sleight of hand, the Canadian Northern was 400 kilometres longer than it had been during the banquet. The final negotiations had indeed taken only a few hours, enough time for the CNoR to buy the line from Mackenzie, Mann & Company; Mackenzie did not reveal that the construction company had acquired the capital stock of the QLLSR the previous June.[62]

Nevertheless, it was a remarkable story. In January 1899, the Canadian Northern had been a minor player, but when Mackenzie made his address in December 1906, it was poised to become Canada's next transcontinental railway.

Mackenzie's old fears, however, haunted him. The night before the banquet, his private secretary, Fred Annesley, arrived with Billy Moore to keep an appointment at Benvenuto. They found Mackenzie in the library, dejected. Spread out in front of him was the *Toronto Week*, whose editorial that day had been critical of his treatment of subordinates at the Toronto Railway Chambers. 'Is it true?' he asked them.

'How many changes have you had in your personal staff in a quarter of a century?'

'None that I can think of,' came the reply. (He had forgotten Porteous.)

The two men told him that of course the editorial had completely misinterpreted his relationship with his staff. 'It is true you speak plainly,' Moore went on, 'You never gloss a criticism; when you differ with us you differ with us as hard as you can, but you give us the privileges you take, and we would not have it otherwise.'[63] In other words, Mackenzie had learned the role of chief executive officer. He delegated authority, listened carefully, but never acted on advice without testing it thoroughly.

And yet here was the powerful millionaire, head of an empire on which the sun never set, sitting alone in his stone mansion on the hill, wounded by an editorial and seeking assurance from his trusted aides. The mask of success had not completely erased self-doubt and vulnerability. The next two years were to revive those doubts and fears.

CHAPTER EIGHT

Dark Moments, 1907–8

People don't remember what they have done, or even what they have
known. What was going on in their heads? Only God knows, and I
mean that literally.

(Mavis Gallant, *Books in Canada* [Jan./Feb.1990] 31)

We don't know exactly what went on or why but we still make judgments.

(Marilyn vos Savant, *Toronto Star* [16 June 1990] M2)

In his *Trains of Recollection*, D.B. Hanna tells a story set on the Saskatchewan prairie. The *Atikokan* sits on a siding. It is night. The
dark, brooding prairie and the ominously silent midnight-blue sky
stretch to infinity. The private car is but a pinpoint of light in the infinite darkness and solitude of a chilly October night. The first fall of
snow is not far away.

A wandering farmer is wearily riding home when he sees the
strange light. He is curious. He spurs his tired horse and rides
closer to discover the glowing window of a railway carriage. Four
men sit around a table, which is covered by a sparkling, white cloth.
Another man appears and disappears with shining silver serving
dishes and bottles of wine. The farmer watches until the meal is finished, the cigars are glowing, and the blinds are pulled. The farmer
can see no more. He is puzzled by the ritual of the meal, and very
impressed by these important men in city clothes sitting at the
table. He is overcome with a feeling of resentment and loneliness as
he wheels round his horse and continues homeward. He is soon
swallowed up by the darkness.

Mackenzie was one of the four men at the table. The second man
may have been Billy Moore, or perhaps Z.A. Lash. The other two
were representatives of financial houses in London. All four had
spent the day examining prairie branch lines of the Canadian
Northern. Next morning, Mackenzie would escort the two bankers

on a rough ride by horse and buggy forty miles north, to inspect the country through which the Canadian Northern Railway hoped to build another branch line.

At first glance there was nothing unusual; each year William Mackenzie made an inspection tour of newly laid tracks. This time, however, there were no tracks. Mackenzie was inspecting Canadian Northern territory before steel was in place. He was in an even greater hurry than usual. Bonds were not selling, and he had to impress these two representatives of British banking houses, whose reports would determine how many bonds he would be able to float in London, and at what price.[1]

Like any good 'once-upon-a-time' storyteller, D.B. Hanna is not specific about time or place. Contextual evidence suggests that this event occurred in 1908, just before the first glimmer of better times began to light up the uncertain night of financial instability that had gripped Mackenzie's empire for the previous year and a half. Those months in 1907 and 1908 were possibly the darkest of his life.

The recessions of 1903 and 1907–8 served as reminders that economic downturns and tight money markets follow periods of overspending and rising expectations. During the first half-dozen years of the century, capital-intensive projects such as railways in North and South America consumed vast quantities of investment money. Enormous sums were spent to overcome natural disasters such as the San Francisco earthquake in 1906, and to pay for wars in South Africa, Russia, and Cuba. In March 1907 stock markets in Europe and North America grew nervous. By October the global economy threatened to collapse. Investment money grew scarce, and yet politicians and voters demanded more railways, especially in the grain-glutted prairies.

Freight cars travelled east full of grain. But tight credit made retailers cautious, and thus westbound freight diminished and railway revenues fell. At the same time, labour and material costs were rising. The insurance investigation of 1906 had restricted investment by Canadian insurance companies. London investment houses were loath to invest in Canadian railways, especially because of the slump in freight revenue. Rails and equipment were scarce, for steel companies and boxcar manufacturers were also affected by tight markets.

The tenacious prairie winter of 1906–7 exacerbated the situation. In January and February temperatures dipped to the minus forties and fifties. Trains came to a standstill, often for days. Snow blew and packed hard in cuts, some up to seven metres deep. Three weeks before the terrible cold and snow immobilized the prairies, the CNoR acquired the Qu'Appelle, Long Lake & Saskatchewan Railway and the company needed more time to reorganize its expanded system and to buy new engines and freight cars. Trains were storm-stayed. Fuel shortages, infrequent passenger and freight service, and decrepit engines drew many complaints. A company snowplow was derailed in January near Elbow, Saskatchewan. 'In an evil hour for Saskatchewan the Canadian Northern bit off more than it can chew in a year,' one Davidson homesteader complained to Laurier in mid-January.[2]

During these winter months of 1907, the Toronto Railway Chambers were frantic with activity. Messenger boys came running along King Street, from telegraph offices at Union Station, to deliver the bad news to Mackenzie as he sat in his glass-enclosed office. The upright black telephone on Fred Annesley's desk rang incessantly. Mackenzie was in almost daily touch with the prime minister and with E.A. James, western manager of the Canadian Northern Railway. In early February 1907 trains ceased running between Prince Albert and Regina for several days. Homesteaders in newly settled areas around Saskatoon were in danger of freezing and starving. 'Make sure that Saskatoon gets enough wood and coal for new settlements on the Goose Lake line,' Laurier cautioned Mackenzie on 7 February. Mackenzie's return telegram informed the prime minister that relief gangs had dug out the railway line as far as Craik, almost halfway between Regina and Saskatoon, and that he had already ordered James to get fuel and supplies into Saskatoon. 'Is there anything further that you can suggest?' the beleaguered Mackenzie asked the prime minister.[3]

On 16 April the Board of Railway Commissioners asked the CPR and the GTPR to lend the CNoR 'every possible assistance.' Finally, on 19 April, the Canadian Northern could declare all its lines open again. Late that month, however, a lingering strike at coal mines in Lethbridge impeded recovery. The CNoR had a backlog of 11 million bushels of grain to be shipped. The railway was accused of placing too much emphasis on construction and not enough on new equipment. In May the prairie snows rapidly melted but investment markets took much longer to thaw.

In Ontario the debate with Adam Beck heated up. On 7 January, four days after the most severe snowstorm of the prairie winter, sixteen municipalities, mainly in southwestern Ontario, voted to buy power from the Hydro Commission,[4] up from the seven municipalities three years before. Beck's movement was growing, in spite of the fact that the Hydro Commission had no supply of power, no method of bringing power from Niagara Falls to Ontario municipalities, and no apparent idea of costs.

The Electrical Development Company of Ontario had invested $14 million in its power generation plant at Niagara and needed more capital. But tight London markets were wary of investing in Ontario utilities, for fear that Premier Whitney might implement what British bankers called the 'almost unlimited powers' of the Hydro Act of 1906.[5] By February 1907 EDCO was in danger of defaulting on its next bond interest payments. Mackenzie planned a February trip to London to promote his flagging securities and to remove himself from the hotbed of Toronto politics and journalism. His family hoped to take him off to the Riviera for a couple of months' rest. On 14 February he left Toronto with Ethel and Katharine.[6] When he reached London James Dunn read the exhaustion on his face.[7]

Although British investors bought Winnipeg land and terminal bonds for the construction of the big Union Station in Winnipeg, guaranteed as they were by the province of Manitoba,[8] Ontario railway bonds were not attracting buyers. The Canadian Northern Ontario Railway was not paying operating expenses, and investors feared that Whitney had become less sympathetic to private investment.[9] At the same time, in an attempt to defeat the Hydro Commission, Pellatt and Nicholls had incited investors' fears in London, and their tactics now worked against Mackenzie and CNoOR directors who decided to borrow money, rather than sell bonds, in the hope that the CNoOR bonds would be more marketable in a year or two.

The third major component (after the Canadian Northern and the Canadian Northern Ontario)[10] of Mackenzie and Mann's railway system was the Canadian Northern Quebec Railway Company (CNoQR), assembled in 1906 from three smaller companies. It ran trains between Quebec City, Montreal, and Hawkesbury, and expected to build lines to Saint John and Halifax. But the CNoQR was only marginally profitable; therefore an issue of its bonds worth $9 million was also expensive to float, especially because the guarantor of its bonds was the Canadian Northern Railway, whose own bonds were unattractive.[11]

Ironically, Mackenzie managed to sell EDCO securities, albeit at a substantial discount,[12] even though the struggle with Beck intensified while he was in London. On 30 April the Hydro Commission signed a contract to buy power from the Ontario Power Company, even though EDCO's offer was almost identical in price and superior in ability to deliver. Beck ignored Whitney's request that he reconsider his decision.[13]

During Mackenzie's visit to London, his lieutenants at the To-ronto Railway Chambers kept him informed of the latest business news. Existing evidence suggests that they carefully screened as much of the gloomy financial news as possible, probably because they were anxious to protect his health. In April Mackenzie ar-ranged to have $1.4 million transferred to Toronto, the final payment of a loan from the Bank of Commerce to one of his companies, but he sent it to the wrong bank in Toronto. Mr. Morris of the Commerce was 'very wrathy,' J.M. Smith wired Mackenzie. But then again, Smith added, these financial arrangements were rather compli-cated. To keep Mackenzie on track, Fred Nicholls and E.R. Wood were dispatched to London.[14]

Mackenzie may not have visited the Riviera, but he did make some social calls in London. Sir Wilfrid and Lady Laurier invited the Mackenzies to lunch one Sunday in May. Mackenzie's hasty hand-written reply on Savoy Hotel stationery was undated. He informed the Lauriers that Mrs. Mackenzie was not with him this time, and that Mrs. Griffin (Mabel) and Mrs. Grantham (Trudie) were in Paris (where they were preparing for the May Drawing Room at Bucking-ham Palace, when all six of Mackenzie's daughters were to be pre-sented). 'I would be very pleased,' he concluded, 'to come to Lun-cheon on Sunday at 1.30 if I may come by myself. Please let me know.'[15]

Neither Mackenzie nor Laurier was a diarist. Railway and power questions must have been on the agenda. In April the Railway Com-mission had turned down the company's request for charters to construct 1,600 more kilometres of prairie railway, many of them in southern parts of Saskatchewan. The two men may also have dis-cussed the shortage of railway equipment. In 1907, to alleviate this shortage and improve existing lines, the Laurier government had provided a guarantee for a new issue of bonds worth over $13 mil-lion.[16] Other topics probably included the Hartney extension from Brandon to Regina, one of Premier Scott's pet projects; the construc-tion of lines north of Superior and through the BC interior to the coast;[17] and the possible use of Dominion disallowance powers to modify the new Ontario Hydro Acts. The two men may have dis-cussed how to encourage Saskatchewan and Alberta to guarantee bonds for branch line construction. Berthiaume's pleading to regain full control of La Presse may also have been on the agenda. No doubt the presence of Zoë Laurier ensured humour and sound advice.

Mackenzie's trip to London that spring was marked more by bluster and bravado than by success. Here was James Dunn, searching desperately for investment fields more fertile than those in London. Mackenzie was 'perhaps the most prominent man in Canada,' Dunn told an investment house in Berlin.[18] There was Dunn dispatching to Canada a representative of an important London banking house that before 1907 had sold large blocks of Canadian Northern securities.[19] There was Mackenzie arriving at Dunn's office in the City with an armload of souvenir copies containing the flattering speeches delivered at the King Edward Hotel banquet the previous December.

Suddenly a telegram from Toronto. His son Alex had attended the Jockey Club races at Woodbine on 30 May. When he returned home, he complained of feeling ill. He was stricken with an attack of appendicitis. In 1907 the operation was not routine, but Alex survived. On 6 June his doctor pronounced him out of danger. That evening, however, at his home on Glen Road in Toronto's Rosedale, surrounded by his wife, his mother, and his brother Joe, he died of heart failure. He was only twenty-nine. His father may have been informed of Alex's illness and assumed that his athletic son would recover. Trudie and Mabel were en route to New York when a ship's steward brought them word of Alex's death. They arrived in Toronto an hour before the funeral, on 9 June. It was a military funeral – Alex had been a lieutenant in the 48th Highlanders – followed by a journey up the Grand Trunk line through Uxbridge, Cannington, and Argyle to Kirkfield. On board the Canadian Northern's three private cars, the *Atikokan*, the *Athabaska*, and the *Balmoral*, were Margaret Mackenzie, R.J., Joe, Trudie and Arthur Grantham, Mabel and Scott Griffin, uncles Ewan and Alex Mackenzie, and the deceased's brother-in-law, Captain Kirkland.

At five in the afternoon the train arrived at Kirkfield. Just three weeks earlier Alex and his wife had spent a few days at Balsam Lake playing tennis, golfing, and boating; as usual, he had been the life of the party. Now he returned for the last time. The body was taken up a specially constructed gravel pathway that led directly into the Catholic part of the Kirkfield cemetery without having to cross the adjacent Protestant burial ground. Ever since his marriage to an Anglican, Alex had not been a practising Roman Catholic, but his mother made sure that he was buried a Catholic. Margaret Mackenzie provided orange lilies from her garden for the Twelfth of July parades in Kirkfield, but her own family must have nothing to do with the religion of Cromwell. Alex would be buried a Catholic. His wife was not at the graveside.

The gravel pathway up the steep hill to the cemetery proved too difficult for the horses pulling the casket. The pallbearers and Kirkfield onlookers had to carry it the last few hundred metres. 'His death seemed to be a blow,' Arthur Hills recalled years later, 'from which those who were privileged to be his intimates could hardly be expected to recover.' Alex had 'qualities of heart,' and an unspoiled, unaffected nature that appealed to all who knew him.

One of the mourners that hot, sticky June day was Sir Henry Pellatt. Many's the time the folks in Kirkfield told the story. They thought for sure that the portly Sir Henry was not going to make it up the hill. In the colourful local idiom, 'he was sweatin' like a hen pullin' rails,' as he lumbered up the gravel road, weighed down by plutocratic girth and immense grief, made more poignant by the absence of his friend and partner, who at that moment was in Liverpool, awaiting the next Atlantic steamer.

'The loss seemed to stagger his father,' Hills recalled. When the ship carrying William Mackenzie pulled into New York harbour a week later, it was met by Margaret, Trudie, and Mabel and Scott Griffin.[20] One can imagine the little party, outfitted in black, hugging each other, bravely trying to conceal their sorrow. More than ever, they must have feared that Mackenzie would succumb to the breakdowns that haunted him in times of stress.

Why Alex? he must have wondered. Just a few months earlier, he had decided that Alex could sign all important documents in his absence. Alex was being groomed to take over the empire. The other two boys were amiable. R.J. was an effective construction boss, respected by workers and adored by his little nieces and nephews; but Rod could never manage a vast empire. His interests were race horses and attractive women. Then there was Joe, the archetypal millionaire's son who loved fast cars and good whiskey.

To add to Mackenzie's personal trials, his eldest brother, Duncan, died in Kirkfield on 3 July, at the age of seventy-four. A few days later, on 6 July, the Kirkfield Lift Lock, the second largest in the world, opened with speeches by officials such as Mackenzie's old friend, Sam Hughes. It was the promise of the Trent Canal that had attracted John Mackenzie to North Eldon in 1836. Now, seventeen years after the senior Mackenzie's demise, the main part of the canal was completed. The lightheartedness of the occasion was scarcely in keeping with the mood of the Mackenzie family.

Mackenzie grieved for his lost son, but only in private. A few days after his return to Toronto, he presided over a meeting of the directors of the Canadian Northern Ontario Railway. It was business as usual. Almost. The directors approved arrangements that he had made in England for the construction of spur lines on the Toronto to Sudbury line; then he had to approve a motion that conferred Alex's signing powers upon one of the remaining directors.[21] The handsome, articulate heir apparent was gone forever.

Shortly after, Mackenzie returned to his place at the forefront of things. Toronto Railway Company employees were asking for a wage hike. At noon on Monday, 24 June, he joined Billy Moore, R.J. Fleming, and representatives of the street railway employees for a 'preliminary canter,' as Fleming put it, in the Toronto Railway Chambers.[22] Workers and management had agreed to establish a conciliation committee consisting of three representatives from each side. If the committee could not come to an agreement, arbitration would follow. The system, established by the new Industrial Disputes Investigation Act, worked to the mutual benefit of both sides. On 13 July Mackenzie, Moore, and Fleming signed a three-year contract with the men.[23] Street railway workers thus continued to be among the best paid and the most continuously employed members of Toronto's work force.

The agreement signed, Mackenzie boarded his private car and, courtesy of the Vancouver-bound CPR, arrived at the Lakehead, where he transferred the Atikokan to a CNoR train.[24] On 15 July he reached Winnipeg, where he announced, in an uncharacteristically subdued mood, that the CNoR would be building no new extensions in the prairies in 1907. Three days later, he met Premier Scott in Regina to deal with the question of the Hartney extension and a railway bridge in Prince Albert.

From Regina, Mackenzie took the Qu'Appelle, Long Lake & Saskatchewan Railway up to Saskatoon, where he announced plans for a $40,000 station on 1st Avenue, a nearby freight shed, and a roundhouse.[25] On 21 and 22 July he was back in Winnipeg, where he held a meeting with homesteaders on the proposed Goose Lake line, southwest of Saskatoon. Mackenzie had intended to postpone construction until 1908, but Scott and homesteaders from Vanscoy and Tessier persuaded him to start grading and tracklaying in 1907. Only seventy-five miles would be built, Mackenzie warned, and only if Dick Stovel, Mackenzie's right-of-way agent, and Mayor Wilson could agree to an entrance route in Saskatoon.[26]

In Winnipeg, Mackenzie defended the CNoR against charges that it had subordinated equipment and service to rapid expansion.[27] He told the press about new stations at Borden, Dalmeny, Lashburn, Lamont, and Brandon, freight sheds at Humboldt, Vermilion, and Vegreville, additions to the roundhouses at Portage la Prairie and Dauphin. He also mentioned roundhouses planned for Winnipeg and Prince Albert, enlarged freight sheds at Edmonton and North Battleford, and construction of repair shops at Fort Rouge. The

CNoR was reducing grades on the railway from Prince Albert to Regina; ballasting and filling was being carried out everywhere; and the line from Brandon to Regina was under construction westward.[28] 'I find the road better every time I pass over it,' Mackenzie boasted to Winnipeg reporters.

On 16 October, when Mackenzie presided over the annual meeting of the CNoR in Toronto, he made the best of an unfortunate year by emphasizing the few positive achievements, such as the recent successful flotation in London of over $3 million in equipment bonds, a new bond guarantee for additional construction, and the increase in the CNoR's capital to $19,250,000.[29] His characteristic enthusiasm shone forth on one subject – he still hoped to fulfil his old dream of building to Hudson Bay.

Immediately after the shareholders' meeting, he took the train to New York and sailed for England. Canadian land and railway bonds were still unpopular. Once again, instead of selling these securities at a large discount, he borrowed short-term money in London and Berlin, at the high rate of 7 per cent interest.[30] He found it almost impossible to sell EDCO bonds in London. Adam Beck was scheming again, this time to limit EDCO sales of power to Toronto and to eastern Ontario.[31] The company was again in danger of defaulting on bond interest payments. In December 1907 it tried to strike a deal with the Ontario government for a guarantee on an issue of EDCO bonds to replace the unguaranteed bonds that Mackenzie was attempting to sell in London. In return, EDCO offered to sell power at cost, plus interest on bonds and dividends to shareholders.[32] Sadly, Whitney's dislike of the sanctimonious Joseph Flavelle, whose newspaper had been a harsh critic of the Hydro Commission, put an end to this sensible proposal.[33]

In January 1908 Beck took the battle one step further: a second by-law now asked ratepayers to make Hydro the sole wholesaler to municipalities. Toronto ratepayers were asked to vote on the question of creating a municipally owned distribution company to compete with the Toronto Electric Light Company. In each case, Beck's options won a majority. English and Canadian bondholders pleaded with Whitney to expropriate EDCO. Whitney refused, partly because of his dislike for Flavelle.[34]

Whitney's relationship with Mackenzie remained cordial. The premier kept in touch with officials of the Canadian Northern, an important source of jobs for his friends and constituents.[35] His warm and witty friendship with Scott Griffin continued throughout 1907 and 1908. (In February 1908 Griffin wryly told the premier that municipal ownership and clean elections were products of disordered brains.)[36] During campaigns launched by EDCO to discredit the Hydro scheme, Whitney blamed Flavelle, Nicholls, and Pellatt, but not Mackenzie.[37] Just before the provincial election campaign began in the spring of 1908, Whitney pushed through legislation guaranteeing $2.5 million dollars of Canadian Northern Ontario Railway bonds for terminal facilities and branch lines.[38] The premier had already made it more difficult for the city of Toronto to expropriate the Toronto Electric Light Company when his government increased the company's capital from $3 million to $4 million, in spite of objections from Beck and the Toronto council.[39]

Whitney did not want to push EDCO into bankruptcy.[40] He was aware that it had invested and borrowed so many millions that its failure would harm Ontario industry, the province's credit rating in London, and his own political career. He was more than pleased when Mackenzie took control of the situation. In January 1908 he began to assemble a large holding company to save EDCO from bankruptcy. He kept the premier informed of the negotiations,[41] and Whitney provided a charter for the new company. On 14 February, Mackenzie announced the creation of a greatly expanded Toronto Power Company, with himself as president and Nicholls, Pellatt, James Gunn, and Jim Grace as directors. The old Toronto Power Company had distributed electrical power within Toronto. The new company was capitalized at $1 million and controlled the Electrical Development Company and the Toronto & Niagara Company, which transmitted power from Niagara to Toronto. Since the Toronto Railway Company controlled the Toronto & York Railway, which controlled the new Toronto Power Company, ultimate control rested with the financially sound Toronto Railway Company. With this move, Mackenzie was uniting transportation with generation, transmission, and distribution, on the model of the Winnipeg Electric Railway. It was the right combination, Ontario style.

Mackenzie made available to the new TPC up to $3 million in Toronto Railway Company securities.[42] Now EDCO was no longer in danger of what Whitney most feared – a 'smash up.' The Toronto Power Company purchased $1,850,000 of EDCO bonds, provided money to meet liabilities and for the next interest payment, due on 1 March. The Bank of Commerce was now an eager supporter.

The *Telegram* called Mackenzie's new strategy a 'deadly menace to the Beck policy,' and *Saturday Night* expressed a widespread concern that the new company might be able to dictate electricity rates in Toronto. Whitney, however, was more than pleased. Mackenzie had stated on several occasions that he had nothing but good feelings towards the Whitney government, and he upbraided colleagues who used the creation of the TPC to taunt the Ontario government.[43] Mackenzie's private chats with Whitney convinced the premier that he was sincere when he promised not to antagonize Hydro in any way. The premier was sure that Mackenzie would now be able to come to an agreement with the Ontario Power Company, the other private power company, in order to supply power at rates even lower than those proposed by Hydro.[44]

Thus, during the first three months of 1908 Whitney and Mackenzie reached an understanding – an 'informal offer,' Whitney called it – that Mackenzie and EDCO, with the Ontario Power Company, would proceed with private generation and transmission of power from Niagara to Toronto and Ontario municipalities. Mackenzie's concession was on rates – the Ontario government, probably the Hydro Commission, would have the power to regulate them. Government would guarantee $10.5 million of bonds and receive power at $10 per horsepower. A few days later, in the legislature, the premier continued to talk positively of negotiations with EDCO.[45]

Mackenzie was certain of success. He had the premier's backing and he also gained influence with the Honourable John Hendrie, one of Hydro's three commissioners. Hendrie's company, the Hamilton Bridge Company, had been awarded a contract to build the Canadian Northern Railway bridge at Prince Albert.[46] Mackenzie was pleased that the city of Brantford, which had been a strong supporter of Beck and the Hydro Commission,[47] had opted to buy power from private companies such as EDCO, which in April 1908 was building transmission lines into Brantford.[48]

So confident was Mackenzie that he began to turn his attention elsewhere. He gained control of the Dominion Brewery, though not without the threat of a lawsuit from its insolvent owners, Case and Miller. Mackenzie had foreclosed on a loan to the brewery, refused CPR stocks as payment, and taken possession of the company. Case and Miller threatened a lawsuit. Mackenzie told them to go to hell, where, one might suppose, they would meet Broach, the Winnipeg union leader, whom Mackenzie had sent there a few years earlier. Even Mackenzie's critics have to admit that he rarely discriminated on the basis of money or rank. He won the case and kept the brewery.[49]

The same issue of the Toronto *Star* that reported the brewery dispute carried a sub-headline, 'Mackenzie The Peacemaker.' In his office at the Toronto Railway Chambers, he had presided over a meeting of the feuding presidents of the Dominion Iron and Steel Company and the Dominion Coal Company, whose president was Sir James Ross, his old colleague. (Mackenzie's attempts to make peace failed; the dispute between these two Nova Scotia coal and steel companies was not settled for another two years.)[50]

Now that the power business in Ontario seemed settled, Mackenzie decided to visit London. At the end of April 1908, accompanied by Margaret, Ethel, and Bertha, he left for England, where his efforts to develop Canada were royally recognized – he was presented to King Edward at Buckingham Palace. The investment climate had improved somewhat since his previous visit at the end of 1907. Bonds, including the latest issued by the Toronto Power Company, were selling. Dunn was interested in selling shares of Mackenzie's newly created Canadian Prairie Land Company. Steam railway securities, however, remained unattractive. The Canadian Northern Ontario Railway was once again forced to borrow money at 7 per cent, and Dunn had little luck selling Canadian Northern Railway securities.[51]

Mackenzie was back in Canada in July 1908 to celebrate the 300th anniversary of European settlement. Quebec City had been founded in 1608 by Samuel de Champlain, the same Champlain who had been part of the folklore of Mackenzie's childhood. In order to turn the Plains of Abraham into a national park, and to remove some of the ramshackle buildings erected on it during the previous century, a fund had been created to collect $2 million. Mackenzie contributed $1,000; Mackenzie, Mann & Company, $3,000. In recognition of Quebec's central role in the history of Canada, contributions came from across Canada and from Britain: Quebec and Ontario each gave $100,000; the Canadian Bank of Commerce, the Bank of Montreal, and the CPR each gave $10,000; King Edward sent a donation; Toronto council contributed $50,000; the Massey-Harris Company, $5,000. Money came from Great Britain for a statue honouring both Wolfe and Montcalm. Pope Pius x sent his best.

The Tricentenary was a grand affair, full of pomp and circumstance. Thousands of Quebec City residents joined guests from across the country and from Britain and France on Dufferin Terrace to cheer and wave Union Jacks and *Tricouleurs* as the ship bearing the Prince of Wales steamed up the St. Lawrence on 22 July 1908. At 4:00 in the afternoon, when the Prince stepped ashore, he was greeted by the governor general, the prime minister, and the premier of Quebec, then taken to a colourful pavilion erected on the Plains. Mackenzie was one of several dozen notables on the stage. As he waited for the prince and the prime minister to assemble, he chatted with guests, among whom were Premiers Whitney and Rutherford, several lieutenant governors, the Speakers of the Senate and House, and representatives of other parts of the Empire. Shaughnessy and Hays were there too. Mackenzie's old friend, Lord Strathcona, surveyed the new battlefield park on the Plains. Lords Grey and Roberts imagined the Battle of 1759. The mayor of Brouage, Champlain's birthplace, was there. So, too, were descendants of Wolfe, Montcalm, Levis, and Murray. They listened to Laurier extol Quebec City's storied past, Champlain's work, Canada's loyalty to the Crown, and the pride that both founding linguistic communities felt for the city that had given birth to Canada. They heard the Prince express his appreciation of French Canadian loyalty, and his pleasure at this, his sixth visit to Canada.

The Prince and the dignitaries paraded through narrow streets and back to the Citadel. During the next few days, Mackenzie attended a round of luncheons, a state dinner, a ball at the legislature, and a display of battleships.[52] One of the highlights was a mammoth pageant on the Plains, during which Jacques Cartier replanted a cross and carried off the Indian chief Donnaconna to the court of Francis I; Champlain, Laval, and Marie de l'Incarnation also made appearances.

During this week of festivities, many important contacts were made. James Dunn discussed underwriting Alberta bonds with Premier Rutherford.[53] Mackenzie spoke to Whitney. Both men had an opportunity to speak to Lord Grey, whose son-in-law was a member of a London banking house floating Electrical Development Company bonds. Whitney said nothing that would have cast doubt on the verbal agreement made a few months earlier with Mackenzie. Mackenzie thus returned to Toronto on the first of August believing that Whitney would honour his promise not to build government transmission lines. Whitney may even have told Mackenzie, as he did his brother, Ned, that he hoped to put that verbal agreement into writing.[54] (Indeed, the basis for that contract was already in writing – before leaving for London in April, Mackenzie had sent over to the premier's office a résumé of the compromise that the two of them had discussed.)[55]

Mackenzie was thus taken completely by surprise by Whitney's announcement in early August that his government was going to build its own transmission lines. He knew, of course, that back in May the Hydro Commission had asked for tenders for construction of transmission lines, but he had grown quite accustomed to Beck's periodic pronouncements that the government intended to build its own lines.[56] Mackenzie may have assumed (or was he told by Whitney?) that this was another ploy designed to assuage supporters of Hydro during the Ontario election campaign of 1908. He must have recalled that Whitney had campaigned in 1905 against government guarantees or any other aid to railway companies. Yet Whitney had found ways to break that promise.

When Whitney made his announcement on 6 August, the deal for construction of the lines had not yet been signed. There was still time to appeal. On 7 August Mackenzie sent a conciliatory note to Whitney. 'Possibly I am mistaken,' he wrote, 'but I understood that in the main you were rather favourable to the plan [government-regulated rates and privately-generated and transmitted power].' He had done nothing since their February meetings, he went on, since both he and the premier had agreed to let the matter rest until after the June election, when negotiations could be continued and concluded. Although the matter was pressing, Mackenzie was the soul of politeness. He knew that the premier was about to leave for England and he had no wish to delay Whitney's trip for 'the preservation of your health is a matter of vital importance to the Province.'[57]

Mackenzie seems to have been satisfied that he could continue his friendly negotiations with Whitney. He had Pogson, his chauffeur, drive him to the National Club, where he had lunch with Colonel Denison and some visiting Conservative English MPs,[58] who doubtless were interested in Mackenzie's progress with Whitney on the issue of private power, and who must have been just as surprised as Mackenzie at Whitney's announcement about the transmission lines.

The next day, 8 August, Whitney wrote a very curt reply to 'Dear Mr. Mackenzie.' He denied that he had promised to postpone a decision on the transmission lines until after further discussions with Mackenzie. He had understood that Mackenzie was to deal directly with Ontario Power Company, but in May, having heard nothing, his government had advertised for tenders for construction of the lines.

Whitney's argument contradicts any evidence in correspondence with Sam Blake, whose law firm, Blake, Lash and Cassels, represented both Mackenzie interests and the Ontario Power Company, and who therefore knew of the proposal to unite the two companies. It also contradicts statements in correspondence with Ned Whitney in February and March, when the premier expressed his pleasure that EDCO, reorganized to include OPC, would be able to supply low-cost power regulated by the Hydro Commission, which would resume its intended role, that of power regulator.[59]

On 10 August, two days after receiving Whitney's letter, Mackenzie wrote another conciliatory letter to Whitney. He had understood that only after hearing from the premier was he to proceed with arrangements with OPC. Now that he had heard from the premier, he was more than willing to complete an agreement with OPC for generation and transmission of power.

To this final suggestion from Mackenzie, Whitney apparently made no reply. On 13 August the government made its decision official – it announced that it had signed a contract for the construction of a transmission line from Niagara to southwestern Ontario and Toronto. Whitney sailed off to England, snubbing Mackenzie. In London, however, he led A.M. Grenfell, Lord Grey's son-in-law, to understand that the Ontario government would safeguard the interests of the British investors in EDCO, but seems not to have told Grenfell that the Hydro Commission had already signed an agreement for the construction of its own transmission line, to be built with bonds guaranteed by the Ontario government.[60] On the basis of his conversation with Whitney, Grenfell's banking house purchased a large number of EDCO bonds.[61]

Back in Toronto that fall, Whitney ignored promises made to Mackenzie and Grenfell. On 18 November he joined Beck and representatives of 250 municipalities in Toronto for the ceremonial turning of the first sod for the new transmission line. There was now little room for accommodation with private interests.

How to explain Whitney's about face? Was it the act of a tightrope walker who loses his balance, and has no choice but to jump to one side or the other? On the one side, he faced Flavelle, Pellatt, and Nicholls, who foolishly and publicly predicted the demise of government hydro power;[62] on the other hand, there was the equally uncompromising Beck, who would have nothing to do with the Toronto-based private power interests. Beck was supported by Chief Maclean's *World* and by John Ross Robertson's *Telegram*. Electoral rhetoric in the spring of 1908 and Whitney's impressive victory at the polls on 8 June may also have influenced his thinking – like many politicians, he was hoist with the petard of his own rhetoric. No matter that he could secure cheaper rates from government-regulated private power. State-owned hydro power in 1908 had electoral appeal.

On the other hand, perhaps rational, linear explanations do not suffice. Historians of Whitney and Ontario Hydro have resorted to the imagery of theatre and fiction, masks and magic, charades and facades[63] in order to explain the creation of Ontario Hydro. Ontario would soon end up with the 'folly,' as the *Globe* called it, of two parallel transmission lines from Niagara to Toronto.

Behind the masks, what was going on? What was Whitney telling Beck? That Mackenzie should be allowed to sell power to municipalities under the supervision of a watchdog Hydro Commission? Or that he was only cajoling Mackenzie into believing that there was room for compromise? What about Albright and the Ontario Power Company? Was he willing to make a deal with Mackenzie and EDCO in order to gain access to the lucrative Toronto market? It seems clear that Mackenzie trusted the premier. But what was Mackenzie telling Pellatt, Nicholls, and Flavelle? Where did Flavelle get the idea that government compromise meant government capitulation? Unfortunately, the few remaining written documents reveal precious little. And the telephone, which Mackenzie started using for long-distance calls as early as 1902 and for local calls long before that, is now as silent as the Sphinx.

On 24 September 1908, just before leaving again for London, Mackenzie tabled the annual report of the Canadian Northern Railway. The railway's growth was modest. Net earnings in May and June 1908 had actually decreased from those of May and June 1907.[64] Prairie railway construction continued to suffer from a shortage of steel. All summer, while Mackenzie was dealing with Whitney he was also under great pressure from Laurier and Scott, who themselves were under pressure from voters and Liberal candidates in the provincial and national elections of 1908. Dr. Tessier of Tessier, Saskatchewan, reminded Scott of the political rewards to be derived from railway construction. 'We are within a very few days of the election,' one of Laurier's MPs on the graded Dalmeny branch line, north of Saskatoon, reminded Scott on 3 August 1908, 'and the territory through which the branch runs should be the backbone of Liberal support.' But if track were not laid, the seat might be in danger. One of the first messages that Mackenzie received on his return to Toronto from Quebec City was a 'Hurry up!' from Scott, who had been too busy campaigning to travel to Quebec. Mackenzie wired back that the CNoR was about to begin laying steel. Scott kept assuring anxious voters that as soon as President Mackenzie obtained steel, tracks would be laid. Mackenzie wired again in mid-August, as Dominion election day approached, that he was still short of rails and that work would be finished as 'soon as rails arrive.'[65]

Through the gloom of the recession, however, a few shafts of sunlight were beginning to penetrate. At the annual meeting on 24 September, Mackenzie announced that the CNoR's gross income had risen from $8,350,198 in 1906-7 to $9,709,463 for the year ending 30 June 1908. The rise was small but unique, for the CPR and the Grand Trunk Pacific experienced a decline in gross earnings during the same period. The company's capital was raised from $37 million to

$50 million. The Laurier government was going to provide bond guarantees for 610 miles (974 kilometres) of new construction in the prairies, at $13,000 per mile. For the first time since its acquisition by Mackenzie and Mann, operating expenses of the Qu'Appelle, Long Lake & Saskatchewan Railway were lower than gross income. During the year ending 30 June, 414,696 acres of CNoR land were sold, bringing in $3,456,758, and the CNoR had come to an amicable wage agreement with mechanics.

In Winnipeg sod-turning ceremonies for Union Station at Main and Broadway took place in June 1908. In early September, Mackenzie was in Calgary to announce a new station. In Saskatoon the company had acquired an entrance route; in Regina the CNoR was to use the big CPR station; and the CNoR and the GTPR planned to build joint stockyards in St. Boniface.

The other two components of the Canadian Northern system, the CNoOR and CNoQR, which at the end of 1908 formed 30 per cent of Mackenzie and Mann's total rail mileage, also showed some improvement. In July the CNoOR officially opened its line to Sudbury, 477 kilometres north of Toronto, and the company hoped to build from Toronto to Ottawa in 1909, to give the CNoR system an independent route from western Canada to tidewater at Quebec. The total value of freight (eastbound grain and westbound manufactured goods) hauled by all three of Mackenzie and Mann's railway companies rose by about 19 per cent, from $5,741,729 in 1906–7 to $6,824,783 in 1907–8.

'Taking this year as a whole,' Mackenzie told the assembled shareholders at the railway's annual meeting that September day in 1908, 'this Railway has a most successful record.'[66] He was not far wrong.

During the fall of 1908 the markets in London at last became interested in Canadian transportation securities. Mackenzie was anxious to catch the rising market, he told Laurier. To save time, the prime minister avoided a debate in the House by passing an order-in-council that provided Mackenzie with a bond guarantee for $8 million to build 974 kilometres of railway, which Mackenzie had already announced earlier at the annual meeting in September.[67]

After obtaining the order-in-council, Mackenzie made haste to London, accompanied by his wife and younger daughters. In November D.B. Hanna joined him there. Banking houses expected that CNoR common stock was about to take a jump in value, and James Dunn wanted a share of CNoR bond sales.[68] An issue of $20 million EDCO bonds was well received this time, partly because the province of Ontario was regarded more favourably in investment circles,[69] and even the announcement of the government transmission line did not cause panic.

Mackenzie was relieved but scarcely surprised. After all, hadn't he predicted, when things were at their darkest, that 'the effects of financial panics in the United States and Canada [were] only temporary'? Canada was a growing boy, he had said, in constant need of doses of investment capital in order to keep him growing.[70] His optimism, voiced early in 1908, before the recession showed signs of dissipating, had helped to bring back better times.

During the recession of 1907 and 1908, the Toronto Railway Company continued to enjoy good returns and continued to have differences with Toronto council. The subjects of dispute remained the same – overcrowding, routes, and stops. Lower courts tended to agree with the city. In May 1906, the Supreme Court of Canada came down with a split decision. In late April 1907, in a decision that set off a spirited debate in the Canadian press, the Privy Council decided in favour of the TRC. In other words, the TRC had the right to choose new routes, the areas to be served, and the number of stops each trolley would make.

A legally separate but overlapping dispute arose in 1906. In May the Ontario Railway and Municipal Board (ORMB) ordered the TRC to build ten to fifteen additional miles (sixteen to twenty-four kilometres) of single track and put into service 100 extra cars. The ORMB set no deadlines, since it wanted the city and the TRC to resolve their differences co-operatively. The TRC proceeded to select certain streets that a former city engineer had approved for trolleys, but council objected. Now the overcrowding case became entangled with the 'choice of streets' case. The city passed an act forbidding the TRC to choose the new routes, thereby contravening the April 1907 decision of the Privy Council. The TRC appealed to ORMB, which gave the company the power to choose routes, notwithstanding the new city act. The city took its appeal to higher courts, including the Privy Council, and lost each time.[71]

In early April 1908 the Private Bills Committee of the Ontario legislature was discussing a bill to annul the decision of the Privy Council and thus to return the choice of routes to the city. On 3 April, Mackenzie was driven over to Queen's Park to present his case against the bill. 'Don't interfere with the efforts of Canadians to get capital in England,' he warned members. C.W. Jefferys' rendition of Mackenzie addressing the committee appeared next day on the front page of the *Star*. It shows Mackenzie *in medias res*. His right hand tucked into the pocket of his trousers, he is emphasizing his points by jabbing two fingers of his left hand in the direction of the committee; on his striped vest rests his watch fob; his grey spade beard is sharply chiselled. He would be fifty-nine on his next birthday, yet appears as fit and energetic as ever. His steely, unfathomable eyes fix committee members, including the dour Adam Beck and the vain Tommy Church.

Sam Blake, Mackenzie's lawyer, listened to his client in admiration. He could not have done a more persuasive job. Ironically it was Blake, as lawyer for the city, who had framed the original street railway agreement in 1891, whose legal jargon was now being debated. Blake and city solicitor Fullerton engaged in some spirited repartee. Fullerton accused Blake of resorting to the Privy Council whenever he wanted to win a case for the TRC. Blake shot back that it was Fullerton who had taken this case to the Privy Council. 'You should take your medicine like men,' Blake advised Fullerton. Mackenzie enjoyed every moment of it. R.J. Fleming, 'minus his beard,' according to Jefferys in the cut-line of his illustration, listened impassively.

So impressive and convincing were Mackenzie and Blake in arguing that investors might be unwilling to invest in a street railway that did not have the right to choose its routes that committee members voted down the bill by fifteen to ten, at the same time recommending to the legislature that the city or ORMB approve routes chosen by the TRC. Mackenzie had won.[72]

The legislature, however, was where Adam Beck held sway, and it ignored the recommendations of the multi-party Private Bills Committee. On the morning of 10 April, the government proposed an amendment to the TRC charter of 1892. Queen's Park was thus ignoring the judgment of the Privy Council. That afternoon, Mackenzie dictated a letter to Whitney, objecting to the proposed legislation. If Whitney would postpone it, the TRC would keep its authority to choose new routes but would lay not one inch of track without the approval of council expressed through a committee composed of representatives of the city and the company.

Whitney was not moved. Four days later the Ontario government passed the bill into law. The city now could choose streets to be served by trolleys. Construction of five badly needed new lines on Adelaide, Bay, University, Richmond, and Wellington, which the TRC was anxious to serve, was held up pending an appeal by the company. In December 1908 ORMB decided that without a shadow of doubt the company had the right to choose streets for its new lines. The TRC had invested a great deal of money, the Board's judgment stated, and the city had invested none. 'The people are suffering,' the Board continued, 'while the City are delaying the company by denying them the streets they require for the new lines.'[73]

Profits, however, were unharmed by this chapter of litigation. The number of passengers rose from a total of 76,958,488 in 1906 to 85,574,788 in 1907, attracted to a transportation system that continued to be one of the best in North America, and also by fares that, at 3 to 5 cents per ride, including transfer, provided what an English photographer thought was the best transportation deal in Canada. In August 1908, after riding the eleven kilometres of the Belt Line on a five cent ticket, A.H. Fisher could only regret 'that other things in Canada [were] not on the same scale of cost as tramcars.'[74]

The TRC's safety record was also admirable: millions of passenger rides per year, yet very few accidents. In 1906–7, the number of cases heard was twenty-two, and in only seven of these was the company found guilty. Dividends were kept at a rather low 6 per cent, perhaps to ensure that the company would remain financially robust in order to act as the guarantor for Electrical Development Company bonds. Mackenzie's remaining 2,164 shares brought him the relatively modest sum of $12,984 in 1907 and in 1908. Toronto city council also benefited, for as gross income rose, so too did the money paid in taxes, percentage on gross income, and pavement rental charges. The Toronto & York Railway had the good fortune to be under a different political jurisdiction. York County was delighted when the company extended its northern line to Jackson's Point on Lake Simcoe in 1907, for a total of 125 kilometres of railway.[75]

In September 1908 Katharine Mackenzie married W.W. Beardmore, scion of the Beardmore family, whose former headquarters, the Beardmore Building, sits today in Toronto on Front Street near Church. Shortly after the wedding, Mackenzie was in Edmonton, where he met author and journalist Agnes Deans Cameron, who had just completed a trip from Winnipeg through the prairies to the Arctic. The Canadian Northern and its two genius promoters had shown great faith in Edmonton, she acknowledged, and had given the charming, cosmopolitan, and earthy town a great push forward by bringing in the railway in 1905.

Mackenzie turned on his charm and impressed Cameron with his 'gentle, kindly, almost retiring' manner. She thought him the 'Cecil Rhodes of Canada' and his eyes 'as inscrutable as the sea.' She admired his ability to discover and focus on the key idea of any proposition, to come to decisions quickly and unerringly, and to calculate accurately the cost of a project. She also admired his monklike simplicity – he travelled without a secretary, dictated letters sparingly, and worked in an office 'bare of adornment.'[76] (Had Cameron been a biographer, she would not have been so enthusiastic about the absence of documents!)

Here was a man in control of himself and his empire. He may have had some lingering doubts about the Canadian economy and the faithfulness of the British investor and he must have experienced moments of grief over his son. As 1908 drew to a close, however, he had to agree with Cameron that Canadians had every cause to face the future with renewed optimism.

CHAPTER NINE

Drinking Life to the Lees, 1909–11

The shadows move, meet and fall apart, but the significance of their gestures is understood only by the initiated.

(Economist [3 Mar. 1990] 46)

Grace Mackenzie's wedding to Count Jacques de Lesseps, on Wednesday, 25 January 1911, united the son of the engineer of the Suez Canal and the daughter of the *'Canadischen Eisenbahnkönigs'* – the 'Railway King of Canada,' a Berlin newspaper's title for Mackenzie. There were titles on both sides: Ferdinand de Lesseps, father of Jacques, had been honoured by Napoleon III; and Mackenzie, with Donald Mann, had been named Knight of the Realm in the King's Honour List, published on New Year's Day, 1911. Now he was Sir William Mackenzie.

De Lesseps, who had inherited his father's title, was a daredevil, a personality trait that appealed to the Mackenzies. He was an aviator who had first come to Canada to participate in the Montreal Air Show in June 1910, the largest in North America to that date. The Count, the second man after Bleriot to fly across the Channel, was the most attractive participant. On 2 July, he made the first solo flight over a Canadian city when he flew over Montreal.

A similar exhibition took place on 13 July in Toronto, where de Lesseps made the first solo airplane flight over the city. The airfield in the town of Weston was later named de Lesseps Field. His first meeting with William Mackenzie was probably at the York Club, in the old Gooderham mansion at Bloor and St. George Streets, where the count was fêted one evening. (The club was in its first year of operation, having been founded by presidents of the three competing Canadian transcontinental railways.) Jacques was invited to Benvenuto, where he met Mackenzie's youngest daughter, twenty-two-year-old Grace, five years his junior. The tall, dark, and handsome aviator was invited to tour the Trent Canal on the Mackenzies' magnificent yacht, the *Wawinet*, which Sir William had purchased in 1903 from the Polson Iron Works in Toronto.[1] When it reached the locks at Fenelon Falls, the local folk hitched up their horses and buggies to catch a glimpse of the yacht and its famous passenger. Local gossip had it that the tour was laid on to catch a count.

If so, it worked. Grace, Ethel, and Katharine were with Jacques when he took the $10,000 first prize at the New York Air Show later that summer. By that time it was clear that Count Jacques and Grace were in love. The French aviator took Grace on a flight over New York City, thus making her the first Canadian woman – perhaps the first woman – to fly. Later that day, he took Ethel and Katharine over New York City. The news of the flying Canadians was flashed to the Toronto press. Their father wired to New York, 'Come home immediately.' Even risk-taker Mackenzie found his daughters' high flying too much. The romance continued, however, and on 14 December 1910 Grace, Ethel, and Bertha left Toronto for London to prepare for Grace's January wedding.

The pair seemed well matched at the time. The wedding caught the attention of newspapers in Canada, the United States, and Europe. The aged and seemingly immortal Lord Strathcona was there with Lady Strathcona. So, too, was Sir Gilbert Parker, whose latest collection of stories, *Northern Lights*, was providing readers with glimpses of the Canadian West, from canoes to railways. Mackenzie's old friend, Monty Horne-Payne, and his wife motored in from 'Merry Mead,' their country estate. From France came numerous de Lesseps relatives, Count Henri de la Rochefoucauld, descendant of the famous eighteenth-century wit, and Baron and Baroness de la Grange. From Farnham, where she had lived in exile since the end of the Franco-Prussian War, the old Empress Eugenie, widow of Napoleon iii, and friend of the de Lesseps, sent her regrets.

Sir William had arrived in London the day before. It was a proud occasion for him, as he escorted the beautiful, dark-eyed bride to the church a few minutes past the appointed hour of 2:00 pm. As they drew within sight of St. James, Spanish Place, near Oxford Street and Manchester Square, they were met by a large and curious crowd, with several bobbies quietly keeping order. They alighted from the landau and walked on the red carpet and under the entrance canopy. The veiled bride took her father's arm. They proceeded through the doors and disappeared into the fashionable Roman Catholic church.

Sir William accompanied the bride up the aisle, preceded by Katharine and Ethel and his wife's niece, Mabel Meagher. Proudly bearing the bride's train was Sir William's grandson, eight-year-old Gilbert Griffin, in Highland costume. The grey stone columns and floor of the old church were enlivened by baskets of flowers. The music of Haydn, Handel, and, for pomp and circumstance, Elgar, filled the church. Each age has its styles and causes. In those self-assured days, skunk fur was in vogue. Lady Mackenzie's black velvet outfit, with matching hat, was trimmed with the black and white fur, as was the bride's going-away dress. And no placards or threats greeted Lady Kilpatrick's sealskin coat.

The guests were entertained later at Claridge's. The newlyweds – the bride wearing some of the pearl, diamond, platinum, and antique-coral jewellery given as wedding gifts – cruised to Egypt, where they passed the statue of Count Ferdinand at the entrance to the Suez Canal. They were later joined by Lady Mackenzie and Trudie. The young couple made Paris their home.

These few years, beginning in 1909, when the twenty months of recession finally vanished, were Mackenzie's golden years. Always a good storyteller, he now told more and more stories of triumph and vision. Journalists listened and wrote articles more admiring than critical. Two of his listeners, an agent for German investment money and an English journalist and novelist, recorded and published his stories. Both Martin Nordegg and Sarah Macnaughtan were keen on stories of Canada's pioneer days and of the emergence of Mackenzie from the backwoods of Ontario to the centre of the world's financial stage. And Mackenzie was delighted to entertain them.

Martin Nordegg arrived in Canada in 1906. He established the German Development Company, which acted as a conduit for German investments in Canadian minerals, timber, and real estate. When he wrote his memoirs, he complained that Mackenzie and Mann were very difficult men, who always got the better of the deal. What he did not know was that Mackenzie was also getting the better of the story. Mackenzie told stories that the European listened to with wide eyes: for instance, that he had borrowed his first $5,000 from a Montreal convent where his wife had gone to school. Had Nordegg retold that story to the folks in Kirkfield, they would have smiled, for they knew that old John Merry was much too poor to send any of his children away to school. In fact, the Kirkfield folk remembered when Margaret Mackenzie had worked as an upstairs maid at Biddy Young's Tavern down on the Portage near Bolsover.

'Ah, Meg Merry, ya needn't stick up yer nose at me,' old Biddy used to taunt Margaret Mackenzie years later, when she could afford her own maids and butlers, 'Many's the time ya potwallopped for me.' Biddy would also on occasion remind Margaret that her mother, Hanora Merry, had once made a dress for little Maggie out of Biddy's red petticoat.[2] Convent? Don't be silly.

Mackenzie first met Nordegg in Ottawa in May 1909. The German was looking for a railway company that would buy large quantities of Alberta coal controlled by the German Development Company (GDC). Nordegg had already talked to the other two big railway companies. Mackenzie and Mann were his last chance. One of the German company's Canadian directors was O.E. Talbot, grandson of Louis Joseph Papineau, leader of the 1837 rebellion in Lower Canada. Talbot sent Nordegg to Billy Moore. The two entrepreneurs were arriving in Ottawa the next day, Moore told Nordegg.

The following evening, as the sun was casting its last red glow as it set behind the deep blue of the Gatineau Hills, Nordegg made his way over from the Russell House past the half-completed Chateau Laurier and Union Station, to the *Atikokan*, parked on a siding in the ramshackle railyards on the east side of the canal. At the entrance to the smoke-filled lounge of the car, he was met by the buzz of conversation and laughter emanating from about a dozen men, including a goodly number of senators and MPs. Mackenzie was in conversation with one of the parliamentarians and failed to see the self-conscious newcomer standing uneasily in the entrance.

Finally Billy Moore took Nordegg over to him. 'Here's the man who represents the German Emperor,' Moore joked to Mackenzie. Mackenzie whirled around and introduced Nordegg to the cigar-chomping Mann.

'Come over here and sit down,' he invited the newcomer. 'Now tell me who you are, where do you come from, what are you doing here?'

Nordegg blurted out his replies, then asked if he could see Mackenzie the next morning.

'Certainly,' replied Mackenzie.

'What time?' asked Nordegg.

'Oh, drop in any time,' was the answer, which surprised Nordegg, for he had heard that Mackenzie was a busy man.

The next morning he became acquainted with Mackenzie's system: no appointments were made; men of influence were ushered into his office promptly; others might have to wait for hours. On guard at the door to Mackenzie's office was his watchdog and private secretary, Fred Annesley, who separated VIPs from mortals. Nordegg was placed in the former category, for he was allowed to enter Mackenzie's office immediately.

Mackenzie was busy discussing railway construction in the West. Without interrupting his discussion, he gestured to Nordegg to sit down. 'I listened with surprise to how easily he disposed of the expenditure of hundreds of thousands of dollars for the construction of a railway branch in the West,' Nordegg later recalled. The large sums were probably named on purpose, in order to impress and intimidate Nordegg.

Once finished with western branch lines, Mackenzie turned to Nordegg, who had entered the *Atikokan* with heart pounding and who by now must have been almost speechless. The two officials – one of them probably lawyer Gerald Ruel – remained in the room to act as Mackenzie's silent witnesses.

Nordegg mentioned the coal fields in Alberta. Mackenzie sent for a large map. Nordegg claimed that he had to point out the location of the mines. Mackenzie was surely feigning ignorance – a few months earlier he had obtained a Dominion government bond guarantee to build a line into his own Alberta coal fields, located at the headwaters of the Brazeau and McLeod rivers.[3] When Nordegg offered to show Mackenzie the engineers' reports, he claimed that he had no time to read them. (Here again, one wonders if one of Mackenzie's own engineers had already gone through these reports and had told Mackenzie that the quality of this coal was high, and that the location, within striking distance of the main line west of Edmonton, was desirable.)

'How many miles of railway would you have to construct to bring out the coal?' Mackenzie asked.

'Oh, about 160,' replied Nordegg.

'You'll need anywhere from $3 million to $6 million depending on whether you're building through prairie or mountains,' Mackenzie told him. (Further intimidation! Mackenzie's estimates were inflated by about 20 per cent.)

Mackenzie continued his grilling. 'How much do you need to equip the mine and build the service town?'

Once again Nordegg had to confess that he did not have access to the necessary $2 million. Mackenzie told him that in 1909 the Canadian Northern was in no position to build the line into Nordegg's mines, but that he would be prepared to buy about 300,000 tons of coal per year. He would pay the going price for western coal and no more, even if Nordegg's coal were better quality.

The scene was vintage Mackenzie. He was in control of the situation from the moment Nordegg entered his private car. He would buy Nordegg's coal at prices he himself dictated. He did not really need Nordegg's coal, he told the German, for Mann and he already controlled two Alberta coal fields. Mackenzie made it clear that without help from Mackenzie and Mann, Nordegg's railway line and the mining town itself might never be built.

'We will amalgamate your coal fields with ours and form a big company,' Mackenzie told Nordegg, who by this time was mesmerized by the speed with which Mackenzie pulled these ideas out of his tall hat. 'That will make it easier for you to get the two millions, and I will give you a contract for a minimum of three hundred thousand tons for three years.'

Without waiting for the speechless Nordegg to say a word or even to nod, Mackenzie rang a bell that summoned Annesley: 'Please ask Mr. Mann to come here. Important.'

The scene that followed illustrates how cleverly Mackenzie and Mann worked their act. That morning it was Nordegg. In his place, one could imagine any number of men – politicians, businessmen, lawyers – who found themselves mesmerized by the wizardry of Mackenzie and Mann.

Mann entered immediately, as if the whole scene had been scripted and he had been waiting in the wings for his cue. Without wasting a second, Mackenzie said, 'Donald, here is a fellow who wants to amalgamate his coal field in the Rockies with our excellent coal fields. What do you say?'

Mann removed the big cigar from his mouth, looked straight down at Nordegg and said, 'It all depends on what he is going to pay for our fields.' (Mackenzie and Mann did have a sense of humour, but it was so incorporated into their deadpan methods of bargaining that people often missed it, or realized too late that, like Nordegg, they had become its victims.)

Poor Nordegg attempted to explain that his proposals had been completely misinterpreted. 'Excuse me,' he said, 'the situation is entirely different. I want you to build the railway and buy our coal.'

'Now, isn't that the same thing?' Mann asked the German, who tried in vain to explain that he never did intend to amalgamate the German coal mines with Mackenzie and Mann's. Mann came back with the novel idea that Nordegg's real intention was to gain Mackenzie and Mann's coal mines free for the asking. Mann was just not going to let that happen.

'Don't let us lose time,' Mackenzie put in. 'We had better get Lash.'

It took Lash a few minutes to arrive. He may have been over at the Russell, or he may have been in the private car itself, but wanted to give Nordegg a few more minutes of suspense.

'Lash,' Mackenzie greeted his famous lawyer, 'I am going to build a railway into that man's coal fields.' (Mackenzie never did master the art of formal greetings and introductions.) 'He is going to combine his fields with ours,' Mackenzie continued, 'and I am going to buy coal from him.'

Lash thought a moment, then decided to let his assistant, the recently hired Phippen, handle the case. Nordegg was shown to Phippen's office, but before he could explain his case, Phippen's telephone rang. It was Mackenzie. Again no formalities: 'Come quick,' he ordered. Poor Nordegg had to wait by himself for fifteen minutes.

'Mr. Mackenzie says you are the hardest fellow he ever dealt with,' exclaimed Phippen, who obviously enjoyed Mackenzie's humour. Nordegg told Phippen that they had not got around to discussing details. 'Well, let's thrash it out,' replied Phippen, the former judge from Winnipeg.

The thrashing resulted in two companies, one west of Edmonton, to be called Brazeau Collieries Limited, comprising Mackenzie and Mann's fields and the German Development Company's northern fields; and a second further south, at the German company's Kananaskis coal field. Shares in each company were divided evenly between Mackenzie and Mann Company and the GDC. The Canadian company was to pay some cash to the German company, since the latter's coal fields were much more extensive.

'Now what is all that?' exclaimed the waiting Mackenzie when they took the preliminary agreement to him. He read it quickly and came up with his usual line, 'You are crazy. I will never agree to that.' Again, as if on cue, Mann appeared. 'Just look what these two fellows want to put over on us,' Mackenzie told his partner.

Mann scanned the document. 'I call that crazy,' he huffed.

'That is exactly what I said,' said Mackenzie.

The two men had played this scene so many times that it came naturally to them. They were two seasoned actors who could go on stage night after night and deliver the campiest lines without betraying the irony that informed this scene with Nordegg. Few other pairs of actors ever walked across the Canadian financial stage so successfully. So intertwined are they in the nation's collective memory that it is difficult to mention one without the other. Thus it comes as a surprise to learn that the partnership was limited to the Canadian Northern family of railways. Mann played only minor roles in Mackenzie's street railway empire.

The bargaining began anew that evening. They arrived at a new agreement. When Nordegg told Mackenzie that the president of his company would have to sign it, Mackenzie told Nordegg to send it over to Berlin. Nordegg knew that Mackenzie was sailing for London in a week. 'Why not go with me to Berlin and have it signed there?'

With characteristic decisiveness, Mackenzie agreed immediately. 'Not a bad idea. I've always wanted to see Berlin. We'll go together,' he announced.

They left Toronto on 21 May 1910,[4] stayed in London a few days, then went to Berlin, where the president of the German Development Company (whom Nordegg never names) met them at the station. Mackenzie was entertained for several days. He was taken to the Berlin opera, where he probably dozed during an aria. The next day he and Nordegg were driven for two hours to the president's country estate. Mackenzie found a supply of whiskey in his bedroom, including a bottle of Canadian Club. The president was out to impress him, but apparently did not know that Mackenzie rarely took a drink.

Before lunch, the president and Mackenzie discussed Canadian coal. Nordegg claimed in his memoirs that the president got the best of the bargaining by pretending not to understand everything that Mackenzie said, forcing Mackenzie to repeat himself, always in a slightly different way, thus allowing the president two or three options on any particular deal. Or he would ask Nordegg to translate Mackenzie's sentence, thus gaining time. The president resorted to telling anecdotes and jokes, one at his own expense while at the Henley regatta in England, which Mackenzie found so funny that he roared with laughter for several moments, slapped his thighs, and had tears of joy in his eyes.

Final details were settled in the hunting lodge of the estate, all in favour of the GDC, according to Nordegg. The president winked at Nordegg when the deal was signed. Nordegg liked to believe that the Germans got the better of Mackenzie, but once the deal was put into operation, he was no longer certain.

The president was a friend of Kaiser Wilhelm, and was a guest on his yacht next day at the Berlin rowing regatta at Grunau. Mackenzie was given a seat in an official box. By prior arrangement, as the Kaiser's yacht passed the box, the president and Mackenzie exchanged hand signals, then the president put his arm on the Kaiser's shoulder, a gesture to prove that he was close to Kaiser Wilhelm. (Nordegg must surely have been exaggerating, since no commoner would dare to breach protocol by placing a hand on a royal shoulder.)

'There is the Indian,' the Kaiser was told, 'and he is the President of the Canadian Railway who had to travel six thousand miles to

Berlin or else his railway could not run.' (Apparently in 1909 some Germans thought that all Canadians were Indians, perhaps the influence of Karl May, the German novelist of cowboys and Indians.) The Kaiser and the president looked in Mackenzie's direction and burst out laughing. Unfortunately Nordegg did not record Mackenzie's reaction. He assumed that Mackenzie was impressed by this close relationship of capital and Kaiser. No doubt he was. What better guarantee of success and security than friends in the upper echelons of German society?

Back in Berlin that evening, Mackenzie signed the agreement, then left for London, where he secured the underwriting of almost $4,000,000 worth of Canadian Northern Ontario Railway bonds,[5] the first time in more than two years that Mackenzie had been able to sell such bonds. The fact that they were guaranteed by railway property and not by government made their sale more noteworthy: investors expressed confidence in the future of the company. Later that year, Alberta-guaranteed railway bonds were welcomed by English investors.

Until 1910 the majority of Mackenzie and Mann's bonds were guaranteed by governments, in what seemed like a sensible and painless method of assisting the construction of a railway. In the 1890s, before Mackenzie's reputation sold bonds, and also during the recessions or 1903 and 1907–8, government-guaranteed bonds were often the only marketable securities. Even in good times government guarantees were welcome, for bond interest might thereby be a half per cent lower than it would be for company-guaranteed bonds, thereby saving the company hundreds of thousands of dollars in interest payments over the life of the bond.

The pressure for government guarantees came from many quarters. Rapid railway development pleased voters. Politicians therefore offered government guarantees to encourage construction of more lines. Richard McBride opened his 1909 electoral campaign by announcing a contract with Mackenzie and Mann for the construction of 960 kilometres of railway in BC.[6] He won in 1909 and again in 1912 with more such announcements. Voters threatened to get rid of any politician who hesitated to guarantee railway construction bonds.[7] 'We the members of the Wardenville Liberal Association,' its president, Robert Campbell, wrote Premier Scott in July 1909, 'would like an explanation from you in regard to your refusal to garentee [sic] the bonds of the CN Railroad through the Cutknife district.' The railway, Campbell complained, had been promised for six years and was a sure thing in the fall of 1908, during two election campaigns, provincial and national. 'The Cutknife district,' he went on, 'has always given a Liberal majority and naturally expects that the Liberal government will help to build this railroad.' One farmer told Scott in 1909 that it would be a 'Regular Kalamity' if the Rossburn extension in southern Saskatchewan were not built immediately.[8]

The political use of railways was not unique to western Canada. In July 1910 Dominique Têtu of Roberval reminded Laurier that he, Mackenzie, and Mann had promised to extend the Quebec & Lake St. John Railway west into Roberval country. 'Le retard du commencement des travaux à l'ouest de Roberval vous causerait une désastre politique absolue,' he warned.[9] When Canadians finally realized by the end of the Great War that there were too many railways, they tended to blame railway presidents and politicians, conveniently forgetting that they themselves had also believed that railways were a panacea for all economic woes.

In February 1910 Mackenzie and his family toured northern Mexico, where he inspected investments – the Monterrey Tramway, Light & Power Company, and the Mexico North Western Railway Company, built to haul timber from the state of Chihuahua.[10] They returned to Toronto, and on 9 March, William and Margaret sailed to England, where he was about to take command of the Royal Line of transatlantic ships.[11] In London he headed for Baltic House in the city, headquarters of the Royal Line, to consult with D.B. Hanna, who had spent the previous month in London organizing the details of the refits and sailing schedules, as well as the official launching of the *Royal Edward*.[12] His inventive mind had helped to create the fantasies printed in publicity brochures promoting 'these really wonderful vessels of the Canadian Northern Steamship Company.'

The official opening took place on 28 and 29 April 1910. Fortunately for posterity, Saskatchewan Premier Walter Scott was on board; he seems to have saved every scrap of paper in his possession, including the official inaugural guest list. In his miniature pocket diary, he recorded his visit to Britain. Sir William met Scott and Jones, London representative of the Canadian Bank of Commerce, at the Cecil Hotel in London on 26 April. They journeyed to Glasgow, where the Royal ships had been refitted. On 28 April the three men, along with Manitoba cabinet minister, Robert Rogers, took a motor tour of Glasgow.

At Greenock the party boarded the *Royal Edward*, joining about one hundred guests and family members, including representatives of the *Daily Express*, the Glasgow *Herald*, and the Edinburgh *Scotsman*; politicians such as W.E. Salisbury and the Lord Mayor of

Bristol; financiers James Dunn and Max Aitken; and Mackenzie's wife, his family, and sister-in-law Annie Mitchell,[13] who probably all agreed with the publicity brochure's message that 'There is nothing more fascinating than a ship, especially the ship in which one is about to take voyage.'[14] The hulls of the *Royal Edward* and the *Royal George* were battleship grey, above which was a broad strip of bright red, and the three decks were painted white. On top were two bright yellow smoke funnels, topped off with a broad swath of deepest blue. They were quickly deemed two of the handsomest ships to sail the Atlantic.[15] Their clean, bold colours were soon captured in eye-catching advertising posters by artist J.E.H. Mac-Donald.

Mackenzie must have been in his glory, showing off his floating palace, part steel, part fantasy, decorated in styles – Louis xv, Louis xvi, and Regency – that recalled other grand empires. The library of the *Royal Edward* was decorated in Regency style, its walls panelled in oak with 'rich but restrained carving' capturing the 'elusive' charm of French châteaux. The smoking rooms on each ship were panelled in mahogany and upholstered in maroon leather. The floor in the dining room was polished teak; its carpets, chair seats, and curtains were old rose pink. A skylight of leaded glass bathed diners in soft light. Each ship boasted a Marconi telegraph office, shops, hairdressers, drug stores, and a first-class ventilation system. Each could carry 350 first-class, 200 second-class and 600 third-class passengers, who enjoyed enclosed cabins, concerts, and fresh food, unusual third-class fare in 1910.

As the *Royal Edward* sailed leisurely down the coast of Scotland, past the mull of Kintyre dotted with sheep and stone cottages, past the Isle of Man and the damp, green coast of Ireland, the Mackenzies must have imagined their own parents setting off from this part of the world eighty years earlier, in crowded, damp, and dim wooden sailing ships. The Merrys and Sullivans, Lady Mackenzie's family, had left Waterford in 1831 aboard the 'Volunteer of Cork.' Little Hanora Sullivan, Margaret Mackenzie's mother, was born as the ship steamed into the Gulf of St. Lawrence. John and Mary Mackenzie, Sir William's parents, had left Scotland in 1832, accompanied by Munro and McLaughlan relatives and connections. They had sought a newer world where they might own a bit of land. Had they predicted that their children would sail the Atlantic in their own luxury ship, fellow passengers would have thought them slightly daft.

When the *Royal Edward* docked at Bristol, the party took the train into London. Two weeks later, Mackenzie helped to launch the ship on its first transatlantic voyage. He had expected to return to Canada with the ship, but business kept him in London. When King Edward died in mid-May, Mackenzie was invited to join other prominent Canadians – James Ross, Sir Hugh Graham, and Joseph Pope, among others – in reserved seats along the funeral route. In Canada that same day, 16 May 1910, all trains from coast to coast stopped for three minutes as the King's body was being lowered into its grave at Windsor.[16] Mackenzie returned to Canada on the *Royal George*, which left Bristol on its maiden transatlantic voyage on 31 May. Within the first month, each ship had set speed records that held for over twenty years.

In early June, Mackenzie was back in Toronto, bringing with him securities worth the incredible sum of $40 million. By 1910 the possibilities of Canada seemed truly great, and Mackenzie's name could now float anything from 12,000-ton steamships to securities worth tens of millions of dollars. The $40 million figure included bonds to construct more railways, steam and electric, to develop steamship lines, and to develop coal and timber in Alberta and BC. One bond issue was not due until 1950. For the first time, continental Europeans were investing in Mackenzie's Canadian empire.

The most speculative bond issue was an 'income charge convertible debenture stock' whose par value was $15 million. It was the first time in the CNoR's history that this kind of high risk security, whose collateral was corporate income – not government guarantees, had been offered for sale. Since net profits were too low to make the issue immediately valuable, investors obviously believed Mackenzie when he told them the railway would be completed in 1913 or 1914, and that as soon as all the component rail and ship companies had been united, the Canadian Northern would rival the Canadian Pacific in corporate wealth. By 1916, he promised, holders of these bonds would have the option of converting them into fully paid-up CNoR common shares of equal dollar value. In 1910 investors shared his optimism.

West coast investments began to appear in Mackenzie's portfolio. One bond issue announced in 1910 was made by a company called the Western Canadian Lumber Company, of which Mackenzie was a director. This holding company controlled thousands of acres of timber, mainly in the Comox Valley of Vancouver Island, perhaps better known now as the setting for Jack Hodgins' novels. The lumber company also owned the largest and most modern saw mill in Canada, on the Fraser River at New Westminster, which sent lumber to the Canadian interior and to Britain, Australia, New Zealand, South America, Japan, and China.

Another bond issue raised money to purchase the vast Dunsmuir empire in January 1910 for a reported $11 million. Mackenzie became president of Canadian Collieries (Dunsmuir). Its other directors were Sir Edmund Walker, Donald Mann, A.D. McRae, vice president of Canadian Western Lumber; and E.R. Wood, whose many directorships included that of the Grand Trunk Pacific Railway. (Here again one wonders if railways co-operated more than they admitted: James Dunsmuir himself was a director of the CPR, and after the change in ownership, the company continued to supply the CPR with 250,000 tons of coal annually.) With the imminent arrival of the Grand Trunk Pacific at Prince Rupert and the Canadian Northern at Vancouver and Victoria, the company's sale of coal would increase greatly. It also owned iron ore on Vancouver Island and in California; real estate (104 houses and a hotel on Vancouver Island); 28 kilometres of railway; land on Denman Island; and property in San Francisco.[17]

During the summer of 1910, Mackenzie, Mann & Company began to assemble a huge whaling company called the Canadian North Pacific Fisheries Limited. One day that summer, a reporter came across Mackenzie in the foyer of the Empress Hotel in Victoria. Ever amiable, approachable, and 'charmingly non-committal,' Mackenzie answered the reporter's questions with an absent-minded, 'I don't know.' And what was he going to do with the Pacific Fisheries? 'Oh, I suppose we shall do a little fishing,' was Mackenzie's droll response. His 'absent-mindedness' was a ploy to get rid of an intrusive reporter, who thought that Mackenzie looked like a pawnbroker – a loaded term.

Canadian North Pacific Fisheries gained a monopoly on Canadian whaling by controlling all eight licences for whaling off the BC coast. The company also acquired two licences for whaling in the western Arctic. In an attempt to regulate the harvesting of an endangered resource, Ottawa allowed only one whaling vessel for each licence. The company was thus legally allowed to operate ten vessels. It operated only four stations, however – two on the west coast of Vancouver Island (at Sechart on Barkley Sound, and one further north at Kyuquot); and two in the Queen Charlottes, at Rose Harbour and Naden Harbour. But it took advantage of the ten licences, including the two for the western Arctic, where it never whaled, to expand its whaling fleet to ten. Each station was able to operate an average of 2.5 vessels, 25 per cent more than the American legal maximum of two per station. The new Canadian company was thus in a better position to compete with the Americans and the Japanese. Existing documents do not indicate whether Dominion inspectors ever communicated this breach of regulations to the Department of Fisheries in Ottawa; nor whether the department would have done anything to prevent the breach, since enforcing the regulations might have harmed the Canadian industry.

About 600 Japanese, Norwegians, and Canadian Maritimers worked on the ships, and about 400 Japanese, Chinese, Haida, and Newfoundlanders worked at the four shore stations. Whale oil and bone were exported to make lubricants, glycerine, typewriter springs, machinery belts, vitamin A, and a medicine to treat diabetics. Despite high operating and licence costs, $100,000 annual interest payments on its debentures, and a decline in demand for whale oil, the company's net profits remained healthy to the end of 1912.[18]

Mackenzie planned to ship these resources on his transcontinental railway. He was in Victoria on 24 June 1910 to sign a final agreement with Premier McBride for the construction of 960 kilometres of railway from Yellowhead Pass to Vancouver, and from Victoria to Barkley Sound. The BC company was to be called the Canadian Northern Pacific Railway, the fourth major component of Mackenzie and Mann's transcontinental system. Premier McBride guaranteed bonds at $35,000 per mile, and the line was to be completed by 1 July 1914. The company's charter also gave it broad powers to operate telegraph and telephone lines, steamships, wharves, warehouses, mines, and express businesses. In return, the premier set two conditions: that the railway not be declared for the general advantage of Canada, thus giving the BC government, not the Dominion Board of Railway Commissioners, control over freight rates; and that Mackenzie not employ 'Asiatic labour.'[19] Mackenzie agreed to both conditions. 'Canada today,' Mackenzie had said two years earlier, 'is a nation in the making,' a 'crucible into which the polyglot peoples of the older countries are pouring.' The term 'Canadian,' he added, would eventually be a compound mix of these various peoples. It was an accurate prediction, but there was apparently little room for Asians in the new multicultural Canada,[20] not an uncommon attitude in early twentieth-century Canada.

By 1910 Mackenzie's ambitions were national and international. He was on the verge of linking the two great oceans and still had hopes of reaching Hudson Bay. His railway companies' most ambitious programs were in BC, Quebec, and Ontario, where the Canadian Northern Ontario was building from Hawkesbury to Ottawa, and on to Sudbury and Port Arthur. Two smaller railway companies, the Quebec & Lake St. John Railway, and the Irondale, Bancroft & Ottawa Railway, were branch lines into the hinterlands of the two central provinces. The CNoOR was building from Toronto to Ot-

tawa and making plans for a line from Toronto to Niagara Falls. Mackenzie was trying to persuade Laurier to lease the Intercolonial
Railway,[21] so as to provide a link with maritime components of the
Canadian Northern system. Construction of branch lines in the
prairies continued under the aegis of several small companies such
as the Alberta Midland Railway, the Canadian Northern Alberta
Railway, and the Canadian Northern Saskatchewan Railway.

By 1910, the fabled Northwest of canoes, fur traders, and Indians
had been pushed north, while in the southern, more populated
third of Canada railways had replaced canoes and grain had replaced furs as the West's chief export. Even the Hudson's Bay Company (HBC), once synonymous with furs and canoes, was quietly
moving into retailing and urban development. In 1869, as part of the
purchase price of Rupert's Land, the Canadian government had allowed the HBC to keep one-twentieth of its land in the fertile belt.
Capitalist values only developed land. Railways were able to arrange such things. In return for creating townsites on HBC land, the
Canadian Northern was given a 50 per cent share of that particular
section. Together the two companies sold this land and profited
from the sales. North Battleford and Fort Frances were joint HBC-
CNoR townsites. So were Athabasca Landing, Elphinstone, Drop-
more, and Demay.[22]

In older fur trade centres such as Edmonton and Winnipeg, the
HBC owned land on which the CNoR wanted to establish terminals.
In 1903 Mackenzie and Mann had purchased twenty-one acres of
HBC land in Edmonton, down on the flats adjacent to the old fort, to
be used as an entrance route to the city. The railway company also
purchased sixty-nine acres of HBC property for its station and yards.
In Winnipeg the same year, Mackenzie and Mann purchased a huge
piece of HBC riverfront property on Main Street adjacent to Upper
Fort Garry, for $350,000.[23] In 1909, with the purchase of the Bay's Fort
Garry Mill property, located on the Red River east of Portage and
Main, the CNoR's Winnipeg terminal property was assembled.[24] In
1911 the railway purchased HBC land in Prince Albert. In towns and
cities, the Hudson's Bay Company was developing retail stores,
which depended on railways to increase the number of consumers
and to transport manufactured goods from Toronto, Montreal, and
Winnipeg.

It was therefore not surprising that HBC's governor, Lord
Strathcona, should appoint William Mackenzie to its board in July
1910. His presence, Strathcona said, would assist the company in
making sound decisions, for Mackenzie knew Canada intimately.[25]

In June 1910 T.H. Skinner, a London-based director of the CPR, was elected deputy governor of the company.[26] The other three members appointed with Mackenzie – V.H. Smith of Morgan, Grenfell & Company, London; Robert Kindersley of Lazard Frères & Company, London; and Richard Burbidge, managing director of Harrods Ltd. – established strong links among retailing, banking, and transportation.[27]

As a member of the board, Mackenzie was finally able to settle a minor difference with the HBC. Since 1903 they had been dickering over the payment for the twenty-one acres in Edmonton. In Commissioner Chipman's worried letters from Winnipeg to London, one catches fleeting glimpses of Mackenzie putting off payment, bargaining for a better deal, promising to have McLeod, western manager of the CNoR, look into the matter, or promising to take the matter up with the board next time in London. Mackenzie insisted on paying the 1903 price of $7,000. The HBC wanted $3,000 per acre. (Thanks to the CNoR, Edmonton real estate values had risen considerably between 1903 and 1910.) Understandably, the Board of Railway Commissioners agreed with Mackenzie that the cost should be based on the price at time of purchase, and in November 1911 he paid the HBC $7,000.[28]

Although he opposed Laurier on reciprocity, Mackenzie remained on good terms with the Liberals; or perhaps it was the unpopular Liberals who needed to remain on good terms with Mackenzie. In 1911, the Dominion government guaranteed close to $40 million worth of construction bonds, mainly for the construction of the line from Montreal to Port Arthur.[29] In early May 1911 Mackenzie was off to London where he attended several meetings of the board of the Hudson's Bay Company to discuss real estate – land sales to churches, schools, and private citizens, and right-of-ways to all three Canadian transcontinentals. Mackenzie, Mann, and Horne-Payne, representing the board of the Canadian Northern Ontario Railway, held their customary fifteen-minute meeting to create a bond to construct the Toronto-to-Ottawa line.[30] Mackenzie met the press of London, and predicted that his railway would be completed from coast to coast by the end of 1914. During an economic boom, nothing seems impossible.

There was one other piece of business. 'Take the first steamer to London,' he wired Nordegg in Canada.[31] In 1910 Nordegg had discovered a coal vein in Alberta at a townsite named for him. He assumed that the mine would belong to the German Development Company, but Mackenzie claimed that the 1909 agreement gave 50 per cent of new fields to Mackenzie, Mann & Company. In London, Mackenzie, Nordegg, the president of the GDC, and London bankers who handled Mackenzie's bonds almost came to blows discussing ownership and sale of the new mine, but the adamant Mackenzie won, after long, heated hours of noisy bargaining.

Mackenzie also won the epilogue to the main drama. The president of the GDC assumed that the Vancouver Island coal acquired by Canadian Collieries in January 1910 would be part of the same fifty-fifty deal which had benefitted Mackenzie, Mann and Company. Mackenzie said no, that the 'West' mentioned in the 1909 agreement did not include BC. Mackenzie and the president had a raging argument. (Mackenzie often forgot to follow the advice posted in the old CNoR station at Water and Main in Winnipeg: 'Let no angry word be heard' and 'take all things by the smooth handle.')[32] Mackenzie, Mann & Company retained complete control of Dunsmuir coal.

While in London Mackenzie attended the coronation of George V in Westminster Abbey on 23 June, one of scores of invited Canadians – Sir Wilfrid Laurier, Lord Strathcona, Whitney, Scott and other premiers, Colonel Denison, Sir Donald and Lady Mann, the Siftons, the Pellatts, Colonel Hughes, the Honourable J.H. Turner, the Honourable J.A. Lougheed, Sir Edmund Walker, and others, including the Honourable Adam Beck, who must have felt slightly uncomfortable among so many titled investors!

Mackenzie returned to Toronto on 5 July, and attended board meetings dealing with railways in Ontario, secret land purchases near Montreal, and utilities in Toronto and Winnipeg. He and Clifford Sifton, who invested in Mackenzie companies, were interested in an oil field in Alberta.[33] He travelled to the coast in September, and noted with pleasure the results of the Dominion election, which saw reciprocity defeated.

By the end of 1911, Sir William could boast that during the year Canadian Northern Railway companies had placed almost $55 million worth of securities on the London market, about 30 per cent of Canadian securities floated in London that year.[34] It was a massive sum, the equivalent in 1990s dollars of over $1 billion.[35] During the boom years, this debt caused few eyebrows to rise. After all, the debt would not have to be repaid for several decades. And the century belonged to Canada.

Between trips to and from London and points west and east in Canada, Mackenzie and his family played their social roles among the small coterie of businessmen, university professors, and esteemed visitors such as Rudyard Kipling, for whom Mackenzie named a town, settled by Hungarians, in southern Saskatchewan. The diaries of George Taylor Denison III, arch arbiter of things fine and correct, paint a vivid portrait of Toronto social life in pre-war days. The crusty old police magistrate, descended from Loyalists and a longtime member of Toronto society, could be merciless in describing the 'vulgar ostentation of the common rich.'[36] That the Mackenzies and other members of the Four Hundred lacked the attributes of the British aristocracy – generations of land, money, and breeding – did not matter. In a country as young as Canada, with families moving from shanties to mansions in one generation, the British model was irrelevant, except for the Denisons or descendants of the French seigneurs.

A model had once existed in a small European country. Pre-war Toronto society was ruled by a constantly shifting élite of merchants whose social position was dependent on income. It was thus similar to seventeenth-century Amsterdam, where a patrician élite created the world's first bourgeois state. Mackenzie's Toronto, like Rembrandt's Amsterdam, was a zesty city, constantly absorbing new members, sending forth its young men to serve in banks, businesses, and parliaments across the country. If these families decorated their fashionable houses with too many Dutch 'browns' and Rembrandt-type art, as artists A.Y. Jackson and Barker Fairley claimed, perhaps it was in unconscious recognition that their spiritual ancestors had resided not in Regency London but in seventeenth-century Amsterdam.

One lovely Indian summer day in the fall of 1911, Sir William stood at the south garden of Benvenuto. With his guests, the Denisons and a member of the House of Lords,[37] he surveyed the booming Toronto spread out below. Over to the west, Casa Loma was just beginning to rise above the ground. Straight ahead, they could see the gothic tower of University College, the pale green dome of the University of Toronto's Convocation Hall, and the steep roof of the Ontario Parliament in Queen's Park. Farther south, the tower of the city hall peered down Bay Street, which was becoming the financial centre of Toronto. The new neoclassical Bank of Toronto at King and Bay streets was barely visible. Mackenzie and Denison could point to several skyscrapers, many soaring church spires, and kilometres of streets lined with elms and maples, their brilliant reds and golds bathed in soft October sunlight. Beyond the sprawling and smoky Union Station on Front Street lay the harbour, sparkling in the mellow sunlight, the same harbour that seventy-five years earlier had welcomed the Scottish migrant John 'Mckenzy' and his family and connections.

CHAPTER TEN

'Honour'd of Them All,' 1912

If you move quickly enough, no one can define you.
(P.E. Trudeau, quoted by B.W. Powe, *The Solitary Outlaw* [1987] 100)

By 1912 Sir William Mackenzie had few detractors. A newspaper in New Orleans said that he and Mann were making Canada 'the country of the twentieth century.' In the British House of Commons he was hailed as 'an authentic specimen of the founders of a great new country, who knew no fear nor discouragement.' The governor of the Bank of England said that there were few men in England or elsewhere in his class. In 1912 the Royal Colonial Institute made him an honourary member; also in 1912 the Winnipeg *Free Press* called him a 'wizard financier' who crossed continents and oceans at lightning speed, at a moment's notice. 'When he spoke of the completion of the CNoR from coast to coast within the next two years,' the paper went on, 'his face lit up with the enthusiasm of a boy.' His 'intense spirit of competition and achievement' was burning inside at a 'white heat.' 'If there were a competition at the Olympic Games for ocean travellers,' Toronto's *Mail and Empire* noted in 1912, 'Canada might well have entered Sir William Mackenzie with a fair expectation of winning first place.'

As if to prove the press correct, during the first two months of 1912 Mackenzie visited Paris, London, New York, Ottawa, Victoria, Winnipeg, Calgary, Halifax, and Quebec City; and also Montreal,[1] where he had been quietly buying up apple orchards on the northwest side of Mount Royal, as well as a downtown block of land bordered by La Gauchetière, Sainte Catherine, Mansfield, and Sainte Monique (today the site of La Gare Centrale, Le Reine Elizabeth, and Place Ville Marie).

Montreal presented special problems: how to bring the Ottawa-to-Montreal passenger line into the centre of a city whose splendid setting on a narrow strip of land nestled between mountain and river made entry of a third railway line almost impossible? The idea of a tunnel under the mountain was as audacious as it was preposterous. On 28 December the press in Montreal got word of the project, one of the most daring since Maisonneuve had founded the city in 1642. Mackenzie and Mann planned to poke a four kilometre tunnel through the volcanic rock of Mount Royal. At one end, on a downtown block they promised to build a large station and a palatial hotel; and at the other end of the tunnel, on the 4,800 acres of farms and apple orchards north of the mountain, a model town. A subterranean electric railway was to be constructed from Rivière des Prairies to downtown Montreal.[2] Financiers were pleased to support the project. In January J.P. Morgan's London investment house announced that it would underwrite $7.5 million worth of bonds for the mammoth project. The Canadian press was rapturous. Maps and illustrations began to appear on front pages across the country.

H.K. Wicksteed, chief engineer of surveys for Mackenzie, Mann and Company, conceived the tunnel idea. Mackenzie must have loved this daring, enchanting, exciting plan to transform Mount Royal into a magic mountain through which electric trains carrying travellers from Ottawa, Winnipeg, and Vancouver, even from the Far East, would glide into the centre of Montreal. The line would also provide a commuter service for downtown workers, thus transforming the farmland into a suburb, thereby netting a handsome profit for the stockholders of the Montreal Tunnel and Terminal Company and the Canadian Northern land company, which owned the orchards of Mount Royal.

Mackenzie was at the pinnacle of business life in Canada. By 1912 he had also reached the summit of his social life. In late April, before sailing again to England, he and Lady Mackenzie spent a weekend with the vice-regal family at Rideau Hall. Conversation no doubt included the Connaughts' imminent visit to Toronto to celebrate the Ontario Jockey Club's week of races and festivities in May, including the awarding of the King's Plate. From 16 to 27 May, the Mackenzies lent Benvenuto to the Connaughts. At Woodbine Race Track, the press noted the 'inclement weather' and race fans such as Lady Mackenzie 'in a blue tailormade [outfit] and hat with flowers.' In the quiet of his study at Heydon Villa, Colonel Denison noted each day's events: '19 May – Helen and I went to lunch with their Royal Highnesses at Benvenuto ...'; '21 May – a dully [sic] rainy day ... Helen, Clare and I went to the concert given by their R.H.'s at Benvenuto'; and '27 May – Helen, Clare and I went to the Duke and Duchess' garden party at Benvenuto – A very large crowd were there.'

One of the highlights at Benvenuto was its art collection, whose quality was largely due to Lady Mackenzie's 'exceptional judgment,'[3] and to her choice of agents in Toronto, Montreal, London, and Paris. When she travelled, she visited art galleries, and managed to avoid an excess of Dutch browns. Sir William had little time to purchase art, but Augustus Bridle, Toronto's social barometer, noted his 'strong taste' for art. He enjoyed the collection and took great pleasure in showing off his Italian, Dutch, French, British, and Spanish masters, including a couple of portraits by Reynolds; a portrait of Lady Westmoreland by Gardner; a portrait of a child by Hoppner, a contemporary and rival of Sir Thomas Lawrence, purchased in 1896 at Christie's in London; and a painting by Fragonard, whose canvasses sold for up to $100,000 in 1912, and who remains admired today. The Mackenzies' Canadian collection included Lucius O'Brien's Canterbury scene, purchased by Lady Mackenzie in 1894; and Otto Jacobi's *The Gipsy Children* and Homer Watson's pastoral landscapes, purchased by Sir William in the 1890s through Charles Porteous, who had acted as an agent for artists of the period. Frederick Verner's *Herd of Buffalo Feeding in a Marshland* and Paul Peel's *Still Life*, winner of a gold medal at the Chicago Exposition of 1893, were also on display. George Inness, an American railway artist, was represented by *Evening Landscape*. For book lovers, Benvenuto's library boasted a fine collection, many leather bound, including *The Chronicles of Canada*, illustrated by C.W. Jefferys; *Canadian Scenery*, illustrated by W.H. Bartlett; a four-volume biography of Napoleon Bonaparte; and a ten-volume set of the works of Guy de Maupassant.[4]

The Princess Patricia, daughter of the Duke and Duchess of Connaught, grew a bit bored by horses, speeches, and art. When the vice-regal couple was visiting the York Club and Convocation Hall, or laying the cornerstone of Grace Church on the Hill, the Mackenzie daughters – Ethel, Katharine, and Trudie – would quietly return to Benvenuto to join the Princess for a smoke in the leather-and-oak smoking room. Neither the press nor Colonel Denison got wind of it.[5] On 27 May, after the departure of garden party guests – the Aemilius Jarvises, the A.A. Macdonalds, the William Mulocks, Lieutenant Governor and Lady Gibson, Principal Hutton, the J.K. Rosses, the Denisons, Oslers, Cassels, and Nordheimers, among others – the Connaughts said goodbye and presented their hosts with a sterling silver champagne cooler, engraved on one side with the vice-regal coat of arms and on the other side with the message, 'To Sir William Mackenzie and Lady Mackenzie from Field Marshall

HRH Duke of Connaught KG, Governor General of Canada, and HRH Duchess of Connaught, May 1912.'[6]

A few days later, in early June, Mackenzie sped out to the west coast to discuss railways with Premier McBride. In Edmonton he called on Premier Arthur Sifton, whose government had recently incorporated the Canadian Northern Western Railway Company to build over 2,000 kilometres of branch lines in Alberta.[7] In Saskatchewan Premier Scott was asking for another mandate from voters who hungered for more surveying, grading, and tracklaying. From Moose Jaw a Liberal candidate wrote to James Calder, Minister of Railways for the province, that 'if the CNoR intend to be one particle of good to us, now is the time and not a month from now.' On 11 June Calder transmitted the message to Mackenzie in Regina. Mackenzie promised to have the grading near Gravelbourg started immediately.[8]

Mackenzie raced back to Toronto. Grace and her first-born, Guillaume, had arrived from Paris to spend the summer in Toronto and at Balsam Lake.[9] Mackenzie was always enormously fond of his children and grandchildren. One day he strolled out the front entrance of Benvenuto, under the broad *porte-cochère* and onto the expansive lawns, where Mabel's son, Gilbert Griffin, and Alex's son, Bill Mackenzie, were launching a toy boat in the large fountain. He watched them with great interest for a few minutes, then asked in his soft musical lilt, 'And just what do you think you're doin'?' The two boys knew how much he loved them. They could see the ironic twinkle in his eyes. He forgave them even when they broke the seals on a rare collection of single malt Scotch carefully hidden at Benvenuto.

On 18 June, Mackenzie attended his wife's garden party,[10] and two days later presided over a meeting of shareholders of the new Canadian Northern Western Railway.[11] A few days later, on the morning of 26 June, Lady Mackenzie and he were off to Montreal where they boarded the *Royal George*. On board was the prime minister, on his way to the Imperial Conference in London.[12] The two men admired each other. Mackenzie had helped Borden to defeat Laurier and reciprocity the previous September. Eighteen of his Toronto colleagues had signed a manifesto against reciprocity in February 1911. Although Mackenzie's name was not among the eighteen, he had expressed himself publicly against reciprocity two weeks earlier in an interview with London's *Standard of Empire*. Rumour had it that Canadian Northern money was behind the Toronto Manifesto. Borden benefited from Mackenzie's financial advice, and had investments in at least one of Mackenzie's companies. And if Borden in 1903 and 1904 had advocated government ownership and operation of railways, he was sufficiently pragmatic to change his mind now that privately owned railways were paying their way.

The next day the ship reached Quebec City where the Chateau Frontenac then the Citadel and Lower Town came into view. It docked to take on more passengers and mail. Then at 4:40 pm, the *Royal George*, looking as if it had just sailed out of J.E.H. MacDonald's poster, eased its way into the St. Lawrence, past the village of Sainte Petronille on l'Ile d'Orléans, where Mackenzie had once spent a few days with Charles Porteous, whom he rarely saw now.

It was Borden's birthday. Mackenzie arranged for the passengers aboard the *Royal Edward* to send congratulatory telegrams to the prime minister as the two ships passed each other beyond Newfoundland. During the next two days the two men spent many happy hours at the bridge table, and they enjoyed shuffleboard with Maude Williams, Donald Mann's sister-in-law; Mrs. Hazen, wife of Borden's Minister of the Marine; Mrs. Nicol Kingsmill; and Borden's wife, Laura. Borden, Mackenzie, and fellow passengers celebrated Dominion Day with a concert and a 'patriotic meeting.' The *Royal George* was in daily communication with Canada and the world. On 3 July the ship's daily broadsheet published news of the devastating cyclone that had pounded Regina three days earlier.

On board with Borden were cabinet ministers Pelletier, Doherty, and Hazen. At some point, perhaps during a game of bridge, J.D. Hazen had a word with Mackenzie. Would he be interested in helping a friend of Hazen's, the owner of the troubled Saint John Street Railway? Hazen stated a price. Too high, Mackenzie told him.[13] The scene is indicative of the casual relationship between business and politics during the early twentieth century, and reminds one of Toronto in the 1890s, when aldermen petitioned businessmen to lift them out of insolvency. In view of the persistent low returns on investment of the Saint John company, under 3 per cent,[14] Mackenzie's decision was sound.

Borden and Mackenzie no doubt discussed Imperial defence, the main topic at the upcoming Imperial Conference. The Navy Question (the 'comedy' of the Navy Question, Rupert Brooke called it),[15] was one of those issues that periodically provoke frenzied debate among Canadians, and which non-Canadians find amusing, perplexing, or dull. The issue had been a factor in Borden's victory in 1911, when a majority of voters rejected Laurier's compromise of a Canadian navy to be used by Britain only during war. Borden's proposal of an outright cash donation to the British navy also incensed some voters, especially many French Canadians, but it pleased many others, especially the business community, which feared the strength of the German navy.

While they took in the sea air out on the decks, or sank back into the comfortable maroon-coloured leather armchairs in the ship's smoking room, Mackenzie no doubt discussed with Borden some of his own ideas about a Canadian navy. He and other Toronto businessmen, including Joseph Flavelle, D.B. Hanna, Edmund Walker, and J.E. Atkinson of the Toronto *Star* were searching for compromise. The Toronto group hoped to make contact with other business groups across the country, both Liberals and Conservatives, to encourage the government to contribute to the British navy, but also to make plans for a genuinely Canadian navy.[16] This business proposal was an amalgam of Liberal and Conservative navy policies. It may have been a response to the alienation of French Canada, which might have accepted financial contribution to an Imperial navy if a Canadian navy were used only for Canadian defence. More likely the proposal implied business fears that the German navy might threaten London's role as a financial centre.

The *Royal George* landed on 4 July at Bristol where Mackenzie was met by James Dunn. From 1909 to 1911, Dunn had underwritten several of Mackenzie's securities, including Canadian Collieries and the Canadian Northern Pacific Railway. Dunn had such faith in the future of the Canadian Northern Railway that in 1910 he had wanted to purchase R.J. Mackenzie's 10 per cent share of stock, hoping to sell it in the next two or three years, when it would doubtless be worth a great deal on the open market.[17]

Most passengers embarking at Bristol had no idea that Mackenzie was on his way to London to create what was to become one of the most successful and prosperous Canadian-owned corporations on foreign soil. During one of their private conversations, Mackenzie and Borden had evidently discussed the large holding company that would unite Canadian companies in Rio de Janeiro and São Paulo. Other than that, the only signs of something momentous were a few cryptic telegram messages between São Paulo, London, and Toronto. Mackenzie and Dunn were about to create Brazilian Traction.

Since 1899 Mackenzie and his Toronto and Montreal colleagues had been investing in street railways, telephones, electric lights, and gas in the two major urban centres of Brazil.[18] Mackenzie's role, as usual, was in promoting the young companies and raising the investment capital in Canada and London, while other men, particularly the American engineer F.S. Pearson and the Canadian lawyer from Kincardine, Alexander Mackenzie (no relation to William Mackenzie) performed managerial, engineering, and public relations tasks on the scene in Brazil.

Frustratons in Birmingham and Toronto, together with success in Winnipeg, had taught Mackenzie and colleagues the benefits of gaining monopoly control of utilities under one large company. And that they did, first in each city. In April 1899 Mackenzie had the São Paulo Railway Light and Power Company incorporated at Queen's Park. A Canadian charter was desirable because it created more investor confidence than a Brazilian charter, and entailed less government scrutiny than a British charter. It gave the company power to operate tramways, lighting, telegraphs, gas, and telephones, and to generate and transmit electrical power. The legal genius of Z.A. Lash ensured that the combination was right.

The other half of Mackenzie's strategy was the successful floating of the company using large amounts of investment money. Making a market for stocks and bonds was no easy task, given the highly speculative nature of the project in a distant land and the immature and volatile nature of the Canadian capital market in 1899.[19] In order to reduce the enormous financial risks involved in handling large Brazilian investments, Mackenzie once again turned to syndicate financing, which spread the risk among individuals representing secure companies, banks, and brokerage houses. The more varied the sources of capital represented by men such as Flavelle of National Trust, Pellatt of Pellatt and Pellatt, and Horne-Payne of British Empire Trust, the greater the possibilities for raising capital. The financing of Brazilian ventures thus followed patterns created earlier in Canadian cities.

The Light, as the São Paulo venture soon came to be known, began to construct its first street car line in 1899. It also constructed a large generating plant at Hell's Gate and absorbed rival utilities companies such as a French-owned, mule-drawn tramway company. In 1900, provisional directors resigned, and William Mackenzie became president with Fred Nicholls as his vice president. (At the time, Nicholls was still president of the Canadian Northern Railway.) In 1902, shares of the once worthless common stock were traded publicly for the first time, reaching $108 by April of that year and rising to $145 in 1906. Even during the recessions of 1903 and 1907, the stock held its own because Mackenzie and the syndicate refused to sell them, thereby creating the illusion that it was unassailable.

In 1904 the Canadians obtained a Canadian charter for Rio de Janeiro Light & Power Company. William Mackenzie's name, together with the success of São Paulo, facilitated the sale of bonds in North America and Europe. In spite of the recession of 1907–8, Rio Light managed to expand, absorb competitors, and consolidate to become as successful as its counterpart in São Paulo. In London, Paris, and Brussels, Mackenzie's boundless energy convinced bankers such as Monty Horne-Payne, James Dunn, and Alfred Lowenstein, a principle shareholder in one of the companies absorbed by Rio Light, that Rio and São Paulo bonds were moneymakers for them and investors. Thus the two companies attracted investors from North America, Britain, and Europe, and by 1912 Brazilian affairs were most successful.

Brazilian Traction, Light and Power Company was created in 1912 in anticipation of the same problems that Mackenzie and his utilities partners were experiencing with 'people's power' in Ontario. In Brazil the 'people' were content with transportation and communications networks controlled by Canadian gringos. But just in case a Brazilian 'Beck' arose, a large and powerful off-shore holding company would be prepared to battle the potentially crippling effects of Brazilian nationalism, populism, and restrictive regulation.

In his desire to keep the deal as secret as possible, Mackenzie forgot to keep the Bank of Commerce, an important source of loan money for the new company, fully informed. In a panic, Dunn sent him a memorandum on 8 July. (He may have been unable to reach Mackenzie by telephone, or he may have considered the telephone no guarantee of secrecy.) He had just received a telegram from Pearson in Brazil; Mackenzie was told to inform the bank about the participation of Alfred Loewenstein and the exact nature of the exchange of old shares for new.[20] (Mackenzie probably went to his grave quite unaware of how much perspiration fell from the brows of his colleagues, his office staff, and especially his wife and family, so that his empire could function as expeditiously as it did.)

On 12 July 1912 Brazilian Traction was incorporated by the Canadian Parliament, and given vague powers to amalgamate with other companies that had similar transportation and communication purposes; those unnamed companies were, of course, the São Paulo and Rio companies. The new holding company was capitalized at $120 million, an indication that its directors had something grand in mind. On 15 July the new company was presented to the public. Brazilian Traction shares replaced those of the older companies at a rate of exchange whose generosity encouraged the rapid trade of old for new. On 15 July Fred Pearson announced that Mackenzie would be president, with himself as chairman. Both names instilled immediate confidence. Other well-known men – Alexander Mackenzie, Horne-Payne, Pellatt, Van Horne, E.R. Wood, D.B. Hanna, and the Lashes, Z.A. and his son, Miller – were also on the board. To expedite the exchange, broker Sir Henry Pellatt, and bankers Dunn and Loewenstein were paid handsomely with shares. As usual, money bought favourable newspaper publicity.

Shareholders responded quickly and positively. By 23 July, when it was obvious that the exchange would be a success, Mackenzie informed the prime minister that everything was moving 'satisfactorily.' By March of the following year, 98 per cent of existing shares of Rio and São Paulo Light had been turned in. Brazilian Traction, Light & Power Company, had made a successful beginning.[21] The holding company would last half a century under that name, and several more decades as Brascan Limited, with its headquarters in Toronto.

During Mackenzie's twenty days in London, he tended other financial and business matters. He attended two directors' meetings of the Hudson's Bay Company[22] and dealt with several issues of bonds.[23] Mackenzie's office in Bond Court House, Walbrook, between London Bridge and St. Paul's, was always busy during his visits to London. Bankers and businessmen called. Dr. George Parkin, Canada's 'Evangelist of Empire,' dropped by on 18 July. Mackenzie had known Parkin since the 1890s when he was principal of Toronto's Upper Canada College and R.J. Mackenzie was a student there. Mackenzie was out. Parkin left a note recommending a young man for a position in some part of Mackenzie's empire. Mackenzie's reply to Parkin the next day was typical. He would be pleased to see the young man if he was willing to 'take his chance of catching me either at the office or at the Savoy. I am unfortunately a little uncertain of my movements ...'[24]

Near the end of July, Sir William and Lady Mackenzie, with the Griffins (Scott had been appointed London manager of the Canadian Northern Steamship Company in 1910), made the crossing from Bristol to Halifax, and on to Toronto. Martin Nordegg travelled with them. In 1912 Nordegg established his office at the Toronto Railway Chambers, down the hall from Mackenzie's.[25] In spite of Mackenzie's tough bargaining techniques, Nordegg continued to admire him and to enjoy his company.

Mackenzie did have his critics, and they seemed to live mainly in Toronto. Council continued to demand that the Toronto Railway Company expand into all annexed areas by building new lines and by amalgamating with its suburban lines within the expanded boundaries of Toronto. Most of the annexed neighbourhoods were served by one of Mackenzie's street railway companies, either the Toronto & York or the Toronto Suburban, but council wanted to provide Torontonians with access to the centre of Toronto at a single fare in order to develop outlying areas. The company, of course, always appeared stingy and uncaring. But often the push for extensions was made by self-styled reformers, one of whom was Chief Billy Maclean, who happened to own a large chunk of real estate called Donlands, on Danforth Avenue east of the Don Valley.[26] Without trolley service, Maclean's land was of little value. It was enough to make Maclean a reformer. A militant reformer. And hell hath no fury like a self-righteous land speculator denied his trolley!

Council wanted to buy a few kilometres of Toronto & York lines running through areas annexed after 1891, and existing evidence suggests that Mackenzie welcomed the city's proposal.[27] Mackenzie and Mayor Hocken had already had amicable discussions, and Mackenzie offered to sell the TRC, the price to be set by mutual agreement or by arbitration.[28] Unfortunately Hocken could not persuade council, which voted down the sale[29] and began to make plans for a municipally owned 'Civic Railway' to run on the Danforth, east of Broadview. (In 1910, Danforth Avenue was not accessible by road from Bloor.) In April 1913 Mackenzie again offered to sell both the Toronto Railway Company and the Toronto Electric Light Company to the city for $30 million. Council gave Mayor Hocken authority to deal with Mackenzie, and in July 1913 the two men signed a draft agreement that the city would buy the Toronto Railway Company as well as portions of radials within the 1913 boundaries of Toronto. Engineers and consultants agreed that the properties were worth the asking price. Council, however, voted down a proposal to submit the Hocken-Mackenzie agreement to the ratepayers, fearing that if approved, the agreement might entangle the city with EDCO, which supplied power to the Toronto Railway Company.[30] The civic will was therefore never tested.

Admittedly there were problems, some serious, such as the riots of December 1910, when the TRC introduced a pay-as-you-enter (PAYE) system. The company was not, however, in a 'permanent state of siege,' as Professors Armstrong and Nelles have argued.[31] It continued to function as well as, and perhaps better than, any other trolley system. In August 1910 two New York consultants observed that the Toronto system was among the best in North America.[32] In 1911 a judge of the Ontario Court of Appeal claimed that the company had one of the best safety records on the continent.[33] From 1910 to 1912, the company continued to expand within old boundaries, adding forty-two kilometres of track and a hundred new cars.[34] Labour-management relations were good. New wage agreements were arrived at without strikes.[35] And the TRC continued to be profitable.[36]

Other Mackenzie electric railways – the Toronto & York, Toronto Suburban, Toronto Eastern, and the Schomberg & Aurora Railway – continued to push out to the hinterlands of Ontario, to Bowmanville on the east, Guelph on the west, and Collingwood and Pefferlaw in the north. Plans were being made to link cities as far away as London and Windsor to Toronto by means of electric railways, all part of the Mackenzie empire.[37] An ecologically sensible transportation system was being created in southern Ontario. At the same time, however, asphalt pavements and the internal combustion engine were growing in popularity.

Magic, masks, and theatre continued to characterize the battles between Beck and Mackenzie. Construction of Ontario Hydro lines went ahead and its power reached Berlin in October 1910 and Toronto in May 1911, five years after Mackenzie hydro first reached the city. In October 1911 Whitney made plans, without consulting Beck, to disband the commission and turn the hydro question over to a government department,[38] only to have Beck put a stop to his plan.[39]

Although the premier could wax wrathful at the advertising campaign waged by private power interests against his government, his personal relationship with Mackenzie and other utilities' entrepreneurs continued to be remarkably warm in private. He enjoyed their companionship at the York Club in Toronto and at Clifford's Inn in London, where Sir Henry Pellatt had established a club for members of the Society of Knights Bachelor.[40] From time to time, Mackenzie seemed to be defending the premier against criticism from the financial press, and even from his own colleagues.[41] It was in the midst of the power debate that Whitney granted the Canadian Northern Ontario Railway two million acres of agricultural land. Whitney and Mackenzie argued from similar points of view on reciprocity in 1911. In the Whitney papers, there are friendly letters from Scott Griffin and Sir Henry Pellatt. Had Beck not been so strong, Whitney and Mackenzie might have worked out a viable compromise.

To counter Beck and Hydro's growing power, Mackenzie and colleagues decided to strengthen the Toronto Power Company. In April 1911 it acquired control of the Toronto Electric Light Company,[42] thus preventing the Toronto Hydro Company, controlled by the municipality of Toronto, from acquiring it. Toronto Hydro, which bought power from the Ontario Hydro Commission and sold it to Toronto customers, had offered only $125 per share, $10 less than the TPC's offer. Mackenzie and colleagues were certain that because of up-front costs (construction of a distribution system within Toronto, for instance), Toronto Hydro would not be able to offer lower rates than those of TELC, especially if voters and taxpayers refused further subsidization of Beck's schemes.

In 1911 and 1912, however, TELC did lose business to Toronto Hydro, which offered rates at less than cost.[43] Pellatt and Mackenzie took steps to make the newly consolidated private companies more cost-effective. In Pellatt's delicately phrased letter of 7 November 1911 urging Mackenzie to fire EDCO's engineer and place TELC's engineer in charge of both companies, there are hints that the old Mackenzie, too rushed to consider organizational details yet keen to tinker, still had to be kept at bay.[44] The reorganization must have worked, for TELC grew after 1912 and remained a tough competitor for Toronto Hydro.

Outside Toronto, the battle with Beck for supplying power to Ontario's towns and small cities was gradually being lost, as more and more municipalities voted to buy from Hydro. On 1 January 1912, thirty-eight additional municipalities voted to join Ontario Hydro, though others – Lindsay, Peterborough, and Kingston – refused, content for several more years to buy power from private or municipal sources.[45]

Despite draconian legislation in 1912 giving the Hydro Commission extensive expropriation powers,[46] Mackenzie was by no means finished. The combination of electric railways in Toronto and southern Ontario with lighting in Toronto meant that in 1912 the Electrical Development Company continued to sell more power (27,000 horsepower) than Beck's Hydro Commission (18,000 horsepower).[47] Ontario municipalities that had opted to be part of the Hydro network – mostly towns and small cities – would not be large consumers of electricity for years. The important battle was in Toronto, where the largest consumer of power was the Toronto Railway Company, which of course bought from Mackenzie's EDCO.

On 25 June 1912, the day before he and Lady Mackenzie left Toronto to join Borden on the *Royal George*, Mackenzie scored a major coup: he acquired control of Dominion Power & Transmission Company, a $25 million holding company controlling fourteen subsidiaries, including a transmission line company, generating plants, and electric railroads. The new company would allow Mackenzie to link Niagara Falls to Toronto and Detroit by means of electric railways,[48] whose source of power would be EDCO. A few months later, Beck belatedly decided that Hydro also should get into the business of urban and inter-urban electric railways.[49]

The year ended badly for Beck and the Hydro Commission. A study carried out for private American electrical utilities concluded that regulated private power would have provided power more economically than the Hydro Commission; that Hydro's lower rates were illusory because it paid no taxes and maintained no sinking fund; and that Hydro's costs had been enormous, while its benefits to Ontario were unevenly distributed.[50]

By contrast, Winnipeg utilities stirred few emotions. The trolley system expanded north, south, and west from the centre, including, in 1912, a line from Elm Park down Pembina Avenue to the six-year-old Agricultural College (later part of the University of Manitoba). In 1912 the Broadway line was extended west to Sherbrook, and new cars were placed in service. A brief strike in 1909 was settled peacefully by a board of conciliation, which included the Reverend Charles Gordon and D.J. O'Donoghue. A second strike in December 1910 resulted from the firing of four conductors and motormen who were caught drinking in saloons while in uniform, but it was relatively peaceful, except for one car burnt at Logan and Arlington by 200 bridge workers not connected with the strikers. They were apparently protesting against rescheduling during the strike.

The company's readiness to expand through thinly populated areas such as Pembina Avenue is indicative of good relations with the city and province. Premier Roblin and the Honourable Robert Rogers supported Mackenzie. Each man was a shareholder in WERC, and each enjoyed the perquisites of association with Mackenzie, including invitations to the launching of the *Royal George*. Even from 1906 to 1912, during the prolonged legal debate on the question of Winnipeg Electric Railway's right to bring power into the city from the Pinawa power plant, Mackenzie remained on friendly terms with Winnipeg mayors. In 1911, while in London for the coronation of George V, Mayor Sandford Evans and Mackenzie worked out an agreement by which the city would purchase Winnipeg Electric Railway for $250 per share.[51] Winnipeg council, however, voted down the deal.

In October 1911, when Winnipeg Hydro first received public power from its plant at Pointe du Bois, it offered rates below cost. Mackenzie's WERC followed suit, and the competition threatened to ruin both companies. A compromise was found. To regulate the power question, the Roblin government created the Public Utilities

Commission, which made both WERC and Winnipeg Hydro accountable (unlike Ontario Hydro) to government. The commission persuaded the two companies to share poles and to arrive at equitable, and profitable, rates that turned out to be lower than Beck's minimum rates in Ontario.[52]

By 1912 WERC was very profitable, growing from ninety-eight kilometres in 1909 to 128 kilometres in 1912. Its return on investment ranged from 11 to 15 per cent. Its dividends, at 10 to 12 per cent, were 4 per cent higher than TRC dividends, a sign that company management had more confidence in the profitability of WERC than in the much-harassed TRC. Mackenzie himself made money from the Winnipeg company. In 1909 he held 18,790 shares (out of a total of 60,000). The 10 per cent dividend gave him an income of $187,960. The same year, his 2,164 TRC shares (out of a total of 80,000) provided him with a dividend payment of only $13,525. In 1911 a combination of dividend income and sale of shares brought Mackenzie over $1 million from WERC,[53] proof of avarice or proof of a well-run company, depending on the theoretical bent of the historian.

A disaster at Pinawa was the only major problem. On 23 November 1909, as afternoon darkness was settling over the city's rush hour, Winnipeg's lights flickered and went out. Trolleys stopped on their tracks. Passengers waited patiently. A penstock had ruptured, flooding the generator. The damage was serious. The city slowed to a crawl for almost two weeks until Pinawa power was restored. When Mackenzie passed through Winnipeg the following January, the Pinawa plant was confidently pumping power into the city.

In early 1912 Mackenzie appears to have had dealings with E.B. Reese, a representative of Morgan interests in New York. Apparently Reese was trying to create a holding company, the Winnipeg Electric Company, a Manitoba version of Brazilian Traction, to consolidate Mackenzie's Winnipeg and Manitoba power empire. The New Yorker may have been acting at the behest of Mackenzie, who was in Winnipeg at the end of January, three weeks before the legislature began deliberations on the 'Reese Bills.' The holding company was not created.[54] Nevertheless, few Winnipeggers in 1912 could ignore the success of Mackenzie's power and transportation companies, for the city's downtown was anchored by the magnificent neoclassical Union Station, fit for a Roman emperor, at Main and Broadway, and by the Winnipeg Electric Railway Chambers, a terra cotta Florentine palazzo fit for a prince, on Notre Dame near Portage. Both buildings remain a proud part of the city today.

By the fall of 1912 Mackenzie was an enthusiastic, slightly spoiled youngster playing with a shiny railway set placed on a map of Canada. If he wanted to link Edmonton and Victoria, it was done. Quebec to Montreal and Ottawa? Or Ottawa and Toronto and Niagara Falls? Done. Ottawa and the Lakehead? Most certainly. Every wish came true as his tabletop toy railway set grew from coast to coast.

. Every fifteen kilometres or so, he created more towns. 'We will open a number of new towns this year and there will be excellent opportunities to engage in business and to buy lots that are likely to increase in value,' Mackenzie informed passengers in broadsheets printed aboard the *Royal George* and the *Royal Edward*. On the prairies, workers grading roadbeds and laying tracks were scarcely finished each section before their temporary living quarters in cabooses or canvas tents were joined by stately, bright-red grain elevators, and by a station, hotel, bank, restaurant, general store, bowling alley, barber shop, and a few wooden shacks. Near Zealandia, on the Goose Lake line southwest of Saskatoon, one brick farmhouse boasted indoor plumbing, a piano, and other 'city conveniences' before the first train arrived.[55] Sometimes the Canadian Northern's advertising, which claimed that the railway had 'pushed the frontier off the map and set the comforts of modern life in its place,' was only slight exaggeration.

As in Manitoba earlier, the names of new towns suggest the sweep of Mackenzie's empire and his personal connections. Kindersley, Saskatchewan, the town that sprang from nothing to 150 buildings in thirty-five days in the fall of 1909,[56] was named for his friend, Sir Robert Kindersley of the Hudson's Bay Company; Camrose, Alberta, called Sparling at its founding in 1905, was renamed for Cameron and Rose McKenzie, whose father, Big Archie McKenzie, completed the Vegreville-Stettler line through Camrose in 1911.[57] Hanna, Alberta, was named after D.B. Hanna; Tisdale, Saskatchewan, for Jo Wheeler's husband; Laura, Saskatchewan, for Prime Minister Borden's wife; and Maymont, Saskatchewan, for Mackenzie's niece, May Montgomery, stepmother of Lucy Maud Montgomery. Wicksteed, McRae, Hanna, Moore, Annesley, and Davidson had their names affixed to streets in the town of Leaside, where Borden's middle name, Laird, also became a street name. Saskatchewan has a town of Canora (CAnadian NOrthern RAilway); the Town of Mount Royal and Winnipeg have streets of the same name. The Montreal townsite also has a Kirkfield Street, and a short, obscure street called 'Mackenzie.' No Canadian town is named in honour of Sir William Mackenzie.

Mackenzie's palatial hotels and railway stations inspired great awe. Designed by New York architects and opened in 1910, the Prince Arthur Hotel on Cumberland Street, Port Arthur, was six storeys high. Its exterior, of Indiana limestone and brick, was decorated with cornices and pilasters; its interior was a tasteful mix of marble, wrought iron, and beamed ceilings. Seventy-nine of its 103 bedrooms boasted en suite bathrooms, a relatively novel idea in 1910. The hotel featured an enclosed rooftop deck, promenade, and palm garden, which provided guests with spectacular views of the twin cities, the bay, and Sleeping Giant.[58] The equally impressive Prince Edward Hotel, with an adjoining station, opened in Brandon in 1911.

In 1910 Saskatoon could boast a handsome two-storey station on 1st Avenue. Its prominent central tower spoke of power and authority; its turrets were Scottish baronial and its pyramidal roofs, French Chateau, a Canadian melange that could be seen in other stations such as the impressive Dauphin station (1912). Calgary's handsome stone station was also built in 1912. Dozens of other stations from Sangudo to Tisdale to Notre Dame des Anges were built in this boom period from 1909 to 1912.

The brightest jewel in the crown was Winnipeg's Union Station, which opened in June 1912. Whenever Mackenzie passed through Winnipeg, he must have revelled in its magnificence: a copper dome glimpsed from St. Boniface across the river, up and down Main Street, and from elegant tree-lined Broadway Avenue; skylights and windows, which allowed rich prairie light to play on interior marble; and the enormous Tyndal stone archway off Main Street, which welcomed travelling salesmen, harvesters, immigrants, and politicians. The building's understated elegance and clean classical lines proclaimed stability and longevity, and soon attracted international acclaim.

In August 1912 Mackenzie announced in Vancouver that the Canadian Northern would push back the sea at False Creek in order to create new land for a station in the grand neoclassical style. It would cost $10 million and would be reached via a tunnel costing $1 million per mile. For Montreal, Mackenzie announced a new and magnificent station to be modelled after New York's Pennsylvania Station. Next to the station was to be a palatial hotel on the site of the Bath Hotel on Dorchester (René Levesque) Boulevard. In Winnipeg a $2 million hotel at Water and Main would replace the old Hotel Manitoba, Winnipeg's grandest until it was destroyed by fire in the late 1890s. In 1911 the Canadian Northern planned to build its Ottawa station on the west bank of the Rideau Canal, on the site of the old Bate warehouse, now the site of the National Arts Centre.[59]

Although as wealthy as Lord Strathcona, Sir James Ross, and Joseph Flavelle, Mackenzie was philanthopically conservative. He donated various amounts of money to many projects including hospitals in Winnipeg and Lindsay; he gave money for university scholarships in Toronto, and to build two churches and a school in Kirkfield. Other projects included the Regina Cyclone Fund, the YMCAS in Toronto and Winnipeg, the Victorian Order of Nurses, the King Edward Memorial Fund for Consumptives, and the Toronto Playgrounds Association. He may also have made a substantial donation to the building fund of Toronto General Hospital.[60] In 1913, he was appointed by the Whitney Government as one of its representatives on the board of the hospital[61] – another indication that some members of the government, including Whitney, continued to support Mackenzie in spite of battles with the Hydro Commission and Beck.

The Canadian Northern provided freight cars to transport relief supplies to fire victims in Chicoutimi (1912); it gave $25,000 to the McGill University Endowment Fund (1911), and $1,000 to the Lord Mayor of London's Titanic Relief Fund (1912). And Lady Mackenzie played roles in various organizations such as the IODE (Imperial Order Daughters of the Empire). Unfortunately Mackenzie and most of his colleagues did not follow the example of American millionaires in establishing permanent foundations to assist charities and the arts.

During the boom from 1909 to 1912, Mackenzie seemed to be everywhere. He spoke to the Canadian Club in Victoria in January 1910 on the subject of 'Canadian Northern Enterprises,' a topical talk, for Premier McBride had just won re-election on a platform of more Canadian Northern lines in BC. He oversaw the return to Winnipeg of the old *Countess of Dufferin*, which had been performing the ignominious role of shunting carloads of lumber in Mackenzie's Columbia River Lumber Company at Golden, BC.[62] In January 1911, a few days after being fêted in Toronto's newspapers on the occasion of his knighthood, Mackenzie clinched a huge real estate deal in Toronto that made him proprietor of a long block of stores on the south side of Queen Street at University Avenue, across from Osgoode Hall. At that time University Avenue went no further south than Queen.

Brilliant sunshine washed over his empire. From Berlin to São Paulo, from London to Victoria, he had become a name. In Brussels one evening in 1910, Martin Nordegg was entertained by a wealthy and world-weary Belgian bachelor in a luxurious apartment filled with art treasures, antique books, and pornography. The Belgian was not interested in investing in Canada until Nordegg casually mentioned the name of Sir William Mackenzie.

'Is that Mackenzie, the President of the Canadian Northern Railway?' the Belgian suddenly sat forward and asked. He was instantly interested in investing. The Mackenzie name had once again worked its magic.

During the fall of 1912, Mackenzie entertained English journalist and novelist Sarah Macnaughtan, who had come to see the country and to interview wealthy men such as Van Horne, Shaughnessy, Mann, Mackenzie, and Denison. While Rupert Brooke abhorred Canadian materialism, Macnaughtan revelled in it and invested money in real estate in Leaside, near Toronto, where a street was named for her. In her memoirs, published posthumously in 1920 as *My Canadian Memories*, she noted the Canadian expression, 'There's a Klondike in every man's brain; keep digging.' She noted also that by 1912 Canada had become aware of its past and enjoyed recounting its history.

In Mackenzie she found the perfect raconteur. At the rambling, timbered summer home on Balsam Lake, he reminisced on the broad verandah with its 'groups of chairs and swinging hammocks and tables piled with books.' As they chatted, water lapped gently against the low stone wall and, above, chattering chipmunks scampered along branches of towering fir trees. They continued their conversation while seated in wicker chairs on the deck of the *Wawinet*, which provided Macnaughtan with a view of 'tranquil sunsets which turned the shimmering gold of the water to silver green as the sun dropped quite suddenly behind the low-lying blue woods that fringed the shore.'

She admired the 'snug little houses and the well-kept gardens' of the new Kirkfield that had replaced the brawling log-shanty pioneer town. She liked the pretty Kirkfield Inn, a three-storey Swiss-style hotel decorated with Persian carpets, a grand piano, golfing pictures, and a billiard room. Lady Mackenzie had built the inn in 1912 on condition that the town vote against licensed hotels. It did. She tore down the two licensed hotels, which had been built by Mackenzie Brothers in the 1880s. Public drinking was banished. Memories of her licensed tavern in Donald, BC, were carefully tucked away. Her attempt to clean up the town, however, was only partially successful. The inn was so grand that the locals took their drinking elsewhere.

The novelist Gabriel García Marquez once said that 'the heart's memory eliminates the bad and magnifies the good, and that thanks to this artifice, we manage to endure the burden of the past.' During these leisurely chats with Macnaughtan, Mackenzie eliminated all harsh memories – the death of his mother, failures in the Klondike and Birmingham, and his periodic bouts with nervous exhaustion. He magnified his accomplishments, inventing a past that was as orderly, secure, and attractive as the new Kirkfield. He told her that he had never taken a holiday in twenty-one years and that he was immune to weakness; he exaggerated his role in putting out a lumbercamp fire in BC in the 1880s; he told her the old chestnut about purchasing the Qu'Appelle, Long Lake & Saskatchewan Railway during two hours of negotiations at Benvenuto in December 1906, and added that he had left for England later that same night.

'There are things that a man is afraid to tell even to himself,' Dostoevsky once wrote. 'Deprive the average man of his vital lie,' says a character in *The Wild Duck*, 'and you've robbed him of happiness as well.' In reshaping his past, Mackenzie was proving his membership in the human race. Mackenzie's successes and failures distinguished him from the crowd, and his tall tales suited his heroic stature. By 1912 he had become the 'Big Jim' of the myth brought from Maine to Kirkfield a quarter of a century earlier. Memory had become his shield, his 'form of self-protection,' to use Timothy Findley's phrase in *The Telling of Lies*. For a man accustomed to rearranging the landscape in order to lay a railway line here, to create a hydroelectric dam there, or to poke a tunnel through a mountain, this rearrangement of memory's landscape is scarcely surprising, as though he believed, like one of the characters in *The Peron Novel* that 'one has to put the mountains where one wants them.' Or as though he agreed with Michael Ondaatje, who claims in *Running in the Family* that 'a well-told lie is worth a thousand facts.'

Mackenzie even invented his mother. Lady Mackenzie hired three Scottish artists, the des Clayes sisters, to paint landscapes and portraits. Sir William's mother, Mary, died in 1852, leaving no photographic record. Gertrude des Clayes was shown photographs of Sir William's deceased sisters. She observed his daughters and granddaughters, and from this collage painted an idealized version of Mary Mackenzie. The successful entrepreneur, argues Michael Bliss in *Northern Enterprise*, is the product of a feckless father and 'the best mother who ever lived.'[63] The unambitious John Mackenzie fits the paradigm. So does Sir William's invention of his mother, who became in memory and on canvas the best mother he never knew. This vital lie in oil hangs today in the Los Angeles home of a descendant of Katie McTaggart, Sir William's eldest sister. The descendant is an actress who makes her living by turning illusion into reality. Or is it the other way around?

That evening, as Mackenzie recreated his past to Sarah Macnaughtan, he must have been aware that the skies were not entirely free of clouds, some of them darkening. After their cruise on the *Wawinet* host and guest returned to the big summer house. As darkness cast a shroud over the lake and the house, they sat watching the flames devour the crackling logs in the huge fireplace. Mackenzie mused that civilization could easily be destroyed by 'a horde of barbarians.'

He did not name the barbarians. The phrase, however, suggests that old doubts, suspicions, and fears were threatening to break their chains and descend from stuffy attics. There were ominous signs that his empire was crumbling. He was preoccupied with falling freight rates. The previous April, the Canadian Northern and the CPR had reduced rates on merchandise shipped between the Lakehead and major distributing centres in Saskatchewan and Alberta. These adjustments had become necessary when the Board of Railway Commissioners ruled that existing tariffs favoured Winnipeg merchants to the detriment of their counterparts in cities further west. Worse still, late in 1911 the board had responded to other complaints by launching a broader inquiry into western rates, which, Mackenzie feared, would produce even further reductions to match rates in Ontario and Quebec. Perhaps the CPR could operate on lower rates, but the CNoR could not, since its economic health was fragile. He would soon have to pay a visit to the prime minister.[64]

And then there was the war scare. What if it should turn into an actual war? More hordes of barbarians unleashed against his empire? War would cut off the money markets of London, Paris, Berlin, and Brussels. He had enjoyed the pomp of the vice-regal couple's visit the previous May, but their cross-country tour after leaving Benvenuto gave the impression of a general rallying his troops. Mackenzie himself had spoken publicly of the German threat to world stability and to Pax Britannica. Even as Sarah Macnaughtan was visiting Mackenzie, she was preparing a speech for delivery to the Winnipeg Canadian Club on 15 October. Her topic? The Balkan Wars.[65]

As they watched the fire burn down, Mackenzie may have reflected on the brevity of life and human relations. In 1909 May Montgomery had died in Prince Albert. Lady Mackenzie's aged mother, the gentle and unpretentious Hanora Merry, born in 1831 as the immigrant ship bearing her parents sailed into the Gulf of St. Lawrence, died in 1910, a couple of months before her granddaughters' flights over New York City. Matthew Perry, manager of the company farm at Dauphin, died in 1910. Dick Stovel, husband of Mackenzie's half-sister, Mary Jane, died in 1911 in a hospital in St. Paul. In 1911, Katie McTaggart died in her home on Colony Street, Winnipeg.[66]

After her glittering wedding and the birth of their first son, Grace's marriage was showing signs of strain. Might she end up like Trudie, whose conversion to the Church of England and marriage to Arthur Grantham had created family tensions and ended in divorce in 1911? Grantham, former purchasing agent for the Toronto Railway Company, remarried and become the successful co-owner of a large hardware business in Toronto. And then there was Rod and those Hollywood types – he had even married one of them – and horse racing and gambling dens. Oh, and that bordello in Winnipeg! And Joe. Poor Joe. Too much, too soon. He had even missed the sinking of the *Titanic* by getting drunk in Paris. If only Alex had lived.[67]

The charred remains of the logs in the fireplace began to shift and tumble. There was something ominous too, Mackenzie thought, in the robbery that had occurred in the *Atikokan* on 2 January 1911, the very day that his knighthood was announced in Canadian newspapers. Were the wealthy and powerful no longer accorded due deference? He had not stayed long at the Toronto celebrations marking his and Donald Mann's knighthood, for there was business in Ottawa. He fell into such a deep sleep en route that his staff let him sleep late on the morning of 2 January, as the private railway car rested in Ottawa. He rose at 10:00 am, dressed quickly, rolled a small packet containing twelve bills worth $500 each in his nightshirt, and tossed it onto the bed. He rushed out through the new Central Station and over to the office of the Honourable George Graham, Minister of Railways, to discuss a host of items including steamship connections through Hudson Bay. His porter found the bills, stole two of them, scattered the rest on the floor, then left the station. He was tracked down to Windsor, Ontario, by two of Mackenzie's detectives. Mackenzie took no action except to dismiss him. He tried to hush it up, but the press got wind of it three weeks later, while he was in England escorting Grace down the aisle of St. James, Spanish Place.[68]

The marriage into the de Lesseps family must have had an unsettling effect. Although the old Count Ferdinand was a hero in France for completing the Suez Canal in 1869, he had been convicted of bribery and fraud in 1892 in connection with the disastrous Panama

Canal project. Along with his son Charles and the famous engineer Eiffel, he had been sentenced to five years in prison. Title, money, and power could not save him. Money and power had not been enough to prevent the decline of the Dunsmuir family on the west coast; nor did it save the life of Charles Melville Hays, who went down with the *Titanic*. Even railway presidents were mortal. In the fall of 1912, Mackenzie's *Royal George* suffered a fate similar to that of the *Titanic* – it was damaged, though not irreparably, by a large rock off L'Ile d'Orléans.

The fire at Balsam Lake had all but died down. As he recreated his past to Sarah Macnaughtan, he could not help but be concerned about the state of the financial markets. In 1912 British investors grew reluctant to invest large sums in Canadian projects.[69] At the end of May 1912, the CNoR had attempted to float bonds valued at almost $7 million in London, but sold only 36 per cent of them. British bond holders, numbering between 40,000 and 50,000, were losing faith in Mackenzie's railway. To raise more money for his Montreal tunnel and station project, he had to float costly short-term securities, another sign that the markets were becoming wary of investing in long-term transportation projects.[70]

Host and guest bade each other good night. But sleep came with difficulty as Mackenzie thought of other problems – the need for economic protection, for instance. In July 1912 he had told the London *Standard* that the Empire should be bound closer by means of two Parliaments at Westminster, one for British local affairs and the other for Imperial matters such as the navy. Preferential tariffs should be placed on non-Empire imports, he believed.[71] In 1912 both the British Empire and his own needed protection.

At the same time, labour was showing signs of discontent. In March 1912 the American union Industrial Workers of the World, newly established in Canada, had organized a strike of several thousand Canadian Northern Pacific construction workers on the line between Kamloops and Hope. The railway company had brought in replacements from Vancouver and Seattle, and the strike had ended, after one month, but not without violence.[72]

The sinking of the *Titanic* in 1912 warned Edwardian optimists that just below the calm surface of civilization lay forces of destruction. The ideas of Freud and Einstein were beginning to challenge old certainties. Stravinsky's music, accompanied by Nijinsky's mad, acrobatic dancing, was redefining traditional harmony and mocking the soothing waltzes of Johann Strauss and Franz Lehar favoured by transatlantic steamships. Cubists were shunning traditional representation. The safe Dutch and Canadian landscapes that lined the walls of Benvenuto were slightly passé as a new age waited to be born. In 1912 the apparently invulnerable Mackenzie found himself in a confusing, ambivalent position. He and his trolleys and steamships and trains and electricity had played an important role in destroying the slower rhythms of the previous century. But change, as V.S. Naipaul points out in *Enigma of Arrival*, leads from creativity to decline to demise.

CHAPTER ELEVEN

Fading Star, 1913–15

[Sir William Mackenzie's] conception of constructing and operating a transcontinental railway was almost a dream; and yet it was a dream that in all probability would have become a reality had it not been for the outbreak of war.

(Robert Laird Borden, *His Memoirs* [1938] 2:60)

Photograph in Mabel's album: Armathwaite, Cumberland, England. The beautiful Lake District. Mabel, two of her young sons, Tony and Bill, and daughter Margaret pose for the camera. Nurse Stafford, a household servant, and a visitor stand stiffly behind the family. Little Margaret holds a kitten and a doll. A black doll. Mabel, pregnant with Peter, stares gloomily at her children. The children are unusually quiet. From the midst of grandchildren and servants peers the face of an old man. He is tugging on Tony's ears. The old man is Sir William Mackenzie. At age sixty-five, he looks haggard and worn. In the previous two years, he has aged twenty. It is Tuesday, 4 August 1914. The family's crystal set has been giving the news. The German army has crossed into Belgium. The German army refuses to withdraw. Britain and her Empire are at war with the Kaiser. 'I'm finished,' Sir William mutters. His face turns ashen.

Mabel never forgot that day. Six weeks later, Peter was born. Peter never forgot that day either, for Mabel told him the story many times during the next half-century. Peter also told the story.[1]

The war was not the sole cause of Sir William's financial problems. It merely exacerbated an already grievously over-extended transcontinental railway empire. Because its construction relied so heavily on debt financing, unprofitability was built into the Canadian Northern from the beginning.[2] By 1914 its earning capacity per mile was lower than that of its two main rivals.[3] Until the outbreak of the Great War, the company had always been able to pay operating expenses and bond interest, but the enormous principal of those bonds would come due one day, with small chance of being repaid, war or no war.

In 1913 railway-backed bonds became unmarketable, and even government-guaranteed bonds were selling for $65 to $70 for each $100 bond. In order to continue laying tracks, Mackenzie turned again to short-term, high interest loans. The CNoR and its sister companies had completed 2,400 kilometres, but there remained 2,712 kilometres of partially completed lines, between Ottawa and Toronto, Ottawa and Port Arthur, and Edmonton and Vancouver. In February 1913 Mackenzie had asked Borden for cash subsidies, arguing, correctly, that the Canadian Northern had received few subsidies.[4] Borden thought Mackenzie's request for $20 to $30 million 'well founded,'[5] and in June 1913 the Dominion government provided a cash subsidy of almost $16 million in return for 10 per cent or $7 million of the railway's common stock. Since this subsidy covered only a small portion of the remaining construction costs, Mackenzie returned to London in October and November 1913 in a futile attempt to float several issues of bonds.[6]

He was back in Canada to drive the last spike of the Canadian Northern Ontario line from Montreal to Port Arthur on New Year's Day 1914, at Little White Otter River, about 400 kilometres east of Port Arthur. The celebrations, beginning at midnight in Port Arthur, were reserved.[7] Further ballasting and bridge work prevented passenger and freight traffic for several more months. Throughout 1914 the Canadian Northern continued to rely on Great Lakes steamers and on the railway lines of the Canadian Pacific and the Grand Trunk to transport grain to Montreal.

A few days after last-spike ceremonies, Mann and Mackenzie were back in Borden's office in the Centre Block. Since government-guaranteed bonds were still not selling, they suggested a large loan. Borden promised nothing. The two men grew 'depressed and resentful.'[8] Their mood was probably more role playing. Their drama, however, was receiving less favourable reviews. Critics agreed with Sir Thomas Shaughnessy that the CNoR 'had pretty well drained the channels through which it might expect to secure any further important loans from the public.'[9]

The government of British Columbia did come through with another guarantee for a bond issue of $5 million, which brought the total BC guarantees to a remarkable $40 million – much greater than any other province,[10] prompting a west coast poet to voice alarm:

> If you're hard up for cash and the future looks blue;
> Don't go to your banker for a thousand or two;

But go to the Government. At least you can try it;
If you ask for enough they're sure to supply it.
This only applies if you're big speculators;
(Not a farmer who wants it to plant his pertaters)
Get after it then on a similar plan
To that of our friends, Mackenzie and Mann.[11]

The two men spent available money on main line construction, on branch lines already under construction, and on the Montreal tunnel project, much to the annoyance of prairie premiers, whose politics was railways 'and then more railways,' to use Premier Arthur Sifton's phrase. A politician who aligns himself with a corporation benefits by its success, Premier Scott lamented, 'but is sullied by its failure.'[12]

Even a scaled-down construction project would cost an estimated $100 million. The total available government-guaranteed securities amounted to less than $60 million. For public consumption, Mackenzie was his optimistic self. In early February he was in Winnipeg to attend the annual meeting of the Winnipeg Electric Railway. There was no crisis, he told reporters. He held up a large map of Manitoba, which showed Canadian Northern territory marked in red. 'Look how the population has followed the CNoR,' he told them. He was planning to build lines into the Interlake district. 'The public want these extensions,' he said. 'It opens up the country.' Financing further extensions was no problem. Why, a new bond issue of $6 million had been released that very day in London. His son, R.J., he told the reporters, had just returned after spending two years in California, where he had made millions in oil. He was to be appointed general manager of the CNoR, in charge of reorganizing all lines west of Port Arthur.[13] Times were tough, and Sir William was at his best, feeding journalists with fantasies of northward extensions and of hungry British investors.

He returned to Toronto, where on Monday evening, 16 February, the Winter Garden Theatre was officially opened. The theatre created the impression that the audience, while watching an illusion on stage, was sitting in a real garden. Outside, chilly winds blew down Yonge Street, past Dundas and Queen. Inside, walls were painted with the spring flowers of an English country garden. Support columns were disguised as tree trunks. For opening night, real leaves and boughs were hung from the ceiling, where electric lights twinkled, as though the heavens themselves watched over performances on both sides of the footlights. On stage, vaudeville actors performed *A Day at Ellis Island* and *A Day in Paris*. The opening was a benefit for the Riverdale Settlement House, a social club for residents of the east side of Toronto, who were mainly working families such as the Callaghans and their ten-year-old son Morley.[14] Toronto financiers who sponsored the opening helped with the ushering. Sir William was there with Grace, who, with Jacques de Lesseps, was visiting Toronto.[15] If he was his usual self at concerts and plays, he took a brief nap in the middle of one of the acts.[16]

The Winter Garden opening was a rare break. During the following ten days, he was back and forth between Toronto and Ottawa. On 18 February he met Borden and asked for a loan of $25 to $30 million. Borden was not enthusiastic. He had problems of his own – a party revolt led by R.B. Bennett, supported by Billy Maclean of Toronto, Stevens of Vancouver, and Nickle of Kingston, who threatened to resign if the CNoR loan were made. On the day that Mackenzie helped to open the Winter Garden, Bennett had lashed out at MPS under the influence of railway companies.[17] Z.A. Lash and Clifford Sifton failed to change Borden's mind. On Saturday, 21 February, Mackenzie met Sifton in Ottawa to plot their next moves.

The following Monday evening, he issued a press release, a defence of railways, especially the Canadian Northern: officials had not lined their own pockets; yes, the railway had received large amounts of land, but all was used quite legitimately to raise money for construction.

The next morning, the Railway Commission decided that the CNoR could no longer increase its capital stock without Parliament's consent. On Thursday and Friday, Mackenzie argued his case so strenuously that Borden found him 'stupidly unreasonable,' and still refused financial aid. The prime minister tried to help him to organize his thoughts. 'Gave McKenzie [sic] memo. of points to which he should address himself and asked for a formal application.' Back in Toronto, Mackenzie received a letter from Joseph Flavelle, congratulating him on his 'fair, lucid and frank statement' on railways, which would 'secure widespread attention, and correct many mischievous, ungenerous and foolish opinions concerning the Canadian Northern Railway.' Mackenzie sent a copy to Borden. 'It speaks for itself,' he told the prime minister, and reflected the thinking of the 'business man of large affairs.'[18] More than likely Flavelle wrote his letter knowing that it would reach the prime minister.

Mackenzie was back in Borden's office the first week in March. 'It is essential that the Company should receive further Government aid,' he pleaded. He had changed his strategy. He realized that Borden could not overcome internal opposition to a government loan.

He was also aware of the difficulties that Finance Minister Thomas White was having in raising money in London. Why not another bond guarantee, say $45 million, to complete construction and pay brokers' fees? Once again, he asked for running rights over the Intercolonial[19] from Quebec City to the Maritimes. He had not given up hope of completing his project.

These meetings in the prime minister's office were often tense. In the corridors of Parliament, however, both Mackenzie and Mann always appeared jaunty and self-confident. 'We haven't made any formal application, it is true,' Mackenzie told reporters, making virtue out of what Borden saw as a lamentable lack of organization. They were still negotiating. A formal application would follow soon. The railway was almost complete, Mackenzie insisted, then added his well-rehearsed line about the best grades to the Pacific.[20] His optimism was remarkable, in view of rumours about a revolution in Brazil and a consequent weakening of the market value of Brazilian Traction stocks and bonds; and news from Mexico, where the rebel leader, Pancho Villa, was poisoning the investment climate.

The second week in March, Mackenzie was back in Ottawa. Throughout the week lights burned late in Borden's office and at Glensmere, his handsome home on Wurtemburg Street, overlooking the Rideau River. On Wednesday, 11 March, Mackenzie and the prime minister emerged into the chill Ottawa air to be greeted by an eerie eclipse of the moon. Perhaps it was the eclipse or Mackenzie's persistence, or maybe even his haggard appearance, that finally moved Borden. By the second week in March, the prime minister was becoming a bit more sympathetic. 'Got a clear understanding of their financial position,' he confided to his diary on 12 March.

The Canadian Northern's application was the talk of Ottawa. 'Fierce invective against Mackenzie and Mann,' Borden noted on 18 March. Having been kept in the dark, R.B. Bennett was 'greatly piqued.' Adam Beck thundered into Ottawa and confided to Borden that Mackenzie and Mann were terribly unpopular. The prime minister thought Beck 'recalcitrant.'

Mackenzie continued his visits to Ottawa during the remainder of March and into April. Lash was often with him. Solicitor General Arthur Meighen, the rising junior member of the cabinet, joined Lash in working out an agreement that would allow the government to support the CNoR. Borden had given Meighen the task of unravelling the corporate finances of the CNoR in order to arrive at a politically acceptable deal, an almost impossible task, given a divided cabinet and a wary public. On one occasion, in late April, Borden left a performance of *Hamlet* at intermission to confer with Mackenzie. The play was a fitting metaphor for his cabinet, which was experiencing its own paralysis of indecision. (Coincidentally, *Hamlet* starred the same Forbes Robertson whom Mackenzie had seen on stage in London in 1896.)

In late April, after weeks of debate and consultation, the Borden government guaranteed an issue of bonds valued at $45 million. In return, Mackenzie, Mann & Company relinquished outstanding claims against the CNoR system amounting to about $21 million. Thirty-one companies comprising the CNoR system were amalgamated into a new company called the Canadian Northern Railway Company, the prairie name for the first time being used to refer to the amalgamated company. The Dominion government claimed 40 per cent, or $40 million worth of stock in the reorganized company. Mackenzie was elated. On Wednesday, 29 April, he strolled down the corridor of the Centre Block and into Borden's office, shook hands with the prime minister, and offered 'warmest congratulations.'[21] He seemed to be back in charge.

Parliamentary debate on the guarantee began on 13 May. Borden introduced the topic. Opposition leader Laurier agreed to support the general aims of the bill. He could hardly do otherwise, since it was his sunny compromise of 1903 that had led to the two new transcontinentals. Meighen made what Borden called a 'masterly speech.' The next day, R.B. Bennett rose in the House. Nearby, in the visitors' gallery, which in the old Commons was just a few metres above the floor of the House, Sir William peered down in silence. His son-in-law, the dapper and sporty Cyril Andrewes, sat beside him. Two days earlier they had been out on the golf course in Kirkfield when a messenger arrived with a telegram from Borden. Could Mackenzie come to Ottawa immediately? The debate was about to begin. The two men had reluctantly left the course and were driven to the Grand Trunk station in Kirkfield. The waiting *Atikokan* was hooked onto a Grand Trunk train and headed for Toronto and Ottawa.[22]

At 3:30 in the afternoon of 14 May, as Sir William watched and listened, Bennett began to hammer away at Mackenzie and Mann, and at fellow Conservative Arthur Meighen, who supported the Canadian Northern since he knew that it was still regarded positively in his home town of Portage la Prairie and indeed throughout most of the prairies.[23] No doubt Bennett knew that Meighen often travelled to Ottawa in the *Atikokan* and played bridge en route with Mackenzie, Cyril Andrewes, and Billy Moore. Could Mackenzie and Mann be trusted? Bennett asked. Why keep this insolvent company alive? It was a strongly worded, explosive speech, lasting two hours.

Fortified by supper, his arms 'waving like windmills,' according to Borden, Bennett resumed his attack. Meighen was the impertinent 'gramophone of Mackenzie and Mann.'[24] Mackenzie listened to the blustering Bennett, whose performance was more riveting than anything he had seen in the Winter Garden. There was certainly no time for a quick nap. When at last Bennett sat down and the stiff and edgy members rose from their seats, Mackenzie and Andrewes made their way downstairs. Mackenzie positioned himself outside the doors of the House. As the MP from Calgary came within earshot, Mackenzie nodded in Bennett's direction. 'Congratulations, Mr. Bennett,' he said. 'That was a very fine speech.' Bennett's scowl deepened. He froze for a split second, then wheeled around and scurried off. Mackenzie and Andrewes headed for the *Atikokan*. Mackenzie must have agreed with Borden that Bennett had great ability and delivered a good speech, but was completely lacking in common sense.[25]

After lengthy debates the bill went to committee hearings, then back to the Commons for its third reading. Thomas Shaughnessy was in and out of Borden's office, advising the prime minister and dining with Bennett, who as a CPR solicitor was probably under the influence of at least one railway company. The vote on the third reading came five days after the sinking of the CPR's Empress of Ireland in the St. Lawrence on 28 May. The government side won easily.

By mid-July, the provisions for the government guarantee of $45 million worth of bonds were drawn up, and Mackenzie sailed to England. On 22 July, Lazard Frères purchased almost $15 million of these bonds. The Mackenzie magic seemed at work again. When war broke out ten days later, however, Lazard Frères was prevented by the British government from selling these securities. However, since the banking house had already purchased them, it honoured the agreement, and thus Mackenzie succeeded in acquiring the last British investment money for Canada until after the war. Unfortunately, there remained $30 million in unsold railway bonds, besides over $2 million for the Mount Royal Tunnel and Terminal Company. Although the actual digging had been completed on 10 December 1913,[26] the tunnel had to be reinforced and the station on Boulevard Dorchester (René Levesque) was nothing more than an excavation.[27]

Thus, the announcement of war that lovely summer's day at Armathwaite was devastating, for the largest source of Canadian investment money was now unavailable. On 5 August, the day after he posed with the Griffins, Sir William sent a telegram to Sir Donald Mann. 'Shut down all work,' he ordered.[28] Mann hesitated. He ordered that all contractors be prepared to shut down. Premier McBride was apoplectic. Have the workers lay a few rails, he pleaded, in order to 'keep up appearances.'[29] Shortly thereafter, Mackenzie sent to Toronto what surely must be the most amusing of messages to come out of wartime London. 'Nothing doing here,' he wired Annesley, his private secretary, 'Coming home.'[30]

He sailed to Canada and headed for Borden's office. Government aid was more than ever necessary. In mid-September he and Lady Mackenzie went west on a six-week business trip[31] to reassure Premiers Roblin and Scott, McBride, and Arthur Sifton. In December 1914, for the first time in its history, the CNoR could not pay interest on one of its short-term bonds.[32] Ottawa was once again abuzz. How to keep afloat the CNoR as well as the Grand Trunk Pacific? Sir Edmund Walker, president of the Bank of Commerce, was called to Ottawa to discuss the question with Mackenzie, Lash, and Borden. McBride telegraphed from Victoria. Premier Scott rushed to Borden's office. Borden made a secret, extra-parliamentary agreement with Walker. If the Commerce lent the CNoR up to $10 million, the Dominion government would guarantee the loans. Borden ordered the printing of an equal amount of treasury notes,[33] and turned these notes over to the Bank of Commerce.

Somehow the last kilometres of railway were thrown together. In September 1914 the North-of-Superior section was ready for traffic, its ballasting having been completed to the satisfaction of the Board of Railway Commissioners. In October the CNoR inaugurated its passenger service between Ottawa and Toronto. In January 1915 the railway was completed to Port Mann on the Fraser River, several kilometres up river from Vancouver. On 23 January an unofficial, hastily arranged last spike ceremony took place at Basque, BC, a little town near Kamloops, on the North Thompson River.[34] Thirty years after he had witnessed his friend Donald Smith drive the most famous of Last Spikes at Craigellachie, Mackenzie drove this now-forgotten Last Spike of the CNoR. The men who surrounded him laughed and smiled as they watched him pick up the wooden mallet. In the photograph his face is hidden by the brim of his felt hat as he bends over in mid-swing. He had no time to pose stiffly. In any case, the art of photography had advanced sufficiently since 1886 so that it was no longer necessary to freeze for the photographer. The joviality was necessary to create the illusion of success. At the very moment that Mackenzie was taking that triumphant swing, his railway and construction companies were gasping for survival.

Mackenzie had hoped to arrange an official Last Spike ceremony for the first week in February, in order to have the Minister of Railways and Premier McBride pose for photographs amidst the splendour of mountains. Rails joined the Fraser to the St. Lawrence, but ballasting and bridging were not complete between Basque and Port Mann. The ceremony was delayed, then postponed for several months when a tunnel caved in near Hope on the Fraser River.[35] Construction crews remained at work in BC and Northern Ontario, ballasting, improving bridges over the North Thompson, building stations, and rebuilding the tunnel. Rolling stock and other equipment had yet to be purchased.

As usual, when the night was at its darkest Mackenzie was busy coaxing the sun to rise. His publicity was modern and sophisticated. (He would have understood the ten-second clip of colour television today.) He arranged for the première of a film. He donated a large collection of Inuit art to the Royal Ontario Museum. He helped to organize an exhibition of art. And he launched the greatest theatrical opening that Canada has seen. For a few brief moments, he was remarkably successful in capturing the imagination of Canadians.

Mackenzie had known Robert Flaherty, explorer, map maker, and photographer, since 1910, when he had hired Flaherty to explore for iron ore in the Nastapoka Islands in eastern Hudson Bay. Flaherty had taken along his camera to photograph mineral deposits. He returned in 1911 with news from an Inuit that the Belcher Islands, lost from European-Canadian maps for two centuries after their 'discovery' by Henry Hudson, contained high quality iron ore. The prospect of rediscovering these islands appealed to both men. 'Go and find out,' Mackenzie had told Flaherty.

Although Flaherty and his Inuit guide failed to reach the islands, he returned to Toronto with more photographs of Inuit. It was obvious that Flaherty was becoming more interested in photographing people than iron ore. He wanted to make a third trip into Hudson Bay, this time by way of Labrador and the Ungava Peninsula. One day in 1913, as he was preparing for his excursion, Mackenzie suggested, 'Why don't you take with you one of those new-fangled things called a motion-picture camera?'[36] (By 1913 the movie camera was no longer 'new-fangled': since 1898 Canadian businesses had used film for publicity,[37] and in 1909 the Canadian Northern itself had hired Britain's Charles Urban to make films promoting British immigration to Canada.)[38]

Flaherty purchased a Bell and Howell movie camera, and studied its use for three weeks in Rochester, New York. To pay for provisions, trading goods, camera, and equipment – 1,000 pounds of chemicals, 25,000 feet of film, and 2,000 dry plates[39] – Mackenzie reached into his pocket and pulled out $1,000. In return Flaherty assured Sir William 'that a film of Eskimo life would be a popular success and that the proceeds from showing it would help defray the considerable expense of his expedition.'[40] Flaherty promised to give to Mackenzie drawings, photographs, furs, ivory, and whalebone carvings, as well as the film itself.[41]

In August 1913 Flaherty left Toronto for St. John's, Newfoundland, and sailed to Baffin Island and Hudson Bay. In November 1914 he returned to Toronto with tales of Inuit near Cape Dorset on Baffin Island. He had also found the Belchers.[42] He presented Sir William with 14,000 feet of film, photographs, drawings, and 360 ivory and soapstone carvings. On 3 January 1915 Toronto's Arts and Letters Club held an exhibition of these photographs, along with scores of Inuit art, which Mackenzie presented to C.T. Currelly, founder of the new Royal Ontario Museum.[43]

In the meantime, the North American press was getting wind of the latest Mackenzie-Flaherty expedition and the rediscovery of the Belchers. On 14 March 1915 the *New York Times Magazine* announced in a headline that 'Sir William Mackenzie's Expedition Has Rediscovered Islands.' The same week, the Toronto *Globe* reported '"Lost Islands" Found Off Shore of Ungava' as a result of 'Sir William Mackenzie's Expedition to Hudson Bay.' The Port Arthur *Evening Chronicle* of 5 April 1915 reminded its readers that Flaherty had spent some of his childhood in that town: 'Port Arthur Boy's Great Achievement – Found the Lost Islands in Hudson Bay,' and 'Mr. R.J. Flaherty in Charge of the Sir William Mackenzie Expedition.' The new Henry Hudson and his sponsoring emperor basked in the publicity.

On 30 March 1915 the movie was given its première at Convocation Hall in Toronto. 'Probably the most remarkable "movies" ever shown in Toronto and surely the first of their kind ever shown in Canada,' extolled the *Globe*.[44] The following Saturday, a special showing of the film took place at the Arts and Letters Club on Elm Street. This time Sir William was there with his family and friends and with members of the club. Augustus Bridle reported that Mackenzie watched the film 'with uncommonly sympathetic interest and an occasional enormous yawn.'[45] The yawn was due more to exhaustion than to lack of interest. During the previous several months, he had been travelling back and forth between Ottawa, Toronto, and Victoria. He was, to be sure, immensely proud of the film, too proud and possessive to suit Frances, Robert Flaherty's new wife, who in her diary called Mackenzie 'His Majesty.'

What Mackenzie witnessed that evening was a documentary showing a day in the life of an Inuit family, beginning in early morning when the family arose in their igloo, lit the oil lamps, ate a breakfast of raw meat, hunted a seal, and processed it. The film included the rituals of feasting and dancing that followed a successful seal hunt. A flirtation scene ended abruptly when the female grabbed a stick and wielded it 'rather handily.' Bridle and other journalists found the film enchanting. 'The photographer has combined beauty and infinite detail with a sense of interest that is rare in moving pictures,' noted the *Globe*.[46] The audience agreed. The Mackenzies gathered around Frances to offer their congratulations. Flaherty was mobbed by members of the Arts and Letters Club. Sir William clasped the film maker's hands; he was so impressed and overwhelmed that he could do nothing but scrutinize Flaherty in silence.

Flaherty and Mackenzie did not have to speak in order to communicate. Movies and railways were both inventions of imaginative minds. Flaherty had encountered an Inuit community on Baffin Island and had recreated that reality by having characters act out typical events over a period of several weeks. And as he would later do in *Nanook of the North*, he rearranged his cinematic bits to create the illusion of one day in the life of an Inuit family. A railway or a hydroelectric project also began with rocks, mountains, prairie, and steel rails, reshaped and edited to create the new reality (or the illusion?) of movement, speed, and power. Of course the two men understood each other. They were both grand illusionists.

During the euphoria of the evening, Lady Mackenzie invited the Flahertys for tea the following afternoon. Frances Flaherty found the Mackenzie daughters, Mabel, Katharine, and Trudie, 'pleasant,' and their husbands 'perfectly impossible.' (Unfortunately Scott Griffin, Billy Beardmore, and Cyril Andrewes kept no diaries to tell posterity what they thought of the irascible Mrs. F.)

Press adulation and the promise of iron ore on the Belchers persuaded Sir William to sponsor his young explorer on one last expedition. The magic of another film might mesmerize investors and politicians. However, Mackenzie did ask Flaherty to cut expenses. Never mind that Sir William was a director of the Hudson's Bay Company. The fur trade commissioner threatened to refuse Flaherty further supplies and transportation if Sir William did not provide the HBC with a letter of credit and pay the $5,000 owing from previous expeditions.[47]

At the end of July 1915, Flaherty, his wife, and assistants embarked on his fourth and final Mackenzie-sponsored expedition. Inadequately financed, it was plagued by a scarcity of food and fuel.[48]

By mid-October 1916 he was back in Toronto with about seventeen hours of film, which he edited and combined with 1914 film footage. While packing the negatives, he dropped a burning cigarette on them. The nitrate film burst into flame. In seconds his work of several years turned to ashes. Sir William probably never saw the 1916 film. Having spent $175,000 on four Flaherty expeditions, Mackenzie could not afford a fifth.

In late August 1915, the annual Canadian National Exhibition opened in Toronto, where each year in the Railway Building (now the Music Building) the three big railways mounted exhibitions. In 1915 the Canadian Northern exhibited the work of three Canadian artists, two of whom, A.Y. Jackson and J.W. Beatty, Mackenzie had commissioned in 1914 to paint Rocky Mountain scenery along the main line of the Canadian Northern. Beatty had already been to the prairies – in 1885 with General Middleton, commander of the forces fighting Riel. For the young and relatively unknown Jackson, the 1914 excursion provided his first view of the West.

C.W. Jefferys was the best known of the three, his illustrations and articles having appeared in the Toronto *Globe* and *Star*, and in *Moon*, *Star Weekly*, and *Canadian Courier*.[49] Mackenzie was probably acquainted with Jefferys, who loved to caricature the railway builder in *Moon* and in the *Star*.[50] In 1907 and 1910, Mackenzie provided the artist with a Canadian Northern 'periodical pass,'[51] which introduced Jefferys to what became his favourite western landscape, the Qu'Appelle Valley. At the 1915 exhibition, Jefferys included work inspired by his 1910 excursion.

In sponsoring artists, Mackenzie was following the example of his friend Sir William Van Horne, who in the 1880s had hired a group of Canadian artists and photographers to record scenery along the line of the Canadian Pacific Railway. Mackenzie's commission coincided with a new interest in Canadian art. Shortly before leaving for Canadian Northern country, Beatty had publicly noted the 'tremendous movement' in Canada 'for the encouragement of a national art.' In early 1914 Beatty, Jackson, Lawren Harris, and J.E.H. MacDonald had moved into studios in the Art Building, located in Toronto's Rosedale ravine, near Yonge Street and Davenport Road. According to Beatty, these artists were searching for a style that would convey the brightness and northern light of Canadian landscapes.[52] The 1914 excursion gave Beatty and Jackson a chance to experiment with the northern light of the Rockies.

Jackson made many sketches, enough to keep him busy for over a year,[53] but only one oil, the enormous *Mount Robson by Moonlight*.

Beatty was more prolific – at the 1915 exhibition five of his oils, including *Evening at Jasper* and nine sketches of Canadian Northern scenery, were on display.[54] Jefferys' two oils at the CNoR show of 1915 were *A Stretch of Farming Country along the CNR*, in which a solitary horseman surveys the rolling prairie in springtime, and *Harvest Fields, North Saskatchewan, CNR,*[55] which depicted the bountiful Saskatchewan harvest.

Mackenzie's patronage gained him publicity. In return, he had, as one art historian puts it, 'put bread' on their tables.[56] He also gave them the freedom to paint what and how they chose, with one proviso – that their subject matter be Canadian Northern country, an area so vast that the proviso was almost meaningless. None of these artists was required to include rails or steam engines, even though they were customary features of previous railway art. Jefferys succeeded in capturing this northern land with vigour, clarity, and toughness, and is admired today as the first artist with a 'new vision' of the prairies, having initiated the necessary artistic process of confronting and imaginatively absorbing an unfamiliar landscape.[57] As patron, Mackenzie created the right preconditions for that vision – free access to the prairies and an almost free range of subject matter.

One of Mackenzie's contemporaries credited him with a 'largeness of vision' in sponsoring Robert Flaherty,[58] who, years later, claimed that meeting Sir William was a turning point in his life.[59] When Sir William suggested the movie camera, Flaherty, by his own admission, knew 'nothing whatsoever about films.'[60] Sir William introduced the movie camera to the man who founded the documentary film tradition, and gave him encouragement, artistic freedom, and money. When the film-maker's interest turned from iron ore to Inuit culture, the patron continued to provide money and arranged for exhibitions of the film. Like art patron Francis Cornish in Robertson Davies' *The Rebel Angels*, Mackenzie 'put money into the hands of living artists ... and gave them what they want most – which is sympathetic understanding.'[61] Fernand Braudel once wrote that capitalism is the sinews of a civilization, and that art is civilization's soul. To his credit, Mackenzie did not overlook the nation's soul.

When the exhibition of paintings opened at the Canadian National Exhibition in late August 1915, Mackenzie was promoting the Canadian Northern Railway, which was finally ready for its dress rehearsal. On 22 August 1915 Mackenzie, his wife, D.B. Hanna, A.J. Mitchell, John Aird of the Bank of Commerce, Ontario Chief Justice

Sir Glenholme Falconbridge, Lady Falconbridge, and others left Union Station in Toronto. The train sped north and west over the vast Canadian Shield towards Winnipeg, where more dignitaries and managers boarded the train, which then sped west at speeds of up to fifty miles per hour. On 27 August it reached Vancouver in the record time of ninety-one running hours from Toronto.[62]

Premier McBride congratulated Mackenzie on overcoming financial difficulties, which proves either that Mackenzie had succeeded in convincing the premier that his finances were in order, or that the premier was also capable of indulging in wishful thinking. On 6 September, when the train arrived back at Union Station, there was nothing but praise for Mackenzie and the railway.[63] The dress rehearsal had worked flawlessly. Mackenzie raced to Ottawa to tell Borden of the trip. But there was no time to bask in praise. Opening night was near. Audience and critics from across the country would have to be impressed. More than ever Mackenzie had to create the illusion of success. If he failed, the play would fold after its first performance.

On 12 October a parliamentary and press train pulled out of Quebec City. It followed the historic North Shore, parallel to the old 'Chemin du Roi,' through Portneuf and Shawinigan, Joliette and L'Epiphanie. In Montreal, Sir Donald Mann conducted a tour through the Mount Royal Tunnel. The train headed up to Hawkesbury, Orleans, and Ottawa, where Senator Pat Burns and about eighty other senators and MPs waited at Central Station.

Accompanied by a large Toronto contingent, Mackenzie joined the excursion at Capreol, north of Sudbury. When the train left Capreol, the engine was pulling fifteen coaches, including three private cars, eight Pullmans, three diners, and a baggage car, a total of 1,190 tons, hauled by one ordinary light engine,[64] because the grades of the CNoR route through the Rockies were, as Mackenzie has often bragged, the best of the three transcontinentals. The rolling stock was 'among the finest' ever to cross Canada, noted one Edmonton journalist on board.[65]

On the train were 'les sommités du monde politique, du monde industriel et de la finance, ainsi que les représentants de tous les journaux du pays'[66] (thirty-five journalists in all, Canadian and American, who used the Canadian Northern Telegraph system to feed to the public instant news of each day's activities). The parliamentarians were from a variety of regions and backgrounds. G.C. Wilson, who represented the riding of Wentworth, near Hamilton, was an ardent supporter of Sir Adam Beck's Hydro Commission; W.G. Weichel represented Waterloo, having defeated Mackenzie

King in the 1911 elections; Senator Thibaudeau's family had arrived at Port Royal in 1605; and G.H. Brabason, from Pontiac riding, had fought under Middleton in the Riel Rebellion of 1885.[67] To take care of any parliamentary illness, Mackenzie enlisted the help of his half brother, Dr. Bert Mackenzie.

It was an excursion 'of truly Sir William Mackenzie proportions.'[68] There was plenty of whiskey, and food from each region of Canada, including three barrels of Prince Edward Island oysters. One car was fitted with a Nordheimer piano to accompany the excursionists in nightly impromptu concerts, during which the senators demonstrated an 'amazing amount of musical talent, opening the eyes of the press and the MPs as to the real value of the Upper House.'[69] Sir William was such an 'ideal host' that one senator wished to become his permanent guest.

In Port Arthur on Thursday, 14 October, the rounds of luncheons, automobile tours, and adulatory speeches began. (Cyril Andrewes avoided the inevitable question 'And what do you think of our fair city?' by heading for the nearest tennis court with an excursionist.) During the one-hour stop, Mackenzie's guests were driven to the CNoR grain elevators, and were duly impressed by their ten-million-bushel capacity.[70] As the train was about to leave at 5:45 pm, one journalist spied a newspaper boy, jumped down to the platform, and sold all the papers to members of the excursion at the unheard-of price of twenty-five cents each. The boy was overjoyed.

On Friday morning the train reached Winnipeg, Canada's third largest city, with a population of 175,000. At Union Station, Premier Norris, who had recently defeated Sir Rodmond Roblin, greeted Sir William. The motor tour took the group down Main Street to Portage, over to tree-lined Broadway, where some of Sir William's grandchildren had been born earlier in the century, then off to Armstrong's Point and Wellington Crescent, over to the business and garment district, and past Mackenzie's Electric Railway Chambers on Notre Dame. The bustling Grain Exchange – the 1915 harvest was the most bountiful ever – was also on the itinerary.

At a luncheon at the CPR's Royal Alexandra Hotel on Main, guest speaker Augustus Nanton, whose association with Mackenzie reached back into the early days of railway contracting in the Northwest, reminded the visitors of the West's generous contribution of money and men to the war. Senator Edwards heaped lavish praise on the Canadian Northern Railway, and W.H. Bennett, MP for Simcoe East, Ontario, assured diners that he was no relation to that other Bennett, R.B.

Early the next morning, the train crossed the provincial boundary into Saskatchewan, passing stately grain elevators painted 'red or old gold.'[71] At Regina, which had grown from a village in the early 1880s to a city of 50,000 in 1915, provincial and municipal officials were on hand, though not Premier Walter Scott, who had chosen instead to travel to Toronto.[72] Some forty automobiles carried excursionists to the farm of H.E. Fields to see his large threshing outfit. Others toured the city hall and the beautiful new legislature in Wascana Park.[73]

Mackenzie and the excursionists reboarded the train and travelled north on the old Qu'Appelle, Long Lake & Saskatchewan line, down into the beautiful, rolling Qu'Appelle Valley named, according to legend, by a voyageur who had heard his name 'as though some comrade hailed him from the rear.' 'Qui appelle?' he asked, thereby naming the valley.[74] As the train climbed out of the valley and headed north into the flat wheat plains, Sir William must have recalled early construction days in 1889 and 1890 when he had helped make roads and streets, in the words of Sir Gilbert Parker, 'on the greenbrown plain, where herds of buffalo had stamped and steamed and thundered not long ago.'[75] Sir William had helped to name such towns as Lumsden and Davidson. If he was in a storytelling mood, he kept the assembled journalists spellbound with stories of wresting timber from the mountains of BC, of risking death from avalanches, of fashioning the ties and erecting the trestles over which his party was travelling.

After several hours, the train glided over the CNoR railway bridge at the south end of Saskatoon, whose population had grown from a few score Temperance Colony folk in 1890, when Mackenzie had first seen the settlement, to what boosters estimated was 30,000 by 1915. As 2,000 people cheered, the train pulled into the handsome CNoR station on 1st Avenue. Motor cars waited. Bunting and flags flapped in the dry wind. And wasn't the afternoon a better time than Regina's morning slot to show off a city? asked the *Phoenix*. The excursionists spent the remainder of the afternoon touring the lovely little city on the South Saskatchewan, admiring its broad boulevards lined with prosperous looking brick businesses and banks, and its fine elm-graced residential streets. They were driven out to the Exhibition Grounds and over to the university, its new greystone buildings proudly encircling a green and leafy bowl.

At 6:30 the next morning, the train stopped in Edmonton long enough to take on coal. At Tollerton, west of Edmonton, even citizens of the nearby Grand Trunk Pacific town of Edson cheered Sir William as he emerged from the train. Edson's brass band struck up 'O Canada.' Smiling broadly, Sir William posed for photographs.

Colour brochure of the
Canadian Northern
Railway, advertising
'Sporting Regions and
Scenic Beauties' to increase
tourist travel on the railway

Tunnel in Rockies near
Jasper, October 1915, taken
during official opening of
the Canadian Northern
Railway

The Kirkfield Inn, 1912–25, built by Lady Mackenzie in order to impose temperance on Kirkfield; she tore down the two licensed hotels and replaced them with the unlicensed inn. The local folk found Persian carpets and a grand piano too grand, and took their drinking elsewhere.

The *Royal George*, which along with its sister ship, the *Royal Edward*, was inaugurated in April 1910 as part of the Canadian Northern Steamship Company. In 1912, Sir William Mackenzie and Prime Minister Sir Robert Borden sailed on the *Royal George* to England.

Smoking room of the *Royal George*

Armathwaite, the Lake District, England, 4 August 1914; when he heard that war was declared, Sir William's face turned ashen and he muttered, 'I'm ruined.'

Ivory carving, part of the Robert Flaherty-Sir William Mackenzie collection at the Royal Ontario Museum, Toronto, as a result of Flaherty's four excursions to the north, sponsored by Mackenzie, 1910–16

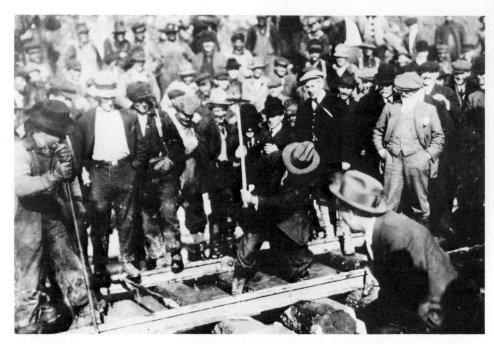

Last Spike of the Canadian Northern, Basque, BC, near Kamloops, 23 January 1915

Official opening of the Canadian Northern Railway, October 1915, the train heading west past the water tower at Capreol, near Sudbury, Ontario

Official opening of the Canadian Northern Railway, October 1915, the welcome at Regina, 16 October 1915

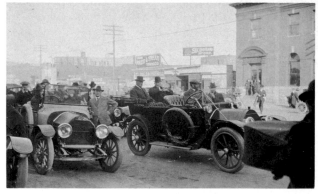

Sir William Mackenzie and Premier McBride, front row left, pose with parliamentarians and journalists on the steps of the BC legislature, 19 October 1915

Sir William Mackenzie, D.B. Hanna, and M.H. McLeod at Spence's Bridge, BC, October 1915, en route to Vancouver

Close-up of Sir William Mackenzie at the legislature in Victoria, 19 October 1915

Christmas at the Mitchells, Lady Mackenzie's sister's family, ca. 1916; Sir William and Lady Mackenzie, seated at right, are not amused.

Photograph of Sir William Mackenzie, ca. 1916, by Elliott and Fry, Winnipeg; by 1916 he was a 'grizzled relic of his former energy,' according to Augustus Bridle.

John Mackenzie, father of
William Mackenzie, ca. 1885

Portrait (1912) of Mary
Mackenzie, ca. 1816–52; Sir
William Mackenzie's
invention of the best
mother he never knew

Local residents had their box cameras; Sir William, his official photographer. He held up babies and tickled them under the chin. He congratulated mothers and shook hands with fathers.[76] At Lucerne, where the railway entered BC, the Honourable Thomas Taylor boarded the train and congratulated Sir William on his great achievement. Premier McBride had promised to meet the train at the BC border but was busy in Victoria denying rumours of graft connected with a submarine deal.

As the afternoon wore on, the train penetrated further into what one journalist called the 'almost overwhelming beauty' of the Rockies, past the snowcapped and moonlit Seven Sisters, sketched by Beatty and Jackson the year before. For most excursionists, this was their first glimpse of the Rockies. They were speechless. Many, including senators, were up before dawn on 18 October. As the train curled around piles of mountains, they peered down walls of rock to the Thompson and Fraser rivers. They marvelled at the imagined construction difficulties. They agreed with their host that the commercial possibilities of the valleys were almost limitless.[77]

From Vancouver, an overnight ferry ride landed Mackenzie and his entourage in Victoria. They posed for photographs on the steps of the legislature. Sir William stands at one end of the front row, next to Premier McBride. As usual, his face gives away very little. His eyes, partly in the shadow of his fedora, are fixed on the camera. The mouth is set firmly, perhaps ready to burst into a smile, a triumphant smile, for he and the railway had made it to the Pacific. If the fists are clenched, it is impossible to know, for the hands are hidden inside the pockets of his overcoat.

After a drive around the beautiful city of 60,000, they were fêted at a banquet at the Empress Hotel, then took the overnight ferry back to a rainy Vancouver where they toured the Fraser sawmills, met BC Liberals in the Blue Room of the (old) Hotel Vancouver, and were given a luncheon by the Vancouver Board of Trade. More than 200 people heard praises heaped upon Mackenzie and Mann. Mackenzie told the guests that he was delighted that his railway had at last reached Vancouver. (In fact, Port Mann, several kilometres up the Fraser River, was the western terminus.) One senator confessed that he had once been sceptical, but now was willing to offer his wholehearted support to the Canadian Northern. Canada needed this railway, for her population would grow to about 90 million by 1940. An MP remarked on the 'splendid optimism' that he had felt between Winnipeg and Victoria. Canada could greatly improve its trade by building even more railways and harbours.[78] At the Hotel Vancouver that day, no dissenting voice was heard.

At 2:30 pm on 20 October, the excursion train pulled out of Vancouver. Mackenzie arranged that on the eastward journey, sections previously traversed by night would now be seen in daylight. The next evening the first CNoR westbound freight train passed the eastbound excursion train. The passing train was loaded with merchandise, Sir William told the parliamentarians and journalists. They were unaware that while their train was speeding eastward, Mackenzie was carrying on negotiations by telegraph with Premier McBride in Victoria and officials of the Great Northern Railway in St. Paul, Minnesota, in order to obtain running rights over J.J. Hill's Great Northern line into Vancouver, the same line that Mackenzie and Mann had sold to Hill in 1901. Those rights were not obtained for another month. A train did pass the excursion train, but it must surely have been empty. Port Mann had no port facilities, and the train could not reach facilities at Vancouver. In his memoirs, published nine years later, D.B. Hanna confirmed that regular freight service to Vancouver began no earlier than April 1916. Nevertheless, Mackenzie succeeded in creating the impression that the new transcontinental railway was already flourishing.[79]

The next morning the train reached Edmonton, a booming capital of over 50,000 people. The excursionists viewed the handsome university campus, the domed legislature, broad Jasper Avenue, and the old fort, then in the process of being removed (and misplaced) from the flats to a less busy site down-river. Sir William was exhausted and remained in the *Atikokan* to rest. An enterprising young reporter from the *Daily Bulletin* knocked at the door, and was welcomed effusively by Sir William, who bowed him into the dining compartment in the centre of the private car, offered him the most luxurious chair, and, to his surprise, opened a box of his best cigars.

Then Mackenzie took a closer look at the reporter and realized his mistake: 'Ah, I mistook you for somebody else, Mr. What's His Name, of the Government.' He realized, however, that here was a splendid opportunity for publicity. He had missed the tour and luncheon, but here was a better way of communicating with Edmontonians. The elusive Mackenzie granted a private interview. He chatted happily for twenty minutes, answering questions, turning back others. Asked about delays on the St. Paul des Métis line northwest of Edmonton, Mackenzie replied, 'I'll come to you for information – How are they getting on?' He was not going to be pinned down. Naturally he boasted about the fine grades and the excellent roadbed. 'The line is built to stay and all railroad engineers agree that there is nothing to surpass it in America.'[80] Had the reporter checked, he would have discovered that Sir William's opinions were shared by engineers and other experts, one of whom had recently called the BC section 'the finest mountain railway in the world in point of construction, grades and curves.'[81]

At 12:45, the train pulled out of the station. Sir William emerged from his private car. The interview had lifted his spirits. With a sunny smile, he waved from the rear platform to hundreds of Edmontonians. The train raced east and south, over the roadbed on which he had driven in a motor car ten years earlier with Sir Gilbert Parker and Sir Edmund Walker, then it crossed into Saskatchewan at Lloydminster, where Barr colonists were beginning to prosper after a dozen years of learning to survive on the prairies. Down through the grain fields and river valleys of Saskatchewan the train raced, on into Manitoba to Gladstone, the birthplace of the Canadian Northern Railway.

Late in the afternoon of Saturday, 23 October, a simple and moving ceremony took place. From a small stage installed for the excursion, Senator Edwards read an address signed by sixty-six senators and MPS, congratulating Mackenzie and the Canadian Northern on the successful completion of the line. 'We had not conceived it possible,' the senator read, 'that a railway possessing the standard of alignment and gradient of your road could have been constructed across Canada within so short a period.'

As he spoke, Mackenzie sank back into his chair. His dream had been realized. 'The evenness of the roadbed,' the senator continued, 'and the facility with which one locomotive has hauled across the continent a train nearly one quarter of a mile in length, consisting of fifteen heavy coaches, fully demonstrates the high standard of construction obtaining throughout the line of travel.' Other speakers, representing ridings across the country, praised the line and wished it success. Senator William Owens alluded to the libellous statements made against the Canadian Northern. He had been warned that the line was not safe and that he would be thrown from his sleeper by the rough roadbed, but had discovered that even at speeds of 40 and 50 miles per hour (64 to 80 kilometres per hour) the road had been completely smooth.[82]

Mackenzie was moved. He stood to reply, spoke a few words, then sank back into his chair in a pensive and quietly jubilant mood. His grand extravaganza had worked its magic. How could Borden refuse further aid now? The war would soon be over. A boom period would surely follow. The Canadian Northern would at last show healthy returns.

By the time the train pulled into Winnipeg at 8:00 pm that evening, Sir William was in high spirits. In the rotunda of the Fort Garry Hotel, across from Union Station, he chatted and joked. At one point, this usually self-contained man was seen to toss back his head and burst into hearty, self-confident laughter.[83] At midnight, the train pulled out of Winnipeg, arriving in Ottawa three days later, on Tuesday, 26 October, shortly after 9:00 pm. It had travelled some 11,500 kilometres and had covered the Toronto-to-Ottawa section in the record time of six hours and forty-five minutes.[84] As his guests expressed their thanks and bade their adieus, the ebullient Mackenzie was now certain that he had succeeded.

He couldn't have been more wrong. The chill late autumn Ottawa wind was a harbinger of a winter long and cold. The 'Guns of August' would not cease pounding for three more years. Newspapers were preoccupied with war news: Zeppelin raids over London and Berlin, naval battles, the annihilation of half a million Armenians, the execution of nurse Edith Cavell, and the death of Rudyard Kipling's son. It was difficult for a mere railway to grab newspaper attention.

The excursion train itself had not been immune to war news, thanks to the news service of the Toronto *Globe* and *Telegram*. At one patriotic concert on the train, the participants collected $500 for the Red Cross. At the Regina station they were greeted by young women selling little tin soldiers to raise money for the Canadian Patriotic Fund, established to help families of Canadians fighting in Europe. Luncheon speeches often made reference to the war.

The war had a personal meaning for Mackenzie. Grace was a volunteer nurse in Paris, as was her cousin Ethel Mitchell. Jacques flew planes for France.[85] (The French government later awarded the two women Médailles d'Argent, and Jacques, a Croix de Guerre.) Lady Mackenzie was honourary president of the Canadian branch of Queen Mary's Needlework Guild, which supplied clothing and other comforts to the Canadian Military Hospital at Shornecliffe, and she presented pipes to the Princess Patricia's Canadian Light Infantry a few days after the commencement of hostilities.[86] She also opened the Kirkfield house to convalescent soldiers.[87] Even R.J. took time out from horses and gambling to set up a military convalescent home in Winnipeg.[88]

Sir William had been one of the incorporators of the Patriotic Fund and had contributed $10,000. He must have been delighted to see the young women in Regina collecting money for it. The Toronto Railway Company had donated $15,000; the Winnipeg Electric Railway, $12,000.[89] The Canadian Northern and its employees would soon donate $100,000 to the fund, which was also supported by royalty, premiers, lieutenant governors, La Ville de Montréal, and Le Séminaire de St. Sulpice. The Canadian Northern Railway gave free passage to anyone connected with the Patriotic Fund or with the Red Cross,[90] and equipped two railway cars as hospital units for Val Cartier Military Camp, near Quebec City.[91] The London offices of the Canadian Northern followed the example of several other Canadian corporations in England and gave paid leave to staff and guaranteed their positions. In an indirect way, Mackenzie contributed to the care of wounded Canadians in France. When Flaherty's film was shown at Convocation Hall, the audience donated generously to a hospital in Paris that tended Canadians.

In the midst of planning the official opening of the Canadian Northern, Mackenzie consulted with Sir Robert Borden, Sam Hughes, and Fred Nicholls about establishing a plant to manufacture 2,000 to 3,000 heavy guns for Britain.[92] With Lash, E.R. Wood, and other Canadian and American businessmen, and with the encouragement of the prime minister, Mackenzie was about to apply for a charter to set up the British American Nickel Corporation of Sudbury to produce nickel for Britain.[93] Mackenzie had interests in a company manufacturing gunpowder, shells, and barbed wire destined for France, some of which was being manufactured in the Winnipeg shops of the Canadian Northern.[94]

Mackenzie predicted that the war would restructure the world's trading patterns. Soon after the outbreak of hostilities, he advised Borden to build up a merchant marine by buying confiscated German ships. Now was the time to open trade with Russia, which, he predicted, would be the next superpower and would need Canadian-made agricultural machinery, mining machinery, and woollen and cotton goods. He also realized that returning soldiers and refugees would need work.[95]

Although preoccupied with keeping the CNoR afloat, Mackenzie found the time to advise the prime minister on governmental appointments. In 1915, he recommended that Premier McBride be asked to join the government, and that Fred Nicholls be appointed Purchasing Commissioner of War Supplies. He also advised Borden that May 1915 would be a good time to hold elections. In spite of the difficult railway situation, the prime minister's diaries make it clear that Borden still respected Mackenzie's opinions and recommendations.[96]

Besides war news, the cross-Canada opening of the Canadian Northern had to compete for newspaper space with other news: in Edmonton, Regina, and Halifax, new lieutenant governors were being installed; the Aberdeens were visiting Canada; Nellie McClung was advocating alcoholic abstinence; and Prime Minister Borden pulled a woman away from a moving train in Halifax. In the States, President Wilson had remarried, to a woman reputed to have Indian blood; and the Boston Red Sox had just won the World Series. The Mexican Opera, Mary Pickford's latest film, and an Australian cadets choir also competed for attention. Even R.J. Mackenzie was grabbing newspaper space while his father travelled across the country – in October 1915, he won $5,000 at the races in Kentucky, then spent the same amount in Milwaukee on a three-year-old filly.[97] Worse still, Canadian newspapers were reporting that the myth of the 'Last Best West,' which Mackenzie had helped to promote, was being satirized in London's West End in a play that explored hardships borne by prairie housewives.[98]

Although most journalists were impressed with the roadbed and the entertainment, a few remained indifferent. Toronto's *Evening Telegram*, for instance, reported nothing. The Toronto *Daily Mail and Empire* also ignored the tour, except for a small photograph of the parlour coach and its Nordheimer piano, even though both papers had been represented on board. Other journalists pointed out some of the problems faced by the railway. The Vancouver *Sun* had ignored the excursion until 29 October, when it printed accusations about the inferior road bed, rails, station houses, freight sheds, and rolling stock; terminal facilities and a ferry link with Victoria were lacking; only a fool, the paper's editor contended, would believe that 'a written contract signed by Sir William and Sir Dan meant anything further than those eminent gentlemen desired it should mean.' He concluded, correctly, that the recent excursion was in preparation for a further demand for government assistance on the part of Mackenzie and Mann.[99] Calgary papers were especially miffed, since arch-rival Edmonton was on the CNoR mainline. In his Calgary *Eye-Opener*, Bob Edwards' only reference to the tour was a cartoon printed the day of the Gladstone declaration (see opposite page), in which a top-hatted Sir William, standing in front of the Ministry of Finance in Berlin, announces: 'I'll just step in and borrow their war fund and put them all on the bum.'[100]

Even the Gladstone declaration was not unanimous. A dozen senators and MPs did not sign. Their silence implied indifference or even disapproval. Ominously too, Borden was beginning to realize that funding the Canadian Northern Railway was an act of folly. As early as May 1915 a few cabinet ministers such as Robert Rogers, once a CNoR supporter, had warned the prime minister of serious difficulties that belied Mackenzie's eternal confidence.[101] Premier

Sir William Mackenzie at Berlin

Cartoon of Sir William Mackenzie about to borrow from the war fund of Germany, in the Calgary *Eye-Opener*, 23 October 1915: Bob Edwards, owner-editor of the *Eye-Opener*, was no fan of Mackenzie.

Scott's absence in Regina must also have worried Mackenzie, although Scott's personal problems may have taken him to Ontario.

As Sir William travelled those thousands of kilometres, he could not forget that the Canadian Northern was insolvent. At the last annual meeting of shareholders, held before his departure, he admitted that for the first time in its history the company had suffered a net deficit, amounting to $1,640,283.[102]

In the long run, it did not matter that journalists like J.S. Crate of the Ottawa *Evening Journal* had nothing but praise for the excursion and optimism for the railway. 'The achievement of Sir William Mackenzie and Sir Donald Mann,' Crate wrote, 'has no parallel in railroad history.'[103] Nor did it matter that the *Financial Post* praised the 'genius of Sir William and his associates' in building this 'excellent line.'[104] Nor that the Toronto *Daily News* praised the 'best grades of any line on the continent.'

The year 1915 was the wrong time to celebrate a railway. No national dream, this one. Financial institutions were sceptical. Steel for peaceful purposes was scarce. Some Canadian Northern branch line trackage had been ripped up and shipped to France, where Canadians, who by 1915 were expert railway builders, were repairing railways. Prospective immigrants to the bountiful prairies or to the busy factories were dying in muddy trenches. So were Canadians.

When Mackenzie called on Borden, on Wednesday, 27 October, the day after the excursion returned to Ottawa, to tell him about the triumphal opening of the railway, Borden noted tersely in his diary that Mackenzie had called. At the very moment of his greatest triumph, Mackenzie's grand illusions, like the myth of the Last Best West, were vanishing.

Two weeks later Sir William met Sir Thomas Shaughnessy and Sir Henry Drayton, chairman of the Board of Railway Commissioners, in Halifax at the funeral of Sir Charles Tupper,[105] whose few months at the top of Canadian political life in the mid 1890s, followed by years of relative obscurity, served as a reminder that fame and fortune are fickle. Two weeks after Tupper's funeral, Mackenzie's daughter, Katharine Beardmore, gave birth to a child incapable of life once cut off from its umbilical cord. In the Kirkfield cemetery, a tombstone inscription reads 'Baby Beardmore, 26 November 1915.'

CHAPTER TWELVE

'An Unjustifiably Sanguine View,' 1915–17

As all historians know, the past is a great darkness, and filled with echoes.

(Margaret Atwood, *The Handmaid's Tale* [1985] 324)

Like two tenacious prize fighters equally matched, Mackenzie and Sir Adam Beck traded punches round after round during the war. In 1916 and 1917 two new hydro acts had given the Hydro Commission the right to order a private plant to deliver excess power to Hydro. The Electrical Development Company's authorized maximum output was 125,000 horsepower, but its generating plant's capacity was 150,000 horsepower. To meet wartime demand, it had diverted extra water into the raceways of its Niagara Falls generating plant. It reported the amount of water used monthly and paid taxes to the Ontario government for all power produced. Neither the Dominion nor the provincial governments had objected.[1] Beck accused the company of stealing water from the Niagara River. In March 1917 Mackenzie complained to Premier Hearst, successor to the late Premier Whitney, that 'Sir Adam has more than once reflected upon my business judgment, and, with strange inconsistency, persistently covets one after another the things I have tried to build up.'[2] Radial railways and electricity in Toronto, where Beck's lackey, Tommy Church, became mayor in 1915, were also bones of contention. Meantime the Hydro Commission was, inevitably, winning more towns and villages. By 1915, 104 municipalities were receiving power from Ontario Hydro, up from 12 in 1910.[3] That year Hydro had reached the 100,000 horsepower limit available from the Ontario Power Company, and ironically was forced to buy 16,000 horsepower from EDCO.

During the summer of 1916, Ontario experienced power shortages. EDCO was selling power in Ontario and, quite legally, to munitions plants in New York. Beck, of course, blamed the shortage on EDCO's exports. Ontario Power Company, Hydro's main supplier, offered to sell more power to the Hydro Commission, at slightly increased prices, which Beck refused to pay. In April 1916 he used the shortage to justify the passage of an act giving the Hydro Commission the right to build its own generating plant at Niagara Falls, thereby abrogating the agreement of 1903 between the Mackenzie group and the Niagara Falls Parks Commission. The agreement forbade the Parks Commission and, by implication, any other government body from taking water from the Niagara River for purposes other than to develop parks.

The 1916 act was a bold and arbitrary move that raised the hackles of both the private power lobby and those who feared for their civil liberties. Particularly exercised was Professor James Mavor, political economist at the University of Toronto and an acquaintance of Mackenzie since the 1890s, when Mavor had worked with Count Tolstoy and Canadian railway presidents to resettle Russian Doukhobors in the prairies. Between 15 July and 23 December 1916, the *Financial Post* printed Mavor's scathing critiques of Hydro and Beck. Mavor lamented the absence of objective inspection of the Hydro Commission and its facilities; the uneconomical character of management, and its tendency to underestimate capital expenditures; its penchant for hiring employees with political connections rather than men with technical expertise; the tendency to price hydro power according to political, rather than technical, arguments; and the absence of properly trained directors. Hydro, he argued, was a tool used by politicians to perpetuate their own power. To do so, they closed the courts to people, thereby violating civil liberties. Beck had become the 'Dictator of Ontario,'[4] which offended Mavor's 'deep-seated intellectual aversion to the expansion of arbitrary state power.'[5]

Mackenzie sent Borden a copy of the Hydro Act of 1916, together with Mavor's introductory article from the *Financial Post*. The act was a dangerous thing, Sir William contended, since it would frighten away American investment money. It was the same argument that Pellatt and Nicholls had used a decade earlier, when the idea of government hydro was first introduced to the Ontario legislature, except that now American replaced British. 'I venture to say,' Mackenzie added, 'that such legislation would be beyond the authorities in any state in the Union' or even in any South American republic. Mackenzie thought Mavor's analysis 'admirable,' and his conclusion, that the acts 'ought either to be repealed or disallowed,' irrefutable.[6]

There was little chance that Borden would try to disallow the act, and Mackenzie knew it. The prime minister had always opposed the use of disallowance; moreover, he needed Premier Hearst's support in the expected Dominion election. Not surprisingly, the Ontario attorney general, who was also a member of the Hydro Commission, proved unco-operative.[7] Without his permission, the case could not go before the Ontario courts. In January 1917 the Queenston by-law permitting Hydro to build its own power plant was voted in by ratepayers, and in May construction began on the 500,000 horsepower plant.

A month earlier the Ontario Power Company had sold its generating plant, transformer stations, transmission lines, and substations to Ontario Hydro, which began to generate its own power. Beck became more unco-operative,[8] and his detractors accused him of deliberately hampering the Allied cause.[9] In November EDCO again applied for disallowance of the water power acts. But Mackenzie realized that the wisest move would be to sell to Beck. In 1917, therefore, the Toronto Power Company opened negotiations with Hydro to sell its generating plant at Niagara Falls.

Mackenzie's offers to sell the Toronto Railway Company to the city had been spurned. Nevertheless, the company, together with its radial companies, continued to reinforce Toronto's economic pre-eminence in southern Ontario. By 1915 the Toronto Suburban had been extended to Woodbridge, a few kilometres beyond Weston, and in April 1917, to Guelph. By 1917 the Toronto & York Radial Railway Company reached north to Sutton on Lake Simcoe, east to Highland Creek, and west to Port Credit, besides a few short lines in the village of East Toronto, a total of about 130 new kilometres.[10]

Henry Ford's assembly line revolution, which by 1914 had made the automobile affordable to people of lesser means, wreaked havoc with street railway revenues in Toronto and elsewhere. 'Tin lizzie' taxis, or 'jitneys,' Yankee slang for a nickel, the cost of a ride, first appeared on the streets of Los Angeles in late 1914 and spread across North America. They followed relatively fixed routes and could be hailed by pedestrians. At first they were unregulated, paying no income tax or street rental fees. In 1915 Toronto was home to 700 jitneys, which helped to reduce TRC revenues by $345,000 from the previous year's gross.[11] Eventually cities across North America, encouraged by trolley companies and unions, found ways to regulate the busy jitneys, which were attracting the most profitable passengers, those making shorter and more frequent trips, especially during rush hours.[12] Jitneys were not the sole problem. Inflation, which pushed up the cost of materials and labour, slowly reduced return on investment during the war.

Once elected mayor in January 1915, Tommy Church wasted little opportunity to harass Mackenzie. At the stroke of midnight on 25 June 1915, he led a motley band of people up Yonge Street to the CPR tracks, south of St. Clair Avenue. Because of boundary changes and annexation, the franchise on a short piece of street railway expired at midnight. The 400 metres in question joined Mackenzie's Toronto Railway Company and Toronto & York Company. The pompous mayor and his band tore up the track, thus inconveniencing commuters transferring from one system to the other. The Ontario Railway Board ordered the city to relay the tracks, and gave the TRC permission to operate north to Farnham Avenue. The Ontario Court of Appeal agreed with the board. The rampaging Church took the case to the Privy Council and lost.[13]

In November 1914 the Railway and Municipal Board had charged the TRC once again with overcrowding and ordered the company to add another fifty cars. The board went so far as to define overcrowding as a 'public nuisance,' thus making it a criminal offence. The TRC appealed the nature of the charge, but Chief Justice Meredith and the Ontario Court of Appeal dismissed the appeal, apparently concluding that overcrowding was indeed a criminal act, akin to bank robbery or murder. The TRC was forced to take the case to the Privy Council, which in 1917 ruled that overcrowding did not constitute public nuisance, and therefore that the TRC could not be charged with a criminal offence.[14]

The company recognized the problem of overcrowding, and in spite of wartime steel and personnel shortages, it tried to alleviate the problem. By April 1915 it had two new cars in service, eighteen under construction, and thirty more on the drawing board.[15] Although most of Toronto's trolleys were no longer factory fresh, there is evidence that the company kept each trolley in a high state of repair, inside and out.[16] By the spring of 1916, it had twenty-three more new cars on the streets.[17] Unavoidable disasters, such as the fire at the King Street car barns, which destroyed 169 trolleys in December 1916, exacerbated the problem. Almost before the embers had cooled, Mayor Church demanded that the company provide 200 extra trolleys.

A two-day strike began at midnight on 10 July 1917. Workers asked for an increase of ten cents per hour. On 1 November 1916 the company had voluntarily raised wages by about 10 per cent, even though the salary agreement did not expire until June 1917. In July, the company refused to raise wages by a further ten cents an hour, so the men went on strike. They agreed to go back to work when the company offered an increase of six cents per hour.

Immediately, Mayor Church announced that he would take action to collect about $50,000.[18] Church's logic was, as usual, impeccable – the city's percentage of gross income had to be paid, no matter if the company had received no income during the strike. Church seems to have set the tone for much of the criticism of the TRC, then and now. Historians Armstrong and Nelles have accused Mackenzie and officials of the company of raising dividends while allowing the system to deteriorate.[19] The truth is somewhat different: dividends had risen to 8 per cent in 1912 and remained at that level until 1918, when they were reduced to an average of 6 per cent, then eliminated for the last three years of the franchise.[20]

Winnipeg saw a similar pattern of extensions, jitneys, and a scarcity of men and steel that culminated in a strike threat. In 1914 the Pembina line was extended six kilometres beyond the Agricultural College to St. Norbert. In the north end, tracks were extended on Arlington, near the CPR yards. The radial companies controlled by WERC also continued to expand.[21] In 1915 jitneys began to eat into revenues, and for the first time gross revenue fell below levels of the year before. In 1917 return on investment had fallen dramatically and dividends were suspended.[22] Shares fell from a high of $269 in 1912 to $36 in 1917. Tickets remained at 1892 levels, and by June 1917 receipts were not sufficient to pay operating expenses and fixed charges.[23] Unfortunately for WERC, employees in 1917 were anxious to improve their earning power. A board of arbitration raised wages by about 12 per cent.[24]

Brazilian Traction survived the war in good shape. Expansion costs were relatively low. Although gas revenues fell, tramway and electric companies saw revenues rise after 1915. Far removed from the motor car centres of North America and Europe, Brazilian trolley riders were not exposed to the sight of jitneys weaving their way through the streets of Rio and São Paulo. In 1915 Mackenzie reduced his shares from about 29,000 to about 12,000, probably because of the financial demands of the Canadian Northern. The sale of these shares earned him over a million dollars. With characteristic bluster, he announced that he had taken a million out of Brazil, a legitimate transaction proof of a 'remarkable public utility operation,' as Brazilian Traction's historian points out, 'in a foreign land which had known neither Canadian capital nor modern electric services.'[25]

During the war it became obvious that short-term solutions would not save the Canadian Northern. Mackenzie discussed government ownership with Borden. There was talk of Cornelius Vanderbilt and other American capitalists buying a large share of the railway.[26] In November 1915 Mackenzie asked the prime minister for a government guarantee of a new series of bonds to replace unsold securities worth over $110 million. But this proposal was also politically unrealistic.

Throughout 1916, however, Borden supported Mackenzie and Mann. When Arthur Meighen advised him to allow an extension of the completion date of the Montreal tunnel and station project, Borden concurred.[27] And the prime minister continued to respect Mackenzie's advice on subjects such as immigration, the homestead system, Sam Hughes, and munitions.[28]

On Wednesday, 2 February 1916, the day before the fire that destroyed the Centre Block, Borden lunched with Robert Rogers and Sir Thomas Shaughnessy at the Rideau Club. It was probably Shaughnessy who made the first suggestion of an official inquiry into the state of Canadian railways, an idea that may already have been on Borden's mind. The CPR president thought that the CNoR and the GTPR should be allowed to go into liquidation. But Borden was still willing to support the two railways by means of parliamentary appropriations and loans from the Bank of Commerce, which, however, was increasingly nervous and had already demanded Mackenzie and Mann's remaining Canadian Northern common shares as security.[29]

If the government continued to support the GTPR and the CNoR, another $20 million would have to be found. Discussions with Mackenzie remained amicable, perhaps because Borden, while favouring government ownership, continued to hope that, given time and interim financing, railways might return to more solid foundations.[30] On 12 April the prime minister and Mackenzie had a frank discussion. The government would probably have to take over the CNoR, Borden told Mackenzie, who 'accepted [the] sit[uatio]n in good part,' Borden confided to his diary, 'but believes he can reorganize finances this summer and consolidate with GT and GTP.' The prime minister was amazed, even somewhat admiring, at Mackenzie's 'exceptional nerve and tenacity' when told that, outside of a miracle, his days as president of the CNoR were numbered.[31]

Borden thought highly enough of Mackenzie to use him as an emissary to meet Sir Sam Hughes in New York in April, when Hughes returned from Europe. It seems that Mackenzie was to introduce the delicate topic of Hughes' resignation as Minister of Militia. A commission of investigation into Hughes and the Shell Committee was about to open in Ottawa, and Borden's other cabinet ministers were up in arms because of Hughes' conduct during the war, as well as rumours that one of his friends was making undue profits from munitions contracts.[32] Few people could handle the mercurial Sam. Mackenzie could, and often did. He did not, however, succeed in persuading Hughes that his resignation might be the best course.[33]

The railway question continued to divide Borden's cabinet. On the one hand, Meighen and J.D. Reid, Minister of Customs, and later of Railways, were usually sympathetic to the idea of interim financing. Sir Clifford Sifton urged Borden to provide further financial support and to leave Mackenzie as president. On the other hand, Borden also valued the advice of Finance Minister Thomas White and Bob Rogers, Minister of Public Works, both of whom thought that Mackenzie should be forced to resign and the railway nationalized.[34]

Even if railways were Borden's only problem – even if there had been no rumours of German naval raids on the British coast, no news of an Easter uprising in Dublin, no Shell Committee problems, and no exasperating Regulation 17, which effectively barred the use of French as a language of instruction in Ontario classrooms – this gentle, sensitive prime minister would have required the wisdom of Solomon to deal with the conflicting railway advice offered by the prima donnas who regularly sang their arias in his office.

Borden probably hoped that a royal commission would not go as far as Shaughnessy had suggested – nationalization of all railways, including the CPR.[35] But at least a commission would postpone the decision for several months. In late May 1916 the cabinet passed an order-in-council setting up a board of inquiry. Borden discussed the choice of investigators with Mackenzie and Mann, with Beatty and Shaughnessy of the CPR, and with Chamberlin of the Grand Trunk Pacific Railway. He could not have handled the railway moguls more judiciously.

At the same time, Mackenzie and CNoR officials were trying to find their own solution. On 31 May 1916 Borden warned Mackenzie that he would provide no more letters of credit to the Bank of Commerce, which was now unlikely to lend Mackenzie more money. Typically, Mackenzie had a counter offer. If the government would sustain the CNoR just a little longer, he was certain that he could find long-term solutions in New York.[36]

Three weeks later, Mackenzie arrived in Ottawa with S.R. Bertron, member of a New York financial house. The two men explained to the prime minister that Kuhn, Loeb & Company was interested in refinancing the CNoR, provided they be allowed to investigate the railway's financial viability. Borden gave this second commission his blessing,[37] and even asked Bertron for his help in finding members for the government's own commission.

A few days later, Borden and Mackenzie met again, this time in Bertron's office in New York. Minister of Railways Frank Cochrane, as well as a representative of the financial house G.A. Read & Company, were present. The five men had a frank discussion about the CNoR. Although Borden made it clear that his government would not consider any more bond guarantees, he seemed as hopeful as Mackenzie that New York money might refinance the railway. Borden and Mackenzie met twice during the next two days. The prime minister was looking for an American businessman to sit on the government commission. Bertron suggested several names, including A.H. Smith, president of New York Central Railway, who agreed to sit. Borden also met E.E. Loomis, also a railway president, and John Platten, president of a trust company, both hired by Mackenzie and Bertron to chair the private investigation of the CNoR.[38]

Mackenzie must have been confident that both commissions would by sympathetic, especially when A.H. Smith was appointed chairman of the government inquiry. Borden announced in early July, during Smith's visit to Ottawa, that the government proposed to appoint Sir Henry Drayton, chairman of the Board of Railway Commissioners, as the second member of the committee; and an English newspaper editor as the third. Before announcing his decision, Borden discussed the two appointments with Smith. Drayton was perfectly acceptable, since during his three years as chairman of the board, he had provided what businessmen considered fair judgments on railway rates cases.[39]

Meantime, Borden provided more letters of credit to the Bank of Commerce to cover interest payments on CNoR bonds.[40] In July and August Sir Donald Mann accompanied Loomis and two representatives of New York investment houses on a trip over the western lines of the CNoR. In September, the Royal Commission set up offices in Ottawa, and Drayton and Smith prepared to inspect railways from Quebec to the west coast.[41] The following October the third member of the commission, W.H. Acworth, a lecturer on railway economics at the London School of Economics, was chosen to replace the English newspaper editor, who had become ill.

During these months, Mackenzie was dealing with the daily operations and long-term plans of the railway. Since he could not obtain an agreement for shared use of the Great Northern station in

Vancouver, he decided to reactivate plans for a terminal on re-claimed land at False Creek. The station, to be built on Main Street, was to be another palace costing $1 million and featuring twelve Co-rinthian columns across the front side; inside, marble, stone, and ornamental plaster would be illuminated by natural light. Pratt and Ross, who had designed Winnipeg's Electric Railway Chambers, were to be the architects; and the Northern Construction Company, Sandy Mann and Big Archie McKenzie's company, was awarded one of the contracts.[42] In Toronto, Sir William made an agreement with the CPR for shared use of the its North Toronto station on Yonge Street at Summerhill, opened in June 1916.[43] In August he travelled to New York to negotiate a $1,750,000 loan to complete the Mount Royal Tunnel and to build a temporary station in downtown Montreal.[44]

From New York, he sailed to England with Ethel, Mabel, and the Hannas. The purpose of the trip is a mystery. Before his departure, Mackenzie had talked with Borden about the need for a higher tariff to protect quality products manufactured in Canada, so as to attract American and British immigration.[45] He may have discussed the nickel question with officials of the British government and met Sir James Dunn, agent for the sale of munitions manufactured in Win-nipeg railway shops. Whatever the reason, the trip was important enough to risk life and limb on the Atlantic. The *Lusitania* had been sunk in 1915. In July 1916 a German submarine had surfaced off Bal-timore. Later that year German submarines sank seven vessels off the American coast.

In Europe, D.B. Hanna joined Sir Clifford Sifton on a troop in-spection in Belgium and France. Sir William probably visited Grace de Lesseps and Ethel Mitchell in Paris, and Horne-Payne at Merry Mead. Accompanied by Hanna and Sir Sam Hughes, he returned to Halifax on 7 October in a new record time of four days and fifteen hours.[46] Mackenzie and Sir Sam probably discussed Borden's latest attempt to curb Hughes' power. During the minister's absence in England, Borden had created a 'Ministry of Overseas Service' to oversee Hughes and Canadian forces in England, thereby defusing the Minister of Militia, who was then summoned to Ottawa.[47] As soon as the ship docked at Halifax, Hughes took a train to Ottawa. Five weeks later, on Sunday, 12 November, Mackenzie visited Bor-den at his home, where they discussed Hughes. Mackenzie agreed that Hughes should resign, and the next day he did.[48] Since neither Hughes nor Mackenzie kept diaries, it is impossible to say whether Mackenzie had anything to do with Hughes' final decision.

The Hughes affair was only one of several pieces of business requiring Mackenzie's attention. He was making plans to purchase six steamers for use on the Great Lakes, using money obtained from the sale of some of the assets of the Royal line to the Cunard Company.[49] (The two luxury liners themselves had previously been requisitioned by the British Admiralty soon after war was declared, and the *Royal Edward* was torpedoed off Gallipoli on 14 August 1915, with a loss of 1,000 reinforcements.)[50] The CNoR was acquiring land for right-of-ways in St. Andrew's Parish, western Quebec, and constructing extensions near Lac St. Jean.[51] The Montreal Land Company was developing land in Mount Royal. Tenders had been called for the Montreal station. By the end of 1916 the concrete lining of the Mount Royal tunnel was almost complete. The railway company was also building one hundred houses for Montreal trainmen.[52]

In December 1916 Sir William travelled to Vancouver Island for an inspection tour of the new line from Victoria to Patricia Bay, where a commuter ferry, manufactured by Davie Shipbuilding at Lauzon, near Quebec City, was expected soon.[53] He inspected the False Creek site of the proposed station, asked for more time to construct the sea wall, and announced that repair shops at Port Mann would be opened in February 1917.[54]

On his return journey, he stopped at Port Arthur, where he was joined by the prime minister, who had been travelling across the country to promote war enlistment. From there to Toronto, Borden and Arthur Meighen, with his little daughter, travelled with Mackenzie and Big Archie McKenzie in the *Atikokan*. Also present was an exhausted R.B. Bennett, who had accompanied Borden on the cross-country campaign.

As Borden and Sir William dined and played bridge, they passed over railway tracks constructed by Archie McKenzie and Sandy Mann. Borden congratulated Archie on the generally good quality of the roadbed. The mood was jovial. Archie drew smiles when he suggested that the often sanctimonious Joseph Flavelle be appointed 'Director General of the National Conscience.' The afternoon wore on and the soft, blue winter light faded. As the train rolled past Sudbury, then south towards Parry Sound, Sir William pointed out some of the two million acres that the Canadian Northern owned, courtesy of the late Sir James Whitney.[55] The land, he reminded Borden, represented millions of dollars of future revenue for the railway, in the form of pulp and paper, mines and farms.

Since the Dominion government held 40 per cent of the common stock of the railway, Borden must have been relieved at the good news contained in the latest annual report of the Canadian Northern, which Mackenzie had with him. For the year ending 30 June

1916, the system seemed to be recovering from the previous year, when gross earnings had fallen by over $5 million. The 1916 report showed gross earnings up by almost $10 million. Although operating expenses had also increased, net earnings had increased sufficiently to cover all but about $250,000 of the railway's fixed charges, mostly interest on bonds.[56] If the railway could continue on the same path, it would be able to pay all its fixed charges in 1917. (Mackenzie, as usual, was somewhat optimistic: on bonded indebtedness of about $300 million, interest debt would have been higher than the $9,621,657 reported in the railway's annual report for the year ending 30 June 1916.)[57]

Anyone waiting at a railway crossing might have caught a fleeting glimpse of the two men sitting at their sparkling white linen tablecloth, facing each other, deep in discussion: the sixty-two-year-old prime minister, handsome and heavy-set, with a bushy white moustache and thick, white hair, which even at that age had not begun to thin; and the smaller and shorter Mackenzie, five years older, with his handsome profile, his grey spade beard, and his bald pate bordered on three sides by thinning grey hair. The most memorable features of both men were their eyes, Borden's deep-set, hazel eyes unfathomable and friendly; Mackenzie's a deep blue with that odd mixture of steel and humour. The two men obviously enjoyed each other's company, even if Borden did find some of Mackenzie's theories 'absurd,' and the man himself at times slightly paranoid.[58] They retired to their beds as the *Atikokan* continued towards Toronto. As Mackenzie drifted off to sleep, listening to the steady clicketty-clack of steel on steel, to the 'long muffled roar of the whistle' (Leacock's phrase), its melancholy wail echoing into woods and across frozen lakes, he may have recalled his pride at the annual meeting a few days earlier, when he had talked about his great transcontinental railway, its superior curvatures and grades, the fact that it served most of the population of the prairie provinces and would soon, once the line to Hamilton was completed, connect with centres producing 70 per cent of all products manufactured in Ontario and Quebec.[59]

In January and early February 1917, Mackenzie continued to pay frequent visits to Borden. On 9 February, just before Borden departed to inspect the battlefields of France and Belgium, Mackenzie went to Ottawa with the kind of visionary scheme that had made him famous, and which a few years earlier he might have been able to realize. He proposed a union of the Intercolonial, the National Transcontinental, the Grand Trunk, the Grand Trunk Pacific, and the Canadian Northern, with himself as president. 'Chimerical,'

Borden labelled the proposal. Strangely enough, Sir Henry Drayton thought it a good one, and John Dafoe, editor of Sifton's *Free Press*, was also hopeful.[60]

The Loomis-Platten report, published in March 1917, found the Canadian Northern Railway sound and its future profitable. It recommended refinancing over a five-year period. In July 1917 two New York underwriting companies and a trust company submitted refinancing plans to Mackenzie, Mann, and Borden. On 2 May the Drayton-Acworth report was submitted to Parliament. The report suggested that Mackenzie and the Board of Directors had taken 'an unjustifiably sanguine view of [the CNoR's] possibilities,' which could lead only to disillusionment.[61] It concluded that the CNoR was worth less than its liabilities, and therefore that its shares were worthless. Drayton and Acworth recommended nationalization of both the CNoR and the GTPR and control by a government-appointed board, with the Dominion government responsible for the interest on the bonded indebtedness of the old companies.

Drayton and Acworth had made considerable errors, confusing subsidies and guarantees, and neglecting to consider land subsidies and cash on hand for construction purposes.[62] To correct these errors of fact and interpretation, Smith, the commissions's chairman, submitted a minority dissenting report recommending that the Grand Trunk become an exclusively eastern railway and the Canadian Northern exclusively western, with traffic exchanges of mutual benefit. He also recommended that Mackenzie and Mann remain in charge of the CNoR. To supervise privately controlled railways, he proposed increasing the regulatory powers of the Board of Railway Commissioners, which would set minimum and maximum freight rates and supervise securities and line extensions.[63] Unfortunately Smith's report was not without its own problems, for it provided no guarantee that the private companies would not continue to drain the public purse.

Mackenzie, Billy Moore, and others tried to explain to Borden that if Drayton and Acworth had included CNoR assets – land and cash – the company's net assets would be as high as $80 million. Naturally Mackenzie and Meighen thought that Smith's report had hit the mark. Even the three government-appointed directors of the CNoR were critical of the Drayton-Acworth report. So, too, was Shaughnessy, for he feared that the CPR would not be able to compete against a huge government-controlled company composed of all major railways except the CPR.

Borden postponed a decision as long as possible. As the snows of Ottawa melted and spring washed over the capital, the prime minister had many other concerns. How would the abdication of the Russian czar affect the war on the eastern front? How many more men would be required to replace those lost at Vimy Ridge? How to handle the anti-conscription riots in Quebec City? Could he get his Military Service Bill through the House and Senate? Could he persuade Laurier to co-operate in a coalition government? Should he provide more letters of credit to the Bank of Commerce in support of the CNoR and the GTPR? Should he consider Shaughnessy's offer to purchase the CNoR?

The first week in June, Borden was still mulling over the three reports. On 4 June he warned Sir William that the government might be forced to take over the CNoR. Sir William told Borden that Lady Mackenzie was very ill and that he would have to spend more time with her. He asked Billy Moore to negotiate in his place. Ultimately cabinet decided that nationalization was the only solution.

Mackenzie rushed back to Ottawa. He arrived at Central Station early on the morning of 14 June. It was a fine summer's day, warm and dry. He was driven down busy Rideau Street, past trolleys and motor cars and sidewalks full of civil servants and politicians and shop clerks. His car turned left onto Wurtemburg Street and into the driveway of Glensmere. A servant opened the door. The prime minister shook his hand. Mackenzie was exhausted from a ten-day vigil at the bedside of his wife. She had just undergone an operation for cancer the day before. Borden also had bad news. He hinted first, then told Mackenzie: the railway had to be nationalized.

It must have been one of the most difficult moments of Borden's political career. Mackenzie had helped to elect him in 1911 and had always been a trusted adviser. Borden admired Mackenzie's 'brilliant initiative, immense resourcefulness and unflinching courage.' Now he was telling Mackenzie that his dreams were at an end. Given Mackenzie's bone-tired exhaustion, there was only one possible response. He bowed his head and wept. He mumbled something about being ruined. The prime minister did his best to console him.[64]

The decision to take over the CNoR created new problems, the most salient being the value of the stock held by Mackenzie, Mann & Company. The resources of the construction company were also stretched dangerously thin. If Borden agreed with Drayton and Acworth that CNoR stock was worthless, then Mackenzie, Mann & Company would be left with millions of dollars of worthless railway stock, and would thus be unable to repay Bank of Commerce loans. Although most bank loans to the CNoR were guaranteed by the Dominion government, Mackenzie, Mann & Company enjoyed no such guarantees. Furthermore, it owed subcontractors hundreds of thousands of dollars. Borden and his cabinet realized that the stability of the Bank of Commerce might be shaken if it lost the entire Mackenzie and Mann account, worth about $10 million.[65] One day a large crowd of anxious depositors gathered outside the bank's headquarters on King Street. They were persuaded by a silver-tongued bank representative that their money was safe.[66] On his deathbed, one old bank official was supposed to have said, 'My dear, I'm not dying of heart failure; I'm dying of Mackenzie and Mann.'[67]

There remained a small chance that the CPR might be able to buy the CNoR. Mackenzie, Shaughnessy, and Aird were in favour. Borden might have agreed to the sale.[68] Mackenzie asked Lash to negotiate with Shaughnessy for the sale of Mackenzie and Mann's shares at $20 million to $30 million.[69] But the Dominion government controlled 40 per cent of the CNoR; it would have been politically inexpedient to sell to the CPR or to operate the CNoR with Shaughnessy.

Throughout these negotiations, Borden continued to rely on Mackenzie and Mann for political advice. The 'Conscription' bill, known officially as the Military Service Bill, was being debated in the Commons. In order to avoid more intense sectional and linguistic divisions, Borden was trying to form a coalition government. In May he sent Mann to Sir Wilfrid Laurier in an unsuccessful attempt to persuade him to join the coalition.[70] When Sir Clifford Sifton proved powerless to bring western Liberals into Union government, Borden turned to Mackenzie to carry on secret negotiations with Saskatchewan's Minister of Railways, James Calder,[71] a powerful western Liberal who was in charge of patronage in his province. Since many prairie farmers were anti-conscriptionist, it was essential to include him in a coalition government.[72]

Premier Sifton of Alberta, James Calder, and Thomas Crerar supported coalition and conscription, but wanted Borden to resign as prime minister. Mackenzie's secret negotiations were to convince them to accept Borden as leader of the Union government, and thus as prime minister. Mackenzie was well placed, for he had remained on close terms with most of the players.

In the meantime, the prime minister was willing to listen to Mackenzie and Moore's continuing critique of the Drayton-Acworth Report. Until the middle of July, Borden considered allowing Mackenzie and Mann to sell their shares to the CPR. By the end of July, however, the government had decided to acquire the rest of the CNoR's stock and to create a board of management to oversee all railways for the duration of the war, even though the CPR would continue to be privately owned. In consultation with Lash, Mackenzie, Meighen, and Aird, Borden and the cabinet drew up details of a bill to acquire the CNoR. Its final version included provision for arbitration to determine the value of Mackenzie and Mann's shares. Their maximum value was established at $10 million, an amount that Sir William had suggested to Borden earlier in July.[73] The bill thus implied that the shares were worth something. Late in August, but only under threat of closure, the House passed the CNoR bill, two days after conscription was made law.[74]

Both bills revived old and bitter memories. If the railway stock was worthless, why was Borden proposing to compensate Mackenzie and Mann? Liberals recalled that Borden had won the 1911 election with help from Toronto businessmen associated with the Canadian Northern and the Bank of Commerce. Now the very survival of the Commerce seemed to depend on the financial largesse proposed by this bill. Laurier's staunchest supporter, Charles Murphy, alleged that Mackenzie and Mann were masters of the Borden administration. Former Liberal colleagues of Sir Thomas White, retired vice-president of National Trust, who had joined Borden in 1911 to fight reciprocity, accused him of using his position as Minister of Finance to help Mackenzie and Mann. The most unlikely combination of opponents to the bill took shape. Laurier, Shaughnessy, the Bank of Montreal, *La Presse* (no longer owned by Mackenzie and Mann), the *Gazette*, and even Laurier's old enemy, Sir Hugh Graham of the Montreal *Star*, joined to fight the bill. Not surprisingly, Mackenzie's support came from Toronto's *Star* and *Globe* and the Winnipeg *Free Press*. Astonishingly, R.B. Bennett defended the bill. Had Bennett now become the gramophone of Mackenzie and Mann? irritated Liberals asked openly. The trip in the *Atikokan* the previous December seemed to have made Bennett a friend.[75]

In September the CNoR Bill moved successfully through the Senate, in spite of rumoured lobbying by the CPR. On 20 September the Borden government took over Mackenzie and Mann's almost 600,000 shares, but allowed Mackenzie to remain president for several more months. Borden even considered Mackenzie as chairman of the government board supervising railways during the war,[76] but wisely decided against that idea.

During the first ten days of October, Mackenzie was frequently in Borden's office. As well as the choice of president of the nationalized Canadian Northern, they discussed Borden's difficulties in making the final selection for Union government. Arthur Meighen objected to so many western Liberals in the proposed cabinet. Calder had become the 'chief negotiator' for Liberal coalitionists.[77] He still wanted Borden to step aside. Mackenzie was Borden's liaison with Calder.

On 10 October Meighen was still adamant against admitting Calder and his prairie colleagues to cabinet. 'Stand pat,' Mackenzie counselled Borden.[78] The cabinet that Borden formed two days later consisted of the prime minister, twelve other Conservatives including Meighen, one Labour representative, and eight Liberals. Meighen was appointed Minister of the Interior, and Calder, Minister of Immigration and Colonization, thereby removing an important responsibility from Meighen's Ministry. Mackenzie had helped to lure Calder into a Borden-led cabinet; he had also succeeded in keeping Meighen as a political and personal friend. By helping Borden to retain the leadership, Mackenzie ensured that neither Chief Justice William Meredith nor Sir Adam Beck, both serious contenders, would become prime minister. It was Mackenzie's old western connections as much as Borden's 'patience and persistence' that had helped to form the new cabinet.

Union government solved Borden's worst fears – that the unified Liberals under Sir Wilfrid might attract enough dissatisfied voters to defeat the Conservatives at the next election. The controversial Wartime Elections Act, passed a few weeks earlier, had given the vote to women in the armed forces and to women related to service men; but by rescinding the vote of Canadians who had arrived earlier in the century from what were enemy territories in 1917, the act had disenfranchised many anti-conscriptionist and pro-Liberal voters, especially in western Canada.[79] Now Union government, with its important western pro-conscriptionist Liberals, made conscription more palatable and electoral victory for Borden more certain. As he had in 1911, Sir William thus played a considerable role in ensuring Borden's victory in 1917.

Throughout the remainder of the year, Sir William and the prime minister arranged a 'clean-up' deal of assets controlled by Mackenzie and Mann. Coal docks, townsites, and two radial railways, the Toronto Suburban Railway and the Toronto Eastern Railway, both controlled by the Toronto Railway Company, were to become part of the Canadian Northern Railway.[80] When Borden was in Toronto in late November, during a hectic and bitter election campaign, he met twice with Mackenzie. The act which had set up an arbitration board to decide on the value of Mackenzie and Mann's CNoR shares gave them the choice of one of three commissioners. The accounting firm of Peat, Marwick and Mitchell had recently provided Mackenzie with a detailed critique of the Drayton-Acworth report. Mackenzie wanted Marwick on the arbitration board. On the morning of Tuesday, 27 November, the early-rising Mackenzie arrived at Borden's private car at Union Station before the prime minister was up. Borden took the inconvenience in good humour. Although he was busy preparing campaign speeches and desperately searching for a modus vivendi to unite feuding Ontario Unionists, he promised to telegraph Mackenzie's suggestion to his cabinet colleagues, who were campaigning throughout the country.[81]

Mackenzie probably had not slept much the night before. Nor many nights before that. His wife was near death. To the last, Mackenzie continued to believe that both his wife and his railway would be cured, by some miracle or other. He sat by her bed at Benvenuto. He may have reminded her of their walks along the old Portage Road to the one-room school in Bolsover, their marriage in the Lindsay rectory, and the arrival of baby Rod. They may have recalled Alex, gone ten years now. From time to time, grandchildren were allowed to tiptoe to the door of the room. When twelve-year-old Margaret Griffin came upon her grandfather in one of the hallways, he hugged her in silence for a few seconds then moved away.[82]

Lady Mackenzie slept fitfully during the last few days of November, as soggy grey skies dissolved into earlier darkness. On 29 November, he decided to take a late-afternoon nap. He removed his suit jacket, loosened his tie, unbuttoned his shirt, and stretched out on the divan in his study. He was just beginning to doze when his sister-in-law, Annie Mitchell, came down the hall and entered the study. 'Come quick,' she whispered. Sir William arrived a moment later, his shirt, tie, and jacket in place. He held his wife's hand. When he finally realized that she was gone, he could contain his grief no longer.[83] A few hours later, the prime minister recorded in his diary, 'News that Lady Mackenzie died today.'

The next day her body was taken to Our Lady of Lourdes Church on Jarvis Street, then transported by train to Gamebridge, where two of her horses were waiting with a light wagon to pull the casket over the muddy Portage Road for a funeral mass in Kirkfield. One or two Presbyterians thought that they overheard the local priest suggesting that Sir William give the church a donation. Sir William was not enamoured of priests, and was reported to have reacted adversely to the suggestion.[84] Whether he really told the priest where to go is perhaps another story.

At the graveside on the hill overlooking Kirkfield, after the Catholic burial rites had been performed, Sir William moved over to his two young granddaughters, Margaret Griffin and Margaret Mackenzie, daughter of his Alex, who was buried nearby. He embraced them and whispered, 'You're the only Margarets I have left now.' The biting, moist December winds quickly dispersed the family. His world seemed as shattered as that of the residents of Halifax, which was destroyed by a ship's explosion a few days later. 'Poor darling,' Grace told Pat Burns years later, 'his life was so sad after mommy died, everything seemed to go wrong.'[85]

His courage and strength pulled him through, and that very night, he travelled to Ottawa. He was in Borden's office the next morning. No doubt the prime minister offered his sympathy. As he had done a decade earlier after Alex's death, Mackenzie rejected self-pity. He had come to discuss something else – the choice of arbitrators for the upcoming hearings, which would decide the value of his railway shares.[86]

CHAPTER THIRTEEN

Unsettling Affairs, 1918–23

When the promoters looked about them they saw the prairie as it would become, not as it was. The vision was millennial, and almost everyone was dazzled by it.

(Ron Rees, *New and Naked Land* [1988] 27)

We had fed the heart on fantasies,
The heart's grown brutal from the fare;

(W.B. Yeats, 'Meditations in Time of Civil War,' vi)

Little Peter Griffin, born September 1914, was sitting on his grandfather's knee one day. Sir William's eyes were laughing. 'Why don't you ever come and see me? Eh?' he asked the boy. Peter looked up into the old man's face. He thought for a few seconds, and then asked, 'What's your name and where do you live?'[1]

It was a question that Sir William Mackenzie had not been asked for two decades. During the years before the war he had become a name in Westmount mansions and prairie sod huts, in business offices from London to São Paulo, and in parliaments and legislatures from Westminster to Ottawa and Victoria. When Mackenzie appeared on King Street, Rue St. Jacques, Portage and Main, or Jasper Avenue, people had stopped and exclaimed, 'By Jove! Mackenzie's back again.' But between 1918 and his death in 1923, his reputation declined, and in 1920 Augustus Bridle called him 'a grizzled relic of his former energy.'[2] Old Canadian battles fought on the Plains of Abraham, at Crysler's Farm, Ridgeway, and Batoche were overshadowed by new battles whose lyrical names – Vimy Ridge, the Somme, Passchendaele, and Flanders Fields – almost masked their carnage. Old monuments to whose building funds Mackenzie and other exuberant nation builders had contributed now seemed tombstones marking a vanished age of glory and enthusiasm. When the war ended, there was little sympathy for men driven to build empires across continents and seas. Canadians who had once enjoyed

Mackenzie's magical performances were now wondering why they had endorsed such grand and expensive visions. Time passed, and many Canadians asked the same questions posed by little Peter Griffin. As the years went on, they ceased to ask. 'There is only one thing in the world worse than being talked about,' Oscar Wilde observed in the preface to *Dorian Gray*, 'and that is not being talked about.'

The arbitration hearings opened in Toronto on 28 January 1918. Sir William Meredith, the government's choice of arbitrator, was a prominent Conservative and a member of the Toronto Four Hundred. As chief justice of Ontario, however, he had recently made decisions unfavourable to the Toronto Railway Company, claiming that overcrowding was company policy. Meredith, Mackenzie must have feared, was likely to be hostile, especially if he suspected Mackenzie's pivotal role in ensuring that he did not replace Borden as prime minister of Canada. It no longer counted that Scott Griffin had once been Meredith's law partner in the 1890s.

But since the choice of the third arbitrator fell to both Meredith and Wallace Nesbitt, chairman of the Ontario Power Company and a friend of Mackenzie's for over two decades, the process was guaranteed to be as fair as possible. They chose Chief Justice Robert E. Harris, a prominent Halifax financier once closely associated with Sir James Ross and other capitalists interested in foreign utilities. In 1915 he had resigned the presidency of Nova Scotia Steel & Coal Company to join the Supreme Court of Nova Scotia.[3] Harris met with Mackenzie's approval[4] even though he and Mackenzie's friend, Max Aitken, were not always on the best of terms.[5] The arbitrators were to hear witnesses and determine the value of Mackenzie, Mann & Company's 510,000 shares. The Dominion government controlled 600,000 shares; the remaining 90,000 were controlled by small investors, the Bank of Commerce, and the government of British Columbia.

The hearings convened on Monday, 28 January. When he arrived at Osgoode Hall, after braving snowdrifts piled deep along Queen Street, the result of a severe winter storm, Mackenzie removed his big winter coat, found the assigned room, and took a seat beside D.B. Hanna at the back of the room.[6] The three arbitrators took their places at the front. Recording stenographers prepared to take down every word. After drawing up an order of witnesses, recording the names of lawyers, and in general setting up the format, the arbitrators adjourned the hearing for one week.

Testimony began on Monday, 4 February. As might be expected, each witness spoke to two audiences, to the three men sitting in judgment in Osgoode Hall, and to posterity, which would stand in judgment for generations. The officials of the railway, and especially Mackenzie, had always understood the benefits of promotion, and by 1918 they were experts in the use of the catchy phrase, the convincing image.

F.H. Phippen, CNoR solicitor and former judge in the Manitoba Court of Appeals, was the first witness. He recreated conditions in Manitoba in the days before the Canadian Northern Railway. Phippen claimed that homesteaders had moved into Dauphin country because the CPR had promised to build its main line there, but were sorely disappointed when the CPR built further south. Mackenzie and Mann's Dauphin line fifteen years later was the long-awaited rail link with the outside world.

D.B. Hanna held the audience enthralled for days. He sounded like the fantastic prose of publicity brochures that he had helped to compose in order to promote the CNoR and Canada. Hanna told Chief Justice Meredith that the history of the Canadian Northern was a 'beautiful story,' and that he spoke about it 'feelingly.' The CPR was the villain, Hanna claimed, because it had imposed monopolistic freight rates on prairie homesteaders and had disappointed communities by altering its route. He painted a picture of the little Canadian Northern so hard-pressed for funds that it had to patch together an old engine to haul its trains up to Dauphin. Company officials could afford very few comforts. He himself had resorted to sleeping on wooden benches. He also claimed that he had introduced the first quality wheat seeds to the Dauphin area.

Mackenzie was no doubt aware that both Phippen's and Hanna's memories were as carefully created and edited as Flaherty's film documentaries or his own well-honed stories. He knew that although the railway had an inauspicious beginning in 1895, he and Mann had been well-established contractors with connections in the upper echelons of Canadian political and financial life. As for myths about the CPR, he himself had helped to create the one about its intransigence. Sir Donald Mann perpetuated that myth on the witness stand.[7] Mann and Mackenzie knew that the CNoR had almost always been friendly with the CPR. Directors of each company sat on each other's boards and founded the York Club; and the two companies exchanged management personnel and shared stations. The Canadian Northern allowed the CPR to enter Edmonton from Strathcona via its line across the North Saskatchewan. While the Canadian Northern officials liked to claim competition with the CPR, that competition appears to have been more rhetorical than real.

There was keen competition in the prairies, but between the CPR and the Great Northern, and to some degree, between the CNoR and the Grand Trunk Pacific.[8] At no time was the Canadian Northern 'bottled up' in western Canada, as officials liked to claim in order to justify the building of the section north of Superior. For years the CNoR had running rights to the Laurentian basin on CPR tracks, and Mackenzie and Mann's company also used the Great Lakes to ship grain to Toronto and Montreal.

Mackenzie must have known that Phippen exaggerated the importance of the northerly CPR route through the prairies. Sir Sandford Fleming's proposed route would indeed have taken the CPR into Dauphin country, but it had been abandoned in 1881, before land around old Fort Dauphin was settled. What attracted homesteaders to Dauphin country was not so much the promise of a railway as the area's fertile soil and plentiful rainfall. Mackenzie also knew that Hanna's story of the old engine was invented, for the company had purchased two new engines from the Kingston Locomotive Works during the railway's first season and at the same time acquired a private railway car. Rarely, if ever, did Hanna or any other official have to sleep on pine benches in a baggage car.

Sir William must have found Hanna's seed story highly entertaining.[9] Hanna claimed that in the spring of 1897 he had purchased 3,000 bushels of wheat seed at his own expense and had it cleaned and shipped to Dauphin. For the first time, farmers in the area had the opportunity to grow grain from top-quality seed. Like any lie, it seems authentic. The truth, however, was different. Before any of his seeds were planted, the rich soil of the Dauphin plains was already producing prize-winning grain.[10] The Dauphin railway had helped to develop the Dauphin area, but it had not opened it. Hanna's memory was 'magnifying the good' more than a little.

Not all the officials of the CNoR were given to 'poetry,' as Meredith one day labelled some of the testimony. W.H McLeod, western manager of the railway, provided a forthright, unembroidered history of the CNoR since he joined it in 1900. He spoke from notes about secondary industries – lumbering, mining, and agriculture – and told his listeners how he had checked the location of the lines to Saskatoon and Edmonton through North Battleford. He had maps and statistics on the amount of grain handled; he exhibited a detailed knowledge of each section from Port Arthur to the Yellowhead Pass; he described the lay of the land, the quality of the soil in each region, and the earning capacity of the CNoR. He got on well with Meredith: 'They tell me,' he told the Ontario chief justice, 'that the wheat that took first prize at the World's Fair [St. Louis in 1904] was grown at Fort Vermilion.'[11]

Mackenzie listened to Z.A. Lash, the silver-tongued lawyer, whose seamless contracts were the envy of businessmen and the frustration of regulators. 'Every transaction between Mackenzie, Mann & Company and the Canadian Northern Railway,' Lash correctly told the arbitrators, 'was absolutely free from any criticism, legal, equitable or ethical.' But Lash also claimed that for constructing the Canadian Northern Ontario from Toronto to Sudbury, Mackenzie, Mann & Company was paid only the actual cost of construction.[12] He knew, as did Mackenzie, that the Canadian Northern Ontario Railway was constructed not by Mackenzie and Mann, but by Archie McKenzie and Sandy Mann of the Northern Construction Company, and that most of the Canadian Northern Railway, especially after March 1902, had been built by subcontractors such as McKenzie and Mann, W.J. Cowan, and Stewart, Foley, and Walsh, who made the usual construction profits, from 10 to 15 per cent of cost. Furthermore, after July 1914 Mackenzie, Mann & Company appear to have made a 10 per cent profit on construction costs incurred by its subcontractors.[13] Lash was telling the truth, but perhaps not the whole truth.

Sir William's almost complete silence throughout the hearings seems curious. His wife's death had been a great but not unexpected blow. The silence had much more to do with his understanding of the art of storytelling. As much as Hanna, Lash, and Mann, he knew how to hold an audience, for he understood the rapport and the suspension of disbelief that unites narrator and listener during a successful story.

Mackenzie had also learned the vital importance of silence in story telling. And by 1918 he knew that the time for stories promoting railways was over. The listeners of 1918 – the three arbitrators and Canadians in general – were no longer willing to suspend disbelief. The high age of railways was over. It did no good to continue to promote them or to justify the vast expenditures that had built thousands of kilometres of track, some of it unnecessary. The Great War concluding in Europe had extinguished any vestiges of Edwardian optimism. Railways were at once the symbol of that old optimism and a painful reminder of its excesses. Thus silence was the most appropriate response.

He was not completely mute, however. During the first week of testimony, Hanna slipped up on the year when the CNoR had purchased the Qu'Appelle, Long Lake & Saskatchewan Railway. Hanna said 1896. 'Nineteen-six,' Sir William corrected him from the back of the room. A few days later Tilley, solicitor for the Dominion government, asked Hanna to locate Kitimat on a map. Hanna stumbled. 'It is away up on the Pacific Coast,' Sir William interjected, 'hundreds of miles up.' Tilley ignored Mackenzie and persisted in questioning Hanna. Sir William reiterated impatiently, 'It is away up on the Coast, about 200 miles north of Vancouver.' That same day, 12 February, he helped Hanna and Tilley to locate the clay belt in Northern Ontario through which the railway ran.[14] In early May, Mackenzie and Premier Oliver of BC had words over the incomplete Vancouver terminals and tunnel. On the witness stand Oliver charged that the Canadian Northern Pacific had diverted funds intended for terminal purposes to railway construction. 'That is a matter between the city and the company to adjust,' Sir William reminded the premier. When Oliver replied that the province did indeed have something to do with the problem, Mackenzie shot back that the province had nothing to do with it.[15] On one or two other occasions, he interrupted proceedings to set the record straight. Mostly, however, he watched silently.

When testimony ended each day at 4:30 pm, the small group of officials drove or walked a few blocks east to the Toronto Railway Chambers, to discuss the day's testimony and make plans for the next day. Twenty years of their lives were being assessed, often critically. They soon realized that Chief Justice Meredith was not objective in the least. He compared the Canadian Northern to the Toronto Railway Company, which he thought the most unpopular thing on earth.[16] They must have suspected that Chief Justice Harris was little better. One day he accused Mackenzie, Mann & Company of transferring money from one account to another on paper only, in order to create artificial sinking funds to retire the principal of bonds. It was a scheme to get rich quickly, the judge stated, because the actual money was non-existent.[17] He offered no proof.

The hearings, Arthur Hills later recalled, were like a game of poker in which 'the cards had been dealt and were to be played with as much skill as each side could apply.'[18] The comparison was apt – railway stories sometimes included poker games played for high stakes in hotels such as the Fort Garry, where hundred dollar bills drifted under gaming tables, detected only by page boys.[19] If they felt that the deck had been stacked against them at the hearings, neither Mackenzie nor Mann resorted to self-pity or to bitterness.

Although Mackenzie said little, he was busy behind the scenes, discussing the hearings and conscription with the prime minister, by telephone or in person. In early April Meredith wanted to hear testimony from Loomis and Platten, who had made the favourable report on the CNoR in 1917. Showing no signs of slowing down though he would soon turn sixty-nine, Mackenzie quickly left Osgoode Hall and was driven to his office, where he talked 'on the long distance phone' to Loomis in New York. He returned to report to Phippen that neither man was able to come to Toronto – Loomis, because he was overworked, and Platten, because he was in Florida. Phippen relayed the news to Meredith.

Most of the witnesses, even the most critical, agreed that construction standards had generally been admirable. Engineers pointed out ballasting problems and the existence of rough tracks on some branch lines, but the picture that emerged was of a railway system built to last. An American engineer who had examined the CNoR for Loomis and Platten in 1916 told the hearings that he found the Canadian Northern 'a magnificently located railroad, built with good grades and in large part well constructed,' with the exception of lines such as the Goose Lake line from Saskatoon to Calgary, where rains had washed out ballast, and parts of the rapidly constructed Port Arthur-to-Winnipeg line. Pierce Butler, the St. Paul solicitor who acted for Mackenzie, Mann & Company, told the arbitrators that 'if the Canadian Northern under proper treatment is not a good railroad, Canada is a failure.'[20] The problem was that Butler was expressing an optimism typical of the days when Laurier was prime minister and when governments, railway companies, and homesteaders all believed that the country's prospects were golden.

The hearings were expected to take about twenty days but lasted fifty and cost an enormous $500,000. One and a half million words were spoken, filling about 6,000 pages of transcription. Mackenzie's few lines would not have filled a page. A total of 211 visual aids, from maps to account books, were exhibited. The three arbitrators concluded that Mackenzie and Mann should receive $16.66 for each of their 510,000 shares, or about $8.5 million.[21] The cheque was made payable jointly to Mackenzie, Mann & Company and the Bank of Commerce.[22] Since Mackenzie and Mann owed the bank about $10 million, they may have received little, if anything, from the settlement.

In September 1918 the two men resigned from the Canadian Northern, apparently without bitterness.[23] D.B. Hanna was appointed president of the nationalized Canadian Northern. Several other officials of the old CNoR – McLeod, Lash, and Hills – joined the board. Hanna remained a close friend and colleague of Mackenzie; too close, in fact, for some of Mackenzie's critics, who accused Hanna of building new stations and terminals on townsites belonging to Mackenzie, Mann & Company, whose mills and mines supplied lumber and coal to the new CNoR.[24] The symbiosis of railway and construction company, meticulously built up over two decades, was not easily destroyed. The nationalized CNoR completed projects initiated during the Mackenzie-Mann years, such as Montreal's temporary passenger station at the corner of Lagauchetiere and Sainte Monique, a handsome terra-cotta building with five entrance arches facing Lagauchetière. The car ferry, *Canora*, was brought from Quebec to Vancouver via the Panama Canal. Shops and yards were built in the town of Leaside, whose street names today bear silent testimony to a business empire long vanished.

Day-to-day operations of the CNoR were no longer Mackenzie's concern. But he remained in charge of all other companies, including the Toronto Power Company, the Toronto Railway Company, Winnipeg Electric Railway, and Brazilian Traction. Sir Adam Beck's 'unremitting campaign' against him[25] was more than enough to keep him busy. During a power shortage in Toronto in early 1918, Borden appointed Sir Henry Drayton as Power Controller in an attempt to bring order to the power situation and to deal with the question of power exports to the States.

Domestic consumers had been encouraged by Beck to 'put in the Hydro,' and were using it in increasing amounts. Hydro had commitments, largely inherited from the Ontario Power Company, to supply power to American munitions plants, which made Ontario Hydro the largest exporter of power in Ontario. The shortage posed a dilemma for Beck. Should he risk the ire of voters by asking domestic consumers to use less power? Or should he cut back on exports and risk the ire of New York munitions plants and the British War Office? He had already illegally reduced power to one American munitions plant. As usual Beck used the Mackenzie company as his whipping boy. The old steam generating plant of the Toronto Power Company, at Front and Frederick, was capable of generating 14,000 horsepower. As long as the generating plant at Niagara Falls provided all the power sold to customers, including the Toronto Railway Company and the Toronto Electric Light Company, there was no reason to reactivate the old plant. Beck, of course, accused the TPC of withholding power.

The impasse lasted until the end of the war, when munitions plants no longer needed extra power. The post-war recession further curbed demand. During the fall of 1920, however, Ontario Hydro was once again short of power[26] and Beck asked Ottawa to cancel EDCO's export privileges in order to force it to sell more power to Hydro. George Foster, Minister of Trade and Commerce, wisely refused. Even Beck's apologists have difficulty explaining his behaviour during these years, when Hydro's spending, especially on the enormously expensive Queenston generating plant, accounted for almost half of Ontario's debt. 'In the name of the people,' notes Professor Nelles in his *Politics of Development*, 'the Hydro-Electric Commission was literally running away with the provincial treasury, and no one had the courage to ask for what purpose.'[27]

Throughout these years, EDCO and its parent company, the Toronto Power Company, continued to be profitable because of wartime demand and, ironically, because of Beck's promotion of electricity. For the year ending 31 December 1918, EDCO's net income was $330,422. In addition to controlling EDCO, the Toronto Power Company controlled six oil wells in Brant County, west of Toronto.[28] It was diversifying into one of the key energy sources of the twentieth century.

Despite the profitable balance sheet, Mackenzie and his colleagues had recognized for several years the futility of competing with Ontario Hydro. In December 1920 R.J. Fleming and Beck arranged for the sale of all generating, transmission, and distribution companies, as well as most radial railway companies, for about $32 million. The only major component not included in the sale was the Toronto Railway Company, whose sale was being negotiated separately with the city of Toronto.[29]

On 1 January 1921 ratepayers voted in favour of the agreement.[30] Shareholders and bondholders of the Toronto Power Company also approved the deal. Lawyers representing the Hydro Commission, Toronto, and the TPC sorted through legal documents representing thousands of parcels of property, including 400 kilometres of rights-of-way.[31] On 16 August 1922 the agreement was signed by Sir William and James Grace, and by Sir Adam and an assistant. On 23 August Queen's Park passed an order-in-council ratifying the agreement and guaranteeing the necessary bonds, about $16 million to pay Toronto Power Company shareholders.[32]

Mackenzie himself controlled few shares of the concerned companies, about ten in the Toronto Power Company, many of whose shares were held by R.B. Angus of the CPR, and about ten EDCO shares, of a total of 30,061, the majority of which were held by British Empire Trust.[33] Nor was Mackenzie a major shareholder in the Toronto Railway Company in 1922, having sold shares to aid other companies such as the Canadian Northern. The sale to Ontario Hydro, therefore, did not benefit him greatly.

The financial health of the Winnipeg Electric Railway was perilous during the last year of the war. According to the agreement of 1892, the company was obliged to pay 5 per cent of gross income to the city each first day of February, besides a $20 tax on each operating street car. On 1 February 1918 the total owed was just under $100,000. The cash-poor company had to borrow money, and Mackenzie and other directors had to provide personal guarantees.[34]

Winnipeg council realized that if it continued to allow jitneys, it would end up with a bankrupt trolley system. In return for improvements in cars and the addition of motor buses on selected streets, the city banished the jitney. During April and May 1918 the company introduced new trolleys, whose lowered frame made entrance easier. By June the company had four handsome 'motor omnibuses,' constructed in Walkerville, Ontario, running in a loop formed by Sherbrook, Westminster, Lipton, and Portage.[35]

Throughout 1918 Winnipeg motormen and conductors, like their counterparts in other Canadian cities, negotiated for increased wages. The war had increased costs for both the company and its employees. On 1 May, when jitneys were banished, the company raised wages to a minimum of thirty cents per hour. Not satisfied, the workers demanded a 55 per cent raise, including a starting hourly wage of forty-seven cents. Understandably, the company resisted, since the existing contract was in force until 30 April 1919. In September 1918 a conciliation board noted that the company had not paid a dividend since December 1915, and that it was actually running a deficit. The board recommended that wages rise to an hourly minimum of thirty-nine cents, a 30 per cent increase, and that fares be increased for the first time in over twenty-five years.[36]

At the annual meeting on 12 February 1919, Mackenzie resigned as president and was replaced by Sir Augustus Nanton. Sir Donald Mann, D.B. Hanna, and R.J. Mackenzie resigned as directors. In 1919 Mackenzie retained only 7,782 shares, worth relatively little compared to his almost 20,000 shares a decade earlier, when WERC stock was selling well above par of $100 on the Toronto and Montreal stock exchanges. A few months after his resignation, the city experienced its famous general strike.

The last years of the Toronto Railway Company were marked by two strikes and many confrontations with Mayor Church over issues such as the number of new trolleys to be placed on Toronto streets. The cash poor company made what improvements it could during the war, converting twenty-five large 'palace-type' cars into PAYE cars that resembled street cars of the 1940s and 1950s, except that passengers entered through a rear door where a conductor collected fares and sold tickets. This time, unlike in 1910, Torontonians adapted peacefully to the new cars, which made their debut in early January 1919 on College Street.[37]

In March 1919 the TRC stopped paying dividends, blaming excessive cost of materials, which had risen as much as three times since 1914, and rising wages, which had doubled between 1916 and 1918. At the same time, the company's average fare remained 3.9 cents, the lowest in North America for a city of its size. On 4 February 1920, at the annual shareholders' meeting in Toronto, Sir William predicted that Toronto politicians would refuse an increase in fares.[38] He was right. Fares remained at 1891 levels to the end of the franchise.[39]

Sir William and R.J. Fleming must have laughed at a cartoon that appeared in financial and transportation publications during the last TRC strike. A woman asked a black child the name of his mule. 'Utility,' was his answer. The puzzled woman asked why. Because, he told her, 'dat mule get mo' blame an' abuse dan anything else in de city, an' goes ahead doin' his level best just de same.' On its back, the overburdened mule carried several heavy loads labelled 'pavement taxes,' 'city percentages,' 'cost of material,' 'wages,' and 'car license fees.' A man called 'City Council' was about to throw a huge bag called 'litigation costs' on top.[40]

The TRC's franchise was due to expire on 31 August 1921, thirty years after Mackenzie, Everett, and Kiely had taken over the old Toronto Railway Company. The next day, the Toronto Transportation (later 'Transit') Commission (TTC) took over operations, raised fares by 40 to 50 per cent, and eliminated discount tickets during rush hours.[41] Since the TTC was owned by the 'people,' it could act against the people in ways that a privately owned company could not.

To determine the value of TRC shares, an arbitration board consisting of Sir Adam Beck for the city, Sir Thomas White for the TRC, and Hume Cronyn, MP from London, acting as chairman, began deliberations in June 1921. One of the solicitors for the TRC was the Honourable N.W. Rowell, who in the mid-1890s had fought against Sunday street cars. Hearings lasted 150 days, more than the Canadian Northern arbitration hearings in 1918, and cost an estimated $2 million. Engineers and lawyers gave evidence on the value of the company's real estate, the condition of the tracks, and the cost of reproducing facilities in order to arrive at a fair evaluation. A Chicago evaluator called the TRC 'well balanced' and 'well designed.'[42] On 31 January 1923, the board awarded the company $11,188,500.[43]

Almost forgotten during strikes and arbitration hearings in Canada, Brazilian Traction continued sound. It had to face most of the problems faced by the Canadian traction companies, including rising costs of materials and labour and a fixed ticket rate. Brazil's deflating currency resulted in decreased dollar earnings, higher prices for imported goods, and demands for higher hourly wages. By 1921 it was obvious that new generating plants would be required for both Rio and São Paulo and the company was thus forced to expand when hard currency earnings were falling and when capital markets were tight. The company could not pay its quarterly dividend from November 1920 until 1922. During this time, Mackenzie's daughter Ethel and her husband, Jim Adams, treasurer of Brazilian Traction in the 1920s, took up residence in São Paulo, from where they would be able to provide Mackenzie with candid reports.[44]

During his final years, Sir William continued to travel. In 1919, soon after his resignation from Winnipeg Electric Railway, he went with two of his daughters, Bertha and Ethel, and F.H. Phippen, on a brief trip to Monterrey, Mexico, where he was still president of the unprofitable Monterrey Railway, Light & Power Company.[45] In May he went to New York,[46] then to England and France for the summer. He attended a meeting of the Hudson's Bay Company in London and motored out to Merry Mead to consult with Monty Horne-Payne about selling stock and extending a loan to the Toronto Power Company. In Paris he and Ethel visited the de Lesseps family. Always a fan of grandchildren, Sir William enjoyed teasing Guillaume, François, Elizabeth, and the newest addition, baby Katharine, known to the family as 'Kiki.'

Back in Toronto, he attended an occasional social event. On a snowy afternoon in December 1919, he and his daughter Katharine were driven out to Heydon Villa, Colonel Denison's residence. Post-war gatherings of Toronto's society lacked the exuberance of pre-war balls and teas. The Denisons, along with too many other Canadian families, had lost sons in Flanders and France. The aging colonel's guest list that day included Sir Thomas and Lady White and Mayor Church.[47] None of the guests seems to have recorded the day's conversations, and the host was strangely silent in his diaries, but one assumes that topics such as personal income tax, introduced by Sir Thomas White in 1917 as a temporary war tax, and street car overcrowding, were discreetly avoided. Mackenzie gave a dinner party at Benvenuto to celebrate the engagement of A.J. Hills' daughter.[48] He kept in touch with old friends and celebrated their achievements.[49] He refused to dwell in the past. In early 1922 he accompanied two granddaughters, Margaret Griffin and Margaret Mackenzie, to England and France. In February, the former railway king, dressed in a bulky melton coat and fedora, posed for a photographer at Versailles with his smiling and elegant granddaughters. Nearby the Sun King's palace stood as a mute reminder of other vanished empires.

Mackenzie returned to Toronto in early May, accompanied by Count Jacques de Lesseps.[50] He made trips to New York, where he called on old friends on Wall Street. In June he attended a showing of *Nanook of the North*, Robert Flaherty's latest film, sponsored by Revillon Frères Fur Company. Mackenzie's claim that he had an investment in the film was true, at least in his early encouragement of the artist.[51] He returned to England in September.[52] In London and Toronto, he ordered half-forgotten stock certificates unearthed in a search for funds.[53] In 1919 the bankrupt Canadian Collieries was handed over to bondholders.[54] Sir Clifford Sifton helped to sell the Inverness Railway & Coal Company on Cape Breton Island to English investors.[55] The Pacific whaling business was taken over by a Toronto-based syndicate,[56] and Cassiar Mining Company near Stewart, in northern BC, was sold.[57] In December 1921 Mackenzie resigned from the committee of the Hudson's Bay Company, leaving behind, it seems, a small personal debt that Governor Sir Robert Kindersley discreetly covered.[58] Kindersley reminded committee members that his old friend and colleague had greatly benefited the HBC.[59]

Several times in 1920, Mackenzie complained to the prime minister that his remaining companies needed government assistance. In June a concerned Borden suggested to Sir John Aird, general manager of the Bank of Commerce, that Mackenzie's friends should help. Eight days later, cabinet made a payment of $30,000 to Mackenzie and Mann,[60] partial payment of the $250,000 security deposit made by Mackenzie and Mann before embarking on the failed Yukon railway affair two decades earlier.[61]

Later in June, the day before the prime minister's birthday, Mackenzie called on Borden at his home on the Rideau River. They discussed Mackenzie's business affairs,[62] no doubt including the Toronto Railway Company strike, still not settled after several days of negotiations. Mackenzie may have cast his mind back to happier days when he had helped the prime minister to celebrate his birthday aboard the *Royal George* in 1912. The circumstances of both men were now altered. The prime minister was about to hand power over to his successor, yet to be chosen. Mackenzie was anxiously seeking the last payment of the Yukon deposit. Having carefully avoided Yukon stories over the past two decades, he was now unearthing that failure in order to acquire money. The meeting was rather brief.

Borden need not have been concerned that Mackenzie would be

reduced to penury. Although businesses like the Toronto Railway Company were no longer paying dividends, Mackenzie's income made him one of the wealthiest of Torontonians. In fact, his income in 1918 and 1919 was $225,000, the highest in Toronto. The next year, it had diminished to $125,700, but rose in 1920 to $165,289, which put him in second place, behind Sir John Eaton ($349,716) and ahead of Sir Edmund Osler ($120,765) and Sir Henry Pellatt ($66,006).[63] Brazilian Traction stock and real estate sales may have been the source of these enviable sums.

It was difficult for Mackenzie to rest. Sometimes in the middle of the night he telephoned Fred Annesley, his private secretary, who lived on Edmund Avenue, near Benvenuto: 'Come quick, I've just had another idea.' Occasionally the disgruntled Annesley thought that Mackenzie was suffering from economic senility.[64] Annesley underestimated Mackenzie, who was still able to generate innovative and practical ideas even though he could no longer sell them to investors. He investigated the potential of a new process to separate metals for use in the mining industry;[65] he invested in telephones and radio (having missed the opportunity of a lifetime years earlier by turning down Reginald Fessenden's request for investment money to develop his radio broadcasting inventions).[66] In 1922 Mackenzie was interested in rubber tires, an ironic but astute investment,[67] which shows that he realized that the twentieth century, no matter who owned it, would run not on steel and steam but on rubber and gasoline.

He enjoyed travelling back to his roots in Kirkfield to talk to the McInneses, Boyntons, Mcdonalds, MacEacherns, Birneys, and Trumans. He continued to have his hair cut and spade beard trimmed in Dan Fraser's barber shop, where he was usually greeted with great bowing and scraping by the assembled men, many of whom had been part of the old Eldon Reserve. Mackenzie's hair floated to the floor and was swept into a corner to join a growing mountain of undulating hair that was removed once a week.[68] One day as his chauffeur, Pogson, was driving him down Nelson Street in Kirkfield, Mackenzie spied a little boy watching the motor car. He ordered Pogson to stop, rolled down the window, and handed little Jack Hughes, a newcomer from England, his first Canadian quarter.[69] Mackenzie continued to do business with Kirkfield stores but would sometimes forget to pay his bills. On one occasion, storekeeper Rod Mackay journeyed to Toronto to collect a bill. One of the maids at Benvenuto let him in and told him to wait for Sir William, whom he could see through the door of his study. Mackenzie was alone, examining notes and ledgers. After a long wait, Mackay began to stir; Sir William looked up and spied his friend. He welcomed him to his study and promptly paid the bill in cash.

On 1 March 1923 Sir William's son R.J. died in Los Angeles at the age of forty-nine. He had invested in railways, real estate, race horses, and American oil wells as well as élite clubs and private schools – the St. Charles Country Club, Winnipeg, and Havergal Ladies College, Toronto. In Kirkfield he owned the family racing stables. His 5,000 shares of Mackenzie, Mann & Company were, of course, worthless.[70] His death was just as mysterious as his life in the Golden State, and rumours circulated that it was suicide. On 11 March R.J. was buried in the Kirkfield cemetery as family members, townsfolk, railway officials, and former associates looked on.[71] His California home near San Francisco stands today as a reminder of this wandering Canadian who enjoyed life and who was remembered in Kirkfield as a boisterous man who said to youngsters, 'Here's five dollars; go buy yourselves all the ice cream you want.'[72] A few months after R.J.'s death, Sir William's brother Ewan died in Toronto.[73]

Other Mackenzie associates and friends had died in the previous years: Big Archie McKenzie in July 1919, while overseeing construction of a power plant on the Winnipeg River,[74] and Newfoundland-born Z.A. Lash, in January 1920 in Toronto. In 1921 Sam Hughes died in Lindsay; Senator Fred Nicholls in Toronto; and Lord Mt. Stephen, one of the last remaining CPR tycoons, in England.[75]

During the summer of 1923 Sir William paid a last visit to England.[76] He sold off bonds, including Barcelona Traction First Mortgage Bonds, and played golf with Sir James Dunn, who continued to act as his agent in England.[77] On his return to Canada, he played bridge and golf with his usual gusto. Some of his friends, including Sir Robert Borden, suggested that he slow down a bit. 'Personally,' Borden told Mackenzie, 'I have found it necessary to make sure that my enthusiasm for the game does not carry me too far.'[78] On 23 October 1923 Mackenzie was at Borden's home on the Rideau, where he played bridge with two former prime ministers, Sir Robert Borden and Arthur Meighen.[79] Young Max Meighen was always fascinated by the object carried by Sir William in his breast pocket, a solid gold toothpick, which he absent-mindedly used from time to time to remove a stubborn particle of food.[80]

The defeat of Meighen's government in the election of December 1921 had cut Sir William off from the highest echelons of power in Ottawa for the first time since the mid-1890s. The new prime minister, William Lyon Mackenzie King, was not likely to feel sympathetic towards a man who had helped defeat the Laurier Liberals in 1911 and who had supported Borden again in 1917 (even if he had found Sir William's daughter Katharine not a bad dancing partner one evening years earlier, when the young Willie King was a member of the Four Hundred).[81] In his *Industry and Humanity*, King had made clear his concern that modern capitalists often failed to understand their employees. Sir William was probably as little impressed with Mackenzie King's book as was King's former employer, John D. Rockefeller.[82]

By 1923 Mackenzie was no longer close to the executives of the Canadian National Railway. When D.B. Hanna resigned as president in October 1922, Mackenzie worried that he might even be deprived of the use of the *Atikokan*, the last trapping of his lost kingdom. Borden and Meighen assured him that the car would be his for life.[83]

Mackenzie turned seventy-four in October 1923. A few days later, he was playing golf at the Toronto Hunt Club overlooking the lake in east Toronto when suddenly he collapsed from an apparent heart attack.[84] He was rushed to Toronto General, where his condition was pronounced grave. He was removed to Benvenuto and though expected to die within a few days, he tenaciously clung to life.[85]

The family gathered. Some made last-minute requests. Almost inaudibly, Sir William directed that several codicils be appended to his will. Lawyers and executors emerged from limousines that pulled up under the mansion's *porte cochère*. Benvenuto would have to be sold for taxes, he suspected, but until then, Grace, Ethel, and Trudie could live in it free of charge, then afterwards at Kirkfield and Balsam Lake. He left money or property to his children and grandchildren, though not to his sons-in-law. As he rested in bed, he decided that Grace and her children would need some extra money, and at Grace's request, he added a line that protected her and her family from any claim or interference from Jacques, from whom she was now separated. He realized that the high-spending Joe might run out of money before the estate was settled, so he left him $500 per month until the will was probated. His signature on the codicils was thin and pale.[86]

During the last ten days, Cyril Andrewes and Dr. Bert Mackenzie, his half brother, sat with him as he laboured between life and death. His imminent death brought forth comments, mostly favourable. Colleagues recalled his toughness, energy, fairness, lack of pretence, and kindness. Sir Donald Mann, who was touring Russia, told the press that 'Sir William did many acts of kindness and charity that the world knew little about. He did not advertise his good deeds.' Sir Edmund Walker remembered Sir William's tremendous energy and courage, and called him 'one of the big minds of Canada.' Like the railway, Sir Edmund added, he seemed to be driven by a steam engine, often to exhaustion. Sir John Aird said that even his enemies would have to admit that Canada was losing 'one of her greatest citizens.' His anger, D.B. Hanna said, was like a spring rainstorm, 'tense for a moment,' and then very quickly calm and sunny. Although he believed that Mackenzie had used the war as an excuse to avoid paying dividends to German investors in the German Development Company, Martin Nordegg always held him in high esteem. Mackenzie, Nordegg recalled, was invariably a tough bargainer, but once he had made a deal, he 'never broke his word.'[87]

The men of the old Toronto Railway Company, though they had been at loggerheads with TRC management at least twice during the last years of the TRC, retained a surprising amount of affection for the old company, for R.J. Fleming, and for Mackenzie.[88] A member of the union told the press that Mackenzie was, in the end, very sympathetic to labour and would be missed by the street railway workers. A former Dominion civil servant who had once worked for the Department of Railways, remembered Mackenzie's loyalty to his old friends.[89] Lord Beaverbrook paid Mackenzie a great compliment: 'I never was a William Mackenzie,' he said. 'I created nothing as he did.'[90]

Behind the accolades, however, the reviews of his life and career were ambivalent. His career had indeed been 'strenuous and picturesque,' but 'not altogether successful.' He had been a great railway builder, but he perhaps had been too sanguine about the future of the country. His amazing ability to raise capital was noted, but 'perhaps it would have been better,' the Canadian Railway and Marine World opined, 'had he concentrated more.'[91]

Few Canadians had not been dazzled by his rise. Augustus Bridle, who had carefully catalogued Mackenzie's career, estimated that nine out of every ten Canadians had once thought Mackenzie a great man. He had been given 'a mandate from this country,' Bridle added, 'to do a great work – and he overdid it.' Mackenzie had staged 'the greatest pageant of industry ever known in Canada,' but when the impresario could no longer pay his bills and the show failed, he had taken 'what he could salvage of the properties and left other men to wrestle with the reconstruction.'[92] Awestruck Canadians who had watched his meteoric rise across the heavens had also watched his dramatic and fiery fall from fortune, which one Canadian historian has called 'one of the most dramatic reversals of fortune in Canadian business history.'[93]

On the night of 4 December it became obvious that he could not last much longer. As he lay dying, someone tried to break into Benvenuto through a window facing Avenue Road, but was apparently frightened off by the crash of breaking glass.[94] The next day, Mackenzie was dead. In Ottawa Sir Robert Borden, who continued to write his diary in French as he had since the Treaty of Versailles negotiations in early 1919, noted poetically, 'Il est tombé de la pluie et de la neige. J'ai travaillé au bureau et au Cabinet. Sir William Mackenzie est décédé. J'ai expedié à son fils Joseph un message de sympathie.'[95] He also sent a floral tribute. Arthur Meighen likewise sent flowers and a message of condolence to Joe Mackenzie: 'Have heard with deep sorrow the tiding of your father's death and send to you and all members of the family my heartfelt sympathy in this sad bereavement.'[96] Prime Minister Mackenzie King had nothing to say in his diary, although he did note in detail Lord Shaughnessy's death a few days later and attended his funeral in Montreal.[97]

The struggle between Catholicism and Presbyterianism flared up at Benvenuto. Mabel wanted her father buried Catholic. Sir William's older brother, Alexander, rose from his bed, where he had been confined since being hit by a TTC street car, and arrived on the arm of his daughter, Viola, who thirty-one years earlier had ridden in the first electric trolley up Church Street. To his horror, he found two priests praying at the coffin. According to Viola, despite his advanced years – he was close to ninety – and the effects of his accident, he roared at the priests, who left so fast they were dizzy.

On the morning of 7 December, Sir William's body was taken down Avenue Road to Union Station, where a Canadian National Railway train awaited the casket and the honorary pallbearers: Sir Edmund Walker, Sir John Aird, C.A. Bogert of the Dominion Bank, R.J. Fleming, Thomas Hall, D.B. Hanna, M.H. McLeod, and E.R. Wood. Also on board were business associates, a representative of Governor General Lord Byng, and Mackenzie's family, except Ethel, who was somewhere on the Atlantic en route from Brazil.

The train travelled up the old Toronto & Nipissing line. In Cannington it stopped to pick up Charlie Cowan, son of contractor W.J. Cowan.[98] It reached a hushed Kirkfield at 12:30 pm. The pallbearers lifted the casket from the train to a horse-drawn hearse. When they passed the public school, Teresa Mcdonald, niece of contractor John Mcdonald, Mackenzie's CPR partner in the 1880s, took her pupils, all eight grades, outside to watch the silent cortège.[99] The route took the mourners through the centre of the town, across the old Portage Road, past the site of the shanty where Sir William was born, then up the steep hill and into the cemetery.

There remained one last problem – how to lower the coffin into the freshly dug grave? Someone was dispatched to Oliver McInnis' hardware store to fetch a set of leather harness. Sir William's coffin was lowered into its final resting place beside Margaret, in the Catholic part of the cemetery. The service was conducted by two Presbyterian clergymen. For fifty years afterward some of his Presbyterian relatives contended, incorrectly, that he was buried in unconsecrated ground.

Mackenzie had come full circle. Born with few prospects, he had become one of the wealthiest of Canadians. But the last cheque that he issued to his Kirkfield estate manager, Billy Mitchell, remained forever uncashed, to be discovered a half century later in Mitchell Lodge in Kirkfield. Grace remained in Benvenuto for a few months, but could afford to heat only one or two rooms. On her wedding day only a dozen years earlier, she had glittered in diamonds and pearls, and had received from the Count an antique gold and enamel snuffbox set in diamonds, a gift to the then Countess de Lesseps by the Khedive of Egypt in 1869. Now Grace was forced to turn to family friend Pat Burns in Calgary, who promised to supplement her income to prevent it from slipping below $5,000 a year. It was a generous offer, but one which Burns could not have made if William Mackenzie had not helped him through his most difficult year, 1907, by buying equity in Burns' Calgary meat business and by lending him money. At Mackenzie's death, Burns owed Mackenzie over $30,000, a small sum compared to the almost $1 million that the bankrupt Sir Henry Pellatt had borrowed from Mackenzie in order to build Casa Loma.

Sir William's complicated estate was finally settled years after his death, thanks to the untiring efforts of his son-in-law, the solicitor Frank McCarthy. His heirs inherited about $800,000, thanks to shares in Burns Meats, Brazilian Traction, and other successful companies; some life insurance; real estate; and art valued at $145,000. The furniture was divided by a random selection of straws. Grace ended up with three pianos, and Pat Burns did not have to send her money after all.

Less than a decade after Sir William's death, the empty Benvenuto was demolished, fulfilling Biddy Young's prophecy that the house of Mackenzie would someday lie in ruin. The beautiful, rambling summer house on Balsam Lake survived in good shape into the 1960s, but after Ethel Adams' death it was deserted and vandalized. Its beautiful Douglas fir panelling was burned in the same fireplace that had warmed Sarah Macnaughtan and Sir William one autumn evening in 1912, when Mackenzie had predicted that hordes of barbarians would eventually invade his empire. The summer house was torn down in the mid-1980s, replaced by a Viceroy house owned by the president of a computer company. In 1927 Joe Mackenzie sold the Kirkfield family home for a dollar to the Sisters of St. Joseph, who lovingly preserved it as a convent until the 1970s, when it became an ill-conceived museum. Today, it is in good repair and functions as an attractive guesthouse, antique shop, and restaurant.

Mackenzie's descendants include two medical missionaries among lepers in Africa, several successful business people, and a number of artists and actors. Their homes preserve memories – the silver tray presented by the mayor of Edmonton in 1905; the champagne cooler given by the Duke and Duchess of Connaught in 1912; albums and framed photographs of Sir William and Lady Mackenzie resting on mantlepieces; a few letters; witty, often self-deprecating stories; and, in Los Angeles, a portrait of Mary Mackenzie, the best mother in the world. And in the Roman Catholic section of the Kirkfield cemetery lie the neglected tombstones of William and Margaret Mackenzie.

Once the leather horse harness had lowered Sir William into his grave, the frenetic little town of Kirkfield began to turn into just another sleepy Ontario town. Except for one difference: for the next half-century, most of the stories told in Kirkfield and surrounding townships began with the line, 'There was a man called Sir William Mackenzie. He had money, a wicked amount of money. The Mackenzies all had money. No, I don't really know how Sir William made his money. He was always in a hurry. They had the first cars and his daughter married a count. His wife, don't you mind, was a Merry. A Catholic. She built the churches, the schools, and the inn. Grand place. Gone now. Burned in '25. Ah, yes, and then there was Biddy Young. Did you ever hear what she told the judge one day? Did I tell you about the time she stood on a soapbox in the middle of Kirkfield and preached against the Mackenzies? No? Say, you in a hurry?'

Notes

INTRODUCTION

1 Augustus Bridle, 'Sir William Mackenzie, Railway Builder' in *Saturday Night*, 14 Jan. 1911.

CHAPTER ONE:
SHANTIES, SCHOOLHOUSES, AND TOWNHALLS

1 Duncan McDowall, *The Light: Brazilian Traction, Light and Power Company Limited, 1899–1945* (Toronto: University of Toronto Press 1988), 55.
2 *Directory of the United Counties of Peterborough and Victoria, 1858* (Peterborough 1859):145–60. (The cost of digging and building several locks between Lakes Simcoe and Balsam was 121,212 pounds sterling, which, at the 1830s exchange rate of $4.00, would be roughly half a million dollars.)
3 Lindsay *Canadian Post*, 11 June 1880. In June 1880 an area farmer, Donald Fraser, ploughed up some Spanish silver coins dated 1723, which suggests that the trail was used by voyageurs, traders, and Jesuits at least until the 1720s.
4 When the author grew up in the same area a century after Mackenzie, stories were still being told about Champlain, the Hurons, and The Portage Road, as though the French explorer had passed through the previous Thursday.
5 NA, RG5–C–1, 3, no. 343, Petition from Eldon and Mariposa to Francis Bond Head, Lt. Gov. Upper Canada, Feb. 1837; and R.A. Mackay, *The Founding of Woodville Presbyterian Congregations, with a Brief Sketch of Pioneers and Pioneer Days* (Beaverton, Ont.: Private Publication 1924), 16.

6 Watson Kirkconnell, *County of Victoria Centennial History*, 2nd ed. (Lindsay: Victoria Country Council 1967), 196; and *Historical Sketch of the County of Victoria* (Toronto 1881).

7 PAO, GS, 6397, 'The Parish Registers of the Reverend John McMurchy.'

8 E.H. Jones, 'Localism and Federalism in Upper Canada to 1865,' in B.W. Hodgins, Don Wright, and W.H. Heick, eds., *Federalism in Canada and Australia: The Early Years* (Waterloo: Wilfrid Laurier University Press 1978), 19–28; D. McCalla, 'Peter Buchanan, London Agent for the Great Western Railway of Canada,' in David S. Macmillan, ed., *Canadian Business History, Selected Studies, 1497–1971* (Toronto: McClelland and Stewart 1974), 197–216; and M.J. Piva, 'Continuity and Crisis: Francis Hincks and Canadian Economic Policy,' *CHR*, 66, no. 2(June 1984):185–210.

9 PAO, RG2, F–3–B, Letter from P.H. Clarke to the Rev. Egerton Ryerson, DD, 15 Feb. 1857.

10 PAO, RG2, F–3–B, 'Annual Report of Local Superintendents and Local Boards of Education, Eldon Township, Victoria County, 1850–1870,' Report for 1866.

11 Grant MacEwan, *Pat Burns, Cattle King* (Saskatoon: Western Producer Prairie Books 1979), 12, 16.

12 PAO, RG2, Series G–1–B, Box 9, Half-Yearly Reports of Lindsay Grammar School, January to June 1867.

13 W.S. Thompson, 'Early Memories and Experiences in Two Hemispheres: An Autobiographical Sketch,' Aug. 1923, quoted in Betty Keller, *Black Wolf: The Life of Ernest Thompson Seton* (Vancouver and Toronto: Douglas and McIntyre 1984), 31.

14 PAO, RG2, Series G–1–B, Box 9, Inspector's Report, 9 May 1866.

15 PAO, RG2, Series G–1–A, 4, Inspector the Rev. G.P. Young's report on the Lindsay Grammar School, 17 Oct. 1867.

16 'Born in Bush Farm Home Became a "Nation Builder",' Obituary of Sir William Mackenzie, Toronto *Evening Telegram*, 5 Dec. 1923, 14.

17 Registry Office, Lindsay, Ontario, Abstract Index to Land Titles, Eldon Township, South Portage Road, East Pt., 1 Oct. 1870 and 24 Oct. 1870; see also PAO, B70, Series B, Reel 2, *Ontario Directory*, 1871, 'Kirkfield'; also author interview with Teresa Mcdonald, Kirkfield, 20 June 1976.

18 G.W. Spragge, 'Colonization Roads in Canada West, 1850–1867,' *Ontario Historical Society Papers and Records* 49 (1957), 10; M.S. Cross and M.N. Duncan, *Some Aspects of Road Financing and Administration, 1791–1958*, pt 1 (Toronto: Ontario Department of Highways 1961), 39–40; and Jacob Spelt, *Urban Development in South-Central Ontario* (Toronto and Montreal: McClelland and Stewart 1972), 102–12.

19 'Born in a Bush Farm Home,' 14; see also PAO, RG52, 1–A, Box 1–A, Victoria Colonization Road, 1857–67.

20 PAO, MU2729, Shanly Papers, A–51–B, Box 62, Envelope 1, 'Financial Report of the Toronto & Nipissing,' 31 May 1881; see also PAO, MU26, Bailey Papers re T&N; also PAC, RG30, 489–94, 1601–3, 2031, 12650: Journals, Land Registers, Ledgers, etc., of T&N.

21 PAO, Ontario Census, 1871, Eldon Township; see also Hunter, 'The Founding of Kirkfield, Ont.,' *Ontario Historical Society Papers and Records* 16 (1919), 53; also *Canadian Post*, 10 Mar. 1865, and E.C. Guillet, *Pioneer Days in Upper Canada* (Toronto: University of Toronto Press 1973), 94.

22 A.R.M. Lower, *Canadians in the Making* (Toronto: Longmans, Green and Company 1958), 259.

23 PAO, RG8, Series 1–6–B, 72, County Marriage Register, Victoria County, 1869–73, 140.

24 The term was first used by Mackenzie in 1895 when he was considering investment in Birmingham, England, transportation: NA, Porteous Papers, MG29 A32, 2, Mackenzie to Porteous, 7 July 1895 and quoted with explanation in C. Armstrong and H.V. Nelles, *Monopoly's Moment* (Philadelphia: Temple University Press 1986), 95.

25 See Mark Casson, *The Entrepreneur* (Oxford: Oxford University Press 1982), 119.

26 *Canadian Post*, 31 Mar. 1876.

27 Spelt, *Urban Development*, 112–13.

28 NA, MG26A, Macdonald Papers, 164,828–31, Laidlaw to Macdonald, 9 Apr. 1879; and PAO, Ontario Sessional Papers, 37 Vic., 36, A1874, 'Return of Correspondence and Papers relating to application of the Victoria Railway Co. for aid,' 4 Mar. 1874, Laidlaw to Lt. Gov.-in-Council, 26 Dec. 1873.

29 PAO, MU20, Bailey Papers, 1877, Laidlaw to Bailey, Sept. 1877; see also *Canadian Post*, 18 Apr. 1879.

30 PAO, MU20, Bailey Papers, 1877, Laidlaw to Bailey, 15 Sept. 1877.

31 PAO, MU20, Bailey Papers, 1880, Kinsman (station agent) to James Ross, 17 Mar. 1880, and Ross to Bailey, 18 Mar. 1880.

32 Lindsay *Victoria Warder*, 26 Sept. 1878.

33 Woodville *Advocate*, 26 Dec. 1879.

34 *Advocate*, 28 Apr. 1881.

CHAPTER TWO: SEEKING NEW WORLDS

1 *Advocate*, 20 Apr. 1882.

2 Lindsay *Victoria Warder*, 8 Feb. 1884; and Kirkconnell, *Centennial History*, 201.

3 *Victoria Warder*, 8 Feb. 1884; and *Canadian Post*, 16 Nov. 1883.

4 *Canadian Post*, 2 May 1884; CACPR, Montreal, President's Office Corre-

spondence, James Ross to Van Horne, 10 Apr. 1884; CACPR, William Mackenzie File (649); D.B. Hanna, *Trains of Recollection* (Toronto: Macmillan of Canada 1924), 117; and Col. S.B. Steele, *Forty Years in Canada* (Toronto: McClelland, Goodchild and Stewart 1915), 189.

5 P. Turner Bone, *When the Steel Went Through, Reminiscences of a Railroad Pioneer* (Toronto: Macmillan of Canada 1947), 89; private archives of Donald Kilpatrick, Vancouver, D.J. McDonald to T.K. Kilpatrick, 13 Oct. 1938; and CACPR, President's Office Correspondence, Ross to Van Horne, 21 July 1884.

6 CACPR, President's Office Correspondence, Ross to Van Horne, 24 Apr. 1884 and 20 May 1884.

7 Rod Stewart, *Sam Steele: Lion of the Frontier* (Toronto: Doubleday Canada 1979), 120–1.

8 Bone, *Steel*, 79, 85, 97; Pierre Berton, *The Great Railway, 1881–1885, The Last Spike* (Toronto: McClelland and Stewart 1974), 295; and CACPR, President's Office Correspondence, Ross to Van Horne, 1 July 1884.

9 *Canadian Post*, 9 Jan. 1885 and 30 Jan. 1885.

10 Private Archives of Karroll Boynton, Kirkfield, Account Book of Albert Boynton.

11 Henry Norman, *Pall Mall Gazette*, quoted in *The Truth*, Donald, BC, 21 July 1888.

12 *Henderson's North-Western Ontario, Manitoba and Northwest Directory and Gazetteer Including The City of Winnipeg, for 1887*, 287.

13 CACPR, President's Office Correspondence, Ross to Van Horne, 11 Nov. 1884; and Calgary *Daily Herald*, 19 Mar. 1885.

14 CACPR, President's Office Correspondence, Ross to Van Horne, 8 Jan. 1885; Bone, *Steel*, 105–6; Berton, *The Great Railway*, 336; also *Daily Herald*, 19 Mar. 1885; Steele, *Forty Years*, 196; Caroline Brown and Lorne Brown, *An Unauthorized History of the RCMP* (Toronto: J. Lewis and Samuel [1973]), 31; and Stewart, *Sam Steele*, 121–5; NA, NWMP *Annual Report*, 1885; and Harold A. Innis, *The Canadian Pacific Railway* (Toronto/Buffalo: University of Toronto Press 1971), 125.

15 NA, A.J. Hills Papers, MG31, E12, 6, 'Manuscript: Articles on Railroading.'

16 CACPR, Comptroller's Office Files, William Mackenzie Files (649).

17 Bone, *Steel*, 124; and C.W. Jefferys' illustration in Joseph Pope, *The Days of Sir John Macdonald* (Toronto: Glasgow, Brock 1915), frontispiece.

18 *Canadian Post*, 20 July 1886.

19 *Canadian Post*, 22 Oct. 1886.

20 O.S.A. Lavallee, 'Roger's Pass: Railway to Roadway,' *Canadian Rail* 137 (Oct. 1962):158. In total, the sheds cost the CPR in excess of $3 million.

21 *Canadian Post*, 22 Oct. 1886 and 5 Nov. 1886; *Victoria Warder*, 3 Sept.

1886, 12 Nov. 1886 and 22 Nov. 1886; and *Victoria Warder, Supplement,* 24 Dec. 1886.

22 CACPR, President's Office Correspondence, Ross to Piers, 20 Jan. 1887; NA, *Arbitration,* 2663; NA, RG12, 863, Atlantic & Northwest Railway, Returns for 1887; Bone, *Steel,* 134; *Victoria Warder,* 11 Mar. 1887; and *Canadian Post,* 8 July 1887.

23 NA, *Arbitration,* 2664; and S. Macnaughtan, *My Canadian Memories* (London: Chapman and Hall 1920), 130–1.

24 MacEwan, *Pat Burns,* 58.

25 *Canadian Post,* 23 Sept. 1887, 11 May 1888, 13 July 1888, 15 Mar. 1889, and 22 Mar. 1889; and *Victoria Warder,* 24 Aug. 1888, 7 Sept. 1888, 15 Mar. 1889, and 19 July 1889.

26 NA, MG19, E29, 3–55, Denison Papers, 1788, Mair to Denison, 28 Feb. 1890; QUA, Mair Papers, Denison to Mair, 29 Jan. 1888; NA, NWMP *Annual Report,* 1889; NA, MG26A, Macdonald Papers, 209113, N.F. Davin to Macdonald, 8 July 1886; and CACPR, President's Office Correspondence, Qu'Appelle, Long Lake & Saskatchewan Railway & Steamboat Company, Thomas Copland, Saskatoon, to A. Hamilton, 5 Feb. 1889.

27 NA, RG15, D–V–I, 1223, file no. 213807, T.S. Higginson to A.M. Burgess, 16 Oct. 1889; NA, RG15, D–V–I, 1223, Department of the Interior, file no. 213807, H.H. Smith, 15 Nov. 1889, R.S. Cook, Report re 'The Pines,' 30 June 1890, and A.M. Burgess to James Ross, 12 Nov. 1890.

28 Bone, *Steel,* 160–1; Edmonton *Bulletin,* 11 July 1891; *Victoria Warder,* 10 Apr. 1891; *Canadian Post,* 5 Dec. 1890 and 23 Oct. 1891; *Victoria Warder,* 6 Nov. 1891; and Edmonton *Bulletin,* 22 Aug. 1891.

29 John Gilpin, 'Failed Metropolis: The City of Strathcona, 1891–1912' in A.F.J. Artibise, ed., *Town and City: Aspects of Western Canadian Urban Development* (Regina: Canadian Plains Research Centre 1981), 259–88.

30 Casson, *Entrepreneur,* 93.

31 PAO, Series D–5, Reels 23–4, *Toronto Directory,* 1891.

CHAPTER THREE: THE ELECTRIC 1890S

1 Author interview with Viola (Mackenzie) Beauchamp, Sept. 1973.

2 NA, A.J. Hills Papers, MG31, E12, 7, 'Biographical Notes.'

3 *Globe,* 11 Aug. 1892.

4 *Monetary Times,* 5 Nov. 1891, 548.

5 CTA, City Clerk's Dept, RG5, D, 'Electric Lighting Investigation,' Box 3, 3; and Toronto *World* and *Globe,* Apr. and May 1891.

6 TCA, *Minutes of Proceedings of the Council of the Corporation of Toronto for the Year 1891* (Toronto 1892), 524–75; Toronto *World,* 17 Apr. 1891; *Globe,* 29 Apr., 18 and 28 May 1891.

7 See *Globe*, 30 May 1891.

8 *World*, 24 Aug. 1891.

9 *World*, 22 July 1891; *Globe*, 22 July 1891.

10 NA, Porteous Papers, MG29, A32, 8, Hughes to Porteous, 8 Dec. 1896.

11 Casson, *Entrepreneur*, 15.

12 Thomas L. Walkom, 'The Daily Newspaper Industry in Ontario's Developing Capitalistic Economy: Toronto and Ottawa, 1871–1911,' PH.D. thesis, University of Toronto 1983.

13 *Globe*, 22 Aug. 1891; and *World*, 24 Aug. 1891.

14 Toronto *Telegram*, 27 July 1891; Toronto *World*, 3, 4 and 5 Aug. 1891.

15 *World*, 27 Aug. 1891.

16 *Globe*, 3 Oct. 1891.

17 TTCA, *The Charter of the Toronto Railway Company ... from April 14th, 1892 to December 8th, 1905* (Toronto 1906); and *Statutes of Ontario*, 55 Vic., Ch. 99, section 2.

18 Senator Forget claimed that the original shareholders of the TRC paid a total of 10 per cent or $600,000 on the total issue of $6 million par value shares (Canada, Senate, *Debates*, 23 Apr. 1902, 289–90, quoted in Armstrong and Nelles, *Monopoly's Moment*, 118). Forget may have meant that of the total of 60,000 shares, 24,000 were sold at 25 per cent of par value [George Cox's figure], thereby raising $600,000).

19 C.A.S. Hall, 'Electrical Utilities in Ontario Under Private Ownership, 1890–1914,' PH.D. thesis, University of Toronto 1968, 125–55 and 161; and McDowall, *The Light*, 50–3.

20 *Globe*, 23 and 26 May 1892.

21 *Globe*, 18 and 21 Nov. 1892.

22 A few years later a working definition of 'permanent' city streets was achieved. See Manitoba *Free Press*, 10 Nov. 1900.

23 *Globe*, 19 Aug. 1892.

24 *Globe*, 23 May 1892.

25 Michael Holroyd, *Lytton Strachey: A Critical Biography*, 1 (New York: Heineman 1968), 50–3.

26 *Saturday Night*, 11 Feb. and 13 May 1893.

27 *World*, 27 Apr. and 13 May 1893.

28 *World*, 18 May 1893.

29 *World*, 22 July 1893.

30 *Saturday Night*, 29 July 1893.

31 *Saturday Night*, 11 and 19 Aug. 1893.

32 *World*, 11 Aug. 1893.

33 Sandra Martin and Roger Hall, eds., *Rupert Brooke in Canada* (Toronto: Peter Martin Associates 1978), 28. Brooke was describing the accents heard in the streets of Ottawa prior to the Great War.

34 *Globe*, 19 Aug. 1893.

35 *World*, 14 Aug. 1893.

36 *Globe*, 19 Aug. 1893.

37 *World*, 19 Aug. 1893.

CHAPTER FOUR: TORONTO, MONTREAL, WINNIPEG, AND BIRMINGHAM TROLLEYS

1 *World*, 25 Aug. 1893.

2 *Globe*, 7 and 12 Sept. 1893.

3 *Globe*, 11 and 18 Sept. 1893; *World*, 11 Sept. 1893; *Saturday Night*, 21 Oct. 1893; and G.S. Kealey and B.D. Palmer, *Dreaming of What Might Be: The Knights of Labor in Ontario, 1880–1900* (Cambridge, Eng.: Cambridge University Press 1982), 109.

4 *Globe*, 2, 7, 10, and 20 Oct., 27 and 30 Nov. and 11 Dec. 1893; *World*, 2 Oct. 1893; *Free Press*, 13 Oct. 1893.

5 Author interview with Susan Payson, Ottawa, 10 Jan. 1986. Although 'tram' is used for the sake of rhyme, read 'trolley' or 'street car.'

6 *Globe*, 8 Jan. 1894.

7 *Globe*, 11 July 1894.

8 J.M.S. Careless, *Toronto to 1918: An Illustrated History* (Toronto: James Lorimer and Company and National Museum of Man, National Museums of Canada 1984), 203; *Globe*, 17 Nov. 1893, *World*, 11 Oct. 1893, and *Monetary Times*, 21 Jan. 1898.

9 *Saturday Night*, 9 Jan. 1901.

10 *World*, 17 Nov. 1893.

11 C. Armstrong and H.V. Nelles, *The Revenge of the Methodist Bicycle Company* (Toronto: Peter Martin Associates 1977), 126.

12 PAO, Whitney Papers, MU3114, Griffin to Whitney, 27 Dec. 1900.

13 Armstrong and Nelles, *Revenge*, 144.

14 *Globe*, 29 Mar. 1892 and 9 Nov. 1893; Montreal *Daily Star*, 1 Apr. 1892; and NA, Porteous Papers, MG29, A32, 16, Memorandum of a Conversation with McKenzie [sic], n.d. [1892?].

15 CWA, Council Minute Books, 19 Jan. and 9 Feb. 1891; and *Free Press*, 20 Jan. 1891.

16 *Free Press*, 20 Mar. 1891.

17 CWA, Council Minute Books, 20 and 24 Aug. 1891; and *Free Press*, 21 and 25 Aug. 1891.

18 *Free Press*, 11 and 14 Apr. 1892.

19 *Journals of the Legislative Assembly of Manitoba*, 1892, 55 Vic. 77–8.

20 PAM, Greenway Papers, MG13, E1, McKenzie [sic] to Greenway, 8 and 9 May 1894.

21 PAM, Greenway Papers, MG13, E1, p. 5168, Sifton to Greenway, 8 Sept. 1892.

22 *Free Press*, 18 July 1894.

23 *Free Press*, 28 Dec. 1892 and 13 Nov. 1895.

24 J.E. Baker, *Winnipeg's Electric Transit* (Toronto: Railfare Enterprises Ltd. 1982); H.W. Blake, *The Era of Street Cars in Winnipeg, 1881–1955* (Winnipeg: Private Publication 1971); PAM, E.S. Russenholt, *The Power of a City: A History of the Development of Winnipeg's Hydro, 1890–1915*, unpub. ms., MG9, 44; *Free Press*, 1895–8; Toronto *Globe*, 1895–8; MHA, Manitoba Electric and Gas Light Co., Minutebook, 1893–5; MHA, WESR, Minutebook, 1899–1900; NA, Porteous Papers, Letterbooks and Daily Journal, MG29, A32, 2, 3, 5, 19, 20, 23, 25, 26, 31, and 32; and NA, Sifton Papers, MG27, II, D15, mic. C–462, 15,833.

25 Thomas P. Hughes, *Networks of Power* (Baltimore and London: Johns Hopkins University Press 1983), 227.

26 *Globe*, 10 Oct. 1896, referring to a letter in Birmingham *Daily Mail*, 21 Sept. 1896.

27 NA, Porteous Papers, MG29, A32, 2, Mackenzie to J. Ross, 5 July 1895 and Mackenzie to Porteous, 7 July 1895.

28 NA, Porteous Papers and Letterbooks, MG29, A32, 2, 23, and 24; and *Globe*, June and July 1895.

29 His biographer has considered that he might have had syphilis, the 'King's Disease.' Construction sites across the country bred social diseases, for which there was no cure, though they usually did not kill the victim. If he had syphilis, however, he probably would not have lived as long and energetically as he did. Besides, he never suffered from skin disorders, cardiovascular complications, incontinence, impotence, walking difficulties, or other symptoms associated with syphilis. See Jay Cassel, *The Secret Plague: Venereal Disease in Canada, 1838–1939* (Toronto: University of Toronto Press 1987), 15–16.

30 For a discussion of the typical entrepreneur, see Casson, *Entrepreneur*, especially 14, 35, 117, and 335.

31 Diary of Jo Wheeler, 1 July 1896; and UBL, Joseph Chamberlain Papers, JC9/2/1K/2, Chamberlain to Sir Wilfrid Laurier, 7 July 1898.

32 Diary of Jo Wheeler, 17 July 1896.

33 NA, Porteous Papers, MG29, A32, 4, Mackenzie to Porteous, 7 Nov. 1896.

34 Diary of Jo Wheeler, 4 Jan. 1897.

35 Asa Briggs, *History of Birmingham*, Vol. 2, *Borough and City, 1865–1938* (London, New York and Toronto: Oxford University Press 1952), 95.

36 Birmingham *Daily Post*, 8 June 1898.

37 Diary of Mabel Mackenzie, 1898–9.

38 *Globe*, 25 May 1893.

39 *Globe*, 2 Dec. 1893.

CHAPTER FIVE: DAUPHIN IRON AND YUKON GOLD

1 P.B. Waite, *Canada, 1874–1896: Arduous Destiny* (Toronto: McClelland and Stewart 1971), 257.
2 *Free Press*, 21 Apr. 1896.
3 NA, Sifton Papers, MG27, II, D15, mic. C–450, Barwick to Sifton, 4 May 1896, 1152.
4 NA, Lake Manitoba Railway & Canal Co., RG30, 1265, Minute Book 25, 30 Jan. 1896.
5 Sandra Gwyn, *The Private Capital* (Toronto: Harper and Collins 1984), 232; and NA, Sifton Papers, MG27, II, D15, mic. C–450, Mackenzie to Sifton, n.d. [July/Aug.? 1896].
6 John A. Eagle, *The Candian Pacific Railway and the Development of Western Canada, 1896–1914* (Kingston, Montreal, London: McGill-Queen's University Press 1989), 71.
7 NA, Porteous Letterbooks, MG29, A32, 25, Porteous to Mackenzie, 15 June 1896.
8 Author interview with Bill Morley, Dauphin, June 1986.
9 J.L. Parker, *The Fort Dauphin Story* (Dauphin: Private Publication 1978); T.D. Regehr, *The Canadian Northern Railway* (Toronto: Macmillan of Canada 1976); E. Ringstrom, *Riding Mountain, Yesterday and Today* (Winnipeg: the Prairie Publishing Company 1981); *Free Press* 1896; *Globe* 1896; NA, Sifton Papers, MG27, II, D15, mic. C–450; NA, Porteous Papers and Letterbooks, MG29, A32, 3, 4, 24, 25; PAM, Greenway Papers, MG13, E1, LB A/835; Greenway, MG13, E1, 8774; and Greenway, MG13, e1, 9197; NA, Lake Manitoba Railway & Canal Co., RG30, 1265, Minute Book 25, 1896–8; and Lake Manitoba, RG30, 10218; NA, Armstrong Memoirs, MG30, B26; and *Debates of the House of Commons and Senate*, 1896.
10 PAM, Greenway Papers, MG13, E1, 9981, Lake Manitoba Railway & Canal Co., Statement of Earnings and Operating Expenditures for month ending 31 Jan. 1897.
11 Cited in Regehr, *Canadian Northern Railway*, 61.
12 In 1895 estimates by Sandford Fleming and by Collingwood Schreiber put construction costs in Dauphin country at between $10,000 and $11,000 per mile (*Globe*, 22 Jan. 1895). Total par value of construction bonds was at least double construction costs. If the bonds had sold at a 50 per cent discount in London, which is an extremely low estimate, Mackenzie and Mann's profit for 1896 was about $200,000.
13 *Free Press*, 10 Dec. 1896.
14 *Debates of the Senate*, 1898, 3rd Session, 8th Parliament, Senator Cox's speech, 30 Mar. 1898, 523.
15 *Free Press*, 11 and 27 Feb. 1896, 4 June and 2 Aug. 1897, 5 and 29 Jan., 10

Mar., 13, 20, and 28 Sept. 1898; *Globe*, 16, 10, and 18 Mar. 1898; Ottawa *Evening Citizen*, 5 Jan. 1898; NA, Ontario & Rainy River Railway Co. Papers, RG30, 1336, 15 and 27 May, and 4 June 1897; NA, Manitoba & South Eastern Railway Co. Papers, RG30, 905, 11 Feb., and 26 May 1898; NA, Ontario & Rainy River Railway Co., RG30, 1336, Shareholders' Meeting, 24 Apr. 1900; NA, Porteous Daily Journals, MG29, A32, 29, 23 Dec. 1898; and NA, Porteous Letterbooks, MG29, A32, 20, Porteous to J. Ross, 12 Aug. 1898.

16 NA, Laurier Papers, MG26G, 80, pp. 24,678–82, Laurier to Mackenzie, 29 July 1898.

17 PAO, Whitney Papers, MU 3122, Dep. Minister Public Works to Whitney, 11 Apr. 1907.

18 *Free Press*, 9 Aug. 1898.

19 *Monetary Times*, 26 Aug. 1898, 279.

20 NA, Sifton Papers, MG27 II D15, mic. C–475, p. 31,218, Mackenzie to Sifton, 21 Oct. 1898.

21 NA, Sifton Papers, MG27, II, D15, mic. C–475, Mackenzie to Sifton, 17 Oct. 1898; and NA, Lake Manitoba Railway & Canal Co., RG30, 1265, Minute Book 25, 1896–8, General Meeting of Shareholders, 15 Dec. 1898.

22 *Monetary Times* 1898; *Globe*, 1897–8; *Free Press* 1897–8; NA, Nipissing & James Bay Railway Papers, RG30, 9465; NA, Porteous Letterbooks, MG29, A32, 25; and Canada, *Statutes*, 1895, 58–9 Vic., Ch. 50, 'An Act to Incorporate the James Bay Railway Company,' 37–8.

23 The spelling and name of the town vary from Fort Wrangell to Fort Wrangel to Wrangel and Wrangell.

24 Roy Minter, *The White Pass: Gateway to the Klondike* (Toronto: McClelland and Stewart 1987); and *Canada Gazette*, 1 Jan. 1898, 1375.

25 *Globe*, 27 Jan. 1897; *Debates of the House of Commons*, 8 Feb. 1898; and D.J. Hall, *Clifford Sifton*, Vol. 1 (Vancouver: University of British Columbia Press 1981), 179–80.

26 Minter, *The White Pass*, 327; Victoria *Daily Colonist*, 17 Feb. 1898.

27 Minter, *The White Pass*, 151.

28 NA, Porteous Letterbooks, MG29, A32, Vol. 20, Porteous to Ross, 1 Apr. 1898.

29 *Free Press*, 27 Jan. 1898; NA, Van Horne Letterbook 54, pp. 592–3, Van Horne to Lord Strathcona, 25 Jan. 1898, cited in Hall, *Sifton*, 1, 332, fn. 79; and *Monetary Times*, 18 Mar. 1898, quoted in Minter, *The White Pass*, 176.

30 *Globe*, 23 May 1898.

31 Minter, *The White Pass*, 275, 327.

32 Eagle, *Canadian Pacific Railway*, 1989, 41–2 and 108–12; Charles and Dorothy Wood, *The Great Northern Railway* (Edmonds, Washington:

Pacific Fast Mail 1979), 258; *Free Press*, 26 and 30 Aug. 1895, 16 Nov. 1896, 15 and 16 Aug. 1898; *Globe*, 11 Sept. 1897, 15 Aug., and 31 Dec. 1898; Victoria *Province*, 23 Oct. and 13 Nov. 1897; Vancouver *Province*, 15 July 1898; *Monetary Times*, 15 July 1898; NA, Porteous Papers, MG29, A32, 3, 19, 20, and 25; NA, Laurier Papers, RG26G, 67, pp. 21,079–80 and 85, pp. 26,400–3; and NA, Sifton Papers, MG27, II, D15, mic. C–484, p. 42,088.

33 TRC Annual Reports in *Globe* 1893–9; and *Monetary Times*, 21 Jan. 1898.

34 *RSW*, June 1899, 186–7; and NA, RG46, 1142, TRC Annual Reports.

35 *Globe*, 3 Jan. 1899.

36 *Globe*, 9 Mar. 1895.

37 NA, Porteous Letterbooks, MG29, A32, Vol. 25, Porteous to Mackenzie, 25 June 1896.

38 James Mavor, *Niagara in Politics* (New York: E.P. Dutton 1925), 29.

39 *Monetary Times*, 15 Mar. 1895, 1195.

40 *Toronto Illustrated: Its Growth, Resources, Commerce, Manufacturing, etc.* (Toronto 1893), 38.

41 NA, Porteous Letterbooks, MG29, A32, Vol. 26, Porteous to J. Ross, 22 Apr. 1897.

42 *Globe*, 29 Apr. and 8 May 1897.

43 *Globe*, 17 May 1897.

44 NA, Porteous Letterbooks, MG29, A32, 26, Porteous to Nicholls, 15 Mar. 1898.

45 NA, Porteous Letterbooks, MG29, A32, 25, Porteous to J. Ross, 4 Feb. 1897.

46 *Globe*, 22 Apr. 1897.

47 Diary of Jo Wheeler, 6 June 1896.

48 Lampman, 'To a Millionaire,' in Margaret Atwood, ed., *The New Oxford Book of Canadian Verse* (Toronto: Oxford University Press 1982), 39.

49 G.M. Adam, *Toronto Old and New* (Toronto: Mail Printing Company 1891, and Toronto: Coles reprint 1974), 144.

50 A.R.M. Lower, *Colony to Nation* (Toronto: Longmans, Green and Company 1946), 309.

51 W. Dendy, *Lost Toronto* (Toronto: Oxford University Press 1978), 184.

52 See Casson, *Entrepreneur*, 93.

53 Dendy, *Lost Toronto*, 184

54 NA, Denison Diaries, MG29, E29, 28; Toronto *Globe* and *Saturday Night*, 1895–8; NA, Porteous Papers, MG29, A32, 26, Porteous to Mackenzie in London, 17 June 1897; Gilbert Griffin, interview taped by Susan Griffin, Oct. 1978; and author interview with Viola (Mackenzie) Beauchamp, Sept. 1973.

55 Author interview with Winnifred Hill, the telephone operator who heard the conversation, Oct. 1976.

56 NA, Porteous Papers, MG29, A32, H.S. Osler to Porteous, 24 Dec. 1898.

CHAPTER SIX: MASKED BALL

1 Quoted by Simon Callow, *Charles Laughton, a Difficult Actor* (London: Methuen 1987), 133.
2 *Saturday Night*, 9 Jan. 1904; and NA, A.J. Hills Papers, MG31, E12, 7, 'Invitations and Menues.'
3 Donald Creighton, *Canada's First Century* (Toronto: Macmillan of Canada 1976), 110.
4 *Niagara in Politics*, 50–1.
5 Hanna, *Trains of Recollection*, 174.
6 Dauphin *Weekly News*, 14 Apr. 1899.
7 *Globe*, 25 Sept. 1899.
8 NA, RG30, 3119, Act Establishing the Halifax & South Western Railway Co., Aug. 1901.
9 Author interview with Jean Shields, Coboconk, Ont., Dec. 1987; and with Bill Morley and other residents of Dauphin, June 1986.
10 Regehr, *Canadian Northern Railway*, 82–3; and *Globe*, 5 May 1899.
11 JJHRL, James Jerome Hill Papers, General Correspondence, 1901, 1–14 Jan., Hill to Mann, 6 Jan. 1901; NA, Porteous Letterbooks, MG29, A32, 22, Porteous to James Ross, 7 Aug. 1900; and *RSW*, Aug. 1900, 245.
12 *RSW*, Oct. 1900, 299.
13 NA, RG30, 1436, Canadian Northern Railway Shareholders' and Directors' Meetings, 20 Sept., 21 Oct., 7 and 17 Dec. 1901; JJHRL, James Jerome Hill Papers, General Correspondence, 1901, 1–14 Jan., Hill to Shaughnessy, 'Confidential,' 10 Jan. 1901; and *RSW*, Feb. 1901, 45–6.
14 Eagle, *Canadian Pacific Railway*, 78.
15 JJHRL, James Jerome Hill Papers, General Correspondence, 1901, 13 Apr.–16 May, Telegram, Mann in Toronto to Hill in St. Paul, 21 Apr. 1901.
16 Eagle, *Canadian Pacific Railway*, 78, following Regehr, *Canadian Northern Railway*, 90, apparently paraphrasing the Arbitration Hearings of 1918, which should be treated less literally. Without doubt there was railway competition and rivalry in the Canadian and American West during the first decade and a half of this century, but much more so between the CPR and its American rival, the Northern Pacific, and to some extent, between the CPR and the Grand Trunk Pacific Railway when the latter built too close to CPR tracks. Shaughnessy was particularly critical of the use of government funds to build the National Transcontinental, the eastern link of the GTPR. He believed that government's role should be limited to encouraging and regulating private enterprise.
17 Eagle, *Canadian Pacific Railway*, 80.

18 Par value of bonds was $20,000 per mile. Provincial and Dominion subsidies were $10,400 per mile ($3,016,000). Even if costs had been as high as $28,000, the construction would still have made some profit, at least $400,000 (NA, RG30, 1436, Canadian Northern Railway Co. Minutes, 29 May 1899, 5 May, and 20 Sept. 1900).

19 *RSW*, Feb. 1902, 63; and *Free Press*, 31 Dec. 1901 and 2 Jan. 1902.

20 The 'measureless west' is a phrase from Charles Mair's description of the 'Buffalo Plains' in *Tecumseh*, Act 4, sc. 7, published in 1886.

21 Regehr, *Canadian Northern Railway*.

22 Eagle, *Canadian Pacific Railway*, 71.

23 NA, Hays Letterbook, MG30, A18, 1, Hays to Wilson, 27 June 1902; and *Globe* and *Free Press*, June 1902.

24 *Globe*, 18 June 1902.

25 *Monetary Times*, 27 June 1902, 1683–4.

26 Claude Bissell, *The Young Vincent Massey* (Toronto: University of Toronto Press 1981), 11–2.

27 *Globe*, June–July 1902; *Free Press*, June–July 1902; *Weekly News*, June–July 1902; *Halifax Herald, Saturday Night*, June–July 1902; PAO, Whitney Papers, MU3115, Scott Griffin to Whitney, 18 June and 8 July 1902; and NA, Hays Letterbook, MG30, A18, 1, Wilson to Hays, 18 June 1902.

28 NA, MG30, A18, 1, Hays Letterbook, Wilson to Hays, 20 Mar. 1902.

29 NA, MG30, A18, 1, Hays Letterbook, Hays to Wilson, 18 Sept. 1902.

30 W.H. Moore, 'The Mackenzie I Knew,' *Saturday Night* (15 Dec. 1923).

31 UTL, TF, Ms. Coll. 1, Sir Edmund Walker Papers, Item 1, In Correspondence, 1867–1912, Plummer to Walker, 4 Oct. 1902.

32 UTL, TF, Ms. Coll. 1, Sir Edmund Walker Papers, Item 35, Journals, 1899–1913, Nov. 1902; and Statement to Bank of Commerce Shareholders, 18 Nov. 1902, in *CAR*, 1902.

33 P. Stevens and John T. Saywell, eds., *Lord Minto's Canadian Papers* (Toronto: Champlain Society 1983), 212: Conversation Minto and Tarte, 22 Oct. 1902, 'Most Secret and Confidential.'

34 NA, Sifton Papers, MG27II D15, p. 101,062, Mackenzie to Sifton, 18 Nov. 1902.

35 *Globe*, 4 Mar. 1903.

36 NA, Hays Letterbooks, MG30, A18, 1, Rivers-Wilson to Hays, 4 Feb. 1903.

37 Henry Borden, ed., *Robert Laird Borden: His Memoirs* (Toronto: Macmillan of Canada 1938), 111.

38 Borden, ed., *Memoirs*, 114.

39 NA, Hays Letterbooks, MG30, A16, 1, Morse to Hays, 9 Dec. 1903.

40 NA, Hays Letterbook, MG30, A18, 1, Morse to Hays, 4 Dec. 1903.

41 NA, Laurier Papers, MG26G, 280:76,816–7.

42 *RSW*, July 1901, 208.
43 *Globe*, 14 Feb. 1899.
44 *RSW*, Oct. 1901, 309.
45 Toronto *Star*, 8 Feb. 1906.
46 *Globe*, 21 Nov. 1905.
47 Donald Davis, 'Mass Transit and Private Ownership: An Alternative Perspective on the Case of Toronto,' *UHR*, no. 3, (1978):97.
48 *Saturday Night*, 26 Oct. 1901 and 25 Apr. 1902.
49 *RSW*, Mar. 1900, 93.
50 J.F. Due, *The Intercity Electric Railway Industry in Canada* (Toronto: University of Toronto Press 1966), 82–5; R.M. Stamp, *Riding the Radials, Toronto's Suburban Electric Streetcar Lines* (Erin Mills: Boston Mills Press 1989), 67–71; *Monetary Times*, 12 May 1905, 1510; NA, Whitney Papers, MU3116, T.W. Ramm to Whitney, 27 May 1905; and *Star*, 5 May 1905.
51 *Free Press*, 20 June 1902.
52 MTL, Baldwin Room, Larratt Smith Diaries, 1886–1905, 22 June 1902.
53 *Globe*, 15–30 June 1902; and *CAR*, 1902, 496–9.
54 Author interview with Gilbert Griffin, June 1976.
55 Author interview with Tony Griffin, Balsam Lake, Sept. 1988.
56 Author interview with Rt. Comm. Francis Lindsay, Sept. 1976.

CHAPTER SEVEN: *LA PRESSE* AND OTHER AFFAIRS

1 NA, Hays Letterbooks, MG30, A18, 2, Hays to Rivers-Wilson, 16 May, 21 June, and 5 July 1904.
2 NA, Edmonton, Yukon & Pacific Railway Co., RG30, 3119, 24 June 1904.
3 *Globe*, 1 Apr., 1904; NA, James Bay Railway Co. Subsidies, 1904–6, RG30, 3119, 8 Sep. 1904; and NA, Hays Letterbooks, MG30, A18, 2, Hays to Wilson, 25 Mar. 1904.
4 PAO, Northern Construction Co., MU5367, D.D. Mann to A.R. Mann and A.C. McKenzie, 5 July 1904; and P. Burns to A.R. Mann, 26 Nov. 1904.
5 Cyrille Felteau, *Histoire de La Presse*, Tome 1, *Le Livre du Peuple, 1884–1916* (Montreal: La Presse 1983), 327.
6 See Laurier Lapierre, 'Politics, Race and Religion in French Canada: Joseph Israel Tarte,' PH.D. thesis, University of Toronto, 1962.
7 Borden, ed., *Memoirs*, 132; Robert Craig Brown, *Robert Laird Borden: A Biography*, 1 (Toronto: Macmillan of Canada 1975), 78–85; and Regehr, *Canadian Northern Railway*, 147.
8 NA, Hays Letterbooks, MG30, A18, 3, Hays to Wilson, 6 Feb. 1905; and 2, Hays to Wilson, 23 Sept. 1904.

9 H. Blair Neatby, *Laurier and a Liberal Quebec* (Toronto: McClelland and Stewart 1973), 146–7.

10 NA, Laurier Papers, MG26, G, 283, pp. 77,251–2, Greenshields to Laurier, 25 Sept. 1903.

11 *CAR*, 1904, 225.

12 Joseph Schull, *Laurier, the First Canadian* (Toronto: Macmillan of Canada 1965), 443; and Felteau, *Histoire de La Presse*, 324.

13 *CAR*, 1904, 223; and NA, Laurier Papers, MG26, G, 348, pp. 93,071–4, Thomas Côté to Laurier, 30 Dec. 1904; and NA, Hays Letterbooks, MG30, A18, 2, [Morse?] in Montreal to Hays in London, cable, 19 Oct. 1904.

14 O.D. Skelton, *Life and Letters of Sir Wilfrid Laurier*, 2 (Toronto: McClelland and Stewart 1971), 87; and J.W. Dafoe, *Laurier: A Study in Canadian Politics* (Toronto: Macmillan of Canada 1963), 76.

15 NA, Porteous Letterbooks, MG29, A32, 23, Porteous to George Blackstock, 26 Nov. 1904.

16 NA, Laurier Papers, MG26, G, 351, p. 93,722, Laurier to Graham, 12 Jan. 1905.

17 NA, Laurier Papers, MG26, G, 348, pp. 93,071–74, Côté to Laurier, 30 Dec. 1904; 349, p. 93,358, Dansereau to Laurier, 3 Jan. 1905; and 351, p. 93,729, Mackenzie and Mann to Laurier, 18 Jan. 1905.

18 NA, Borden Papers, MG26H, 449, Diaries, 25 Aug. 1917.

19 NA, Laurier Papers, MG26, G, 407, pp. 325–9, Berthiaume to Laurier, 19 Mar. 1906.

20 *Northern Lights* (Toronto: Copp Clark 1909), 41.

21 *Daily Edmonton Bulletin*, Sept. 1905.

22 SAB (Saskatoon), Scott Papers, M1.V.14, Railways, 1901–9; M1.IV.112, Libel Cases: McInnis; and D.H. Bocking, 'Premier Walter Scott: A Study of His Rise to Political Power,' MA thesis, University of Saskatchewan, 1959.

23 *Daily Edmonton Bulletin*, 25 Nov. 1905.

24 Toronto *Star*, 19 June 1906.

25 NA, RG30, Canadian Northern Ontario Railway, Directors' Meeting, 10 July 1906.

26 Lindsay *Weekly Post*, 3 Aug. 1906.

27 *Monetary Times*, 27 Oct. 1906, 610.

28 NA, Hays Letterbooks, MG30, A18, 3, Hays to Wilson, 9 Nov. 1906; and Wilson to Hays, 20 Nov. 1906.

29 PAO, Whitney Papers, MU3114, Griffin to Whitney, 27 Dec. 1900.

30 NA, Porteous Papers, MG29, A32, 11, W.T. White, general manager National Trust, Toronto branch, to Porteous, 17 Mar. 1903.

31 OHA, Toronto Power Company File, Income Tax, 1916–17.

32 Frederick Nicholls, 'Niagara's Power: Past, Present, Prospective,' in *Empire Club Speeches* (Toronto 1905), 159–70.

33 W.R. Plewman, *Adam Beck and the Ontario Hydro* (Toronto: Ryerson Press 1947), 85.

34 *Globe*, 8 and 9 Apr. 1895.

35 See 'A Chat about Lawn Tennis,' *Massey's Magazine*, 2 (July–Dec. 1896):58–60 in which he talked about the formation and growth of Ontario tennis clubs in places such as Uxbridge and Lindsay, Ontario.

36 PAO, Whitney Papers, MU3114, Griffin to Whitney, 27 Dec. 1900.

37 PAO, Whitney Papers, MU3117, Whitney to Griffin, 24 Aug. 1905.

38 PAO, Whitney Papers, MU3118, Whitney to Griffin, 16 Feb. 1906.

39 NA, Sifton Papers, MG26, II, D15, mic. C–539, p. 101044, Mackenzie to Sifton, 20 Mar. 1902.

40 Kenneth Buckley, *Capital Formation in Canada, 1896–1930* (Toronto: McClelland and Stewart 1974), 4–5; and NA, Porteous Letterbooks, MG29, A32, 21, Porteous to James Ross, 6 Oct. 1899; and Porteous to Ross, 17 Oct. 1899.

41 PAO, Whitney Papers, MU3118, Pellatt to Whitney, 9 Jan. 1906; Whitney to Nicholls, 11 Jan. 1906.

42 *Monetary Times*, 3 Aug. 1906, 157–8.

43 PAO, Whitney Papers, MU3119, Nicholls to Provincial Secretary, 24 Mar. 1906.

44 PAO, Whitney Papers, MU3118, Aemelius Jarvis to Whitney, 21 Feb. 1905; and Pellatt to Whitney, 9 Feb. 1906.

45 PAO, Whitney Papers, MU3118, Whitney to Griffin, 16 Feb. 1906.

46 *Star*, 19 June 1906.

47 *Monetary Times*, 14 Sept. 1906, 356–7.

48 *Star*, 17 Apr. 1906.

49 *Star*, 10 May 1906.

50 *Globe*, 1 Dec. 1906.

51 NA, Denison Diaries 1901–9, MG29, E29, 29, 4 Dec. 1906.

52 MHECA, WERC, file 2, 9 June 1906.

53 *Free Press*, 29 June 1906.

54 Armstrong and Nelles, *Monopoly's Moment*, 193–6; and Nelles, 'Public Ownership of Electrical Utilities in Manitoba and Ontario, 1906–30,' in *CHR*, 57 (1976):461–84.

55 *Star*, 6 Apr. 1908; and NA, Electric Railways, RG46, 1147, Winnipeg Electric Railway returns, 1907 and 1908.

56 *Free Press*, 31 Mar. 1906; PAM, Autobiography of Andrew Scobie, MG14, C101; and PAM, R.R. Rostecki, 'Walk for Labour,' essay, University of Winnipeg, 1973.

57 *Free Press*, 3 Apr. 1906.

58 See Paul Craven, *'An Impartial Umpire': Industrial Relations and the Canadian State, 1900–1911* (Toronto, Buffalo, London: University of Toronto Press 1980).

59 Craig Heron and Robert Storey, 'On the Job in Canada' in *On the Job: Confronting the Labour Process in Canada* (Kingston and Montreal: McGill-Queen's University Press 1986), 15.

60 Hector Charlesworth, 'Sir William Mackenzie,' *Saturday Night*, 15 Dec. 1923.

61 New Orleans *Daily Picayune*, 27 Sept. 1908.

62 NA, QLL&SR, RG30, 1363; and SAB (Saskatoon), Scott Papers, M1.IV.137, file 1, Railways: Canadian Northern Railway, 1906–16, Pugsley to Scott, 21 July 1906.

63 W.H. Moore, 'The Mackenzie I Knew' in *Saturday Night*, 28 Dec. 1923.

CHAPTER 8: DARK MOMENTS

1 Hanna, *Trains of Recollection*, 190–9.

2 NA, Laurier Papers, MG26G, 444, pp. 118,448–53, T. O'Flynn to Laurier, 19 Jan. 1907.

3 NA, Laurier Papers, MG26G, 446, Mackenzie to Laurier, 6 Feb. 1907; Laurier to Mackenzie, 7 Feb. 1907; and Mackenzie to Laurier, 7 Feb. 1907.

4 *CAR*, 1907, 517.

5 PAO, Whitney Papers, MU3123, Chaplin, Milne, Grenfell to Whitney, 10 Aug. 1907.

6 *RMW*, Mar. 1907, 17.

7 NA, Dunn Letterbooks, MG30, A51, 252, Dunn to Martin Schiff, 28 Feb. 1907; and *RMW*, Mar. 1907, 17.

8 NA, RG30, 10218, CNoR Indentures, 15 Apr. 1907.

9 PAO, Whitney Papers, MU3122, Sir Mortimer Clark to Whitney, 2 Apr. 1907.

10 Regehr's title, *The Canadian Northern Railway, Pioneer Road of the Northern Prairies*, is misleading, since his book deals with all four components of Mackenzie and Mann's transcontinental system, which became the Canadian Northern Railway only in 1914. Until 1914 that name designated only the prairie component.

11 NA, Dunn Letterbooks, MG30, A51, 253, Dunn to Schiff of Nationalbank für Deutschland, Berlin, 11 May 1908.

12 PAO, Whitney Papers, MU3123, Whitney to F.W. Taylor, Bank of Montreal, London, 5 July 1907.

13 *CAR*, 1907, 517

14 BA, William Mackenzie file, A31, Smith to Mackenzie, 18 Apr., 22 and 23 May 1907.

15 NA, Laurier Papers, MG26G, 441. (The volume number indicates the year. Context indicates the time of year.)

16 *CAR*, 1907, 142.

17 *RMW*, Sept. 1907, 665.

18 NA, Dunn Letterbooks, MG30, A51, 252, Dunn to Martin Schiff, 28 Feb. 1907.

19 NA, Dunn Letterbooks, MG30, A51, 253, Dunn to Mackenzie, 3 Apr. 1908.

20 *RMW*, July 1907, 499; Lindsay *Weekly Post*, 14 and 17 June 1907; Toronto *Star*, 7 June 1907; NA, A.J. Hills Papers, MG31, E12, 6, pp. 7–8; and author interviews with Teresa Mcdonald, June 1976 and with Roy Steele, July 1976. The hen-rail image is courtesy of Myrtle Fleming, my mother.

21 NA, RG30, CNoOR, Minutes, 1259.

22 *Star*, 25 June 1907.

23 *RMW*, Aug. 1907, 607.

24 *CAR*, 1907, 46.

25 *RMW*, Aug. 1907, 599–600.

26 *RMW*, Sept. 1907, 665; and Saskatoon *Daily Phoenix*, 22 July and 30 Dec. 1907.

27 *CAR*, 1907, 143–8.

28 *CAR*, 1907, 144.

29 *CAR*, 1907, 47 and 143.

30 Regehr, *Canadian Northern Railway*, 215, 305; and NA, Dunn Letterbooks, MG30, A51, 252, Dunn to Martin Schiff, Berlin, 16 Dec. 1907.

31 Merrill Denison, *The People's Power: The History of Ontario Hydro* (Toronto: McClelland and Stewart 1960), 65–6.

32 PAO, Whitney Papers, MU3123, E.R. Peacock to E.E.A. DuVernet re an EDCO memo 4 Dec. 1907.

33 PAO, Whitney Papers, MU3123, Whitney to E.C. Whitney, 4 Dec. 1907.

34 C.W. Humphries, *James Pliny Whitney: Honest Enough to be Bold* (Toronto: University of Toronto Press 1985), 167–8.

35 PAO, Whitney Papers, MU3124, Whitney to Moore, 11 Feb. 1908.

36 PAO, Whitney Papers, MU3124, Scott Griffin to Whitney, 1 Feb. 1908.

37 PAO, Whitney Papers, MU3124, Whitney to E.C. Whitney, 3 Jan. 1908.

38 *CAR*, 1908, 294; NA, RG30, 1259, Canadian Northern Ontario Railway, Shareholders' and Directors' meetings, 13 June 1908.

39 H.V. Nelles, *The Politics of Development* (Toronto: Macmillan of Canada 1975), 275–6.

40 *CAR*, 1908, 300.

41 PAO, Whitney Papers, MU3124, Whitney to Ned Whitney, 7 Feb. 1908.

42 Mavor, *Niagara in Politics*, 123.

43 *CAR*, 1908, 301.

44 PAO, Whitney Papers, MU3124, Whitney to E.C. Whitney, 27 and 28 Feb., and 6 Mar. 08.

45 *CAR*, 1908, 301.

46 SAB (Saskatoon), M1.IV.137, file 1, Railways: Canadian Northern Railway, 1906–16, Scott to Donald Mann, 15 Sept. 1908; and Mann to Scott, 26 Sept. 1908.

47 *CAR*, 1907, 517.

48 *Star*, 4 Apr. 1908.

49 *Star*, 15 Apr. 1908.

50 David Frank, 'The Cape Breton Coal Industry and the Rise and Fall of the British Empire Steel Corporation,' *Acadiensis* 7, no. 1 (Autumn 1977):10–13.

51 NA, Dunn Letterbooks, MG30, A51, 253, Dunn to Martin Schiff, 11 May 1908, and Dunn to William Mackenzie, London, 22 June 1908; NA, RG30, 10225, Toronto Power Company Trust Deed; and NA, RG30, 1259, Canadian Northern Ontario Railway, Directors' Meeting, 20 July 1908.

52 *CAR*, 1908, 241–51.

53 NA, Dunn Letterbooks, MG30, A51, 254, Dunn to Rutherford, 12 Aug. 1908.

54 PAO, Whitney Papers, MU3124, Whitney to E.C. Whitney, 24 Mar. 1908.

55 PAO, Whitney Papers, MU3126, Mackenzie to Whitney, 7 Aug. 1908.

56 *CAR*, 1907, 523.

57 PAO, Whitney Papers, MU3126, William Mackenzie to Whitney, 7 Aug. 1908.

58 NA, Denison Diaries, 1901–9, MG29, E29, 29, 7 Aug. 1908.

59 PAO, Whitney Papers, MU3124, Blake to Whitney, 21 Mar. 1908; and Whitney to Ned Whitney, 18 Mar. 1908.

60 PAO, Whitney Papers, MU3126, A.M. Grenfell to Whitney, 17 Nov. 1908.

61 PAO, Whitney Papers, MU3126, Grenfell to Whitney, 17 Nov. 1908.

62 Toronto *News*, 17 Feb. 1908; and PAO, Whitney Papers, MU3128, W.J. Hanna to Whitney, 26 July 1909.

63 See, e.g., Nelles' phrase 'exciting fictional world' in *Politics of Development*, 277.

64 *RMW*, Sept. 1908, 627; and *RMW*, Nov. 1908, 773–4.

65 SAB (Saskatoon), Scott Papers, M1.IV.137, file 1, Railways: Canadian Northern Railways, 1906–16, Scott to Alex Robertson, Delisle, 27 Apr. 1908; Dr. Tessier to Scott, 6 May 1908; G.E. McCraney, MP, to Scott, 3 Aug. 1908; Scott to McCraney, 8 Aug. 1908; and Mackenzie to Scott, 19 Aug. 1908.

66 *CAR*, 1908, 566.

67 NA, Laurier Papers, MG26, G, 538, Laurier to Fielding, 15 Oct. 1908.

68 NA, Dunn Letterbooks, MG30, A51, 254, Dunn to Mackenzie, 15 Oct. 1908.

69 PAO, Whitney Papers, MU3126, 29 Dec. 1908.

70 *CAR*, 1907, 23.

71 *CAR*, 1907, 23, 106, 352–3; *RMW*, Apr. 1910, 305; *RMW*, June 1910, 499.

72 *CAR*, 1908, 292; and *Star*, 3 and 4 Apr. 1908.

73 *RMW*, Jan. 1909, 51.

74 RCSL, A.H. Fisher Collection, Letters, 1908, Fisher to Mackinder, 28 Oct. 1908, 68.

75 *RMW*, June 1907, 431; and NA, RG46, Electric Railways, 1142, Toronto Railway Company, Annual Report, 1907.

76 Agnes Deans Cameron, *The New North: An Account of a Woman's 1908 Journey through Canada to the Arctic*, ed. David Richeson (Saskatoon: Western Producer Prairie Books 1986), 18, 293–5.

CHAPTER NINE: DRINKING LIFE TO THE LEES

1 NA, Railway Misc., RG30, 9258, file 1038–1, 'Mackenzie Steam Yacht.'

2 T.D. Regehr, ed., *'The Possibilities of Canada Are Truly Great!': Memoirs 1906–1924 by Martin Nordegg* (Toronto: Macmillan of Canada 1971), 127–41; *Monetary Times*, 1 Dec. 1906; and author interviews with Weldon and Vina Neale, July 1987, Roy Forman, Jan. 1977, Roy Steele, Oct. 1976, and Ellen McRae, May 1974. For a serious retelling of the convent story, see Regehr, *Canadian Northern Railway*, 29.

3 Regehr, *Canadian Northern Railway*, 88.

4 *RMW*, June 1909, 433.

5 *RMW*, Aug. 1909, 595; and NA, CNoOR Co., RG30, 1259, Shareholders' and Directors' Meetings, 25 June 1909.

6 *CAR*, 1909, 587.

7 See PABC, Premiers' Papers, GR441, 163, file 15, Railway Files, N–W, Steward Citizens' Association to McBride, 1 June 1911.

8 SAB (Saskatoon), Scott Papers, M1.IV.137, file 2, Railways: Canadian Northern Railway 1900–1916, Campbell to Scott, 12 July 1909; and Alex Weinmeister to Scott, 17 June 1909.

9 NA, Laurier Papers, MG26G, 631, Têtu to Laurier, 16 May 1910.

10 *RMW*, Mar. 1909, 189.

11 *RMW*, Nov. 1909, 855; *RMW*, Apr. 1910, 321; Winnipeg *Telegram*, 7 Apr. 1910; and NA, RG30, III, J, 1183, Minutes of Shareholders' Meeting of Canadian Northern Steamships Ltd., 22 Feb. 1910.

12 *RMW*, Mar. 1910, 221; and May 1910, 381.

13 SAB (Saskatoon), Scott Papers, MI.XI.77, Pocket Diary, 1910, file 2, 87,112–13.

14 RCSL, Publicity brochure called 'Royal Line to Canada,' ca. 1910.

15 R.M. Parsons, 'The Royal Route to Canada,' part 1, in *Ships Monthly* (Sept. 1984), 19.

16 *CAR*, 1910, 50.

17 Michael Bliss, *Northern Enterprise: Five Centuries of Canadian Business* (Toronto: McClelland and Stewart 1987), 351; *CAR*, 1910, 605–7; *RMW*,

May 1910, 381 and July 1910, 555–9; Winnipeg *Free Press*, 20 June 1910; and NA, RG30, 10223, Bond Mortgages: Canadian Northern Railway Systems, 6 Aug. 1910.

18 Robert Lloyd Webb, *West Whaling: A Brief History of Whale-hunting in the Pacific Northwest*, 9–13; Wray Vamplew, *Salvesen of Leith* (Edinburgh and London: Scottish Academic Press 1975), 138 and 162; Adam Shortt and Arthur Doughty, eds., *Canada and Its Provinces*, 22 sec. 11, *The Pacific Provinces*, pt. 11 (Toronto: Glasgow, Brook 1914), 475; *CAR*, 1912, 620; Canada, *Sessional Papers*, no. 22, 44, 1910; Vancouver *Sun*, 31 Jan. 1914; Victoria *Colonist*, 19 July 1953; NA, Dept. of Marine and Fisheries, RG23, 1081, file 721, pt. 19, fo. 5C, R. Brown to A. Johnston, 23 May 1912; NA, Dept. of Marine and Fisheries, RG23, 242, file 1536, pt. 3, memo 22 Nov. 1910, memo 29 Nov. 1910 and L. Rissmuller to Dept., 22 Nov. 1911.

19 PABC, Premiers' Papers GR441, McBride, 140, Canadian Northern Railway, Mackenzie (in Victoria) to McBride, 17 Jan. 1910.

20 *Canada West Magazine*, ca. early 1908, quoted by A.D. Brodie in *The Westminster*, 12, no. 3 (Mar. 1908), 141, 150.

21 PAO, Whitney Papers, MU3126, Whitney to Ned Whitney, 14 Jan. 1909.

22 HBCA, A.12/L, Misc/92, Townsite Agreements Canadian Northern Railway Co., 1911–12.

23 HBCA, A.1/160, Minute Book, 1910–12, HBC Committee Meeting, 25 Apr. 1911.

24 HBCA, A.12/L, 109/1/6, Canadian Northern Right of Way, 1903–11, C.C. Chipman to W. Ware, 12 Feb., 12 Mar., and 22 June 1909; HBCA, Abstract of Letters, A.1/199, 1909–11, Chipman to Ware, 6 Apr. 1909.

25 HBCA, File: 'Sir William McKenzie [sic],' Extracts from Proceedings of a General Court of the Hudson's Bay Co. held 4 July 1910.

26 *RMW*, July 1910, 565.

27 David Monod, 'Bay Days: The Managerial Revolution and the Hudson's Bay Company Department Stores, 1912–1939,' in *Historical Papers/Communications historiques, 1986* (Ottawa 1987), 173–96.

28 HBCA, File: 'Sir William Mackenzie,' (Land Correspondence file 5, Division 109/1/6), letter L.1/478, Land Commissioner James Thomson to F.C. Ingram, Secy., HBC London, 23 Nov. 1911.

29 *CAR*, 1911, 275–6 and 639; NA, CNoR, Mortgages, RG30, 10220; and NA, CNoOR, RG30, 1259, Directors' Meeting, 15 Apr. 1911.

30 NA, CNoOR, RG30, 1259, Shareholders' and Directors' Meetings, 17 June 1911.

31 Regehr, ed., *Possibilities*, 168.

32 Quoted in Cameron, *The New North*, 6.

33 NA, Sifton Papers, MG27 II D15, mic. H-998, Sifton to Mackenzie, 4 Apr. 1911; and Sifton to Mackenzie, 8 Aug. 1911.

34 *CAR*, 1911, 641 and 633.

35 By comparison, in 1987 'Chunnel' construction was projected to cost 13 billion dollars over several years.

36 D. Gagan, *The Denison Family of Toronto, 1792–1925* (Toronto: University of Toronto Press 1973), 90.

37 NA, Denison Papers, MG29, E29, 30, diaries 1909–23, 19 Oct. 1911.

CHAPTER TEN: 'HONOUR'D OF THEM ALL'

1 *RMW*, Feb. 1912, 76; and Mar. 1912, 137.

2 *CAR*, 1911, 641.

3 Toronto *Star*, 19 Jan. 1927.

4 AGOL, *Catalogue of Highly Important Old and Modern Pictures and Drawings* ...; for Fragonard today, see *The New Yorker*, 18 June 1990, 10.

5 Author interview with Cyril Andrewes, second husband of Gertrude Mackenzie, Oct. 1975.

6 *RMW*, May 1911, 485; and June 1911, 531; *Star*, May 1912 and 19 Jan. 1927; and NA, Denison Papers, MG29, E29, 30, Diaries 1909–23, May 1912.

7 *CAR*, 1912, 588.

8 PABC, GR441, Premiers' Papers, 163, file 15, McBride Railway File, N–W (and misc. proposals and petitions), McBride to president of Revelstoke Board of Trade, 7 June 1912; UAA, Pearce Papers, MG9/2/6/3–21, Pearce to J.S. Dennis, 12 June 1912; SAB (Saskatoon), M2.53, Calder Papers, Railways: CNoR: 1908–17, Hugh Maher to Calder, 11 June 1912 and Calder to Maher, 15 June 1912; SAB (Saskatoon), M2.29, Calder Papers, Elections: Saskatchewan, 1912, J.A. Sheppard to Calder, 13 May 1912 and Calder to S.C. Wright, 12 June 1912; SAB (Saskatoon), Scott Papers, M1.IV.137, file 2, Railway: CNoR 1906–16, W. Holwill to Scott, 21 July 1912.

9 *RMW*, July 1912, 350.

10 NA, Denison Papers, MG29, E29, 30, Diaries 1909–23, 18 June 1912.

11 PAA, 84.388, Box 1, Canadian Northern Western Railway Company 1912–13, Shareholders' Meeting, 20 June 1913.

12 NA, Borden Papers, MG26 H, 449, Diaries, June–July 1912.

13 UNBA, J.D. Hazen Papers, Hazen to Doherty, 18 July 1912, quoted in Nelles and Armstrong, *Monopoly's Moment*, 115.

14 *CAR*, 1907, 83.

15 Martin and Hall, eds., *Rupert Brooke in Canada*, 59.

16 R.C. Brown and R. Cook, *Canada, 1896–1921: A Nation Transformed* (Toronto: McClelland and Stewart 1974), 205–11; and *CAR*, 1912, 40, and 86.

17 NA, Dunn Letterbooks, MG30, A51, 252, Dunn to Mackenzie, 28 Feb.

1910; 254, Dunn to Mackenzie, 25 Jan. 1909; 257, 23 Feb. 1910; 258, Dunn to Mackenzie, 18 Apr. 1910; 258, Dunn to Secretary, Canadian Northern Steamships, 22 Apr. 1910; 261, Dunn & Fischer Co. to F.S. Pearson, 9 Nov. 1911.

18 The history of Canadian involvement in Brazil has been recorded in two admirable books: C. Armstrong and H.V. Nelles, *Southern Exposure: Canadian Promoters in Latin America and the Caribbean* (Toronto, London, Buffalo: University of Toronto Press 1988); and Duncan McDowall, *The Light: Brazilian Traction, Light and Power Company Limited, 1899–1945* (Toronto: University of Toronto Press 1988). The material on Brazilian affairs comes from these two sources, as well as from primary documents in the Brascan collection, Toronto.

19 See Armstrong and Nelles, *Southern Exposure*, Ch. 7 for a description and analysis of the problems faced by men like Mackenzie, James Dunn, and Max Aitken in selling securities in Canada and in Britain during the first decade of the century; and McDowall, *The Light*, Ch. 2, for a discussion of the strategies and risks involved in finance capitalism, with reference to Brazil.

20 NA, Dunn Letterbooks, MG30, A51, 263, Dunn to Mackenzie, 8 July 1912.

21 McDowall, *The Light*, Ch. 5; NA, Borden Papers, MG26H, 449, Diaries, 26, 27, 28, and 30 June, 1, 3, 4, and 23 July, 20 and 22 Nov. 1912.

22 HBCA, A.1/161, Minute Book, 1912–15, Directors' Meetings, 12 and 23 July, and 12 Nov. 1912.

23 NA, RG30, 1259, Canadian Northern Railway, Directors' Meeting, 10 July 1912; and *CRMW*, Aug. 1912, 410.

24 NA, Parkin Papers, MG30, D44, Mackenzie to Parkin, 19 July 1912.

25 *CRMW*, Sept. 1912, 458.

26 John C. Weaver, '"Tomorrow's Metropolis" Revisited: A Critical Assessment of Urban Reform in Canada, 1890–1921' in G. Stelter and A. Artibise, eds., *The Canadian City: Essays in Urban and Social History* (Ottawa: Carleton University Press 1984), 462.

27 *RMW*, July 1911, 685; and *CRMW*, Oct./Nov. 1912, 530.

28 *RMW*, Nov. 1910, 969.

29 *RMW*, Dec. 1910, 1071.

30 *CAR*, 1913, 417–8; and TTCA, Bion J. Arnold and J.W. Moyes, *Report on the Toronto Railway Company*, July 1913. TRC and TELC were buying about 50,000 h.p. from EDCO.

31 Armstrong and Nelles, *Monopoly's Moment*, 132.

32 TTCA, *Report of Messrs. Jacobs & Davies on Street Railway Transportation in the City of Toronto*, 25 Aug. 1910, 20.

33 *Star*, 3 Feb. 1911.

34 *RMW*, June 1910, 499.

35 See, e.g., *RMW*, Aug. 1912, 419.

36 NA, RG46, 1142, Annual Reports of Toronto Street Railway, 1909 to 1912; and *Star*, 19 Jan. 1911.

37 *RMW*, July 1909, 501 and June 1912, 310; and *CRMW*, Nov. 1912, 559.

38 PAO, Whitney Papers, MU3128, Whitney to Griffin, 18 July 1909; MU3128, Whitney to F.W. Taylor, manager of the Bank of Montreal, London, 13 Dec. 1909; MU3130, Griffin to Whitney, 14 Nov. 1910; MU3130, Whitney to Griffin, 26 Nov. 1910; MU3130, Pellatt to Whitney, 28 Nov. 1910; and MU3132, Whitney to A.J. Matheson, 28 Oct 1911.

39 *CAR*, 1909, 609; PAO, Whitney Papers, MU3131, W. Moore to Whitney, 10 Mar. 1911; and MU3130, Whitney to Griffin, 26 Nov. 1910.

40 *CAR*, 1911, 616.

41 Nelles, *Politics of Development*, 292–7; Toronto *Globe*, 21 July 1909; and PAO, Whitney Papers, MU3128, Whitney to W.J. Hanna, 22 July 1909.

42 *CAR*, 1911, 449; and *RMW*, Mar. 1912, 144.

43 Nelles and Armstrong, *Monopoly's Moment*, 191.

44 PAO, Pellatt Papers, MU3823, file 41, Pellatt to Mackenzie, 7 Nov. 1911.

45 See, for instance, Elwood Jones and Dyer, Bruce, *Peterborough, The Electric City* (Burlington, Ont.: Windsor Publications 1987), 50.

46 *CAR*, 1912, 356–7.

47 The Hydro Power Commission had 100,000 h.p. available and 44,000 h.p. under contract from the Ontario Power Company, but the quantity actually used was only 18,000 h.p. (*CAR*, 1912, 355). The Toronto Electric Light Company bought 15,000 h.p. annually from EDCO, and Toronto Railway Company bought 12,000 h.p. annually (*CAR*, 1907, 516).

48 *Star*, 25 June 1912.

49 *CAR*, 1912, 358–9.

50 *CAR*, 1912, 359; and R.P. Bolton, *An Expensive Experiment: The Hydro-Electric System of Ontario* (New York, 1913), quoted in Nelles, *The Politics of Development*, 405.

51 PAM, W. Sanford Evans Papers, MG14, B28, Box 10, 'Winnipeg Electric Railway Company, Statement by Mayor Evans re Offer of the Company to Sell to the City of Winnipeg,' 20 July 1911.

52 H.V. Nelles, 'Public Ownership of Electrical Utilities in Manitoba and Ontario, 1906–30,' *CHR*, 57 (1976):461–71; and *RMW*, June 1912, 305.

53 NA, RG46, 1147, Annual Reports of Winnipeg Electric Railway, 1909–12.

54 J.E. Rea, 'How Winnipeg Was Nearly Won,' in A.R. McCormack and I. McPherson, eds., *Cities of the West* (Ottawa: Carleton University Press 1975), 74–87.

55 NA, Armstrong Memoirs, MG30, B25, 231.

56 *CAR*, 1909, 536–7.

57 *CAR*, 1911, 641; and author interview with Elizabeth (McKenzie) Brodie, Oct. 1977.

58 *RMW*, Mar. 1910, 197; and Oct. 1910, 856.

59 J. Richards and J.M. MacKenzie, *The Railway Station, A Social History* (Oxford: Oxford University Press 1986), 57; Regehr, *Canadian Northern Railway*, 326–31; *RMW*, Oct. 1910, 855; Nov. 1910, 929; May 1911, 429; Oct. 1911, 953; Feb. 1912, 70; Oct. 1912, 511; and *CAR*, 1911, 641.

60 The amount his donation to the Toronto General is unknown. Flavelle and Cox each gave $100,000; J.C. Eaton, $361,589; Lash and Walker, $20,000 each; the CPR and Donald Mann, $10,000 each; Nicholls and Pellatt, $5,000 each; 'Anonymous' gave $300,000 (*CAR*, 1913, 348). Mackenzie? Yet that amount is out of line with donations of Mann and Walker, etc. As well as donating money to the Toronto Playgrounds Association (1910), he sat on its board. The specific amounts and projects are as follows: $5,000 to the Regina Cyclone Fund (1912), $10,000 to the Winnipeg YMCA (1910), $2,000 to assist the Vancouver Cadet Corps to reach Australia (1912), $2,500 to the VON (1912), $10,000 to the King Edward Memorial Fund for Consumptives (1912), $500 to the Canadian Club Movement (1910), $10,000 to the Toronto YMCA and YWCA (1910), $500 to the erection of a tower in Halifax commemorating the 150th anniversary of the establishment of self-government in Nova Scotia (1909), $500 to the South African Memorial Association for the erection of a memorial in Queen's Park (1909), and 1,000 pounds sterling to the Habitation Fund of the Society of Knights Bachelor (1911).

61 *CAR*, 1913, 348.

62 *Free Press*, 6 Nov. 1915; and author conversation with David Harris and John Baker, Winnipeg, 16 Feb. 1990.

63 Michael Bliss, *Northern Enterprise: Five Centuries of Canadian Business* (Toronto: McClelland and Stewart 1987), 350.

64 H. Darling, *The Politics of Freight Rates* (Toronto: McClelland and Stewart 1980), 35–44; Regehr, *Canadian Northern Railway*, 336–8; K. Cruikshank, 'The Limits of Regulation: Railway Freight Rate Regulation and the Board of Railway Commissioners,' PH.D. thesis, York University 1988, Chs. 6–7; and NA, Borden Papers, MG26H, 449, Diaries, 7–8 Oct. 1912.

65 *CAR*, 1912, 255.

66 *RMW*, May 1909, 349; Aug. 1911, 761; and Dec. 1911, 1149; and author interview with Kathleen Bowley, Peterborough, July 1988.

67 *RMW*, July 1909, 507; Sept. 1911, 865; Jan. 1912, 26; *Free Press*, 30 Mar. 1910; and author interviews with Winnifred Miller, Oct. 1976, and with Nonnie Griffin, July 1980.

68 *Star*, 26 Jan. 1911; *Globe*, 27 Jan. 1911.

69 Bliss, *Northern Enterprise*, 373.

70 *CAR*, 1912, 151–7.

71 *CAR*, 1912, 111.

72 D. Avery, 'Canadian Immigration Policy and the 'Foreign' Navvy, 1896–1914,' in M.S. Cross and G.S. Kealey, eds., *Readings in Canadian Social History*. Vol 4: *The Consolidation of Capitalism, 1896–1929* (Toronto: McClelland and Stewart 1983):47–73; and *CAR*, 1912, 601.

CHAPTER ELEVEN: FADING STAR

1 NA, Borden Diaries, MG26H, 449, Diaries, 14 Mar. 1914; author interview with Peter Griffin, Aug. 1977; and photograph album of Mabel (Mackenzie) Griffin.

2 F. Lewis and M. MacKinnon, 'Government Loan Guarantees and the Failure of the Canadian Northern Railway,' *The Journal of Economic History* 47, no. 1 (March 1987):175–96.

3 *CRMW*, Apr. 1914, 172.

4 NA, Borden Papers, MG26H, 27, Private Memorandum, Mackenzie to Borden, 21 Feb. 1913.

5 NA, Borden Papers, MG26H, 449, Dairies, 21 Feb. 1913.

6 PAA, 84.388, Box 1, 'Canadian Northern Western Railway Company, 1912–1913'; NA, RG30, 1259, 10211.

7 *CRMW*, Feb. 1914, 73; and Augustus Bridle, *Sons of Canada* (Toronto: J.M. Dent and Sons 1916), 74–5.

8 NA, Borden Papers, MG26H, 449, Diaries, 22 Jan. 1914.

9 NA, Borden Papers, MG26, H, 27, Shaughnessy to Borden, 27 Feb. 1914.

10 PABC, Add. Ms. 347, 1, file 1/2, McBride Correspondence: Confidential, McBride to Mackenzie (coded telegrams), 9 Feb. and 11 Mar. 1914.

11 NA, Borden Papers, MG26H, 27 [ca. Feb. 1914].

12 *CAR*, 1913, 631; and SAB (Saskatoon), Scott Papers, M1.IV.137, file 2, Railways: Canadian Northern Railway: 1900–16.

13 *CRMW*, Jan. 1914, 31; and *Free Press*, 10 Feb. and 14 Feb. 1914.

14 Philip Marchand, 'Morley Callaghan,' Toronto *Star*, 26 Aug. 1990, A12; and telephone interview with Barry Callaghan, 22 Nov. 1990.

15 *Star* and *Globe*, 17 Feb. 1914; MTL, Scrapbooks, T686.2, 4, 58; *Globe*, 23 Oct. 1916; and NA, Denison Papers, MG29, E29, 30, Diaries 1909–23, 5 Feb. 1914.

16 Bridle, *Sons of Canada*, 76.

17 *Globe*, 17 Feb. 1914.

18 NA, Borden Papers, MG26H, 28, pt. 2, Flavelle to Mackenzie, 24 Feb. 1914; and Mackenzie to Borden, 28 Feb. 1914; and NA, Borden Papers, MG26H, 449, Diaries, 17, 18, 19, 25, 26, and 27 Feb. 1914; and NA, Sifton Papers, MG27 II D15, C–593, 159,587, Mackenzie to Sifton, 20 Feb. 1914.

19 *CAR*, 1914, 737; and NA, Borden Papers, MG26H, 28, pt. 2, Mackenzie to Borden, 5 Mar. 1914.

20 *Globe*, 6 Mar. 1914.

21 NA, Borden Papers, MG26H, 449, Diaries, 10–14 Mar., 23 and 29 Apr. 1914.

22 Author interviews with Mrs. R. Barkwell, Lindsay, Ont., Jan. 1988, and Cyril Andrewes, June 1976.

23 NA, Borden Papers, MG26H, 28, pt. 2, J.B. Maclean to Mann, 18 Mar. 1914.

24 Roger Graham, *Arthur Meighen: The Door of Opportunity*, 1 (Toronto: Clarke, Irwin 1960), 81–2.

25 NA, Borden Diaries, MG26H, 449, 25 Feb. 1913; and author interview with Cyril Andrewes, June 1976.

26 *CAR*, 1913, 693.

27 Regehr, *Canadian Northern Railway*, 364; and *CRMW*, July 1914, 322.

28 PABC, Premiers' Papers, GR141, McBride, 141, 'Canadian Northern Railway,' Mann to McBride, 15 Aug. 1914.

29 PABC, Add. Ms. 347, 1, file 1/2, McBride Corresonpondence: Confidential, McBride to Mann, 7 Aug. 1914.

30 Author conversation with Tony Griffin, Oct. 1988.

31 *CRMW*, Oct. 1914, 470.

32 Regehr, *Canadian Northern Railway*, 397 and 406.

33 R.C. Brown, *Robert Laird Borden, A Biography. 2: 1914–1937* (Toronto: Macmillan of Canada 1980), 6, 12, and 41; and NA, Memoirs of Robert Watson Sellar, MG31, E5, 4, 159–60.

34 *CAR*, 1915, 753.

35 PABC, GR441, Premiers' Papers, 141, file 5, McBride, 'Canadian Northern Railway,' T.H. White, chief engineer CNoPR, to McBride, 2 Feb. 1915; Mann to McBride, 5 Feb. 1915; and BCARS, GR441, Premiers' Papers, 426, Clipping Book, Legislative Assembly, 1915.

36 BBC Sound Archives, London, Eng., Robert Flaherty, 'The Odyssey of a Film Maker,' MT 14516; and 'Portrait of Robert Flaherty,' T1 9897.

37 Donald Brittain, 'Dreamland,' NFB history of Canadian cinema, 1895–1939.

38 Peter Morris, *Embattled Shadows: A History of Canadian Cinema, 1895–1939* (Montreal: McGill–Queen's University Press 1978), 244–7.

39 Alan Cooke, 'Robert Flaherty, Filmmaker and Explorer,' unpub. ms., 1962, 11.

40 Cooke, 'Robert Flaherty,' 12–13.

41 BLCU, Robert J. Flaherty Papers, 'Proposal for Third Mackenzie Expedition 1913–1914,' Flaherty to Mackenzie, 26 May 1913; and author interview with Werner Zimmerman, Guelph, May 1983.

42 Robert and Frances Flaherty, *My Eskimo Friends* (New York: Doubleday 1924), 124–5.

43 Jo-Anne Birnie Danzker, *Robert Flaherty, Photographer/Filmmaker* (Vancouver: Vancouver Art Gallery 1979), 19; letter from Valerie Grant, De-

partment of Ethnology, Royal Ontario Museum, 13 Mar. 1984; and A. Calder-Marshall, *The Innocent Eye: The Life of Robert J. Flaherty: A Biography* (Harmondsworth, Eng.: Penguin Books 1983), 69, fn. 2.

44 *Globe*, 31 Mar. 1915.

45 Bridle, *Sons of Canada*, 67–8.

46 *Globe*, 5 Apr. 1915.

47 HBCA, A.12/FT Misc./260. 'McKenzie [sic], Sir Wm. – Expedition, 1915,' N.H. Bacon, Fur Trade Commissioner, Montreal to F.C. Ingram, Secretary of HBC, London, 28 Jan. 1915; and F.C. Ingram to N.H. Bacon, 18 Mar. 1915.

48 Cooke, 'Robert Flaherty,' 17.

49 Robert Stacey, *C.W. Jefferys* (Ottawa: National Gallery of Canada 1985); and Robert Stacey, *Western Sunlight: C.W. Jefferys on the Canadian Prairies* (Saskatoon: Mendel Gallery 1986).

50 See, e.g., the 6 June 1903 issue of *Moon*, which featured Mackenzie the jockey riding in 'The Race for the Pacific Stakes.' In April 1908, Jefferys had been kinder when he sketched a determined Mackenzie speaking to the Private Bills Committee, for the Toronto *Star*.

51 Courtesy of Robert Stacey, director of the Archives of Canadian Art, Toronto.

52 *Star*, 28 Feb. 1914.

53 NA, J.E.H. MacDonald Papers, MG30, D111, 1, A.Y. Jackson to Thoreau MacDonald, 5 Oct. 1914.

54 *Evening at Jasper* is now in the permanent collection of the Winnipeg Art Gallery. In 1981 a companion piece was sold at D. & J. Ritchie Ltd., Toronto, in 1981 for $7,500 (*Arts West*, 7, no. 2 [Feb. 1982], 11).

55 Stacey, *Western Sunlight*, 35, 80, 82.

56 Dennis Reid, *Our Own County Canada* (Ottawa: National Gallery of Canada, and National Museums of Canada 1979), 437.

57 Ron Rees, *Land of Earth and Sky: Landscape Painting of Western Canada* (Saskatoon: Western Producer Prairie Books 1984), 36–9.

58 J.L. Rutledge, 'Flaherty of Belcher Island,' *Maclean's*, May 1915, 26.

59 BBC Sound Archives, MT14516, R.J. Flaherty, 'The Odyssey of a Film Maker,' first broadcast 24 July 1949.

60 Calder-Marshall, *The Innocent Eye*, 55.

61 Robertson Davies, *The Rebel Angels* (Markham, Ont.: Penguin Books Canada 1983), 144.

62 *CAR*, 1915, 754; and *CRMW*, Sept. 1915, 351.

63 *Globe*, 6 Sept. 1915.

64 Saint John *Standard*, 19 Oct. 1915.

65 Edmonton *Daily Journal*, 18 Oct. 1915.

66 Montreal, *La Presse*, 12 Oct. 1915.

67 Vancouver *Daily Province*, 18 Oct. 1915.

68 *Manitoba Free Press*, 15 Oct. 1915.

69 *Standard*, 15 Oct. 1915.

70 *Globe*, 15 Oct. 1915.

71 NA, J.E.H. MacDonald Papers, MG30, D111, 2, 'A Glimpse of the West,' n.d. [1918 or 1925].

72 SAB (Saskatoon), Scott Papers, M1.IV.137, file 2, Railways: Canadian Northern Railway: 1900–16, Mackenzie to Scott, 13 Oct. 1915; Scott to Mackenzie, 14 Oct. 1915.

73 Regina *Leader*, 18 Oct. 1915.

74 'Qu'Appelle' by J.C. Hodgins in *Saturday Night*, 12 Jan. 1889.

75 Sir Gilbert Parker, 'Qu'Appelle,' in *Northern Lights* (Toronto: Copp, Clark 1909), 102.

76 Ottawa *Evening Journal*, 19 Oct. 1915; Winnipeg *Tribune*, 25 Oct. 1915; and *Globe*, 25 Oct. 1915.

77 *Tribune*, 25 Oct. 1915; Saskatoon *Phoenix*, 19 Oct. 1915; and *Evening Journal*, 19 Oct. 1915.

78 *Tribune*, 25 Oct. 1915; *Daily Province*, 20 Oct. 1915.

79 *CRMW*, Mar. 1914, 119; *CAR*, 1915, 755; *Daily Province*, 22 Oct. 1915; BCARS, Premiers' Papers, GR441, 141, file 5, McBride, Canadian Northern Pacific Railway, R. Budd, St. Paul, to McBride, 6 Nov. 1915; and W.H. Macleod to McBride, 8 Nov. 1915; and NA, Arbitration Hearings, RG30, 2187, 11 Feb. 1918, 594–5.

80 Edmonton *Bulletin*, 22 Oct. 1915.

81 *CAR*, 1915, 711; and NA, Borden Papers, MG26H, 29, Collingwood Schreiber, general consulting engineer to Borden, 12 Aug. 1916.

82 *Evening Journal*, 27 Oct. 1915; Winnipeg *Evening Tribune*, 25 Oct. 1915; and *Manitoba Free Press*, 25 Oct. 1915.

83 *Manitoba Free Press*, 25 Oct. 1915.

84 *Standard*, 27 Oct. 1915; and *Evening Journal*, 27 Oct. 1915.

85 *CRMW*, Dec. 1915, 466; and *CRMW*, Jan. 1916, 13.

86 *CRMW*, Sept. 1914, 423.

87 *CRMW*, July 1915, 259.

88 *CAR*, 1916, 239.

89 *CAR*, 1914, 226–7 and 231.

90 *CAR*, 1916, 793.

91 *CRMW*, Oct. 1914, 472.

92 *CAR*, 1915, 234.

93 Nelles, *The Politics of Development*, 353–5; *CAR*, 1916, 534; and NA, Borden Papers, MG26H, 449, Diaries, 22 Jan. 1915 and 23 Apr. 1915.

94 NA, Dunn Letterbooks, MG30, A51, 270, Dunn to Mann, 29 Dec. 1914; Dunn to Mackenzie, 21 Jan. 1915; and Dunn to Mann, 8 Apr. 1915.

95 NA, Borden Papers, MG26H, 192, Mackenzie to Borden, 15 Dec. 1914; and Mackenzie to Borden, 27 Jan. 1915.

96 NA, Borden Papers, MG26H, 449, Diaries, 6, 16, and 28 Apr. 1915.

97 *Daily Bulletin*, 13 Oct. 1915; and *Evening Tribune*, 26 Oct. 1915.

98 *Star*, 19 Feb. 1914. The play was actually produced the year before, but its challenge to the myth did not close with the production.

99 Vancouver *Sun*, 29 Oct. 1915.

100 Calgary *Eye-Opener*, 23 Oct. 1915.

101 NA, Borden Papers, MG26H, 449, Diaries, 18 and 24 May 1915.

102 *CAR*, 1915, 753.

103 *Evening Journal*, 26 Oct. 1915.

104 *Financial Post*, 30 Oct. 1915.

105 *CRMW*, Dec. 1915, 466.

CHAPTER TWELVE:
'AN UNJUSTIFIABLY SANGUINE VIEW'

1 Fleming to Beck, reprinted in the *Mail and Empire*, 27 Mar. 1917.

2 Mavor, *Niagara in Politics*, 127–9; and *The Mail and Empire*, 23 Mar. 1917.

3 Denison, *The People's Power*, 124; and *CAR*, 1913, 408.

4 *Financial Post*, 15 July to 23 Dec. 1916; and TF, James Mavor Collection 119, Box 63, 'Appeal to the Public: A Protest Against the Confiscatory Legislation and the Arbitrary Conduct of the Hydro Electric Commission of Ontario,' [1916].

5 Nelles, *The Politics of Development*, 405.

6 NA, Borden Papers, MG26H, 210, Mackenzie to Borden, 24 July 1916.

7 *CAR*, 1916, 511.

8 Armstrong, *The Politics of Federalism*, 76–84.

9 Mavor, *Niagara in Politics*, 129–30; and *The Mail and Empire*, 27 Mar. 1917.

10 Due, *The Intercity Electric Railway Industry*, 86; *CRMW*, May 1917, 197; *CAR*, 1915, 548; NA, RG46, 1143, Annual Reports of the Toronto Suburban Railway; and NA, RG46, 1144–5, Annual Reports of the Toronto & York Radial Railway Company.

11 NA, RG46, 1142, Annual Reports of the Toronto Railway Company.

12 *CAR*, 1915, 548; and Donald Davis, 'Competition's Moment: The Jitney-Bus and Corporate Capitalism in the Canadian City, 1914–1929,' *UHR*, 18, no. 2 (Oct. 1989):103–22.

13 *CAR*, 1915, 649; and *CRMW*, Aug. 1916, 336.

14 *CRMW*, Sept. 1917, 369; and Oct. 1917, 406.

15 *CRMW*, June 1915, 234; and Dec. 1915, 483.

16 TTCA, 'Report to the Ontario Railway and Municipal Board on a Survey of Traffic Requirements in the City of Toronto and Service Furnished

by the Toronto Railway Company,' by C.R. Barnes, assisted by J.H. Cain and J.M. Campbell, Toronto, 1914, 49.

17 *CRMW*, Apr. 1916, 155.

18 *CRMW*, Jan. 1917, 28; and Aug. 1917, 328.

19 Armstrong and Nelles, *Monopoly's Moment*, 265.

20 NA, RG43, 1142.

21 NA, RG46, 1149.

22 NA, RG46, 1144–5.

23 *CRMW*, Sept. 1917, 364.

24 *CRMW*, July 1917, 285.

25 McDowall, *The Light*, 202.

26 NA, Borden Papers, MG26H, 449, Diaries, 14, 17, and 18 Mar. 1915.

27 NA, Borden Papers, MG26H, 29, Borden to Mackenzie, Biltmore Hotel, New York, 14 Aug. 1915.

28 NA, Borden Papers, MG26H, 449, Diaries, 25 Jan. and 5 Apr. 1916.

29 NA, Borden Papers, MG26H, 449, Diaries, 6 Dec. 1915, 2 Feb., and 6 Apr. 1916.

30 NA, Borden Papers, MG26H, 449, Diaries, 4 Apr. 1916.

31 NA, Borden Papers, MG26H, 449, Diaries, 12 Apr. 1916.

32 Brown, *Robert Laird Borden*, 54–5.

33 NA, Borden Papers, MG26H, 449, Diaries, 5, 11, 12, and 15 Apr. 1916.

34 NA, Borden Papers, MG26H, Vol. 449, Diaries, 13, 14, 15, and 28 Apr. 1916.

35 NA, Borden Papers, MG26H, 449, Diaries, 24, 25, 27, and 30 Apr. 1916.

36 NA, Borden Papers, MG26H, 449, Diaries, 31 May 1916.

37 NA, Borden Papers, MG26H, 449, Diaries, 19 June 1916.

38 NA, Borden Papers, MG26H, 449, Dairies, 26–8 June 1916.

39 Regehr, *Canadian Northern Railway*, 414.

40 NA, Borden Papers, MG26H, 449, Diaries, 4, 5, and 7 July 1916.

41 *CRMW*, Oct. 1916, 408.

42 *CRMW*, Mar. 1916, 100; Apr. 1916, 145; and Sept. 1916, 358.

43 *CRMW*, July 1916, 287.

44 *CRMW*, Oct. 1916, 409.

45 NA, Borden Papers, MG26H, 449, Diaries, 20 Aug. 1916.

46 *CRMW*, Nov. 1916, 448.

47 Brown, *Robert Laird Borden*, 57.

48 NA, Borden Papers, MG26H, 449, Diaries, 12 and 13 Nov. 1916.

49 *CRMW*, June 1916, 247; and NA, Minutes of Canadian Northern Steamships Ltd., RG30, III, J, 1183, Directors' Meeting, 16 Oct. 1916.

50 *CRMW*, Sept. 1915, 363.

51 NA, Laurier Papers, MG26H, 29, Giraud à Laurier, le 22 nov. 1916.

52 *CRMW*, Nov. 1916, 452; and Dec. 1916, 490.

53 NA, Minutes of Canadian Northern Steamships, Ltd., RG30, III, J, 1183, Directors' Meeting, 21 Aug. 1916.

54 *CRMW*, Jan. 1917, 22.

55 NA, Borden Papers, MG26H, 449, Diaries, 20–1 Dec. 1916.

56 *CAR*, 1916, 792–3.

57 Later Drayton and Acworth took exception to Mackenzie and Mann's accounting methods. The Drayton-Acworth report accused the CNoR of moving $5 million in interest into the capital fund, thereby reducing fixed charges and the net deficit. Drayton and Acworth may have been closer to the true figure than Mackenzie's accountants.

58 NA, Borden Papers, MG26H, 449, Diaries, 22 Dec. 1916.

59 *CAR*, 1916, 792–3.

60 NA, Borden Papers, MG26H, 449, Diaries, 29 Dec. 1916, 12, 21, 24, 27, and 29 Jan 1917; 1 and 9 Feb 1917.

61 Canada, *Sessional Papers*, 20g, 52, no. 12, 1917, xxxviii and xl.

62 Regehr, *Canadian Northern Railway*, 421–8.

63 *CRMW*, June 1917, 216–19.

64 Brown, *Robert Laird Borden*, 96; and NA, Borden Papers, MG26H, 449, Diaries, 4 and 14 June 1917.

65 Regehr, *Canadian Northern Railway*, 441.

66 Author interview with Sam Weir, QC, Queenston, Ont., Oct. 1977.

67 Author interview with W.E. Greening, Montreal, Nov. 1976.

68 NA, Borden Papers, MG26H, 449, Diaries, 21 and 22 June 1917.

69 NA, Shaughnessy Letterbook, no. 112, 62, Shaughnessy to Lash, 4 June 1917, cited in Regehr, *Canadian Northern Railway*, 433.

70 NA, Borden Papers, MG26H, 449, Diaries, 20 and 21 June 1917.

71 NA, Borden Papers, MG26H, 449, Diaries, 16 Aug. 1917.

72 Brown, *Robert Laird Borden*, 103–5; and Graham, *Arthur Meighen*, 159–63.

73 NA, Borden Papers, MG26H, 449, Diaries, 10 July 1917.

74 NA, Borden Papers, MG26H, 449, Diaries, 28 and 30 Aug. 1917.

75 Brown, *Robert Laird Borden*, 97; Graham, *Arthur Meighen*, 157; NA, Borden Papers, MG26H, 449, Diaries, 9 June, 18 July, 21, 22, 23, 25, and 28 Aug. 1917; and NA, Foster Papers, MG27I, D7, 6, 23 Aug. 1917.

76 NA, Borden Papers, MG26H, 449, Diaries, 2 Oct. 1917.

77 Brown, *Robert Laird Borden*, 108.

78 NA, Borden Papers, MG26H, 449, Diaries, 5, 6, and 10 Oct. 1917.

79 Brown, *Robert Laird Borden*, 99–110.

80 NA, Borden Papers, MG26H, 449, Diaries, 17 and 25 Oct., 1, 8, 9, and 10 Nov. 1917; and NA, Meighen Papers, MG26I, 10, 5795–8, Mackenzie to Reid, 8 Nov. 1917.

81 Brown, *Robert Laird Borden*, 120; NA, Borden Papers, MG26H, 449, Diaries, 26 and 27 Nov. 1917.

82 Author interview with Margaret (Griffin) Norman, St. Clere, Kemsing, Kent, England, May 1988.

83 Author interview with Winnifred (Mitchell) Miller, daughter of Annie (Merry) Mitchell, Oct. 1976.

84 Author interview with Gilbert McInnis, Lindsay, Nov. 1987.

85 GAA, Pat Burns Papers, 1442, Box 36, file 487, La Contesse de Lesseps (Grace Mackenzie de Lesseps) to Pat Burns, 8 May 1929.

86 NA, Borden Papers, MG26H, 449, Diaries, 1 Dec. 1917.

CHAPTER THIRTEEN: UNSETTLING AFFAIRS

1 Author conversation with Peter Griffin, Tony Griffin, Kitty (Gordon) Griffin, and Margaret (Griffin) Norman, Aug. 1988.

2 Augustus Bridle, *The Masques of Ottawa* (Toronto: Macmillan of Canada 1921), 254 and 260.

3 David Frank, 'The Cape Breton Coal Industry and the Rise and Fall of the British Empire Steel Corporation,' *Acadiensis*, 7, no. 1 (Autumn 1977):13–14.

4 NA, Borden Papers, MG26H, 449, Diaries, 20 Dec. 1917; and 139, Borden to Mackenzie, 17 Jan. 1918; *CAR*, 1920, 195–7.

5 Armstrong and Nelles, *Southern Exposure*, 117, 128.

6 *Star*, 28 Jan. 1918.

7 NA, RG30, Arbitration Hearings, 2187, pp. 393, 2672, 2684.

8 Eagle, *Canadian Pacific Railway*, 79, 86, 93, 97.

9 NA, RG30, 2187, p. 404.

10 *Free Press*, 3 Aug. 1897; and 16 Sept. 1897.

11 NA, RG30, 2187, p. 1643; Fort Vermilion is located in the fertile Peace River Lowland in northern Alberta; McLeod may have been confusing it with Vermilion, which emerged in 1905 as a village when the CNoR reached the area 190 kilometres east of Edmonton.

12 NA, RG30, 2187, pp. 2510–4.

13 NA, RG30, 1166, Directors' Meeting, Canadian Northern Ontario Railway, 2 June 1916.

14 NA, RG30, 2187, pp. 754–88.

15 *CAR*, 1918, 929; and NA, RG30, 2187, p. 5171.

16 NA, RG30, 2187, 109.

17 NA, RG30, 2187, p. 4673; NA, Borden Papers, MG26H, 449, Diaries, 12, 20, and 21 Feb. 1918; 6 and 11 Mar. 1918; and 29 Apr. 1918.

18 NA, A.J. Hills Papers, MG31, E12, 6, Manuscript: Articles on Railroading.

19 Author interview with Margaret Bell, Kirkfield, Sept. 1987.

20 NA, RG30, 2187, pp. 5383 and 6392.

21 *CRMW*, June 1918, 248.

22 *CRMW*, Oct. 1918, 442.

23 NA, Minutes of the Canadian Northern Steamship Co. Ltd., RG30 III J, 17 Sept. 1918; and NA, CNoOR, RG30, 166, 27 Sept. 1918; and NA, Borden Papers, MG26H, 449, Diaries, 9 May 1918.

24 Montreal *Gazette*, 19 Apr. 1920, quoting F.S. Cahill, MP from Pontiac Riding, Quebec.

25 Nelles, *Politics of Development*, 373.

26 Armstrong, *Politics of Federalism*, 83.

27 Nelles, *Politics of Development*, 410, fn. 33; and 413.

28 OHA, TPC, Income Tax 1917–18; and TPC, Statistics, Reports, 31 Dec. 1918.

29 Denison, *The People's Power*, 154; *CRMW*, Jan. 1921, 30–2, and Oct. 1921, 549; and TTCA, 'Financial History of the Toronto Transit Company and the Toronto Railway Company,' 25 July 1932.

30 *CRMW*, Feb. 1921, 91.

31 *CRMW*, Mar. 1922, 146.

32 *CRMW*, Sept. 1922, 478.

33 OHA, TPC, Income Tax, 1917–20; and OHA, TPC, 1917–20, list of shareholders, 31 Dec. 1921.

34 Baker, *Winnipeg's Electric Transit*, 57.

35 *CRMW*, May 1918, 206 and 207; and July 1918, 307.

36 *CRMW*, Nov. 1918, 502–3.

37 *CRMW*, Feb. 1919, 83.

38 *CRMW*, Apr. 1919, 206; and Mar. 1920 144.

39 PAO, RG3, Records of Prime Ministers' Office, Drury General Correspondence, Box 29, 'Toronto Railway Company,' 1920, Church to Drury, 12 May 1920; and *CAR*, 1920, 340.

40 *Wall Street Journal*, reprinted in *CRMW*, Dec. 1920, 675; Winnipeg Railway Company's 'Public Service News'; and *CRMW*, Feb. 1921, 95.

41 *CRMW*, Sept. 1921, 486; and *CAR*, 1921, 426.

42 *CRMW*, Oct. 1921, 547; Nov. 1921, 606; Dec. 1921, 659; Feb. 1922, 100; Mar. 1922, 146; Apr. 1922, 207; July 1922, 372; Sept. 1922, 478; Oct. 1922, 533; and Feb. 1923, 83.

43 *CRMW*, Mar. 1923, 127–30.

44 McDowall, *The Light*, Ch. 7.

45 *CRMW*, Apr. 1919, 207; and May 1919, 265.

46 OHA, Bonds: TPC, 1905–19, J.M. Smith to R.J. Fleming, 18 May 1919.

47 OHA, Bonds: TPC, 1905–19, Mackenzie to Horne-Payne, 30 May 1919; Mackenzie to British Empire Trust, 31 May 1919; and Horne-Payne to Mackenzie, 4 June 1919; *CRMW*, June 1919, 305; July 1919, 391; and Sept. 1919, 487; HBCA, A.1/163, Minute Book, 1917–19; NA, Denison Papers, MG29, E29, 30, Diaries 1909–23, 7 Dec. 1919; and author interview with Kiki (de Lesseps) Hicks, Victoria, BC, Mar. 1988.

48 NA, A.J. Hills Papers, MG31, E12, 5, Journals, 10 Jan. 1921.

49 NA, Dunn Letterbooks, MG30, A51, 281, Dunn to Mackenzie, 20 Jan. 1921.

50 *CRMW*, June 1922, 314.

51 Toronto *Telegram*, 15 June 1922.

52 *CRMW*, Oct. 1922, 507.

53 NA, Dunn Letterbooks, MG30, A51, 283, Dunn to Mackenzie (cable), 14 Nov. 1921.

54 *CRMW*, Jan. 1920, 20.

55 *CRMW*, Sept. 1920, 482; and NA, Sifton Papers, MG27II, D15, mic. H–998, Sifton to Mackenzie, 19 Nov. 1918.

56 *CRMW*, Nov. 1920, 622.

57 *CRMW*, Aug. 1919, 436.

58 HBCA, A.1/213, London Minutes, Extracts, 1920–3, 20 Dec. 1921.

59 HBCA, 'Sir William Mackenzie' file, Extract from Proceedings of a General Court of the Hudson's Bay Company, 30 July 1922.

60 NA, Borden Papers, MG26H, 449, Diaries, 3 and 11 June 1920.

61 NA, Meighen Papers, MG26I, 58, Petition, 8 Sept. 1920.

62 NA, Borden Papers, MG26H, 449, Diaries, 27 June 1920.

63 *CRMW*, Oct. 1919, 541; and Nov. 1921, 581.

64 Author interview with J.C. Annesley, Montreal, Oct. 1976.

65 NA, Dunn Letterbooks, MG30, A51, 284, Dunn to Sir Cecil Budd, 3 and 5 Apr. 1922.

66 Author interview with Gilbert Griffin, Oct. 1977. Fessenden had been a member of the Ross government Power Commission in 1903.

67 NA, Dunn Letterbooks, MG30, A51, 285, Dunn to Mackenzie, 16 June 1922.

68 Author interview with Cecil Nicholls, Argyle, Ont., Dec. 1987.

69 Author interview with Jack Hughes, Kirkfield, June 1976.

70 PAO, Will of R.J. Mackenzie, RG22/305, York County, 7 Jan. 1924, Grant No. 48898; and NA, Meighen Papers, MG26I, 43, pp. 25,143–5.

71 *CRMW*, Apr. 1923, 176.

72 Author interview with Rt. Comm. Francis Lindsay, Balsam Lake Drive, Ont., Oct. 1977.

73 *CRMW*, July 1923, 335.

74 *CRMW*, Aug. 1919, 436; and author interview with Elizabeth (McKenzie) Brodie, June 1976.

75 *CRMW*, Jan. 1922, 28; and Dec. 1921, 642.

76 *CRMW*, Aug. 1923, 386 and 387; Oct. 1923, 469.

77 NA, Dunn Letterbooks, MG30, A51, 284, Dunn to Mackenzie, 7 Apr. 1922; and 287, Dunn to Mackenzie, 1 May 1923.

78 NA, Borden Papers, MG26H, 277, Borden to Mackenzie, 5 Dec. 1923.

79 NA, Borden Papers, MG26H, 449, Diaries, 23 Oct. 1923.

80 Author interview with Peter Griffin, Balsam Lake, Ont., Aug. 1988.

81 C.P. Stacey, *A Very Double Life* (Halifax: Formac Publishing Company 1985), 37.

82 W.L. Mackenzie King, *Industry and Humanity* (Toronto: University of Toronto Press 1973), especially D.J. Bercuson's introduction, xx.

83 NA, Borden Papers, MG26H, 449, Diaries, 23 Oct. 1923; and NA, Meighen Papers, MG26I, 61, Borden to Mackenzie, 30 Oct. 1923.

84 *CRMW*, Dec. 1923, 588.

85 BA, Sir William Mackenzie, 100.45, Miller Lash to Sir Alexander Mackenzie, 22 Nov. 1923; and Lash to A. Mackenzie, 26 Nov. 1923.

86 PAO, Will of Sir William Mackenzie, RG22/305, York Co., 25 Jan. 1924, Grant no. 49474.

87 Regehr, ed., *Possibilities*, 136.

88 *CRMW*, Dec. 1921, 662.

89 Archives of Mrs. Kathleen Bowley, Peterborough, Ont., A.W. Mackenzie to Sir William Mackenzie, 24 Aug. 1921.

90 Quoted in Bridle, *The Masques of Ottawa*, 258.

91 *CRMW*, Jan. 1924, 31.

92 Bridle, *The Masques of Ottawa*, 255, 256, 259.

93 McDowall, *The Light*, 214.

94 Author interview with Cyril Andrewes, June 1976.

95 NA, Borden Papers, MG26H, 449, Diaries, 5 Dec. 1923.

96 NA, Meighen Papers, MG26I, 61, p. 34,890, Meighen to Joe Mackenzie, 5 Dec. 1923; and 99, p. 56,492–4, Meighen to Sir Edward Kemp, 5 Dec. 1923.

97 NA, King Papers, MG26, J13, Diaries, Dec. 1923.

98 Author interview with Alan Cowan Bell, Kirkfield, Sept. 1987.

99 Author interview with Teresa Mcdonald, Kirkfield, June 1976.

Selected Bibliography

Armstrong, C., *The Politics of Federalism*. Toronto: University of Toronto Press 1981

Baker, J.E., *Winnipeg's Electric Transit*. Toronto: Railfare Enterprises Ltd. 1982

Barker, T.C. and M. Robbins, *A History of London Transport*, 1. London: Allen and Unwin 1963

Berton, P., *The Great Railway, 1881–1885: The Last Spike*. Toronto: McClelland and Stewart 1974

Birnie-Danzker, J., *Robert Flaherty: Photographer/Filmmaker. The Inuit 1910–1922*. Vancouver: Vancouver Art Gallery 1979

Blake, H.W., *The Era of Street Cars in Winnipeg, 1881–1955*. Winnipeg: private publication 1971

Bliss, M., *A Canadian Millionaire*. Toronto: Macmillan of Canada 1978

–*Northern Enterprise: Five Centuries of Canadian Business*. Toronto: McClelland and Stewart 1987

Bocking, D.H., 'Premier Walter Scott: A Study of His Rise to Political Power.' M A thesis, University of Saskatchewan 1959

Bone, P.T., *When the Steel Went Through*. Toronto: Macmillan of Canada 1947

Borden, H., ed., *Robert Laird Borden: His Memoirs*. Toronto: Macmillan of Canada 1938

Breen, D., *The Canadian Prairie West and the Ranching Frontier*. Toronto: University of Toronto Press 1983

Bridle, A., *The Masques of Ottawa*. Toronto: Macmillan of Canada 1921

– *Sons of Canada*. Toronto: J.M. Dent and Sons 1916

Briggs, A., *History of Birmingham*, Vol. 2, *Borough and City, 1865–1938*. London: Oxford University Press 1952

Brown, R.C., *Robert Laird Borden: A Biography*, 1 and 2. Toronto: Macmillan of Canada 1975, 1980

Buckley, K., *Capital Formation in Canada, 1896–1930.* Toronto: McClelland and Stewart 1974

Calder-Marshall, A., *The Innocent Eye: The Life of Robert J. Flaherty: A Biography.* Harmondsworth, Eng.: Penguin Books 1983

Cameron, A.D., *The New North.* Saskatoon: Western Producer Prairie Books 1986

Careless, J.M.S., *Toronto to 1918, an Illustrated History.* Toronto: James Lorimer and Co. and the National Museum of Man 1984

Casson, M., *The Entrepreneur.* Oxford: Oxford University Press 1982

Craig, G.M., *Upper Canada: The Formative Years, 1784–1841.* Toronto: McClelland and Stewart 1977

Craven, P., *'An Impartial Umpire': Industrial Relations and the Canadian State, 1900–1911.* Toronto: University of Toronto Press 1980

Darling, H., *The Politics of Freight Rates.* Toronto: McClelland and Stewart 1980

Davis, D.F., 'Mass Transit and Private Ownership: An Alternative Perspective on the Case of Toronto,' *Urban History Review,* no. 3 (1978):60–98

Dendy, W., *Lost Toronto.* Toronto: Oxford University Press 1978

Denison, M., *The People's Power: The History of Ontario Hydro.* Toronto: McClelland and Stewart 1960

Due, J.F., *The Intercity Electric Railway Industry in Canada.* Toronto: University of Toronto Press 1966

Eagle, J.A., *The Canadian Pacific Railway and the Development of Western Canada, 1896–1914.* Kingston: McGill–Queen's University Press 1989

Filby, J., *Credit Valley Railway.* Cheltenham: Boston Mills Press 1974

Flaherty, R. and F. Flaherty, *My Eskimo Friends.* New York: Doubleday 1924

Fleming, H.A., *Canada's Arctic Outlet: A History of the Hudson Bay Railway.* Berkeley: University of California Press 1957

Frank, D., 'The Cape Breton Coal Industry and the Rise and Fall of the British Empire Steel Corporation,' *Acadiensis* 7:1 (Autumn 1977):3–34

Graham, R., *Arthur Meighen: The Door of Opportunity,* 1. Toronto: Clarke, Irwin 1960

Hall, C.A.S., 'Electrical Utilities in Ontario under Private Ownership, 1890–1914.' PH.D. thesis, University of Toronto 1968

Hall, D.J., *Clifford Sifton,* 1 and 2. Vancouver: University of British Columbia Press 1981, 1985

Hanna, D.B., *Trains of Recollection.* Toronto: Macmillan of Canada 1924

Hughes, T.P., *Networks of Power: Electrification in Western Society 1880–1939.* Baltimore: Johns Hopkins University Press 1983

Humphries, C.W., *James Pliny Whitney: Honest Enough to Be Bold.* Toronto: University of Toronto Press 1985

Kealey, G.S. and B.D. Palmer, *Dreaming of What Might Be: The Knights of Labor in Ontario, 1880–1900*. Cambridge, Eng.: Cambridge University Press 1982

Kirkconnell, W., *County of Victoria Centennial History*, 2nd ed. Lindsay, Ont.: Victoria County Council 1967

Lewis, F. and M. MacKinnon, 'Government Loan Guarantees and the Failure of the Canadian Northern Railway,' *The Journal of Economic History*, 47, no. 1 (March 1987):175–96

Lower, A.R.M., *Canadians in the Making*. Toronto: Longmans, Green and Company 1958

MacEwan, G., *Pat Burns, Cattle King*. Saskatoon: Western Producer Prairie Books 1979

Macnaughtan, S., *My Canadian Memories*. London: Chapman and Hall 1920

Martin, S. and R. Hall, eds., *Rupert Brooke in Canada*. Toronto: Peter Martin Associates 1978

Mavor, J., *Niagara in Politics*. New York: E.P. Dutton 1925

McDowall, D., *The Light: Brazilian Traction, Light and Power Company, Limited, 1899–1945*. Toronto: University of Toronto Press 1987

Middleton, J.E., *Toronto's 100 Years*. Toronto: Toronto Centennial Committee 1934

Minter, R., *The White Pass, Gateway to the Klondike*. Toronto: McClelland and Stewart 1987

Monod, D., 'Bay Days: The Managerial Revolution and the Hudson's Bay Company Department Stores, 1912–1939,' in *Historical Papers/Communications historiques, 1986* (Ottawa, 1987):173–96

Morrison, D.R., *The Politics of the Yukon Territory, 1898–1909*. Toronto: University of Toronto Press 1968

Morton, D., *Working People*. Toronto: Summerhill Press 1990

Neatby, H.B., *Laurier and a Liberal Quebec*. Toronto: McClelland and Stewart 1973

Nelles, H.V., *The Politics of Development*. Toronto: Macmillan of Canada 1975

– and C. Armstrong, *Monopoly's Moment*. Philadelphia: Temple University Press 1986

– *The Revenge of the Methodist Bicycle Company*. Toronto: Peter Martin Associates 1977

Panitch, L., ed., *The Canadian State: Political Economy and Politics of Development*. Toronto: University of Toronto Press 1977

Passer, H., *The Electrical Manufacturers, 1875–1900*. Cambridge, MA: Harvard University Press 1953

Piva, M., *The Condition of the Working Class in Toronto, 1900–1921*. Ottawa:

University of Ottawa Press 1979

Plewman, W.R., *Adam Beck and Ontario Hydro*. Toronto: Ryerson Press 1947

Pursley, L.H., *Street Railways of Toronto, 1861–1921*. Los Angeles: Electric Railway Publications 1968

Rees, R., *New and Naked Land, Making the Prairies Home*. Saskatoon: Western Producer Prairie Books 1988

Regehr, T.D., *The Canadian Northern Railway*. Toronto: Macmillan of Canada 1976

– ed., *'The Possibilities of Canada Are Truly Great!': Memoirs 1906–1924 by Martin Nordegg*. Toronto: Macmillan of Canada 1971

Richards, J. and J.M. MacKenzie, *The Railway Station: A Social History*. Oxford: Oxford University Press 1986

Russell, E.T., *What's in a Name*. Saskatoon: Western Producer Prairie Books 1973

Russell, V., ed., *Forging a Consensus: Historical Essays on Toronto*. Toronto: University of Toronto Press 1984

Schull, J., *Laurier, the First Canadian*. Toronto: Macmillan of Canada 1965

Stacey, R., *Western Sunlight: C.W. Jefferys*. Saskatoon: Mendel Gallery 1986

Stevens, G., *History of the Canadian National Railways*. New York: Macmillan Company 1973

Sturgis, J., *Adam Beck*. Don Mills: Fitzhenry and Whiteside 1978

Thompson, A.S., *Spadina: A Story of Old Toronto*. Toronto: Pagurian Press 1976

Index